VALUE
LANGUAGE
&
LIFE

*And God saw every thing that he had made,
and behold, it was very good.*

—Genesis 1:31

VALUE LANGUAGE & LIFE

An Essay in Theory of Value

JOHN T. GOLDTHWAIT

Prometheus Books
Buffalo, New York

To the memory of
Charles F. and Isabel T. Goldthwait

BD
232
. 615
1985
14 8149
7-b. 1990

Published 1985 by Prometheus Books
700 East Amherst Street, Buffalo, New York 14215

Library of Congress Catalog Card Number: 85-61566
ISBN 0-87975-284-X
Printed in the United States of America

Contents

1

Preface

What is value?

What is that which all good things have in common?

What is that whose presence certifies to us the good when there is good present, or whose absence (or possibly whose opposite) certifies the bad?

The consciousness of value has been with mankind throughout his concern with Being, with Creation, since the time when an early spokesman set down the words, "God saw every thing that he had made, and behold, it was very good." From that time, the above questions have been posed, but not conclusively answered.

Most persons want their conduct to be morally good. The more reflective among them also have a second desire, namely, to be able to know what is the property of goodness that their conduct seeks to realize, and in so doing attain confidence that judgments with respect to their own conduct and that of others are well founded. I believe that this second moral impulse has been responsible for many persons embarking upon philosophical inquiry. Others have been moved to undertake it by a need to understand value in its various settings, such as in the arts. It is my hope that this book will carry these inquirers one or a few steps forward.

It is evident to me that the questions listed above are spurious. They are founded upon a model for the construction of questions that is very useful in some inquiries, but ill-adapted to this one. In other words, they are founded upon the often false assumption that if a word exists, there is an object, a substance, that it names and that man has somehow encountered—although if a "What is———?" sort of question must be asked, man must have inconveniently mislaid that object. Rather, I take a strong clue from twentieth-century linguistic philosophy and conclude that a more proper way of inquiring into value is to ask, "When writing or uttering value-judgmental sentences, what are we using our language to do?" It turns out that the previous questions could be dissolved to this, that it can be answered, and, I believe, that the answer can supply much that was desired with the impulse to ask the initial questions about value and the good.

In considering the nature of the propositions with which we express our

3

value judgments, I have first had to put together a new theory about the ontology of propositions; the application of existing theory alone did not suffice. I have also examined concepts, and produced a practical understanding of what these are; though far from complete, it is consistent with everyday usage of the noun *concept* and is helpful to my task. These steps prepared me to analyze the difference between our fact-assertive propositions and our value-assertive propositions, thereby developing an answer to the question of the difference (the conflict) between fact and value, or the question of "the place of value in a world of fact."

In an effort to explain my position without entangling myself in metaphysical problems that would needlessly delay a fruitful result, I have turned to a method suggested by the phenomenologists. This consists in recognizing the function in consciousness of a framework of various modes, some of which we have been accustomed to recognizing as imputing existence, and others not. It is easier, and as it turns out, immensely more explanatory, to assume merely that any content of consciousness exists *as a content of consciousness*, in some mode or other, the mode usually being evident—and to let the metaphysical problems rest with that.

As a result of the study, I should say (as an approximation) that when we utter fact-assertive propositions we are informing ourselves about our world, and when we utter value-assertive propositions we are orienting ourselves toward it, normally with action in prospect. The need to regard value-assertive propositions as either true or false, as having truth-"value" (ugh!), drops out. Since value assertions possess other characteristics of propositions, we have imputed that one to them also. Common experience shows us otherwise. Yet we crave a standard, like the easy dichotomy of True-False, to apply to those value judgments that govern our conduct. Searching for the bases of our moral choices, I have concluded that they are *intuitions*—not traditional moral intuitions but read-offs of all sorts from any objects of consciousness. Nevertheless, just as we are free to choose what to do, we are free to choose what structures of these intuitions shall serve as the reasons we select for what we do.

Thus far, this statement seems to leave us in the intolerable relativism from which Plato, deploring Protagoras, tried to rescue us. However, in practical fact, it leaves us facing the responsibility of controlling our own fate: we must find ways of orienting ourselves to the world that shall save us and serve us, that shall be the basis of a global morality free of the conflicts that cultural studies, and the day's news, show us on all sides. The compensation for the dread with which at times we see this responsibility is the knowledge of our entire freedom, our independence from criteria that (we have often supposed) we could never understand. Rather than being free only to obey some unfathomable external power or principle, we are free to make a world that we all want. We will surely get that world sooner if we accept this view of value and conduct in our minds and in our actions than if we wait until mankind settles down to a single set of moral dictates based on one of the social, national, or religious dogmas that are competing today for final dominance.

Historic value theories are known by certain names. If the present doctrine should be referred to, I suggest that it be by the characterizing epithet, "the framing-concept theory of value." As to why this phrase is apt, I invite the reader to find the answer in the pages that follow.

John T. Goldthwait
Plattsburgh, New York

1

How the Difference between
Fact and Value Enters Our Discussions

By the time we discover for ourselves, reflectively, the difference between ourselves and our world, that world has become one of bewildering complexity. When the awareness of this difference joins with our own curiosity to engender in us a desire to come to terms with this world, and understand both it and ourselves, we tend to locate ourselves within it by some sort of scheme of dimensions. For example, we place ourselves at 44° 36′ north latitude, and 73° 26′ west longitude, or at the corner of Madison Avenue and Seventy-Second Street, or at the intersection of actuality and possibility. Another set of such coordinates is suggested by saying that we dwell at the meeting point of fact and value.

As soon as we locate ourselves according to such a scheme, we operate with it as best we can. Often, we then discover that we have already been operating with it without knowing or saying so. Occasionally we discover further that we regard ourselves as understanding our place in the world according to our scheme just so long as we succeed in the operations that are based on it, but when we are forced into explanation of the dimensions of our scheme (such as those we call *fact* and *value*), we become perplexed all over again. We then try to set our perplexity at rest by attempting satisfactory explanations of these terms.

It is my aim in the present study to arrive at an increased understanding of the coordinate in the last-mentioned scheme, above, which we know as *value*. Such an understanding could enrich life and heighten the appreciation of its events. But in order to orient and analyze *value*, I shall first have to come to some accommodation with *fact*, just as someone who wishes to explain *width* would do well to give at least brief attention to *length*. Before I finish, I shall look again at *fact*, in order to portray the two in what we shall have seen, through our development of the concept of *value*, to be their actual relationship.

In recent thought, *fact* and *value* have been brought together as a pair, but as somehow a contrasting pair. It is this that suggests to me that it may be proper to regard them as dimensions, as coordinates. The field within which they appear together is as broad as the mind itself, our whole consciousness. It is necessary to assume, of course, that each of us has consciousness, and it seems rather difficult indeed to deny it, in any other than a verbal sense. We allege ourselves to be conscious with greater confidence than we allege ourselves to know the nature of fact or the nature of value, or that there are entities external to consciousness, or indeed almost anything else. I shall therefore take *consciousness* as the frame of my inquiry, human life aware of itself and its world, the presence that posits a place for itself in the world and that questions the nature of the dimensions by virtue of which it locates itself.

Something that we want, then, for the convenience of our inquiry into *value*, is to find a way of accommodating to *fact* in terms of consciousness, so that the separate problem of the nature of fact need not first be settled before we study value, even though we shall need from time to time to give the bearings of value with respect to fact. To attempt to accomplish this accommodation, I shall borrow from phenomenology a way of expressing things, although I am mindful that thorough phenomenologists will disown much that I undertake in this work. Thus I shall speak of certain *modes*, or *ways of appearing*, purposing by that expression to speak of appearing things as phenomena of consciousness, whether or not the conscious being attaches to them a belief in their existence external to consciousness. For example, some things appear in my consciousness in that mode of appearing that is common to physical objects. Other things appear in the modes of objects dreamed of, of objects hallucinated, of objects deliberately imagined (pictured mentally), of objects held to be ideal only and not physical, and still others, in other modes of appearing. It shall occasionally be necessary to indicate an object that is held in mind in first one, then in another, of two or more modes of appearing. I shall treat the objects of any of the ways of appearing as being on a par with one another. The term *exists* shall mean only "appears in consciousness," nothing more. Hence, it may be used for items of any of the modes of appearing (e.g., "Elephants exist in India"; "Dragons exist in dreams"). I shall thus avoid dependence upon the reality of an unproven external world, but I shall treat it as a reasonable explanatory assumption, explicitly noted, where invoked. These means are adopted for the convenience of exposition; I hope by their use to leave metaphysical questions open rather than to presuppose solutions that could perhaps bias our findings about value.

Consciousness has a number of features that are germane to the present study. We can tiptoe around the question, much controverted in this century, whether there is or is not a subject or an ego who has that object that is the object of consciousness. I should like to make note, however, that I depend heavily upon certain features or functions of consciousness, namely, purposiveness; reason, or rationality; subarticulate thought; and language, or articulate thought. A reader unwilling to grant me one or more of these is likely not to grant me credence. However, I do not see how I can base my study on much less than I catalogue here.

My methods of inquiry are mixed. I find much usefulness in attention to features of words and language, means of inquiry usually associated with the analytic schools of the present century. In applying these I believe I am uncovering the funded knowledge and belief of the users of our ordinary, day-to-day language. Despite this, I do not insist that the ordinary person is always in possession of the truth, or that if an interpretation of a passage of ordinary language is a correct one, the passage necessarily contains the truth. Rather, I tend to accept the correct interpretation of a linguistic expression as at least an accurate representation of what the user of the expression means, presupposes, or implies, whether he is articulately aware of it or not, and I suggest that once we gain the implicit message, we do well to test it by such other criteria as we may be able justifiably to bring into play. I do not consider that the goal of a philosophic search is always a truth somewhere apart from the mind, waiting to be discovered. After all, human history, including the history of philosophy, is partly that of an endeavor to construct something that is not already present, and hence a new structure built is often as worthy an end as a discovery. Although as I proceed I shall be making a number of excursions into areas of linguistic inquiry, these are always undertaken for the sake of clarifying what is to be said about value.

Again, in my inquiry I often attempt to examine exactly what it is that is present to consciousness, what may be justifiably said of it, how it became present, and what the processes are by which consciousness holds it and perhaps adapts to it or manipulates it. There is something of the phenomenologist's approach to this, although I do not make a commitment to the phenomenological as the only method proper to philosophy. Further, some of my vocabulary will be considerably at odds with that of the phenomenologist, for I desire to keep it as close as feasible to that of the general reader. For example, that latter will probably accept the special use of *exist* introduced above (p. 00), whereas the former will probably regard me as playing fast and loose with the word.

A characteristic of my method is signaled by one of the terms that I frequently use, namely, the term *experience*. During much of my essay I will be attempting to describe how in fact things happen, and yet these shall often be events that are not open to the scrutiny of the eye or ear. I shall speak of this test of the truth of my description or narration as *experiential*, not as *empirical*, and shall reserve the latter word for occasions when its usual connotation of the sensory, the overtly physical, is appropriate. The method implied is that of the exposition of things that "happen" in respect to our consciousness, even though there may be no overt, sensible signs of their happening. In the sense in which I shall employ the word *experiential*, a person's knowledge of the workings of his own mind or presentations of his own consciousness may be applied as a standard for the justifiability of an assertion, and also, in fact, for the justifiability of linking to a linguistic expression one, rather than another, of the available meanings. This *experience* can thus be a sort of common ground underlying both the analysis of verbal expressions and the recording of the presentations of an ongoing, living consciousness.

Throughout the centuries of Western philosophy, considerable effort has been devoted to the attempt to understand the principal valuative terms, such as *good, right, virtue, beautiful, evil, wrong, vice, ugly,* and others. There has been unending controversy over the proper definitions or understandings of these terms. Despite this controversy, I shall assert, and attempt to explain and demonstrate, that there is generally speaking a great deal of agreement in one most important respect pertaining to discussions of these things. This is not agreement upon some principle. Rather, it is similarity in the linguistic behavior of people performing evaluations. It is agreement in the way we use language in connection with the valuative terms and the judgments involved in arriving at them. I shall shortly present a statement expressing that agreement, offering it as a true generalization from experience. In other words, it is based on experience and it is true of the overwhelming majority of instances from which it emerges or to which it may properly apply. Yet since language is the familiar, taken-for-granted, and continuously regenerated thing that it is, there are so many instances that there is no possibility whatsoever of enumerating them or of getting a statistically significant sampling of them. For what would be the number of instances of sentences in language constituting a statistically significant sample of all the declarative sentences that have ever been formed, in all of the world's languages? This predicament having been acknowledged, the best I can do is to work out the logic of my generalization, while asking the reader to accept it for the reason that his experience of encountering sentences will come close enough to matching my generalization that he can substantially verify it for himself, so far as anyone will ever be able to verify it.

The generalization that I venture is this: Although there is great disagreement and there are many different beliefs as to what values are, *there is general agreement as to which among the statements that are made are the statements that essentially express value judgments.*

This generalization, before being supported, needs a bit of annotation. The crux is hardly the assertion that there is great disagreement as to what values are, for this is so patent that its iteration is hardly helpful. Rather, the important and relatively new part of the claim is that there is general agreement as to which statements express value judgments. This is a claim about language, not about values themselves. Further, I point out that the basis of the claim is behavior rather than testimony, for there actually is relatively little discussion, either in treatments of value or treatments of other problems, of just precisely which statements are those expressing value judgments and why. Occasionally, value judgments, embedded in contexts with other statements, are identified as such; but most authors have no purpose in going beyond their mere identification. Therefore they do not carry out much, if any, further examination of the relation between values and statements that express judgments of value. Rather, the place where the data leading to my generalization can be found is simply the vast total body of statements, some of which really do express value judgments, and the body of verbal or situational contexts within which they are found. In other words, I must look to the employment of value judgments in discourse, rather than theoretic analyses, to support my generalization; and the sign for which I must look is simply the acceptance, implied in context if not explicit, that such-and-such a statement expresses a value judgment—that the statement is treated in its context as a "value judgment" rather than as a "statement of fact."

Let us look at some ordinary sentences to see what we can observe that relates to the above generalization.

List I

(1) This is a good electric fan.
(2) Paula sings well.
(3) Anderson is a good lawyer.
(4) The portrait over your mantel is a good painting.
(5) The weather is bad today.
(6) His new wife cooks poorly.
(7) Forbes was a bad judge of human character.
(8) Anderson is a bad lawyer.
(9) Thomson is a better quarterback than Schmidt.
(10) Democracy is the best form of government.
(11) For some crops, an unusually wet summer is worse than an unusually dry summer.
(12) Today I am worse than I was yesterday.
(13) Leach certainly uses his backhand in the right way.
(14) Advertising is the right way to go about establishing a market.
(15) It is right to return a freely performed favor.
(16) Beach shoots his baskets the wrong way.
(17) Putting all my money into a single investment was the wrong thing to do.
(18) It is wrong under most circumstances to tell a lie.
(19) You should save money in youth to make your old age secure.
(20) One ought always to attempt to save endangered human lives.
(21) One ought to hold to his word of honor always.
(22) One ought not to spend immediately everything one earns.
(23) One ought not to get drunk at his or her spouse's birthday party.
(24) One ought never to break a marital vow.

(25) Chopin was a marvelous composer.
(26) Williams is a superior surgeon.
(27) She was an excellent woman and a surpassing wife.
(28) Never have I seen such foul weather.
(29) His prospects before the bar are dismal.
(30) Only a cad would behave as he behaved.

I submit that each of the statements of List I is an expression of a value judgment. Although there may be one or a few which the reader might not classify as such, I think he will be in general agreement, and will grant that all or the preponderant majority of these sentences express value judgments. If the reader can agree to that much, then the auspices are good that I shall be able to justify my generalization to him.

Let us now look at some statements of another sort. The sentences of this second list have been coordinated with those of the first:

List II

(1) This is an electric fan.
(2) Paula sings operatic selections.
(3) Anderson's profession is that of lawyer.
(4) The painting hanging over your mantel is a portrait.
(5) The weather is cloudy and rainy today.
(6) His new wife does his cooking.
(7) Forbes attempted many times to judge human character.
(8) Anderson makes his living as a lawyer.
(9) Thomson and Schmidt both play quarterback.
(10) Democracy is a form of government in which citizens express their wishes through voting.
(11) Some crops will not grow to as full a maturity in an unusually wet summer as they will in an unusually dry summer.
(12) Today my activity is more limited by my debilitated condition than it was yesterday.
(13) Leach scored many points using his backhand.
(14) Advertising is one way to go about establishing a market.
(15) Often one has an opportunity to return a freely performed favor.
(16) Beach generally aims for an imagined spot on the backboard when shooting baskets.
(17) By putting all my money into a single investment I left myself with no provision for emergencies.
(18) Plank would tell a lie only with the greatest reluctance.
(19) If you save money in your youth, you can make your old age secure.
(20) Mr. Skutnik successfully attempted to save the human life that he saw endangered.

(21) Jones attempted always to hold to his word of honor.

(22) Dale was in the habit of spending immediately everything that he earned.

(23) Even though he was the host, Corson got drunk at his wife's birthday party.

(24) To commit sexual infidelity is to break a marital vow.

(25) Chopin was a composer for the keyboard.

(26) Williams is a brain surgeon.

(27) She had both the role of a woman and that of a wife.

(28) Never before have I seen weather in which the rain came down so hard, the wind was so strong, and the seas were so high, as today.

(29) It is not likely that he will be able to earn a living by practicing law.

(30) The persons who knew him all censured his behavior.

A difference in nature between the sentences of List II and those of List I is obvious at once. To elicit the nature of that difference, I will begin by suggesting that nearly all readers of the two lists will believe not only that there is a difference, but also that they have some measure of knowledge of the nature of the difference. We may, however, expect diverging opinions about what the difference is, and I believe that the respondents to the question will fall into three groups. One group will suggest that the difference is best expressed by saying that the sentences of List I are subjective, whereas those of List II are objective. A second group will affirm that those of List I are matters of opinion, whereas those of List II are facts, or "matters of fact," matters that can be settled. I will agree, provisionally and in the main, with both parties, but I will say that these descriptions do not bring out the essential difference, the difference that actually constitutes the principle of division between the sentences of List I and those of List II. I will therefore side with still a third group, namely, those who affirm that the sentences of List I express value judgments, while on the other hand the sentences of List II are statements of fact. And I shall now undertake to explicate the nature of this distinction and of the propositions that participate in it.

At this stage, I can offer another generalization, one that will help to explain the first. Although the second, like the first, is gathered from experience, the circumstance will emerge that when it is suitably qualified there is good logical ground for it which tends to give it strong logical confirmation. There is also support for it from the nature and use of language. Finally, the generalization implies one or two metaphysical principles such that, if we find them acceptable, they also strongly support the generalization. Thus we may be able eventually to justify this second generalization about as strongly as we are ever able to justify any beliefs about things we take to be actualities, or objects in the real world, which we must regard sentences to be, at least in part. But our exploration of these arguments for the second generalization will not be complete until much later.

The second generalization is that *every declarative sentence principally expresses either a value judgment or a fact.*

To discern the plausibility of this generalization, I suggest comparing the parallel items in Lists I and II. Although there may be one or two items in either list about which the reader senses vagueness or ambiguity, unclarity or imprecision, again I have recourse to the general tendency of each list. If the reader will withhold judgment temporarily from any individual items that do not seem clear-cut or that he disputes, I believe that he will concur that in general, pair for pair, on the one hand we have a rendition of a value judgment, and on the other, a fact. After we accustom ourselves to noticing, for any important sentence, whether it purports principally to state a fact or a value judgment, we will find that classifying it as one or the other according to its evident meaning is a tremendously useful tool for analysis and criticism, helping to detect and correct ambiguity and vagueness and to show logical relationships—or lack of them—among the structures of sentences that are offered for our belief.

Of course, something that one must show, when saying that any *a* is also either *b* or *c*, is that the item *a* is not a third thing instead, neither *b* nor *c* but *d*. With regard to my second generalization, I must demonstrate that there is not some third kind of statement, besides expressions of value judgments and statements of fact, to which any declarative sentence excluded from one of those categories could belong. Of course, there are other ways of classifying sentences; and sentences that are either expressions of value judgments or statements of fact according to the present scheme of classification can also be classed according to other schemes, like long versus short, or loose versus periodic, or analytic versus synthetic, or smooth versus awkward. Sentences can also be classified grammatically, but I have already confined my generalizations (so far as they concern sentences distinct from propositions) to sentences that are declarative, that is, they express assertions, rather than questions, commands, or other sorts of utterances. My first support for the second generalization, then, is simply that in my experience I have found declarative sentences always to be expressions of either facts or value judgments, and I have never found any third class. Although I have encountered some few sentences that put a difficulty in the way of their classification, the problem with them is that of choosing between those two classes, not that of identifying a third class of a different nature from either of those two. In addition to this evidence, I can add substantiation of another kind, one that in its way is intuitive, and to whose validation I invite the reader to apply his own experience. That is, that as a user of language I see purpose to these two ways of using assertion, but have no experience of the recognition of a need or occasion to employ assertive sentences for some third purpose, which would warrant generating a third kind of declarative statement. However, upon any occasion when I have originated a declarative sentence, I find myself quite able to affirm of it that with it I had mainly wanted to accomplish one or the other of two things: to state the fact of the matter, or to express an evaluating judgment upon it.

It is also a part of my message to indicate that statements in being either factual or valuative are essentially or principally not both at the same time. This can be debated, in respect to certain vague or possibly ambiguously worded sentences, or even a few very carefully contrived sentences generated for the purpose of being the exception. However, when a sentence is composed as usual, so as to accomplish but one purpose, this duplicity of demeanor will not characterize it. In brief, when someone wants to express a value judgment, he consciously or unconsciously chooses language that will accomplish that single purpose, rather than a dual one; and similarly, when he wants to express a fact.

Now the average person, using what the twentieth-century analysts call "ordinary language," probably holds, or at least operates according to, a material-realist metaphysics and a referential semantic. This is the readiest interpretation of the evidence contained within the English language. He operates as though there really is a material world containing physical objects, and if he is aware of the epistemological criticisms of this belief, he is willing to chance it that the belief is true even if unprovable. He believes that most of his words work referentially, symbolizing things that of course are not words, but are "objects" or entities outside his own mind. He believes that whole declarative sentences describe states of affairs, and that when they describe them accurately, they are true. It is to neutralize these assumptions, as well as others that might be put in their place, that I am assuming the existence of consciousness, that "objects" (objects of attention or awareness) appear in consciousness, and that they appear in different modes, so that we can speak about "things" without overtly or covertly implying metaphysical existence or nonexistence, or other metaphysical views, about the things that may or may not be *outside* of consciousness. However, I believe that the presuppositions of everyday language do include those mentioned, and I am further suggesting that much light can be shed on the nature of fact and value by examining the way people speak about these "things," even if it should turn out upon more critical investigation that they are not "things" at all—that they are not denizens of a world conceived as lying outside consciousness.

Let us try to accommodate the word *fact* while bearing this outlook in mind. The everyday conception of *facts* is that they are objective, rooted in actuality and reality, and that they are the tests of statements that purport to impart facts. The TV character Sergeant Friday constantly enjoins people, "Just give us the facts, ma'am." Ordinary people often say such things as "I didn't really go there at all. I went straight home, and that's a fact." In such manners of speaking there is shown little awareness of the difference between a state of affairs and a linguistic expression. Which component is the *fact*— the travel homeward or the sentence stating the travel homeward? Philosophers are now hard at work untangling the possibilities here, but as I interpret everyday language, it is the understanding of the users of such phrases that there is somehow an objective reality *somewhere* underlying such a statement, that there are real things like tables and chairs and events outside consciousness, that sentences can be composed to inform others of what one has observed among these real things and events, and that the words used "stand for something" and can assert states of affairs.

Because I wish my discussion to remain close to everyday language and to do as little violence to it as possible, while making adjustments or corrections to its presuppositions to enhance understanding, I shall continue to treat *fact* as conveying *somehow* the objectivity that can correct misstatements. I shall, however, separate *fact* from another of the meanings that arise for it in everyday language, namely, the meaning "a sentence that is true." In the locution cited in the previous paragraph, ". . . that's a fact," the pronoun *that* may be interpreted to have as its antecedent either the event reported or the report, the preceding clause itself. I believe that further discussion would probably move the speaker of such a sentence to distinguish between his spoken sentence and his going home, and this should, I think, justify the interpretation that at bottom he regards something other than the sentence to be the "fact." Where needful, I shall simply say *true sentence* or the like to signal this latter meaning. But that which is treated as objective and which may undergo interpretation, rather than the interpretation itself or the expression of the interpretation, shall be *fact* for me.

In the popular vocabulary, *object* is regarded as meaning a physical thing (as in "He espied an object in the distance"; "The study was furnished not only with desk and chair but with objects collected in his travels"), then more intangibly as a purpose, or as that which gains the regard of an individual ("Her neighbor was the object of her curiosity"; "The object of Cato's highest hopes was the destruction of Carthage"). The trend of this extension is toward the application of it that I shall usually make, i.e., as the object of attention or awareness or consciousness, anything that may be entertained in the mind. This may include what we understand as events, as well as physical objects, and also what we understand as "ideal objects," mental objects such as numbers and abstract figures, which are not subject to physical erosion or change. An *event* I shall take to be anything that has or had or shall have a time before which, a time during which, and a time after which it appears. Thus, I shall consider both "objects" and "events" to be presentations to consciousness, regarding all these as lying within the strictures of metaphysical and epistemological vocabulary that I have imposed on myself. If I am successful in my attempt to communicate, it shall not matter if we believe that sentences are about actual objects and events out there in an external universe that is independently real of our awareness, or that they are about objects of consciousness only, such that we hang back from imputing objective existence to them independent of our own and any other consciousness.

Thus, in the sense of everyday language and under the qualifications now introduced, we may suggest in rather loose language that *fact* is a term encompassing anything that occurs; and that we may take *occur* to mean *is present* (as in "Veins of coal often occur in association with shales and other carbonaceous strata"), just as it also means *happens*. Either sort of occurrence may serve to ground the truth of descriptive declarative sentences, granting merely that the wording is adequate to the subject matter. Thus, *fact* includes anything that may ground the truth of a descriptive declarative sentence, anything that is an occurrence either as a static object (including ideal objects) or as a dynamic event, against which a realist might attempt to test its truth. This conception of *fact* at first glance seems pretty comprehensive. We shall see, however, that it does not exhaust the universe.

We are influenced in our orientation toward *fact* by another strong tendency of our use of language, namely, that of reification or hypostatization. While it is not usual to analyze a physical object into separate "before's" and "after's"—though it may be done—we often do condense events, phraseologically, into determinate objects, or "things." We speak of "a baseball game," which is not one physical object but an event of some hours' duration, taken part in by a few dozen people manipulating various discrete physical objects, and clearly having a "before," a duration, and an "after." We speak of the Hundred Years' War as a single, even if long-lasting, event, talking about its causes with just as much confidence that it is a "thing" as we talk about the causes of blisters, stalactites, or gold ores. The word *object* has already shown us that we move in thought from the physical thing to the mental "thing," a purpose, and then from that to the abstraction, the "object of attention," or the still more obvious reification, i.e., "an ideal object." The importance of this tendency for our study is, in part, that pre-reflectively we already regard facts as things somehow, which may properly be said to have properties and descriptions; and that we embed in our language myriad expressions for handling them as though they *are* entities, or things, whether they are or not. This enables us to use them (or our ideas of them) as the standard for truth or accuracy of statements. Contemporary critical philosophy, of course, issues us many cautions about these practices. Analogously, we speak of "values," possibly an even more obvious reification than "facts," and this has set the value theorists to searching for and attempting to define *the good* and, later, *value,* as though value is an independently existing object in an outside world, about which descriptive sentences can be composed and tested if only we are patient enough in our search to persist until we unquestionably have found it, and if only we are astute enough, upon finding it, to recognize it for what it is. Actually, this reification of *the good* and of *value* has tended to obscure what we really mean in applying the word *value*.

Now we may come to understand another important term. A *statement of fact* is a sentence purporting to express an assertion (or a denial) of what is the case concerning a state of affairs or an event. The statement, a declarative sentence, is a linguistic configuration, in contrast to the state of affairs itself or to an event that the sentence may record. In everyday situations, ordinary persons need not and do not separate the two threads, the linguistic expression and the matter it symbolizes. They are aware that the total combination has, for their purposes, a strong connotation of the idea *truth*. But a statement and its truth are two different things. Therefore, in order to remove the misleading idea of *truth or falsity* as a determinant of the *kind* of sentence that we employ to assert facts, I shall introduce and consistently apply the phrase *fact-assertive statement* (*fact-assertive sentence* or *fact-assertive proposition*) so as to identify the kind of sentence we have been calling a "statement of fact," and to set deliberately aside the consideration whether the statement mentioned has been tested and confirmed to be true, or tested and found to be untrue, or has not been tested. In my usage, a fact-assertive statement bears the purport of expressing a fact, that is, of reporting a state of affairs or an event, but it should *not* be considered certified as true by virtue of what it is called. Some fact-assertive statements we know to be true; others we know to be false; and of yet others, we know them to be of undetermined truth-sign, even though they may be of crucial importance.

In this chapter I have attempted to propound, and to a small extent demonstrate, the usefulness of turning to *statements*, expressions in language, in order to learn about things that are not statements, namely, in this instance, those things that we call *values*, or that which we call *value*. I have sketched a widespread, though incomplete, uncritical, and quite untechnical, understanding of the idea of what a fact is, against which we may and often do compare *value*. I have affirmed that the way the difference between fact and value enters our discussions and thought is in two kinds of statements, those expressing facts and those expressing value judgments—and that *we regularly recognize the difference between the two*. I have suggested that we operate, whether knowingly or not, in the fashion of using the one kind of statement to express or represent facts, and we understand them as having that function; and in turn, we operate also in the fashion of using the other kind of statement to express and convey value judgments, and we do in fact understand *them* in turn as having *that* function. The reader has no doubt noticed that occasionally I have used the word *proposition*, without explanation. This important term can hardly be taken without examination in an inquiry that turns to propositional expression as explanatory of other things. Rather, we must investigate what it implies or presupposes for our inquiry, for we can neither do without it and confine our topic entirely to statements or sentences, nor use the term *proposition* fruitfully, without understanding its relation to the subject at hand, and particularly the relation between propositions and sentences that are statements. This must be the subject of our next chapter.

2

Propositions

For our study of value we are going to need the concept of *proposition* as an instrument for pulling together and organizing a number of other concepts. That there are such things as propositions, or that they are needed, has been questioned. However, the proposition evidently has some sort of ontic status, at least pragmatically speaking, for discussion is much more facilitated when the term is admitted than when it is expunged, and those employing it seem to believe they are talking about something rather than nothing. In order to push my inquiry further, then, I shall have to establish an orientation for propositions, for there is an important connection between propositions and value judgments.

There are certain things that we have long believed about propositions. There is a connection between propositions and sentences, yet this holds true for only some sentences, not all. Propositions appear not to have a direct relation or connection with sentences that are commands, questions, exclamations, performatives, and other sorts; rather, their connection is with the declarative sentences. Yet they are again not simply the same thing as declarative sentences or statements, for we acknowledge that the same statement in writing or speech may express two different propositions, and again that two different declarative statements may express the same proposition. Both sentences and propositions may be said to be true or false, and of both of them it may be said that a given one may be either true *or* false but not both true and false under given conditions. Both statements and propositions may be regarded as potential objects of belief; it is idiomatic to say either "I believe that statement" or "I believe that proposition." Thus in these various ways, both statements and propositions may figure as objects of consciousness and objects of attention.

On the showing made thus far, summarizing the things that are "common knowledge" or common conceptions of the proposition, we have mentioned three separate entities—the sentence, the statement, and the proposition. The sentence is fairly easy to lay hands on; it is a certain sequence of words, either in speech or in writing. Sentences are of several kinds, and among them only the declarative sentence is decisively interesting to an inquirer into the nature of the proposition. A declarative sentence is also fairly readily specifiable—it is a sequence of words that declares, or affirms, or (as is more often said) asserts, rather than questions, commands, exclaims, confers, or something else. Now then, a sequence of words that asserts, that is, a declarative sentence, is ordinarily called a statement, in contrast to a question, a command, and so on. So a statement is also readily specifiable in the objective realm; it is a certain sequence of words, specifically, the kind that asserts. A *caveat* is useful, however; the word *statement* is often made to serve as a synonym either for *sentence* or for *proposition*. Thus it possesses an ambiguity not characterizing the two between which it lies.

But what about a proposition? It seems not to be a sequence of words, or at least not any fixed sequence of words, for we "know" that a variety of sequences of words, of sentences, is capable of expressing the same proposition. For a given proposition, there is one sequence, we suppose, and very likely more than one, in each of the 800 or more natural languages of the world that expresses it. Hence we infer that a proposition is not a sequence of words, but something that is conveyed in common by all members of a set of sequences of words, a set whose number of members we never ascertain since few of us are fluent in all the world's natural languages, and since we cannot take into account the particulars of all possible languages whether extant or not. Again, the fact that a single sequence of words may on different occasions convey different propositions tends also to make us infer that the proposition is something independent of wording, possibly a thought that the sequences of words express, or possibly the meaning of the sequences of words. At any rate, by the time our thinking has reached this stage we have by inference pushed the proposition way out of sight, so that it has become a kind of ghost of the sentence or sentences with which we began. It has acquired a spooky character, yet it haunts us so constantly that it tends to lead us even to believe in the existence of spooks.

Now, I am as open as anyone to the possibility of intangible realities and even to the reality of totally mysterious entities, but I do not believe in adopting these as the explanations of common experience until after the possibilities of tangible explanatory entities have been exhausted. Further, I believe that such an explanation can be found, and can be found to suffice, for the proposition.

In looking further into what can be known about propositions, we can specify more fully the things we have already listed as commonly agreed knowledge about them; and to guide the development of our inquiry, we can ask the very useful question, "In just what ways do propositions enter into experience?"

Perhaps the most evident way in which propositions enter into human experience is that on certain occasions people talk about them. As a discussion begins to move from casual conversation to serious talk or controversy, it frequently happens that someone labels a significant statement a proposition, and in doing so directs special attention to it. Others ordinarily fall in with the usage; after one speaker has shown his willingness to engage in serious consideration of a given statement that he has designated as a proposition, it is hardly imaginable that anyone else would say, "Oh, no, that statement is not in fact a proposition at all." Evidently, the labeling of a key statement as a proposition gives that statement a certain status, a dignity elevating it above others. But that added dignity is hardly enough alone to induce speakers to create, by referring to it, a whole category of statements—"propositions"—separated off from the great remainder of the statements. In fact, there appears to be no clear differentiation in form or characteristics between statements that are propositions and statements that are not or might not be. Any statement may be labeled a proposition, although some listeners might see little point in singling out trivial statements for that designation and might wonder why anyone would "propose" or "propound" a trivial statement for consideration or debate.

Rather, it is this last matter that is important in determining which statements come to be known—for a time, at least—as propositions. The propositions are the statements that are selected for primary roles in discussions, as statements that comprise the structure of the discussions and without which the discussions would be substantially different. The statements that speakers come to call *propositions* are important to them, important to the purposes they have in carrying on discussion (such purposes as establishing truth, discovering worthy beliefs, or enforcing one's own already-fixed beliefs upon others). What distinguishes propositions from statements that are not propositions (although they *could* be) is this fact about them, that they are *treated* as propositions; and since statements are potential grist for the mill of consideration, all statements are in that sense potential propositions. Thus while there exist statements that are not now propositions, it would be idle to attempt to identify them, since singling out a statement would give it the special attention that characterizes serious consideration—and the statement selected would *ipso facto* become a proposition.

In a similar vein, we should notice that it is not necessarily the actual labeling of a statement as a proposition, but rather it is the *treatment* of the statement, with respect to the serious consideration of it, that is the core of the conferral of proposition status upon that statement. If two persons are debating the advisability of accepting the statement "We should write our Congressman to urge immediate passage of the Conservation Bill" as a maxim for their day's plan, they are treating the statement as a proposition regardless of its label. A third person happening upon the discussion could properly label the statement a proposition in his own mind, without using the term in the hearing of those discussing it; or he could label it a proposition in their hearing without its striking them as odd that he should do so. Hence, whatever else the statement may or may not be, and whether labeled as such or not, in the experience of these speakers the statement is a proposition.

If, however, any statement is potentially a proposition, we may ask ourselves how it could be that, as we have said, some sentences may convey two propositions rather than one. Here, notice that we shift our terminology back to *sentence* rather than to *statement*. Actually, it would not be unidiomatic to affirm that a single sentence may convey two statements rather than one, or even that a single *statement* may convey two propositions rather than one. This circumstance serves to remind us that the term *statement* is (like most important everyday terms) ambiguous. When we do say that the same sentence may convey or "make" two statements rather than one, we have shifted from our understanding of a statement as a sequence of words and are actually using the word *statement* as a synonym for *proposition*. Let us simply decline to fall into this trap, and revert to *sentence* as our designation for a sequence of words (arranged in an appropriate grammatical and semantic way), a linguistic phenomenon. Now we can notice how it is that a given sentence may convey two propositions. First, the sentence may contain a word that is ambiguous in its sentential context. "The boat is fast" may convey that the boat, when moving, moves rapidly, or that the boat is securely tied so that it cannot move at all. *Fast* has both the meanings of *rapid* and of *fastened*. Second, the sentence may be so constructed that relationships among its words and phrases are left vague, as in this example from a book: "The problem does not seem to have been discussed on purpose . . . ." This statement says either that potential speakers unwittingly omitted to discuss the problem, or that they were aware of the problem but intentionally refrained from discussing it—or even that speakers did discuss the problem without intending to discuss it! A third way is that the sentence may depend upon situational context for determination, as "I prefer coffee," when spoken once by James and once by Thomas respectively means either "James prefers coffee" or "Thomas prefers coffee." Furthermore, the same sentence may "convey" two propositions simply by being a compound sentence: "James smoked and Thomas drank" conveys (1) "James smoked" and (2) "Thomas drank" as well as the conjunctive affirmation of these. Thus it is already ambiguous to say "The same sentence may convey two different propositions." What is important here is not the emphasis upon ambiguity but the indication that in cases of ambiguous declarative sentences, to utter the observation that one sentence may convey two propositions is a convenient way of identifying and handling that ambiguity. And, consequently, it is clearly a way in which propositions enter the experience of human subjects.

What of the converse, i.e., instances of two sentences conveying the same proposition? There is nothing mysterious here. It is simply one way to explain translatability, to explain the flexibility of language in the form of synonymous sentences. When we say that both "Il pleut" and "Es regnet" mean "It is raining," we may and occasionally do add the idea "These sentences, from different languages, all express the same proposition." Thus we see that this discussion in which the term *proposition* figures is another way in which propositions enter human experience.

It is illuminating to notice that not only does conferring the term *proposition* upon a declarative sentence seem to elevate it in dignity, but we seem to assign dignity principally to those statements that are crucial in arguments, namely, premises and conclusions. In everyday affairs we rarely identify the elements of formal arguments; we perhaps do so more in our vocational transactions if we are members of certain vocations, such as lawyers, legislators, or logic teachers. But when we do so, we are moving from the less formal to the more formal, a movement which has its affective elements in such things as an increase of dignity and its explicitly sought purposes in such things as greater exactness of thought and statement.

Finally, it may be said that when we are intent upon deciding whether to add an item to our store of beliefs, we may use either of two families of locutions to explain to ourselves or to others what it is that we are about. We may say that we are attempting to establish whether that item is *true,* or we may say that we are attempting to decide whether that item is something that we shall be inclined or be compelled to *believe.* Both of these manners of speaking are quite common. In connection with each, and possibly more customarily in connection with the second, we are likely to say that the candidate for belief is a *proposition.* We may also call it a *statement* as a synonym for *proposition* rather than *sentence,* for we generally (though not universally) classify objects of belief not as linguistic configurations (sentences as such) but as mental configurations, propositions that we think, speak, or write. Hence here is yet another way in which propositions enter into human experience. And while there undoubtedly are still more, the set concluding with this example should serve to typify the lot.

By now one fact about the proposition stands forth very clearly, instanced in all of our several ways in which propositions figure in our thinking. In every case the proposition has a function of emphasizing that precision is needed, and to employ the word introduces a dignity of treatment that may be expressed in some formula such as "This matter is worth thinking through in exact terms." The proposition is mentioned—or better, perhaps, the word *proposition* occurs or would occur—in discourses where we are aware that exact rather than vague thinking is desirable, and where we are actually embarking on the project of making our thinking more exact than it was at first. Thus we use "propositions" to clarify ambiguities, to explain linguistic phenomena such as translatability and linguistic equivalence, to focus attention upon logical structure, and to emphasize the importance of fixing belief in carefully considered ways. One is hard put to think of counterexamples, and I suggest that the evidence for this characterization of the proposition— that it is a device for gaining precision—is strong.

Now we can consider what implications for the proposition this characterization of it may have. What is the nature of a device for gaining precision? Certain things might in a sense be classified as precision devices which are in the material realm—planes, micrometers, fine machining tools, things that are used to bring other materials to a realized form with great exactness. In the case of the non-material devices of the sort, however, precision devices (such as formulas for precise definitions) are by nature rules. They instruct us in mental or intellectual techniques that we may apply in numerous situations of resolving mental or intellectual problems and, especially, confusions.

From this consideration, we now can begin to see more fully what a proposition is. A proposition is an entity of a certain sort that has a close relation to a sentence and arises from the need for rendering employment of that sentence precise. In fact—and I shall develop this description forthwith—a proposition is a sentence treated according to certain rules in a manner that maintains or adds to the precision of discourse in which that sentence occurs. I shall call these rules Rules of Propositionality, and I shall set them forth as fully as I can.

Before beginning to list rules, however, I must hasten to state that for a proposition to be treated in a certain way, it may in the process be modified. On some occasions the wording of a sentence and its corresponding proposition may be exactly the same; but on other frequent occasions a sentence that is singled out for propositional treatment must be reworded. It will be consistent with normal usage if we refer to the product of such modification as the proposition, although it will bear the same sort of relation to the original as a squared beam bears to a tree trunk, or a baked loaf bears to a pan of dough. It will be the same matter that was originally procured but something has happened to it. Its original has a greater or lesser resemblance, depending upon particular circumstances, to what it becomes once it has undergone the appropriate methodical treatment to adapt it better to human purposes. Sometimes the final wording of the proposition is identical to that of the original sentence so that the difference between the specimen as sentence and as proposition is not tangible. On the other hand, sometimes the rewording may be drastic. Our definition of *proposition,* once fully elaborated, will apply with full appropriateness to either sort of sentence.

It is also pertinent to remark before embarking on the rules themselves that when one or more of the Rules of Propositionality is applied, the users of the sentence in question may or may not actually have used the term *proposition.* Similarly, it is conceivable, though I should suppose it rare, that someone may actually use that word while yet failing to apply any Rule of Propositionality. This would most likely occur, I should think, when the individual simply does not actually know the meaning of the word *proposition* or its conventional employment in our language, for surely if he does know its meaning and applies it to an appropriate linguistic entity, he shall at least be singling out that entity and giving it the kind of special attention which the conventional application of the term signals. Regardless of whether the speakers in a given discussion have used *proposition,* if their discussion was to be subjected on another level to an analysis as to its import, it would be highly idiomatic for that analysis to contain the word *proposition,* and rather likely that it would do so. This second-level usage of the word *proposition* is confirming evidence of the interpretation here offered.

It should be evident by now that the Rules of Propositionality have not heretofore been formulated in any public fashion, much less adopted by any authority and declared binding upon any constituency. Rather, they are detected implicit in the ways in which persons use the resources of their language. Their force is the common one of linguistic convention. Their users are no more aware of them than most of us are aware of the rules for pronoun agreement in our own language even while using those rules correctly—that is, while speaking according to the conventions of that language. Those being the circumstances, it is surprising how much regularity we can elicit from the practices of speakers, to formulate in the pattern of rules; and it is the more surprising that while the rules may be understood as descriptive, like the "laws" of nature, people nevertheless also actually "obey" them or conform to them in order to achieve a desired precision in their discussions. Thus the Rules of Propositionality actually do function both descriptively and prescriptively—although once they have been identified as prescriptive, some rebellious individuals will no doubt set out systematically to violate them.

The basic thrust of the rules is this: "Treat an indicated sentence as though it is a proposition." This is the Principle of Propositionality. It epitomizes some six separate rules, the application of one or more of which is constitutive of the kind of special attention that makes a sentence a proposition.

The First Rule of Propositionality is:

> A sentence *S* to be treated as a proposition is to be cast in declarative form.

This rule is in conformity with common knowledge about propositions—which is to say, with standard usage of the term *proposition* in the English language (and presumably in any natural language into which the present discussion can be adequately translated). It singles out the *sentence* as the product of propositional treatment which may be either written or spoken or both and may be imagined or conceived in the mind, whether in written or spoken form or both. Evidently sentences may also be stored in the mind or remembered, for we succeed in recalling them after periods in which they are not actively in consciousness. If a sentence is to be regarded as a possible object of belief, it must be in declarative form.

The first rule, however, does not command, "Take only declarative sentences for treatment as propositions." An exclamation, a question, or a command, and at that not necessarily a complete sentence, can in fact communicate a proposition even though it is couched grammatically in language that is nominally devoted to other things: "You generous fellow!" "Can one really prefer one's own mere comfort to the faithful discharge of a duty to secure the health of one's father?" "Don't call *me* a thief!" These three sample locutions are not written as declarative sentences, yet each clearly conveys a proposition. They are produced otherwise than as declarative in order to achieve an emphasis that is not attained, respectively, by "You are a generous fellow," "One ought not prefer one's own mere comfort to the faithful discharge of a duty to secure the health of one's father," and "I am not a thief." In fact, one of the effects of a precision process is the neutralizing of emotional emphasis that characterizes the latter versions of each of these pairs, for emotional neutrality generally is an aid to accomplishing the pertinent cognitive purposes. Thus we can see that the First Rule of Propositionality does not require us to confine our attention to sentences that have occurred in discourse in the declarative form, but it tells us what to do with locutions of other forms when we take the propositional sort of interest in them. And of course if there are various possibilities rather than a single propositional implication (say, for example, "Although I *am* a thief, you ought not call me one!"), the very process of rewording will tend to bring such ambiguities to light and thus partially fulfill the purpose of propositional treatment.

Again, propositions may originate in locutions that are not grammatically complete sentences, so that they cannot actually be classified as declarative, imperative, or something else. Indeed, they may originate in forms that are partly non-linguistic. "Fire!" the shout goes up. On hearing such a cry in a public place, one is likely to think "Something has caught on fire." Under certain circumstances, such as within a confining enclosure, one might further think "I ought to leave rapidly." While the single word does not convey a single determinable proposition, most listeners will derive at least one from it, and probably will then set about securing verifying evidence for that one. Just as in many situations, in this one the situational context has much to do with the proposition that one derives; on a target range, for example, it probably will be quite different from those suggested above. In some cases, involving two different persons, two locutions are required to generate a single proposition: The used car customer asks, "How many miles has the car been driven?" and the salesman replies, "Twenty thousand." Only when enough material has been supplied, either in statement or in context, can the First Rule of Propositionality be fulfilled.

Finally, we have to look in another direction to find still another way to generate propositions within the linguistic framework. In the sentences we have examined so far, we have made relatively little change in their sense, in order to render them worthy of proposition status. However, we have used rather short and simple sentences. Even at that, the kind of exfoliation of propositions that must now be acknowledged can be illustrated by "I ought to leave rapidly." This set of words actually yields two propositions, which we are unlikely to discriminate unless our purposes induce us to make finer distinctions than the ordinary. The first is simply "I ought to leave," and the second is "The manner of my leaving should be rapid." For ordinary purposes—certainly including those of a person who is in close quarters, upon hearing the shout "Fire!"—such a degree of discrimination is probably pointless, but when we are examining the whole structure of a complex sentence in a discussion of considerable importance, we may in fact want to explore many discriminable nuances and examine each for its potential truth, believability, arguability, approvability, or the like. To elicit all the possible second-level propositions conveyed by a long sentence is likely to yield as many or more propositions as there are words in the sentence, and is one form of what we have come to call "unpacking" the sentence.

The Second Rule of Propositionality is:

> A sentence *S* which is to be a proposition is to be treated as though it has a claim upon belief.

Whereas the First Rule was concerned with form, this rule requires a certain attitude and corresponding behavior on the part of originators and recipients of the sentence in view. The application of the rule assumes the possibility that words arranged in declarative sentences can communicate states of affairs or events. Thus the sentence is taken as a representation of something other than itself; by means of the sentence, some element of a state of affairs or an event is brought under special attention. To apply the Second Rule is to enter seriously the inquiry whether *S* is true or false, or is deserving of belief.

The Third Rule of Propositionality is:

> Disregard the features of *S* that do not contribute necessarily to the principal assertion contained in *S*.

Features of the sort mentioned are such things as certain aspects of its mode of statement and its adjunct meanings, rather than its central meaning. Features to disregard include grammatical features other than those facilitating declarative expression; linguistic features (features of the specific natural language in which the sentence is rendered or of its translations into other languages, assuming always that the content remains stable despite translation); rhetorical features (features tending to achieve persuasion in ways other than those ways in which assertions *per se* are persuasive); poetical features; and strictly ornamental features. Some art, some judgment on things not easily decided objectively, is required in observing this rule.

The Fourth Rule of Propositionality is:

> Heed particularly the features of S that constitute its basic content, being careful to omit nothing that is vital to its whole principal assertion.

Features to heed include those of what the user of ordinary language will regard as the *basic content* of the sentence, the main message. While this rule tends to narrow down from a larger potential total the number of separate declarative sentences that will be implied by a sentence of some complexity, it does not actually require that a maximum be placed on the amount of content that may be treated propositionally. Rather, it leaves to determination within each discourse, according to the specifics of that discourse, the number of assertions that are ultimately to be taken as the basic content of S. Hence S eventually may appear as grammatically and logically simple or compound or complex, and as comprising unrelated elements, or else as comprising certain sentence elements together with one or more relations between them. This sort of effect of the Fourth Rule is the kind of result for which propositions have been devised in the first place.

So far from there being any formidable difficulty to practitioners of serious discussion as to what is the basic content of a sentence rather than its ancillary content, it is probably the widespread recognition of the basic content of sentences that has led to the general view that there is a "thing" that is a proposition, that two separate sentences thus say the same "thing," that it is this "thing" that remains stable when a sentence is translated into another sentence in a different language, and so on. There has seemed to be some quiddity that lurks just out of sight and is embodied temporarily in the disguise of now one, now another of these linguistic costumes. We shall shortly be able to disabuse ourselves of such a notion of "the real proposition" that is "lying behind" the various sentences expressing it.

The Fifth Rule of Propositionality is:

> Treat S as unitary even though S may have variant particular expressions.

The sentence S may have not only a number of translations into many natural languages that preserve the content of S throughout all the permutations of translation; it may also have more than one expression within a given language ("The highway is beside the river"; "The river is beside the highway"). This rule calls for treating all these versions as making a single assertion of a state of affairs, and prescribes indifference of treatment to the various translations so long as they are equivalent translations. The usual application of the rule is to settle upon a single wording of S and employ it as though it alone expressed S; that, of course, is merely a convenience of exposition employed by the originator and recipients of S. Actually, when giving serious consideration to S, one does not think all exemplars of S but rather thinks a token of S, one exemplar, one statement into which other exemplars may be translated without substantial change in the meaning of the source sentence (say, S in French) and the target sentence (say, S in English).

Even within the one language in which a discourse or discussion takes place, there may be in circulation alternative wordings of S. When this is so, and yet the variant wordings do not effect a substantial change in content (for example, the pair "'Lucy' is a girls' name"; "'Lucy' is a feminine name"), then such differences are to be disregarded. The two wordings may be treated as though they are but one—S is handled as though unitary, despite alternate wordings or the encroachment of synonymous expressions. On the other hand, as between two sentences, so long as differences in the apparent basic content are distinguishable, the two sentences should be regarded as expressing two separate propositions. ("At age eighteen, a person is old enough to vote"; "At age eighteen, a person is legally an adult." Even though both sentences are true in a given locality at a given time, so long as differences in their content, in "what they say," are distinguishable, they are not alternate versions of S but two separate propositions. Very difficult questions involving theory of meaning, which could be brought in here, had best be left alone, while we take the practical way out—that when someone can discriminate a difference, then there is a difference, and any disputants should then choose, as between the two possibilities, which one it is that sets forth the issue between them.)

The Sixth Rule of Propositionality is:

Recast S so as to remove uncertainties of meaning.

Applying this rule not only acknowledges that "the same sentence may convey more than one proposition," but also lets us dispose of the fact as an anomaly arising out of ordinary ambiguity. There is little need to amplify the statement of the rule since many techniques for improving upon ambiguity, amphiboly, vagueness, and the like, are widely known. Those persons who are concerned with S for important reasons will, of course, guard against any changes in the substance of S occurring by virtue of these changes of wording, to the extent that the substance has already been established. Where it has not, of course, their modifications upon the original of S are instruments for their use in their endeavor either to decide what S means in this context or to decide what is true, what to believe, or what description of an occurrence which S concerns is an acceptable description. It is permissible, though by no means required, to modify the original of S by omission of some or all of the elements that are to be disregarded, since presumably these will be of no effect upon an investigation concerned with the basic content and substance of *S*. There is normally a considerable portion of any serious inquiry that is devoted to making terminology more exact and to ascertaining just what it is that is being investigated; this is all consistent with the thesis that the introduction of the proposition as a more worthy expression than the unconsidered sentence, as in fact an instrument of making precise a sentence that has caught attention and attracted inquiry, is indeed the origin of the proposition.

The recognition of the Rules of Propositionality now enables us to round out the ontology of the proposition. But first, to do so, we must briefly consider the ontology of a sentence, for a proposition is a sentence treated in a certain way, namely, by the Rules of Propositionality. Let us consider, then, how a sentence enters experience.

One way a sentence may appear in consciousness is in the form of markings on a surface, handwritten or printed letters of an alphabet or characters in a symbol system. However, it is evident historically and anthropologically that these have followed the development of spoken language, so that we may consider the graphic sentence as a coded representation of the spoken or heard sentence. Thus, at its base a sentence is a collection of vocal sounds. What distinguishes the sentence from any collection of vocal sounds is meaning, and meaning with certain characteristics. A single word may have meaning; a sentence, however, has meaning with a certain completeness, which differs for the various kinds of grammatical sentences. That which constitutes a collection of meaningful sounds as a sentence, rather than merely a word or phrase, is meaning having the appropriate kind of completeness, and so long as an originator or a recipient of the sounds hears it as complete in such a way, it is for him a sentence of the kind whose complete meaning he detects. Since we are interested in the sentence as a base for the proposition, we need look only at the declarative sentence, and say that it is based on a collection of sounds such that its user (its originator or recipient) apprehends in it that kind of completeness that the grammar teacher calls "a complete thought," a full rendition of grammatical subject and predicate, with nothing present that leaves an unfulfilled grammatical expectation (such as a transitive verb lacking an object). Thus a sentence is relative to the person who apprehends it as such. The user of the sentence brings something to it; without him, it is not a whole object of consciousness of the kind we may legitimately label a sentence. The sounds represented by "Life is short" make a sentence for me, but if I do not know Spanish, I do not know whether the sounds represented by "La vida es corta" make a sentence in that language or not, and for me they cannot be a sentence until I have more knowledge. All told, then, for an appearance in consciousness to be a declarative sentence, it must consist in sounds apprehended as units of linguistic meaning (words) arranged in coherent groupings (phrases or other functional parts of sentences) with meanings formed by their grouping, associated with the units independently, and apprehended as a grammatically complete rather than a fragmentary affirmative or negative assertion. Thus the sentence in its ontic entirety has objective and subjective elements. That is, the sentence, as an object of consciousness, has an element that can be intersubjective, which is the concrete form of sounds or of markings representing sounds; and over and above the concrete form, it has elements contributed by the user of the sentence, namely, the meanings imputed to the words and phrases, the imputed completeness rather than incompleteness, and the imputed functioning of the whole as a sentence rather than as mere miscellaneous vocalizing.

Now we can note the ways a proposition appears in consciousness. A given proposition consists in those expressions that are present in consciousness as sentences, in both the objective and subjective aspects of sentences, together with the taking up by cognizant persons of the propositional attitude and the carrying out of the kind of correlative behavior that characterizes that attitude. In other words, a proposition is a sentence that is treated according to the Rules of Propositionality. All the features of the declarative sentence remain with it; in addition, with some of its appearances in some consciousnesses, there appears the behavior of special treatment which, for that sentence and for that user, constitutes it a proposition.

An individual apprehending the sentence in question takes it as one in which he has greater than average cognitive or epistemological interest. Something about this sentence is at issue for him and, in his view, is yet to be established, whereas that is not the case with other sentences that have entered his consciousness. This element of interest in the sentence, or concern for it, on the part of one or more subjects, is a second element in the structure of the proposition, for without that interest on his or their part, the sentence would simply remain a sentence and not be accorded the status of a proposition.

To accord propositional status to the sentence, to adopt a certain stance or attitude toward it, is already to treat the sentence *S* in a distinctive way. Further distinctive treatment for *S* consists in the application of some number of and possibly all of the Rules of Propositionality. Certain acts performed by the participants in a discourse in which *S* is an issue, or is a significant structural member, are events comprising the behavior of these participants vis-à-vis sentence *S*, and are a part of a collection of such acts that eventually comprises a total behavioral component of the proposition. These acts include the shearing away of irrelevant expressions, the identification of features of *S* that do enter into the issue under examination, the acceptance (often by letting them go unremarked) of variant versions as expressing the one proposition, and the like. And the collection includes acts performed by all those who take part in inquiry concerning *S*, whether or not separated by space or time from the first inquirers who discuss *S*. Thus when *S* becomes a proposition, it may indeed have a long and complex life as such, imaginably enduring as a proposition for the life of a civilization or longer (for example, "Pleasure is the good").

A glance at the application of the Sixth Rule shows that two of the components are affected by its application. The revision of *S* to make it more fitting as an object of treatment as a proposition contributes acts of proposition-behavior to the total collection just mentioned. It also contributes specific concrete expressions—statements in speech, writing, or print—to the body of expressions of *S*, and necessarily contributes to a numerically plural and possibly, at a given time, still increasing number of those expressions. These variant expressions of *S* simply become part of the total body of material expressions of *S*. Their ever more precise sentential meanings become part of the total body of mental representations of *S*. Thus the proposition whose ontic status we are describing is a growing thing throughout a period of time (this is no more odd than the ontic status of, say, a tree or an elephant or a body of law), and it is this growth, looked at from the viewpoint of the refinement of the item being discussed, that has the principal practical effect of fulfilling the purpose of the proposition, that of rendering a sentence, and the discussion centering upon it, more precise.

The behavioral component of the proposition bears a closer look. We distinguish between the *ontic status* of *a* proposition, one we have been denominating sentence *S*, on the one hand, and the *meaning* of the term *proposition* on the other hand. Let us remind ourselves that the wording of a casually encountered sentence and of the proposition which that sentence yields when it is treated by speakers as a proposition may be exactly the same, or it may be different. On the supposition that the wording remains the same, the version that the speakers use later in time, treating it with care in ascertaining its exact meaning and perhaps labeling it a *proposition*, is indeed a proposition; and it is just this treatment on their behalf that has made it a proposition, for otherwise it remains indistinguishable from what it was at the outset, merely one sentence among others. And although we might suppose that when the wording of an original is altered, the difference between the original sentence and the proposition formed later is the difference that constitutes the second version a proposition, that in fact is not so. That difference is a by-product rather than the product. It is still the *treatment by the speakers* who have discussed the original sentence and established the second version as a result that constitutes the second version a proposition. They have not "reworded the original sentence so as to make it into a proposition," for there is no flag, no identifying mark or characteristic, no overt sign that shows that some expressions are propositions while others are mere sentences. The reworded version that is a proposition in a discussion by A and B could be the casually encountered sentence that is attended to but not subjected to any special attention at all in a conversation between C and D. It is solely the history, as it were, the treatment by users of the precise sentence, that constitutes the sentence a proposition. The case is similar to that of a garden hose treated as a siphon to empty a puddle, but not continued in that use. Just as it retains its status as a garden hose, a sentence remains a sentence when special interest in it ceases and its life as a proposition is over.

Looking further at the behavior of speakers in a discussion of a proposition, we may note that one of them may be the originator of sentence *S*, or may have discovered it in an existing context; and one of them, who may either be the same or a different one, may first refer to *S* as a proposition. These facts patently make the being of a proposition relative to certain users. It is even conceivable that if A and B are talking together, *S* is a proposition to A but not a proposition to B, who lets A talk on while he himself gives closer attention to other things. However, the relativity of the proposition as an entity to individual minds is neither in itself a disproof that it is real or actually occurs, nor an objection to assigning the proposition the ontic status that I claim it actually occupies. For the ontic status of *S* is one thing, and is relative to A or B or C who consider *S*, but the meaning of the word *proposition* does not suffer from the same variability. *Proposition* continues in conventional usage to mean any sentence treated in the fashion of the rules given here.

The behavior of A and B when carrying on their discussion is *ipso facto* a part of the being of the proposition that they investigate. It is at least that part of their total behavior that is carried on in accordance with the Rules of Propositionality, and it may also include other acts besides, acts that are in the spirit of treating *S* as a proposition but that are not covered by the rules, acts that perhaps could not be anticipated nor commanded. However, if there is such additional behavior by A and B, it is all part of what makes *S* a proposition. This behavior can be conceived of independently of any theory of meaning that may or may not be based on behavior, and it should be clear that the recognition of the behavioral component of the entity that is a proposition is a different thing from a commitment to a behavioral theory of meaning (which says, "What a sentence means is what people do, that is, how they behave, when they regard it to be true," or the like).

In this connection it is not amiss to note that one of the speakers in a discussion may control the behavior of another by injecting the word *proposition*. If A utters something as a more or less casual comment—an unexamined thought—but B responds by saying "Oh, really? Now let us examine that proposition," then B has implicitly put A under an obligation to obey the Rules of Propositionality. Characteristically, A will rise to the defense of his statement, often by striving immediately to make more clear what he has just said in the sentence at issue, which B has called a proposition. If A and B now find themselves engaged in a controversy, the basic behavior of both may become competitive. However, the rules of the game of controversy evidently include the Rules of Propositionality, for A and B will pretty fully behave in accordance with the latter. In their competition to justify opposing views, conducting themselves as adversaries, they will nevertheless include sequences of mutually acceptable, and in fact accepted, behavior in the form of speaking according to the Rules of Propositionality and other conventions of civilized, constructive discussion. The competitive behavior is no part of the total structure of the proposition, but according to the Rules of Propositionality the behavior is indeed a part of the structure of the proposition they discuss.

While we are considering, perhaps for the first time, the matter of obedience to the Rules of Propositionality, we would do well to remind ourselves that not only are these implicit rather than explicit rules, founded on convention rather than on deliberate adoption by individuals or by parliamentary bodies, but also that the rules are more or less well recognized by speakers and writers, in proportion to the amount of experience with and knowledge of linguistic practice that they possess. In this respect these are rules for the performance of a skill, rather than for the fulfillment of an obligation or the achievement of social acceptance. They are like certain rules in learning golf or tennis, not the regulations of the game, but rules for operating, like "Keep your eyes on the ball" and "Don't bend your back when making a swing." No player ever absolutely culminates his mastery of rules of this sort, for the more of them he absorbs into his practice, the more of them he becomes aware of. He may hear of them from the more experienced, or he may (as we do with the Rules of Propositionality) learn them by observing others putting them into practice. Consequently, when I say that the treatment of sentence S in propositional fashion is a component part of the actual proposition, I cannot realistically say that *only* when all of the rules are applied has S reached the status of a proposition. Just as we speak of "his game of golf" or "his game of tennis" in terms of the skills—the embodiment in action of rules for performance—of an individual, we must recognize that for one player "his game of golf" may be a far more developed thing than for another. We know some poor chaps, of course, of whom it is appropriate to say, "He *has* no game of golf," only slightly exaggerating the miserable showings they make on the golf course. Similarly, a speaker in a discussion may do no more than take the propositional attitude toward a sentence, hardly applying and possibly not successfully applying the Rules of Propositionality, but we need to understand what it is that he is working with; and even if his adoption of the pertinent attitude of giving enhanced status to the sentence concerned is the only change he has effected, he has nevertheless constituted S a proposition. That, of course, is the ontic status of S relative to him. It may be none such to others, or it may be profoundly a proposition, a highly elaborated and sophisticated product of insight and skill.

It has been the practice, following various theorists on the problem of meaning, to speak of separate kinds of meaning (denotation-connotation, emotive-cognitive, denotation-comprehension-signification-intension, and so forth). To speak of meaning at all not only involves ambiguity among the members of these categories until he who speaks of it clears them up; it also involves the ambiguity between meaning as a subjective factor with the individual user of the term (his intentions, proposed or intended meaning), and meaning as a characteristic of the term independently of its user. For convenience, in the present work I write as though meaning belongs to a term, rather than its user, although where greater strictness is required both must be taken into account. I also speak (somewhat oversimply) of two kinds of meaning, referential meaning and conceptual meaning.[1] These two phrases appear to me to make an adequate distinction among kinds of meaning for my general purposes, and I do not see that I must attempt any full discussion of the nature of meaning. However, I must acknowledge that in introducing the behavioral component *as part of the proposition itself,* I have also introduced another, previously unnoticed, kind of meaning of a term. That is, the word *proposition* embraces within *its* referential meaning not only the sets of physical marks or sounds, in all their history, that comprise a sentence undergoing propositional treatment, and their mental or conceptual correlates (the marks or sounds as they are thought or are present to consciousness), each with its own conceptual meaning (thoughts, mental events, whatever they may be), but also this behavioral factor. I propose to call it *correlative behavioral meaning.* Thus, when I am thinking the word *proposition,* evoking its meaning for my own attention, I have to include within that attention certain behavior patterns exhibited by those who entertain propositions, thus making these patterns part of the referential meaning of the term *proposition.* In turn, when I am thinking "proposition *S,*" the name of an individual proposition, I am to think it as having been the object of these behavior patterns as well as the other aspects of it that I know. And when I think of the term *correlative behavioral meaning,* I am to include within *its* reference not only that behavior which is according to the Rules of Propositionality, but also other forms of behavior that are patterns associated with other words and phrases (which, like *proposition,* possess correlative behavioral meaning), whatever these may be. When I am talking about correlative behavioral meaning, in other words, it is a referent; but as a feature *of the proposition* it is not simply referential meaning but a newly recognized kind of meaning.

That behavior according to the Rules of Propositionality is a part of the meaning of the term *proposition* is further demonstrated by the fact that this behavior travels with the word *proposition* rather than remaining with the speakers throughout all utterance. It is manifested on occasions when treatment of a particular sentence, according to the Rules of Propositionality, is appropriate, and at no other time. It is so well understood, although not articulately known, by users of the word *proposition* that they know how to perform according to the Rules of Propositionality whenever they inject the word *proposition* fittingly into a discussion or hear it injected by someone else. But, of course, a speaker may discuss a sentence in the spirit of the propositional attitude and with the application of the Rules of Propositionality without anyone saying "proposition," just as a bridge player may apply the rule called the Blackwood Convention without anyone's saying "Blackwood Convention." Nevertheless, the behavior consisting in discussion in that spirit and in the application of those rules is a part, and indeed the determining part, of the meaning of the term *proposition*.

Thus a proposition is no ghostly entity haunting our serious discourse, but rather a collection (perhaps inconceivably large) of events and objects in the experience of one or more rational beings, funded by individual or group experience, consent, and convention, and existing retrospectively in the groups' or individuals' memory, presently in groups' or individuals' attention, and prospectively in their future experiences.

Correlative behavioral meaning of a term is narrow and determinate. It may be reduced to rules more or less specifically and easily, as we have done with the correlative behavioral meaning of *proposition*. It is not simply all the behavior of the persons who in this case, for example, are carrying on a serious discussion, as is clear in the instance of those who are competing to have their own assertion win out over that of an opponent. Rather, it is one part or aspect only of that behavior, an aspect that is correlated more closely to the word in question *(proposition)* than it is to the person using the word or introducing the sentence at issue. It is present or absent according to the presence or absence of the referent object (the proposition), and not with different individuals who enter or leave the discussion.

Can we support with additional examples the claim of the discovery of a previously unnoticed kind of meaning? I should think we can, if we can produce one or more terms whose meaning includes an associated behavior, no matter what else it includes. That is to say, if we can produce one or more items whose ontology has a component of associated behavior, as well as other components such as physical-meaning components ("referential" meaning "physical" in this instance) and mental-correlate components (conceptual meaning). I believe that a telling example is the word *danger* in one of its common applications. Unlike *proposition,* whose referential objects are pretty homogeneous, *danger* denotes no one sort of physical thing. Physically, a danger may be such things as a sharp edge, a swiftly moving projectile, a poisonous substance, or a source of radiation. Therefore, the conceptual meaning of the term *danger* will not include the concept of a single physical entity present in all cases where the word *danger* may properly be applied, but rather will be the concept of a characteristic, probably a dispositional property, borne in mind by a person present in the situation in which the word *danger* is or would be properly used. This conceptual meaning is evoked by the cry "Danger!" or the word printed in red on a sign. The recipient of the communication "Danger!" adopts an appropriate mode of behavior associated with the word, including taking on an attitude of watchfulness, looking about for such things as sharp edges or sources of radiation, carrying out measures of avoidance—warning others, removing children from the scene, and the like. Again, these stay or travel with the word *danger*, not with the individual or his changing moods, passions, intellectual furniture, or other aspects of his particularity. This kind of behavior is different from the behavior that ensues upon baleful contact with sharp edges (bleeding), swiftly moving projectiles (crumpling to the ground), poisons and radiation (becoming sick and seeking medical treatment). This is behavior that is part of the meaning of *danger,* not part of the meaning of *knife, bullet, arsenic,* and so on. And again, there can be knives, bullets, poisons, and atomic blasts without anyone using the word *danger;* but on the occasions of these, danger-behavior may indeed be carried out, and it would be fitting and appropriate for someone actually to use the word.

In my references thus far to behavior, I have written in a fashion applicable only to overt behavior. It seems true to experience, however, to go further than that. I should wish to include among the kinds of correlative behavioral meaning not only overt behavior but also a type of behavior that would probably be admitted under that term only as a courtesy by behavioral scientists. This is an activity that we know for ourselves, although we know little of it as occurring with anyone else. It includes "behavior" that takes place within one's mind—thinking, supposing, analyzing, verbalizing, hypothesizing, guessing, envisioning, planning, appraising; all sorts of things, in other words, whose occurrences are signaled by some inner change. These functions may in fact have an origin in overt behavior, and I have therefore, in the above, posited speakers in a discussion who carry out the overt behavior of applying the Rules of Propositionality. Whether or not the same sort of thing carried on by a single person has its origin in overt behavior, it is at least analogous to such behavior and I think I am thereby justified in terming it *internalized behavior* or *internal behavior,* or even *mental behavior.* It is necessary to acknowledge that the Rules of Propositionality may be applied by a solitary thinker as well as by a plurality of individuals in open discussion. Similarly, other instances of associated behavioral meaning may consist in internal or internalized behavior as well as in overt behavior. And while this must be acknowledged for truth to our subject matter, on the other hand, we can reach only an approximation rather than exactness in our description. I am satisfied to call for only that degree of exactness that enables an individual to be sure of his own subjective events. When *he* is sure that *he* has (for example) changed his mind, or has left off daydreaming and begun to plan, that suffices for the applications I expect to make of this kind of language. The special case of this endeavor to reach subjective exactness is one that permeates the present exposition; I seek to produce descriptions that my reader can recognize as approximating his own experience, and as containing truth to that extent, regardless of his knowledge of the mental activity of others or of his recognition of the need to qualify generalizations about human minds taken universally or about any possible mind.

In the above treatment, I have traced out the ontic status of a proposition in its respective components of physical expression, the mental correlate to the physical expression, reception of the mentally apprehended physical expression, as a *sentence,* cognition of the meaning of the sentence, and, from the sentence, generation of the proposition through adoption of the propositional attitude toward it and application to it of the Rules of Propositionality. That is a set of strata or of levels of entities such that there must be content on all of them in order for a proposition to exist and enter experience. The actual particulars taking their places on the respective levels for a single proposition may be tremendously numerous and in fact innumerable (if one takes the future into account, it may be, practically speaking, infinite). The proposition itself is a single entity whose singularity is determined by the meaning of the sentence on which it is based, as qualified by steps of precision, and whose status as a proposition in addition to being a sentence is determined by the treatment accorded to it by individuals who concern themselves with it. The proposition thus has components of its being on some five levels, and has possibly an innumerably large number of particulars on nearly every one of the levels. The previous example, "Pleasure is the good," may serve as an extreme illustration of this. The proposition "Pleasure is the good" consists, on the physical level, of all the speakings and writings of the original Greek of the words of this sentence, in the various dialects that Socrates in his linguistic musings is apt to point out; to these must be added all instances of someone speaking or writing the sentence in Latin and other languages into which it is translated. On the level of mental apprehension of the sentence, it includes every instance of an individual producing or reproducing mentally the sounds or the markings that make the sentence for him in his language or languages. On the level of the cognition of the meaning of the sentence, the particulars include all the instances of anyone not only having the words available physically and mentally but of also recognizing what they say, what they mean; and this will include the various precising versions as well as the simple four-word (in English) sentence. On the distinctly propositional level, there will be fewer particular instances, in that not everyone familiar with the sentence may accord it the status of an issue to be explored or deliberated, but there will still be more events of this (that is, of discussion of "Pleasure is the good" as potentially believable, for example, or of analysis of it as to what it says) than any one human mind can know of. When we consider that in the future people are very likely to go on saying "Pleasure is the good," and thinking the words, and apprehending when they assert something, and recognizing the thought that they express, and debating their statement as an issue, we can justifiably claim that here is one more instance of the human mind comprehending that which it cannot image. Yet throughout all these many particulars on five levels, there is the unity of meaning bonding all these particulars together into just one proposition, individually different from others like "Salvation is the good" or "Pleasure is a qualified good." It is this unity of meaning that cements disparate elements (sounds or markings, thoughts, attitudes, events of behavior) into a single ontological entity. While our former notion of the proposition probably had it a linguistic entity, a mental entity, or possibly (noministically) a physical entity, we now see that for something to be a proposition it must participate in many forms of being or modes of appearing in consciousness. Still more importantly, we see that for our understanding of at least one prominent feature of the intellectual life we must be willing to abandon a much too compartmentalized notion and accept a view of it that makes it partly internal and partly external. It is not like a pebble in the pocket or like a thought in the mind, pure and simple. Rather, it is more like a net thrown by a fisherman, partly spreading on the beach and partly reaching into the sea. It transcends the internal-external bifurcation. In this it has promise, for it is an exemplar of a solution of problems that the internal-external distinction breeds. The proposition, as conceived of here, reaches from a mind into the external world that we posit, and then further from that world to another's mind; the behavior and attitudes of both enter into, and in this limited way unite in, one and the same object, the proposition that they discuss. It is not a discrete unit (like a coin) but a continuity (like credit).

No doubt problems will arise with this understanding of the proposition, just as with any other. I believe, however, that it can accommodate other, narrower views of the proposition. The principal effect of the description is to remove the proposition from the realm of subarticulate thought, on the one hand, and from the realm of intangible existent entities on the other, and no doubt most of the problems that are left over after one adopts this view of the proposition will arise with respect to its relations in those two directions. However, if we hold this view of the proposition, there are certain things that we are left free to do. We can continue to treat the proposition as testable, something whose truth can be confirmed or disconfirmed, or whose assertability can be warranted by strong or weak support, or the like. In other words, we can hang on to our favorite theory of truth. We can in fact either retain or remove the idea of truth with respect to propositions; we can continue to define the proposition as being true or false, or we can let it be something we can merely entertain and contemplate, leaving its truth-relations undetermined and even unposited. We can reify the proposition in general or certain individual propositions, treating them as the "thing behind the sentence," as we usually do now, or we can keep ourselves reminded that a proposition is a growing and developing thing like a living tree, even one whose top is not visible from our position near it on the ground. We can in fact continue to investigate the question whether it has become the basis of tautological truth only by virtue of convention, or whether there is some other foundation for what is objective so that there is a basis more objective than convention for the apparent solidity of the truth-claims of tautological or analytic propositions. We can also apply the proposition—and propositions in general—to the external world, regardless whether we regard the external world as a certain reality, or as merely suppositional, or as totally private, or whatever. We do not need any further answer to the question of the nature or ontological status of propositions before we inquire, without risk of bias, into the question whether one's own real world is also the public world, and whether the public world once granted is a real world or a humanly constructed fiction or whatnot. In reifying a proposition, we can selectively cut it loose from its history, even though our view asserts, in a sense, that it *is* its history; in doing this, we can be inventive, creative, speculative, and philosophically ingenious. Or we can cling to the history of the proposition and claim that any understanding of it without full attention to its history is faulty. We can treat a proposition as private—and surely all of us must have certain private propositions—which by design or happenstance belongs to ourselves alone and has the whole history of its special consideration solely within our own consciousness. Or we can treat the proposition as public, and can, if we wish, declare that it isn't "really" a proposition unless it *is* public, transferable, in a metaphorical way of speaking, from one mind to another. I am suggesting that my description does not destroy the proposition in the frameworks of those who have entered controversies on the nature of propositions, but rather supplements the general views of many of the contestants, while rendering it unnecessary to embrace an idealistic or mystical view of the nature of the proposition. The price of acceptance of my description, I believe, is not giving up a favorite view of the nature of ideal or mental objects, for there is still plenty of room in the investigation of subarticulate thought for us to furnish the mind with ideal or mental objects. Rather, the price is that of according to the human mind in general the scope and power to construct propositions over not only whole lifetimes of individuals but whole lifetimes of cultures. And I think the history of Western culture shows an ample number of examples in which this has in fact been done, so that we may justifiably extend credence to the ability of the human mind to operate at this degree of complexity.

The importance of this description of the proposition to the search for value has to do with the relation of the proposition to things non-propositional, of course. Now, since we can slice away considerations of the truth or falsity of a proposition, and of relation or unrelatedness of the proposition to a real world, we can see that a major subject of debate in philosophy is and has always been the question of whether there *is* a basis of relation of a proposition to the world that it "describes," and if so, what the nature of that relation is. Hence the problem introduced in this book may be understood in terms of the investigation of the relation of value-asserting propositions to any values, real or otherwise, that may have been said to be the subjects or the content of such propositions. We can see also that our pre-reflective and our philosophical tendency to contrast value with fact *may* be an expression of our pre-reflective impression that there indeed is a *quid* that is the subject of the value-asserting propositions, and also that there *is* a posited contrast between the nature of the subject matter of the valuative propositions and that of the fact-assertive propositions, even though we are far from having it settled what the facts are that fact-assertive propositions might assert. The project in value theory, viewed from this angle, is the inquiry into the nature of "value" or "values" as themselves, not propositions, and also into the nature of the relation, if any, of these to value-assertive propositions.

3

The Natures of Factual and Valuative Assertions

In the first chapter I noted the difference between sentences that state facts and sentences that convey value judgments, and I sketched the evidence of its recognition by those who use language. I will now attempt to exhibit the general shared nature of statements that express facts, and then, through a parallel analysis, to show the general nature of statements that express value judgments.

We may notice in this light a nineteenth-century usage that made explicit what the man in the street still today takes to be the case with respect to "values," even if not to "facts." Works in logic and grammar termed all indicative declarative sentences *judgments*. The word has process-product ambiguity; it can mean the act of producing or the product of the act (that is, judgment itself, contrasted with *a* judgment). But what act, and what product? Frege distinguished between a thought, the acknowledgement of the truth of the thought, and the sentence expressing the thought.[1] The sentence is the product, and the process of judging was for him the acknowledgement of the truth of what the sentence expresses. The recognition of the truth of the thought occurred intermediately between the apprehension of a thought and the assertion of this thought. Regardless whether the process or function of judgment is conceived of as applied to a linguistic entity such as a sentence expressing a thought or to a prelinguistic entity or event, the key notion of judgment seems to have been that it was a recognition of truth. Thus if there is a moment of apprehension of a thought or a meaning that is not the same as the recognition of truth of that thought or meaning, then the judging or recognition of truth is conceived of as performed independently of the apprehension. The assertion, after the recognition, is yet a third thing. The judging, then, is some sort of process of deciding something about an apprehension, after which one is willing to affirm and before which one is unwilling to affirm the thought, affirm what one's sentence expresses. Thus there can be judgment without assertion, and regardless of the prudence of the thing, there can also be assertion without judgment.

Even with this distinction between judgment and assertion we have not yet ascertained in full the relevant senses of *assert* and *assertion*. There are two. To elicit them, let us imagine an amateur magician impressing a friend with some parlor tricks. He borrows his friend's pocket watch, and in full sight wraps it in a napkin. He asks, "Where is the watch now?" The friend replies, "In the napkin, of course." He has seen the watch being wrapped, and has been satisfied from what he has seen that it has not been surreptitiously removed. The magician asks, "Are you sure?" The friend replies, "Yes." The magician: "Why don't you pick up the napkin and feel its weight, or tap it on the table, to make sure the watch is still in the napkin?" The friend does these things, now beginning to be unsure that his eyes have not deceived him; but on feeling the solidity of the watch through the layers of cloth and upon making a muffled rap on the table with the wrapped object, he says, "Yes, the watch is still in the napkin." Our point is that in order to make these replies, he has been invited to reflect upon something on which ordinarily he would expend no reflection at all; and he has decided—judged —that the state of affairs actually is as he at first perceived it to be.

Then the magician closes his fist about the little packet of cloth, and without opening his hand he first passes it into an open drawer, then into an open cabinet, then into an empty wastebasket, and finally into the open fireplace, without making any move as though to deposit the packet in any of these places. Then with the handkerchief still in evidence in his hand, he asks the friend, "Where is the watch now, do you suppose?" The friend, pretty well convinced that he will be found wrong no matter how he answers, says, "The watch is in your hand, wrapped in that napkin." Presto, the magician unfolds the napkin and shows it to be quite empty. The friend says, "I knew that would be wrong—that was just a guess." The magician then passes his hand a second time into the open fireplace, without the napkin in it this time, and brings forth the watch.

In this second stage of the parlor trick our friend has again made a statement about the whereabouts of the watch, but has labeled his statement a guess. As our knowledge of magicians and parlor tricks informs us, the statement will almost certainly be disproved even though he cannot understand how it can be false. But he has offered an *assertion*, "The watch is in your hand, wrapped in that napkin," which expresses a state of affairs, not knowing whether it is true or false. He has withdrawn his previous judgment of its truth, but it is still possible for him to make what we call an *assertion*. I should like us to conceive that in this fashion a sentence can *assert* an actual or possible state of affairs, or, as it were, *propose* one to us, without sides being taken on the matter of whether it is true or false. In this sense asserting is the constructing of a declarative sentence in such a way that it invites its recipient to see it as a collection of words having "declarative" function, to see it as related to some state of affairs or event outside itself and as offering a scheme of entities and relationships that may be entertained by the mind.

For it to have been asserted is not for it to have been *received as true*; it need not even have been *originated as true*, as we have just shown. It may be originated as a hypothesis for testing, as a wishful thought, or even as a deliberate lie. What makes it what it is, is its being constructed so as to have that peculiar force of invitation to be considered as indicating a structure of things. Whether or not it truly indicates a structure of existing things, or even of things appearing in some consciousness, is yet to be determined. It is assertion in this sense that makes the difference between a declarative sentence and a mere nonsensical stream of words, or a sentence fragment, or a question, or a command, or some other sort of string of words. It is what makes the difference between a sequence of words that informs and one that does not. It is the notion, "to compose verbal symbols into a pattern of the kind that may admit of the assignment of truth-signs (*true* or *false*), in contrast to other patterns that are not amenable to assignment of truth-signs." For this sense of *assert*, there is no requirement that the truth-sign actually assigned is *true*. The assigning of one or the other of the truth-signs specifically is no part of its meaning and is no requisite to this process, or to its product being labeled *assertion*. I shall call this the *grammatical* sense of *assert*.

Of course I concede that most offerings of sentences are ones in which judgment is *not* withdrawn or suspended, and we generally assume (unless there are signs to the contrary) that sentences offered to us are offered as though previously judged by their originators to be true. This gives us our other sense of *to assert*, which is the notion, "to express as though that which is expressed is true, or is believed." This is the core meaning of such definitions or senses of *assert* that place it in opposition to *deny*. Obviously the concept of *truth* is crucial to the meaning of the word *assert* or *assertion* taken in this sense. I shall term this the *epistemological* sense of *assert*.

These two senses are both present in combination in the ordinary understanding that speakers of the language have in their everyday situations. It is under unusual circumstances, arousing our caution, that we begin to suppose that we might hear a declarative sentence that is not offered as true by its originator. Awareness of these two senses of *assert* and *assertion* will enable us to see how it can be that sentences in certain contexts might be assertions in the one sense but not the other, or how there might be something that we call an *assertion* that has the distinctive features of a declarative sentence or proposition, but need not have a truth-sign. This will help us to understand more fully the fundamental difference between fact-assertive propositions and value-assertive propositions.

In the twentieth century in popular language we have pretty much left behind the practice of calling factual declarative sentences *judgments*, probably because we consider the assumption that they are almost universally proposed as true to be wholly justifiable. We do not believe we need to focus on the process of judgment, of decision, in considering what we offer to others in the way of factual sentences. Yet in the case of the valuative statements, we have clung to the use of the word *judgment*. When one of them comes under discussion, we quite commonly refer to it as a "value judgment" or a "judgment of value." One speaker does not refer to another's factual sentence as a "judgment of fact," but readily calls it a "statement of fact." On the other hand, he is unlikely to call the other's valuative sentence a "statement of value," but customarily calls it a "value judgment"; and this phrase is especially likely to signal that it is upon differing valuative judgments that a controversy turns. The aggregate of speakers, in establishing their linguistic conventions over long periods of time and use, tends to signal what is important to them, and the notion of a judging remains under attention of this kind for expression of value, whereas it does not for expressions of fact.

Now the difference in these usages that involve our two key notions, fact and value, is an informative one. *Statement* in "statement of fact" refers to the language of the locution. It suggests the originator's process of selecting words and constructing the vehicle of his expression. It capitalizes on the process-product ambiguity and leaves the thought of *a* statement, a structure of words. On the other hand, *judgment* in "value judgment" does not focus upon language, but rather upon a mental act —a decision—in respect to the subject matter itself of the proposition spoken about. The pattern of this comparison suggests that the speakers who mold our language are responding to some felt difference in the two subject matters, i.e., fact and value, which is evident to them on the subarticulate level and which may prove to be a genuine difference that we can exhibit once we bring it into the daylight of deliberated examination.

The folk wisdom, then, that has given us our phrases *statement of fact* and *value judgment* (or *judgment of value*) has probably operated on the view that normally when one is going to say something, one decides first what to speak about, and then what to say about it, and how to say it (deciding either beforehand or simultaneously with the utterance). If one cares anything about accuracy, one attempts to ascertain precisely what the state of affairs or the happening actually is that one intends to assert and then selects wording to reflect this content accurately to its recipient. Hence, all three elements—language, state of affairs or event as subject matter, and judgment of the originator—are present in the ordinary declarative assertion. The logical, though not necessarily temporal, priority calls first for apprehending the entity or event with which one is concerned, then selecting the expressions that can convey it, and finally performing the utterance that conveys it. Now in everyday circumstances and for workaday purposes, people do not encounter much difficulty in apprehending the factual objects, and there are only a few kinds of instances (although there are some, and those may be important) in which these objects themselves permit much deviation of interpretation, that is, much latitude of judgment in ascertaining what they are. Thus it is not usually very important to pay special attention to the interpreting or judging process that leads to statements of fact (so this folk wisdom goes). But on the other hand, people frequently disagree about values and are well aware that for the testing of challenged statements about values, there is no easy answer. Consequently, attention is drawn to the matter of doing the judging, of deciding "what the value actually is." You are your judge of values, and I am mine, and we do well to remind ourselves of this circumstance. In sum, when it is a *fact* that one is expressing, attention may normally dwell more profitably on forms of statement in language than on the method of ascertaining the fact; but when it is a *value*, one should not lose sight of the method of ascertaining the nature of the thing that will be the subject of the assertion, and it seemingly merits more attention than the selection of the forms of statement. While an account of folk wisdom can be only a surmise and is not likely to be either proved or disproved, these suggestions are in keeping with the general view that facts and statements of fact are objective, while in contrast, values and value judgments are subjective.

A further circumstance tending to confirm these conjectures is the relative frequency of occurrence of the phrases being compared. I believe my reader will concur in noting that the phrases *value judgment, judgment of value,* or their equivalents actually occur in usage in ordinary discourse much more often than the phrases *statement of fact, factual statement,* or their equivalents. Still more significant: Even though actual occurrences of statements of fact are far more numerous in daily discourse than valuations, the phrases embodying the word *value*—and thereby emphasizing the judging process—occur in a far higher proportion in relation to the number of actual articulated value judgments than the phrases that mention the factual in proportion to the number of statements of fact actually expressed in discourses. In other words, in proportion to their rates of occurrence, value judgments attract attention and linguistic recognition far more often than statements of fact.[2] This picture seems also to indicate that the ordinary speaker is far more aware of the relativity of value assertions to the source or the method of obtaining them than he is of the relativity of facts to the method of origination or source of factual assertions. He is aware of the far greater subjectivity involved in performing judgments upon value and offering statements about them for others to accept.

Such is the pattern of general usage, as I see it, in the employment of the two key phrases—a pattern that is beyond the scope of descriptive, scientific study. However, without having to know how many events the history of language contains that would substantiate the interpretation given (billions, surely), we can take a clue from it to improve the precision with which we deal with the respective concepts. Both expressions can easily be made more precise if each borrows something from the other. Granting that *some* interpretation, and in that sense some judging, normally operates and is logically presupposed in producing propositions that purport to state facts, we can understand the phrase *statement of fact* as intending *statement of a judgment of fact*. The chief reason the addition seems verbose or idle, I suggest, is merely that nobody believes he has to do much judging when he perceives a thing that he takes to be what actually is or what actually happens (making exceptions, of course, for baseball referees, physicians, traffic policemen, research scientists, gourmet cooks, and actually just about all of us when carrying on our more exacting pursuits). Similarly, *value judgment* can become *statement of a judgment of value*. These longer phrasings, as well as showing the parallelism that exists between the two kinds of statement, are more fully descriptive of the two sorts of declarative sentence than their popularly used short versions. But "judging," as the mode of their generation, is not to be accepted without criticism, and much of our duty in the remainder of this inquiry has to do with the ways in which statements of judgments of value are generated.

We have still further refinements to make in our vocabulary for our inquiry into value. In a preliminary way, I shall remark that the noun *statement* has, as already noted, the process-product ambiguity; statement can be either the process of reaching a worded version of a communication, or the sentence that is reached as the product of the wording process. In addition to that, it has also the ambiguity of being sometimes substitutable for *sentence,* and sometimes for *proposition.* In the immediately preceding discussion I have made intentional use of that latter ambiguity, and shall in all that ensues; whenever I employ *statement* I shall intend the scope of the term to include both sentences and propositions—that is, to include ordinary declarative sentences of the sorts that provide context while not undergoing special attention, and also the other sentences that are treated according to the Principle of Propositionality. I do not abandon the view of the proposition that I have explained in the previous chapter, but there are things I must say about discourses that may consist of either or both, sentences and propositions, and the "product" sense of *statement* is perfectly suited to this use.

Another refinement of our working vocabulary has to do with the circumstance that sentences and propositions have the capacity to be true or false, but not both. We shall shortly examine the possibility of testing propositions against the subject matter that they express, in order to distinguish true ones from false ones. The consideration of the true-false distinction raises the thought that it is possible that a proposition might fail in its function of expressing fact or value—it might, for example, stand as an attempt to state a fact that does not actually do so, and thus actually fails. Yet we shall need a term by which to know it independently of its failure or success, and especially by which to know it before we have put it to the test. For this purpose, let us employ the expressions *fact-assertive proposition* and *value-assertive proposition,*[3] and let us retain the understanding that these are defined, *not* in terms of truth and falsity (like *fact* as a sentence, in popular speech), but rather, in terms of what their subject matter is. Thus, a fact-assertive proposition is a proposition whose originator or proponent attempts (unless his intent is fraudulent) to express accurately what *is* the case, what *is* the state of affairs or the happening—but the proponent could either succeed or fail. Thus a fact-*assertive* proposition could be either true or false. Knowing that the proposition is fact-assertive in nature is quite a different thing from knowing that the proposition is actually true. Knowledge of its truth or falsity is *not* requisite to recognizing that it is fact-assertive in its purport, its verbal statement, or its proponent's evident intention. For that matter, a lie is a fact-*assertive* proposition without being required *per impossibile* to be true in order to be a lie. Obviously the success of a lie depends on something other than the property of being-either-true-or-false,[4] and so does the success of a fiction; yet either has the same form as other fact-assertive sentences. The communication in each of these cases does not depend for success in fulfilling the intent of the originator upon the truth or accurate descriptiveness of the proposition; but it does depend for success in communication on the fact-*assertiveness* of the proposition. Thus, grammatical fact-assertiveness is quite a different property of a proposition from its factuality, its truth.

Following the pattern of the fact-assertive proposition, we could suggest that in parallel fashion a value-assertive proposition is one whose proponent attempts accurately to express a value. But since we do not as yet have a determination as to what value is, we must concede that this is hardly a definition or even a clarification of the phrase *value-assertive proposition*. However, we must move to the definition of *value* in stages, rather than in a leap from our present point of advance. The definition of *value-assertive proposition* shall—oddly, it may seem to the reader—be offered before that of *value*; and to arrive even at that nearer goal, we must again travel the route of everyday language. Therefore let us now turn to a further examination of those sentences that are popularly called *statements of fact* and *value judgments*, and that I shall regularly term *fact-assertive* and *value-assertive propositions*.

But are values states of affairs, or events, that an observer can perceive and describe, as he perceives and describes those states of affairs or events to which we devote *fact-assertive* statements? And are they equally independent of the apprehending and interpreting, or judging, processes of their originator?

I am far from prepared to affirm either of these theses; I am prepared to say, further along, that values do not answer either of these descriptions. They share a *grammatical* nature with facts, but they do not share the objectivity of facts; or at least, if they do, the method of discovering and exhibiting their objective nature is as yet unknown. I believe there is ample theoretic reason to suggest that there is no such objectivity of value or values. Consequently, it does no good to propose that a logical way for the value theorist to proceed would be first to define values, then to show how statements reporting on values can accurately describe values themselves, then finally to elicit by this means the proper test for the truth of value-assertive propositions. The disagreement on the nature of values has heretofore left this procedure fruitless or produced deceptive or perplexing results. Exposition will be more clear, more brief, and more productive if we first examine the characteristic kinds of linguistic expression of each.

It has been convenient to consider the meaning of words under two general headings, the conceptual and the referential, to which I have added for some cases the behavioral correlative. We may point out that these sorts of meaning are not the only components of the burden carried by verbal symbols. For the individual word there is also a general concept about the function of that word, the sort of thing we know grammatically as its part of speech. Nouns are, for example, naming words, and we learn what words are the naming words by their functions when put into action by speakers and writers. Now I would like to suggest, on the level of the whole sentence, that there are concepts of this sort. A sentence achieves, as a part of its burden, a property that I shall call its *framing concept*, which is held in common by many different sentences. The framing concept has grammatical equivalents in the concepts of *question, exclamatory sentence*, and *command* or *imperative sentence*, and in the one to which we have substantially confined our interests, the *declarative sentence*. Yet, as I have pointed out, the latter in turn is divided into two kinds, each with its own subordinate framing concept. One is the fact-assertive, and the other is the value-assertive.

The underlying concept of the declarative sentence in general is simply that of assertiveness, which I have identified as a property achieved by a certain kind of construction that the language affords to its users as a resource, and that its users in turn may follow in constructing individual sentences. This duality of assertiveness is not intended to beg the question of affirmation or denial, for a sentence in respect to its construction can be assertive rather than questioning, or exclamatory, and so on, yet be negative, that is, be a denial of some positive statement. And again, the assertion conveyed through the assertive sentence can potentially be either true or false. Now the difference between the *fact-assertive* and the *value-assertive* declarative sentences lies in another underlying concept, different for each of these classes of sentence, even while they continue to share assertiveness and declaration. The operative underlying concept for each of these kinds of assertion, their *subordinate framing concept*, is understood and used both by the originator of the statement and by its recipient. The underlying subordinate framing concept shared by all fact-assertive sentences is the concept of *what is*, in a broad, atemporal, and epistemologically loose application of the word *is*. This is the identifying feature of "statements of fact," i.e., fact-assertive sentences and propositions. It is held in common with those that are true and those that are untrue, and is a more fundamental thing to understand about them, therefore, than their truth-sign or factuality. On the other hand, all value-assertive statements are based on the concept of *what ought to be*.[5] This is the identifying feature of "value judgments," i.e., value-assertive sentences and propositions; it is their distinctive framing concept, against which they are constructed. It is these two underlying concepts that, respectively, give their distinctive general natures to all fact-assertive sentences and propositions and to all value-assertive sentences and propositions. For the two parallel kinds of statements, *these are the defining characteristics.*

It is not difficult to show the commonalty of the concept of *what ought to be* in the typical forms of value expressions. Some typical patterns of value-assertive propositions are these:

List III

   (1) *X* is good.
   (2) *X* is right.
   (3) *X* is better than *Y*.
   (4) *X* is bad.
   (5) *X* is wrong.
   (6) *X* is worse than *Y*.
   (7) Trait *T* is a virtue.
   (8) Habit *H* is a vice.
   (9) Act *X* is a good act.
(10) Act *Y* is evil.
(11) One ought to perform act *X*.
(12) One ought not to perform act *Y*.
(13) One ought to be of the character *C*.
(14) One ought not to be of the character *D*.

The patterns exhibited by the items of List III are not, of course, propositions but rather, propositional functions. They have blanks to be filled in, such as "*X*" or "Act *A*" or "character *C*." These patterns are reached inductively, by abstraction from actual value-assertive sentences that occur constantly in anyone's experience. "*X* is good" is the pattern in common of "This kind of luggage is good"; "'All in the Family' is good" (said of a television series); "Bicarbonate of soda is good" (answering the question "What should I take for this indigestion?"); "Little Tommy is good" (". . . so why can't you be good, Johnny?"); "Fifty-yard-line seats are especially good"; "Paul Muni was a very good actor of the heyday of the Hollywood film"; "Misfortune, since it instructs us, is actually good." Similarly, the other items on List III are abstracted from innumerable day-to-day instances of actual locutions.

Now, however, it is our concern to move in the other direction—from the propositional functions of List III and their like, once elicited from everyday speech, back to statements of the familiar kinds using the term *ought* but fully parallel to the propositional functions with which we begin.

Although the last four items on List III are less frequently represented in everyday discourse than others on the list, they serve best for us to examine first since they demonstrate our point most clearly. That point is that for every value-assertive sentence, represented by these and other sentence patterns, one or more equivalent sentences employing the phrase *what ought to be* can be devised which, without altering the substance, show the involvement of the original with what ought to be. Each such equivalence confirms my claim that *what ought to be* is the foundational concept of all value judgments, and indeed does lie at the base of every valuative proposition. For example, the propositional pattern "One ought to be of the character *C*" says in effect "What ought to be the case is a state of affairs in which everyone is of the character *C*." An instance of a proposition exhibiting this pattern is "One ought to be a good sport," from which, without any change of meaning (although at some stylistic cost), we can readily reach the rewording "What ought to be the case is that each person is a good sport."

Expressions that are negative but otherwise of the same pattern have similar though negative equivalents. "One ought not to be of character *D*" represents, for example, the proposition "One ought not to be a spoilsport," or alternatively, "What ought not to be the case is that persons are spoilsports." A benefit of this sort of transformation from idiomatic language to stricter language is that if variants of the fuller linguistic expression are to be found that seem to depart from the original version, these are useful for eliciting the precise intended meaning of the originator of the proposition as originally advanced. Thus, this procedure is an instrument for precise and clear discourse.

Taking another item from List III, one that involves an act rather than a state of affairs,[6] we may propose as a sample covered by "One ought to perform act *X*" the proposition "One ought to exercise unbiased selection when voting." An equivalent is "What ought to be is a state of affairs such that whenever voting is taking place, those voting are exercising unbiased selection," or more simply, "What ought to be done when voting is to exercise unbiased selection." As for the negative, "One ought not to perform act *Y*," an instance is "What ought to be is a state of affairs in which homicide is not (or, is never) committed," or "What ought not ever to be done includes committing homicide."

Now, referring still to List III, we are ready for the slightly more involved items.

"*X* is good" is equivalent to "*X* is as it ought to be." Few expressions of actual discourse are as simple as "*X* is good." Most expressions of goodness are somehow qualified, or fitted into a setting, or the like. But we do occasionally encounter sentences as simple as "Serenity is good" or "Contentedness is good." These say, "What ought to be the case is that each person has serenity (or contentedness)."[7] We more usually encounter something like

"Peace of mind is a good thing to have." Here "peace of mind" is X, and "to have" mildly qualifies "good thing," probably more for emphasis than to limit the idea expressed. The interpretation is easy to produce: "It ought to be the case that one has peace of mind," or "What ought to be is the possessing by everyone of peace of mind."

"X is right" may be said of an X that is an action, or of an X that somehow embodies a principle, such as a moral principle. An example is "Supporting my minor half-brother was the right thing for me to do." This may be rendered indifferently as "It ought to be the case that I support my minor half-brother," or "What I ought to have done was to support my minor half-brother," or "To support my minor half-brother was what ought to have been my action." We are probably most interested theoretically with "X is right" as it occurs in ethical contexts; but such senses of "X is right" as "X is the correct answer" or "X is the right play to call when it is fourth down and the goal is thirty yards distant" can also be translated, with indications of the situational context, in the terms proposed: "X is what you ought to have written in the blank"; "X is the play the quarterback ought to have called."

Comparatives and superlatives are readily translatable. "X is better than Y" means "X is more the way it ought to be than Y." "Abel plays the piano better than Bradley" means "Abel plays the piano more in the way that a pianist ought to play than Bradley does." "I am the greatest," a superlative often heard in sporting circles not long ago, has as its equivalent, "I am, of all prizefighters, the most like what a prizefighter ought to be." "X is bad," "X is wrong" can be treated in patterns opposite to the patterns for "X is good" and "X is right": "Poverty is bad" is "There ought to be no more poverty" or "A state of poverty is a state of life that is not as it ought to be." "Murder is wrong" is "persons ought not to commit murder." "Greene is worse than Browne for sentence length" is "Greene writes, as to sentence length, even less the way one ought to write than Browne does." If it should happen that the reader differs with me on the appropriateness of any of these specific translations, this is evidence that he understands what I am endeavoring to exhibit, the fact that the *ought* concept underlies the value-assertions; it is also evidence that the ordinary language may harbor vagueness or ambiguity. Such should not be surprising, for ordinary language is fitted to handle ordinary situations, and not characteristically situations in which greater-than-average precision is required. Thus we see that making the concept of *ought* explicit can be an aid in eliciting meanings from value-assertive sentences.

Many judgments of value are expressed in language that is more particular than the extremely broad words such as *good* or *bad* in the above examples.[8] Words like *virtue* and *vice, admirable* and *abhorrent* carry not only emotional connotations of liking or disliking but also valuative connotations, expressing their classification with regard to what ought to be. "Trait

T is a virtue" says that *T* is a characteristic of the kind that persons ought to have, or that persons having that characteristic are as they ought to be with respect to it. "Habit *H* is a vice" says that persons possessing *H* are not, in that respect, as they ought to be.

In that *ought* is a concept, it is patent that the propositions employing it for a basis are not *ipso facto* expressions of emotion. Of course, language is quite capable of conveying both concepts and feelings in one and the same word, and, of course, persons are inclined to dislike what they believe ought not to be and to like what they believe ought to be, or to believe that what they like is what ought to be and that what they dislike is what ought not to be; but clearly the emotional basis does not explain the evaluative propositions. For there are, on the other hand, ample occasions with which everyone is familiar, when one likes what he has decided ought *not* to be and dislikes what he has conceded ought to be the case. If it were not so, language need not contain the instruments for expressing valuation that it does, over and above its instruments for conveying emotion. The view of the logical positivists that evaluative judgments are simply emotive expressions was never successfully established, because the positivists did not recognize that the concept *ought to be* underlies the value terms, and that it is in fact a cognitive concept, not merely the natural sign or artificial symbol of a feeling. It is the end product of intellection, not of emotion.

To overcome the unwelcome effect of the stilted prose of the renditions just tendered, I ask the reader to bear in mind that the equivalent I have supplied in each case has one purpose only, namely, to show how the meaning of the value-assertive propositional form applies to the realm of what ought to be. I do not at all claim that speakers actually speak such cumbersome sentences. I should, rather, suppose that the familiar patterns have become the most used because they are easy to enunciate and seem to carry the desired messages quickly and without misunderstanding in ordinary situations. But there are instructive features of the equivalent expressions. First, the equivalent is a fuller expression that means the same thing as the familiar pattern—or at least, as one of the things it may mean if it is vague or ambiguous. Second, and consequently, it has the same degree of warrantability. We have gained nothing and lost nothing epistemologically by making the translation. Finally, from these patterns we can legitimately infer of any other value-assertive patterns that they too may be understood in an appropriate equivalent explicitly expressing the concept of *what ought to be*.

The propositional forms of List III are by no means all of the possible forms of value-judgmental statements, but represent a sampling only, and a very small sampling at that. They are common forms of the expression of value judgments, but there is no limit to the number of ways that a well-developed natural language has of expressing value judgments. For this reason, a proof (by deduction or by a "perfect induction") of what I claim, that value-assertive propositions are based on the concept of *what ought to be*, can never be final. All that can be done is to appeal to the reader's experience of language. I believe, however, that "once he gets the feel of it," he will agree that it is in fact his own purpose, when he utters value-assertive statements, that he is expressing, among other things, his own conception of how the world ought to be, in some specified respect. He will find that others are doing the same, and that to apprehend someone's value-assertive utterances in this guise is to understand them more fully. Therefore, over a period of time he will come to consider this claim as more and more confirmed by his experience.

Again, my intent in supplying equivalents in terms of *what ought to be* for sample sentences having each of the patterns of List III is not to lay before the reader a one-to-one correspondence, deductively arrived at, from the familiar wording to the wording of the equivalent. Given the richness of cognitive and emotive connotations as well as literal meanings of the developed natural languages, we recognize that unless we stipulate meanings in remarkable and highly impractical numbers in a discussion, any sentence will tend to evoke slightly differing meanings in the minds severally of all those who receive it. The equivalencies given above are therefore not the ultimate in precision. Rather, they will have performed their purpose if they lead the reader to think something like this: "Yes, if I had said 'One ought to be of character *C*,' I should have meant something very close to 'What ought to be the case is that everyone is of character *C*,'" or perhaps "If I had said that, I would have meant that most people ought to be of character *C*." Interpreted as before, the latter version would be compatible with, say, "If I had said that, I would have meant that most people ought to be good sports, but not everyone, for there are some things that are too much to expect of quite small children." Modifications of this sort will no doubt be made by different individuals according to specific beliefs and circumstances, and according to the degree they possess of the tendency to be cautious and precise in statement. That surely happens in discussion and controversy. However, what these modifications characterize will still be sentences that relate to the concept of *what ought to be*. I believe that the dependence upon that concept will be seen in every reasonable variation among the allegedly equivalent expressions, when these are full and faithful to what the originator intends or appears to intend by his value-assertive propositions.

Of course there are some gray areas and ambivalent cases. I have heard a colleague state, as the premise of an argument, "Teaching is not a competitive occupation," from which he drew a conclusion as to whether universities should allocate rewards based on measurements of merit. His listeners did not accept his assertion as factually true. However, they understood his argument by interpreting his premise as an expression of the value-assertion, "We ought to regard teaching as not a competitive occupation." This intention on the assertor's part was implicit in the fact that his conclusion was in the *ought* mode: "Therefore there *ought* not to be rewards based on measurements of merit." Without the *ought* taken as part of the premise, his argument would have committed the fourth-term fallacy, introducing new material in the conclusion. We have a tendency to put premises of this sort in phrasings that obscure the *ought* that we are expressing, and thus we seem to argue from fact-assertive rather than value-assertive premises. To offer a value-assertive premise, we are aware, is to offer something that an opponent can claim is merely subjective and open to difference of opinion. A famous example of a proposition often challenged on the basis of fact is "All men are created equal." When this proposition is understood as being framed in the *ought* mode (confirmed by the preceding wording, "*We hold* these truths to be self-evident . . ."), the counterinstances paraded as disproof are seen to be irrelevant to what is being said. The assertion is, "All men ought to be regarded by government as created equal." Thus the famous Declaration may be taken as the statement of an ideal, a description of the way the Founding Fathers believed a society ought to be and the way they intended to attempt to make it, rather than the way it was at the time when they wrote.

It becomes apparent that to look upon declarative sentences (statements, propositions) as being divided into the fact-assertive and the value-assertive is a very useful tool of interpretation. Paraphrasing is a long-established technique for rendering thought overt, explicit, and precise; these two modes are open to the paraphraser for every declarative sentence, and only these two, unless assertion itself is not a part of the intent of the original (as, for instance, when a declarative is used for the purpose of asking a question). Although probably no two people, owing to the richness of language and individual experience, will translate given texts in exactly the same way, reasonably objective paraphrases of value-assertive propositions can be produced and agreed upon; and if two interpreters differ, they shall perhaps have located substance, rather than merely the uses of words, upon which they have differences.

Let us revert again to List III and a consideration of the condition that I have identified by calling it "what ought to be," and even "the realm of what ought to be." It is patent that sometimes "what is" *is* "what ought to be," and that sometimes "what is" is *not* "what ought to be." The general equivalent of "This is good" (that is, when *good* does not have a special meaning evident in context) is "This is as it ought to be." "This is bad" is "This is not as it ought to be." The former is a case in which what *is* and what *ought to be* coincide, and the latter is a case in which they do not. Psychologically, it is usual that expressions that things as they are coincide with the way they ought to be have strong connotations of pleasure, and likewise that assertions that the way things are is *not* the way they ought to be have strong connotations of displeasure. This is quite possibly what misled the positivists into taking emotive meaning as the only important meaning of valuational statements as such. Since the *ought* is not detectable empirically, by the means they admitted as the instruments of obtaining knowledge, they could hardly do other than turn to emotion—physically felt, at base at any rate—for the meaning of valuative assertions.

I believe that, in building our personal or public bodies of beliefs, and hence our communicative discourses, we more often proceed from an awareness and a consciousness of "what is" to a consideration of "what ought to be," than the other way around. We first of all size up a situation for what it is, *then* we judge how it ought to be, probably using our cognizance of the way it is as the point of departure for our judgment of how it ought to be. Thus we may say, perception precedes reaction; cognition precedes valuative judgment. This is the more characteristic order, but not necessarily exclusively the order. There may be times when a sequence is discernible such that an individual first judges how a state of affairs ought to be, then acts so as to learn how it actually is and to learn how to bring about the situation that his valuation calls for. Two observations pertain to that less frequent occasion. First, order is relative to a time scheme, and while the order (1) judgment favoring a conception, (2) action, (3) realization of that conception may be imputed to a certain occasion, on full inquiry we may find that the judgment actually had as its object some previously cognized existing state of affairs, so that actually the more characteristic pattern is obtained although not initially evident. Surely this often occurs. Second, however, I shall also observe, as a supposition that is probably unprovable by the nature of the case but may nevertheless augment understanding, that I see no reason why there cannot be pure cases of the *less* characteristic order. I believe I have observed some cases of that sort, which I should call instances of creativity. Surely painters, poets, sculptors,—creative artists of any sort—are examples *par excellence* of the person who first exerts a judgment as to what ought to be—namely, his work of art—and then he acts; later when it has become a *fait accompli,* he observes before him the state of affairs that he had judged ought to exist. The relations of this interpretation of value assertions and values to aesthetic concerns will be examined in a later chapter.

There was mention above of a "translation" of the word *good* in applications in context, where something more specialized than "as it ought to be" would be its equivalent. The concept *as it ought to be* underlies every use of *good* where its central meaning remains unimpaired, but it is true that through stipulating a special meaning, we sometimes thrust that central meaning far aside. We say, for example, "This light bulb isn't good any more," meaning one and only one thing, that the bulb will no longer give light. Yet "capable of giving light" is not itself an adequate expression of the central meaning of the word *good.* A person might say of emptied beer cans that "they're still good" if what he has in mind is melting used metal down for re-use—though the cans cannot be refilled, they are still as they ought to be, relative to his special purpose. Thus, even when context determines a highly specific meaning, the general and central meaning, while not conspicuous, remains present. Another way in which we express the underlying meaning of *as it ought to be* is the use of more specific words to convey meanings of the desired sort. We say *right, better, excellent, superior, satisfactory,* or we use terms that convey a special meaning but also carry the connotation *good—pleasant, interesting, impressive, appropriate, effective, successful, humane, helpful,* and innumerable others grading off into more and more special contexts and uses. Another circumstance we must notice is that many sentences contain terms having highly value-toned words even though the purport of the sentence is fact-assertive. This bespeaks our need for both kinds of expression in interpretation and communication, and suggests that if some of its words are so value-toned as to confuse or compete with factual import, the sentence should be divided and reworded, or at least the presence of strong value overtones should be noted.

One more fact is implicit in the discussion above. The terms *what is* and *what ought to be* are polar terms, but polar terms in a special way. It would be more usual to say that *what is* and *what is not* are polar terms, terms that are understood in relation to one another. *What is not* is understood in negation to *what is*. When *is* is taken as asserting existence, then *what is not* is taken as meaning what does not exist. However, as pointed out above, *what is not* does not by any means necessarily coincide with *what ought to be,* nor does it necessarily exclude *what ought to be.* Rather, *what ought to be* is understood in terms of *what is;* and therefore that which it names, that which ought to be, must be regarded as potentially equally extensive as what *is* and may be even more extensive, since one particular of what *is* may give rise to more than one particular of *what ought to be. What ought to be* includes both what ought to be that *is,* and what ought to be that *is not. What ought not to be,* in parallel fashion, includes *what ought not to be but is,* and *what ought not to be and is not.* The crucial fact is that just as *what is* when taken as denoting the existent (the real) is all-embracing, the phrase *what ought to be* is of at least equally extensive scope and is therefore the broadest phrase available for us to apply, among all the words or phrases that express the central meaning of our valuative assertions. It is therefore the only term that is fully suitable, and its concept is the only concept that is fully applicable, for expressing strictly the underlying meaning of all our valuations. The terms used in ethics—for example, *good* and *right*—while valuative indeed, cannot be broad enough for use across the whole spectrum of value judgments and assertions; the definition in ethics of the normative as relating only to obligation cannot apply to that entire spectrum, and similarly for key terms in other fields of values. Rather, a master concept and term are required, within the framework of which these are all understood, and the concept that fills the need is *what ought to be.*

It is usual on one or another of our theories of truth to say that the objective test, the test according to reality or what is, is the proper test for fact-assertive propositions. Under a copy theory of truth, if a fact-assertive proposition correctly expresses a state of affairs as objectively perceived, we say that it is true and is a part of the total body of knowledge. The other theories of truth propose different tests of truth, but for the most part have in common with the copy theory some kind of reference to objective actuality or an objective, empirical or logical framework. Now, if the value-assertive propositions are about values just as fact-assertive propositions are about facts, it would seem to follow that one would look at the values themselves to see whether the value-assertive propositions were true, just as one looks at the entities or events themselves to see whether the fact-assertive propositions are true. However, it is the current situation that no way of doing this has reached acceptance. This circumstance suggests that the realm of value is metaphysically unlike the realm of fact, of entities or events; that there is thus theoretical reason why a test of truth of the sort suggested is not applicable; and indeed, that the concept *truth* may itself not even be applicable to value-assertions even though we understand them to be assertions. In order to explore these problems, we will, in succeeding chapters, have to survey truth in propositions, and then concepts and reference.

4

Value-Assertive Propositions:
Their Tests and Their Truth

Although in the second chapter we acknowledged the role of the idea of truth in the explanation of the proposition, our exposition of fact-assertive and value-assertive statements thus far has assumed nothing about the truth of specific assertions or of kinds of assertions. The relationship of truth to the distinction between fact-assertive and value-assertive propositions is not definitive. Nevertheless, the idea of truth is important to it, because the value-assertive propositions borrow a semblance of authoritativeness from a characteristic of the fact-assertive propositions, which, on examination in the light of experience, we find them not at all equipped to support. This characteristic is the amenability of the fact-assertive propositions to bear a truth-sign, *true* or *false*. There are important consequences of the relationships between the respective elements that may be modified by the adjectives *true, untrue, existent, nonexistent, fact-assertive,* and *value-assertive,* which warrant a reappraisal of the ways we talk about truth. We must now examine these relationships, asking ourselves what it is that value-assertive propositions assert, whether they might properly be tested by the familiar ways of testing fact-assertive propositions, and whether we should introduce any reservations as to whether and in what way it is possible for them to be true.

The assumption about facts that is made in the culture has the word *facts* stand for things that are independent of or unaffected by our knowledge of them. Accordingly, when we shape a proposition, we select linguistic symbols and arrange them so that they will parallel the facts, the actual states of affairs or events, and we test the truth of any proposition by its accordance with the facts that it is thus expected to express. When the proposition is in complete accordance with the facts, so understood, we classify it as true and give it the truth-sign *true.* If the proposition significantly falls short of an appropriate degree of correlation with the facts that its originator purposes to express, we classify it as false and give it the truth-sign *false.* Thus the content, the specific subject matter, that which is not the proposition but what the proposition represents, is thought to serve as the test of the truth of the proposition. This is, of course, the copy theory of truth.

A more critical understanding of the relation between propositions and their subject matters, one that is compatible with the fundamental assumptions acknowledged at the start of the present study, would modify the above popularly held description as follows. We are aware of certain appearances to our consciousnesses that we take to be appearances of external objects or of otherwise objective entities (perhaps ideal objects). We compose our propositions by selecting elements appearing in consciousness as linguistic symbols, and by arranging these in such a way that they parallel the set of other appearances that we are concerned to express. When we have arrived at a sentence that is satisfactory by the test of the nearness of the linguistic parallel to the set of appearances that supply its subject matter, then we call that sentence *true*, and if our sentence falls short, we call it *false*, bestowing the truth-signs accordingly. Thus, once again, with the caution in mind that we ought not to take an appearance in consciousness as a guarantee of the existence of a perfect correlate of that appearance in the realm of external existence, we nevertheless test our proposition according to that which supplies its subject matter—whether or not we still wish to call that subject matter "the facts."

The familiar kinds of declarative sentences and propositions fall within the descriptions just given, while exhibiting variants that distinguish them from one another. They include matters of experience expressed in synthetic sentences and propositions, matters of the relations among ideas expressed in analytic sentences and propositions, and definitions. While it cannot be my purpose to lay out theories of each of these kinds of propositions, I believe it will be helpful to sketch for each the ways in which it can be alleged that an examination of the subject matter or referent can serve as the test of truth.

In the epistemological tradition, synthetic propositions have most conspicuously included empirical propositions, that is, propositions based on sense experience. However, there is no need to confine them to such things, for surely the sentences that tell what one has dreamed, or imagined, or conceived, or supposed independently of sense experience are synthetic, for there is nothing logically necessary about those modes of appearance in consciousness. Yet there is an amenability to truth, for one can either accurately or inaccurately report a dream or an imagined scene, and so on. One can suppose a physical principle or conceive a geometrical principle, and produce a proposition that describes it accurately or inaccurately. Thus there is a test for the truth of any proposition concerning appearances in these modes, and the test involves the specific appearances, the subject matters, of the propositions produced. I can say, for example, that I have been spending some time reflecting on the nature of a world in which any mind could, at will, operate time bidirectionally instead of remaining in unidirectional time; and that report can be true or false, according to whether I *have* been conceiving of such a world, that is, according to the subject matter of the proposition and by reference to it; that subject matter test is a separate thing from questions about whether such a world is possible or what the logical implications of such a world would be. It seems that in this way any sort of synthetic proposition can have a truth-sign assigned to it by virtue of what its subject matter is, and that that is our standard way of arriving at a truth-sign for such a proposition.

The effect of the preceding sketch of testing the truth of synthetic propositions is to identify the subject matter of such propositions as one or more referent objects, and to apply the test by inspecting the referent objects. Similarly, for analytic propositions, if we specify their referent objects or subject matters in certain appropriate ways, we can say the same thing about their tests for truth. The basis of their truth is the tautology; an analytic proposition is assigned the sign *true* when its subject is identical to or contained within its predicate. The explanation of this test by subject matter depends upon what is taken as the subject matter of the proposition. If it is the words or symbols of the proposition, then a simple inspection of the written or spoken version will suffice. If it is concepts or objects, then the truth-sign is assigned according to what the concepts or objects of the subject term and the predicate term *are*, even though definitions of the terms for these concepts or objects may be employed for the cases of propositions whose subjects and predicates do not merely consist of the very same symbols. One need not go and look at the object designated by a subject or predicate term to verify such a tautology; rather, one needs to know the use of the symbols, so as to know whether the concept or object designated by the subject term of the proposition is the same as or a component of the concept or object designated by the predicate term (hence the employment of the definitions). This is not the usual way of speaking about analytic propositions, but it is merely an effort to emphasize what we do usually say about them when we are taking for granted the meanings of our symbols. This much of the test of analytic propositions is a test of the truth of the proposition by considering what its subject matter is.

Now let us glance at the special case of definitions. We will be able to draw a special point from it, beyond the more general point now being supported. Consider the definition: "A diaskeuast is an editor." There is a long-standing controversy about what the subject of a definition is. Is it, in this case, diaskeuasts, or is it the word *diaskeuast?* Again, is a definition capable of being true or false—or on the other hand, is it an imperative, commanding us to use or to understand a word in a certain way? There are at least three ways in which this definition may be said to be true, even if we want also to claim that the definition commands its recipient. First, the statement "A diaskeuast is an editor" is synthetically true, because diaskeuasts actually are editors; they are not cooks or physicians or chauffeurs: look among editors, and you will find diaskeuasts. Second, the statement is true because the predicate is identical to the subject—regardless whether we mean by this the predicate word, the predicate concept, or the predicate object, so long as we mean something of the same ontic status respectively by both "predicate" and "subject." Thus, the definition is tautologously true, analytically true. Finally, the statement is true as a linguistic report, in the often recommended interpretation that says a definition is a statement of how people actually use words. Users of the word (when any can be found!) actually do use *diaskeuast* interchangeably with *editor*. Thus, just as with the other kinds of statement, this one is tested for its truth by an examination of its subject matter, depending upon which of its guises we elect to recognize. That is, it is tested by examination of the person who *is* a dieskeaust; or of the concept or whatnot that the analytical proposition is about; or of the words *diaskeuast* and *editor*. But further, notice the happy sort of ambiguity we have in this instance, that of a definition of a thing belonging to the world. It exhibits in itself two sorts of truth—analytic and synthetic—about three sorts of subject matter. As an assertion about relations among concepts, it is analytic. As an assertion about real objects (a person, the diaskeuast), and also as an assertion about linguistic terms and the persons who use them, it is synthetic. And on each of the pertinent criteria of truth, about each of the appropriate subject matters, the assignment of the truth-sign in every case is the same, namely, *true*. The truth-situation with definitions, then, argues that we actually do use more than one kind of criterion of truth in our ordinary discourse, and get along quite successfully and evidently without bothersome internal contradiction or mental conflict when we do so. I shall be wanting to bear this in mind below when I invite my reader to consider truth-signs applied to value-assertive propositions.

What past history suggests is that the search for "the good" or value has taken the form of inference by analogy. Those sentences and propositions that have declared truths of the world of experience and of conceptual or ideal fact have been about certain identifiable referents or subject matters; they have been testable by inspection or examination of those subject matters in their appropriate ways; and they have on that basis supplied us with true propositions. It should be the case, as we have concluded by analogical inference, that we need only to inspect and examine the values, generate correctly the propositions that accurately express them, and then justify what we say by referring back again to the referent values as the suitable tests of our propositions. In such a way we could expect to become well acquainted with value or values, and we should become able to generate and test propositions about them, eventually accumulating enough of these that by abstracting or generalizing we would be able to define *value* satisfactorily with a definition that would have truth rather than falsity, and would have realized its truth-sign in the three disparate ways outlined above.

Obviously it would be of the greatest usefulness to us if we could apply the same test pattern to value-assertive propositions, just as we apply it to fact-assertive propositions. However, either the project will be conceded to be fruitless in the very acknowledgement of its illogical nature, or if we can somehow rescue its logic, we will find ourselves generating tautologous statements that can be logically warranted but are empty of the kind of knowledge that we would like to find in them.

With respect to the first alternative, it is obviously inconsistent to say that we will test the truth of propositions about *what ought to be* by ascertaining whether they conform to what *is*, either in the world or in consciousness. For if we were to find a statement that someone claims expresses a value judgment, such that the statement conforms to what is, we will know only that we have found a fact-assertive proposition that is true factually. We will have left ourselves behind, so to speak, as to our crucial purpose, the testing of our proposition as value-assertive.[1] Even acknowledging that the proposition might be one of those that report the pleasing circumstance that what is coincides with what ought to be, we have no way of knowing by virtue of this test.

But if, instead, we make changes in the structure of the test on account of our awareness that we are moving from the testing of statements of "what is," in the world or in experience, to the testing of statements of "what ought to be," we will probably end up with empty words. The natural way to try to accomplish this would be to remind ourselves that we are talking about judgments of values, and from this to take a clue for a modification of the form of our test, namely, to say that values are what are to be communicated in our statement, and that language must be made to match them in order to communicate them accurately, and then that the way of testing is to check against the subject matter, to see whether the language of the value-assertive proposition actually matches the values that are to be communicated. If so, we might then conclude that the specific value-assertive proposition is true, and if not, not. But, alas, what are values? Where shall we look to find them? Whose description, whose theory of value shall we take to be the authoritative one? Among philosophers and non-philosophers alike there is as yet no agreed-upon way to settle disputes about values, which is to say that there is no agreed-upon definition of *value*. Therefore, there is no way to identify values as they occur in the world and no way to test the truth of reports of value judgments. It is precisely this uncertainty that has set our problem for us in the first place. Thus we see that we cannot test valuative propositions or statements by referring to certain referents in the world or in consciousness. We cannot test them empirically, in the accustomed manner of testing synthetic propositions, for the objects that appear in consciousness as the objects of our world are irrelevant to what we are testing.

If we attempt to test our value-assertive propositions as logical propositions, what we have to fall back on is tautologous truth and the meanings of terms. But when we do that we have left the world of natural fact and entered the world of arbitrary symbolism. Consequently, what we can test is not what certain propositions say that values *are*, but rather, what people *call* them, in language; and the tests available are the tests in terms of the consistency of the logical system embodied in the language concerned, not tests in terms of consistency with some extralinguistic realm. The test is, so to speak, a test of the machine, rather than a test of the finished product issuing out of the machine; and we are not getting the result we desire.

Finally, the special case of definition is the one whose successful test we most wish to obtain. We can see that if we had a successfully tested definition of *value,* it would be at once an instance of logical, analytic truth and of experiential, synthetic truth, as well as an accurate report of its use in the language. This would bind together the world of language with the world of being. But what is lacking is some principle of relation under which we might expect propositions that describe value to yield the test result *true* by one or both sorts of tests and for reasons as good as those that support our beliefs in the relations of other sorts of subject matter with the language through which we describe and discuss them. What this works out to is that we want to be able by acts of the mind to look on a sufficiently precise proposition, the satisfactory result of our inquiry, now as analytic and again as synthetic, without violence to either logic or our experience. That is, we want to look on it as a definition. In the case of the definition, "A diaskeuast is an editor," we can find a parallel proposition that we consider synthetically true, such as "A diaskeuast is a person who reads manuscripts, adjusts and revises them, and makes them ready for publication." Insofar as an actual diaskeuast is a person who does these things, our definition is synthetically true. Consulting the linguistic conventions shows us that when persons use the expression *diaskeuast* they use it interchangeably with the expression *editor;* hence the definition is true in the role of that other sort of synthetic proposition which is a report on the use of language. And finally, since the linguistic facts are as they are, we know that the subject term and the predicate term of the definition are exactly interchangeable, hence that the definition is tautologously true. Thus examination of one or another body of fact is what gives the definition its truth. But our difficulty in the case of an attempt to define *value* is that we are, as it were, fishing in different waters. The principles that are assumed by means of which referential truth, linguistic report, and therefore tautological truth are brought into convergence in our paradigm definition are not so clear in our linguistic practice and convention for our vexed notion of *value.* The folk wisdom has not provided us with a dependable framework, but only with the weak analogy that leaves the underlying problem unresolved.

Nevertheless, there is much that we can say about value-assertive propositions at this stage of our inquiry. We can say (*a*) that they have the same *outward form* as fact-assertive propositions; (*b*) that having the same form, they appear to operate as items of potential belief in the same fashion, in respect to the appraisals that people make as to whether or not to believe them; (*c*) that this operation on the part of the propositions consists in the suggestion to the recipient by their similar form that he is receiving a proposition about something as real as states of affairs, or something that is real in the same way as states of affairs are real; and thus (*d*) that he is receiving a proposition that can be believed and handled in the same way as propositions about states of affairs; and therefore (*e*) that he is receiving something that can be tested in the same way as propositions about states of affairs. This is the analogy of the value-assertive propositions to the fact-assertive propositions that has probably been a major force in leading philosophers into errors about value. It has led them to seek value as though value were a *quid,* the very gold that the philosopher's stone should produce, and to experience considerable bafflement when they have been unable to find the substantial thing called *value*; or else it has led them wrongly to consider this or that thing (such as pleasure) to be the very stuff of value; or on a lesser scale it has induced their confidence that there is a single and totally satisfactory answer to the question "What is it that is valuable?" But while many a philosopher will tell us most confidently what he believes value to be, most will also confess that there is little agreement among themselves and no well-established consensus as to what value finally is.

It is possible that the present investigation may bring us closer to "the truth about what value really is." Far be it for the writer to hang back from making the happy announcement of that result if indeed it were to accrue. But before going so far, I believe I can record some additional facts— continuing to write descriptively of the way users of language do actually employ it, as well as of typical events of our experience of things other than language—that will enable us very readily to handle value *judgments* them- selves. There are some facts whose recognition enables us to understand more fully than we generally have in the past what it is that we actually *do*: (*a*) when we make value judgments, (*b*) when we accept for our own beliefs the value-judgmental propositions of others, (*c*) when we test value-assertive propositions, (*d*) when we make use of them, and, very importantly, (*e*) when we are uttering or writing value-assertive propositions and pressing them upon others, hoping for the acceptance by those others of what we ourselves assert in matters of values.

What is important for the present is to notice well that the fact-assertive propositions, whether analytic or synthetic, *can be tested,* and that it is of the nature of such propositions that there is theory relating distinct types of tests respectively to these two distinct types of fact-assertive propositions.[2] This is an added fact about fact-assertive propositions, not merely a repetition of the characteristic already mentioned in the definition of the proposition such that it "can be true or false"—that is, that it is the case with any such locution that either it is true or it is false. The doctrines classifying fact-assertive propositions into these two types are arrived at through theory. Theory provides us with kinds of tests suited to the types, and practice carried on consistently with theory provides us with actual tests and actual decisions as to whether a given proposition *is* true, after its kind. While not every fact- assertive proposition is tested, and while in some respects the tests can never be exhaustive and hence finally conclusive, in theory we may and in practice we do conclude that fact-assertive propositions are determinable as to their truth or falsity.

The importance of this is to bring out, by contrast, the circumstance that things are quite different indeed with the value-assertive propositions. *Value-assertive propositions cannot be objectively tested.*

The Romans had the proverb, "De gustibus non est disputandum"—"there is no disputing of matters of taste." Matters of taste lead to judgments of taste, whose propositional vehicle is the value-assertive proposition. While doubtless there was plenty of actual disputing about taste among the Romans, there was no deciding, hence (the proverb reminds us) dispute was futile. The same is the experience of modern conversants when dealing in matters of taste, of morals, of etiquette—and in brief, of all kinds of issues that have their expression in value-assertive propositions. Although we are well aware of the possibilities for testing fact-assertive propositions after their kind, we are so unaware of any possibility of doing the same with value-assertive ones that we have enshrined our pessimism on the subject in proverbs and in subjective and relativistic doctrines: "Everyone to his own opinion," "You have your opinion, and I have mine," "I have as much right to my opinion as you have to yours." Shortly we shall be examining the basis and validity of these doctrines. For the moment let us sum them up in the way they are often summed up in popular language: Value-assertive propositions are by nature *matters of opinion.*

The concept of a matter of opinion is nothing mysterious. Among fact-assertive propositions, some are said to be matters of opinion, and some are not. There are some fact-assertive propositions such that, although it may be known how to test them or what kind of test to apply, the test has not actually been applied. It perhaps requires use of materials or locations that are not accessible, or it may be too expensive, or too risky, or the matter may be too trivial, or there may be other hindrances. Some untested propositions may indeed be such that we do not have a clear idea of precisely what test would resolve the truth-question for them. Thus fact-assertive propositions fall into two groups, those that have been satisfactorily tested, and those that have not; and the tested ones, being tested, are not matters of opinion. Among untested fact-assertive propositions some of them are such that there seems to be evidence for both truth and falsity, evidence sufficient to make either claim superficially plausible. The evidence may lean to one side, but so long as the leaning is not decisive and the alternative may be seen as having a significant even if lesser degree of probability, then the issue of the truth of the proposition is classified as a matter of opinion. This status, of course, changes with time and knowledge. At one time the general nature of the moon's surface was a matter of opinion, and propositions like "The moon's surface is all hard rock" and "The moon's surface is largely deep, loose dust" were carefully weighed. The matter has now been removed from among matters of opinion by actual exploration. Thus fact-assertive propositions are usually either not matters of opinion at all, or are matters of opinion by virtue of the relative inaccessibility of the evidence that would decide their truth, and this inaccessibility is subject to change.

What we have now said, then, makes it come to something very simple for value-assertive propositions. It is simply the case that they are *all* matters of opinion.

If there was a theory of the specific reference of the word *value* that was both true and widely recognized, so that through it the nature of value was finally known or agreed, then we could avail ourselves of that theory in testing value-assertive propositions and in solving value disputes. Whatever the theory alleged value to be, we could hold a given value-assertive proposition up in its light, so to speak, to see whether the proposition accurately reflected the referent state of affairs with respect to value. If so, we could call the proposition true, and if not, we could call it false. (This would entail, of course, that the conventionally established meaning of *value* would be different from what it actually is, according to the claim I shall make about it in this volume.) But there is no such true or widely recognized theory. Consequently any evidence suitable for answering the truth-question for value-assertive propositions is either nonexistent or in this sense inaccessible. Since this is the epistemological circumstance at present, it remains the case that all value-assertive propositions are matters of opinion. Of course I must acknowledge that we can conceive of there being such a thing as a body of value that is a body of reality, and that we might someday come to know it, and that then it might be the case that the desired evidence would no longer be inaccessible. But I will give reasons toward the end of this chapter to explain why I do not believe this to be the case—why it is theoretically impossible.

This result may come as a disappointment to some readers. It is the long-standing wish of many of us that problems of the truth of value assertions could get straightened out, rather than remain indeterminate. But I can no more apologize for this outcome than Galileo could apologize for the motion of the Earth, for it is simply the case. To recognize it does not leave us any worse off than we were when we believed as before, that there were truths in the realm of values that could be found if only we could discover the arcane key to their hiding place. We shall still operate on the same basis as we always have, with no less success at least and possibly with more. If it is to be more, then we will earn the gain by further understanding, to which some further features of value-assertive propositions will help to lead us.

The circumstance that value-assertive propositions are beyond demonstration and proof raises for us certain questions important both to our philosophy and to our daily life. Plato made the point in his admirable and now too little studied dialogue *Phaedrus* that the orator must first know his audience and also must assure himself systematically of the truth and wisdom of his message, before deserving the right to occupy the position of practitioner of the persuasive art. Most of us agree, and exercise our consciences as fully as our self-discipline commands, when we are attempting to persuade others to our beliefs. But at the present stage of this inquiry we must notice that when those beliefs for which we are seeking assent are value-assertive propositions, we are put in a difficult position. We can ascertain which of our fact-assertive beliefs have been verified and pass these to an audience with confidence; but chances are that the dominant purposes of those speeches, discussions, and conversations in which we most hope to be persuasive are the very ones whose main points are value-assertive propositions, not fact-assertive ones. Yet if all value-assertive propositions are matters of opinion, and are beyond the pale of test and possible demonstration, what are we in conscience to do? Fall silent?

Again, we have acknowledged above that the form of value-assertive propositions is analogous to that of fact-assertive propositions. This generally goes unnoticed by the general public, the persons who do not keep abreast of logic, semantics, epistemology, and other practical branches of philosophy. These persons are little enough articulate about, and usually only vaguely conscious of, the difference itself between the fact-assertive and the value-assertive. Thus a speaker who is aware that the structure of the value-assertive is analogous to that of the fact-assertive proposition is aware of something possessing persuasive force of which his typical listener is ignorant. Specifically, if I offer to my hearer a value-assertive proposition in the same grammatical and syntactical form as the fact-assertive propositions that I also have offered him, and that he has indeed found on the whole to coincide with his own beliefs, then I know that I am habituating him to believe what I say, and that I offer him my value-assertion in the guise of a proposition that is *similar to* propositions that are about something accessible, propositions whose truth-evidence is accessible and can be definitively tested. Hence the odds are heavily in my favor that he will hear my value-assertion quite uncritically so far as its being forever a matter of opinion is concerned, and that, provided it does not openly conflict with some other proposition to which he is greatly attached, he will accept it. Is it fair of me to use this method to achieve persuasion?

Or keeping in mind the questions just raised, let us look for a moment at ourselves as the recipients rather than the originators of value-assertions. We hear (for example) a speech by a national figure on a matter of importance to us. We approve his citation of facts in his fact-assertive statements, and we concur in his analysis of the existing state of affairs. But then he begins his peroration with a value-assertive proposition that is obviously his principal thought. Recognizing it as value-assertive, we immediately discount it, remarking to ourselves that it is no better than a matter of opinion, that there is a radical distinction, rather than any necessary connection, between such a proposition and those having factual content. We therefore opt to disregard this speaker's valuative conclusion, saying that it is no better than that of any other person, including his most formidable opponent. Are we treating him fairly?

The three questions just presented exhibit, in a simplified fashion, certain problems of human communication. They are not, however, problems that distress very many of us. In usual situations, either as speaker or as recipient of value-assertions, we do handle such matters somehow, and most often, I suppose, we handle them satisfactorily to ourselves. Few speakers refrain from uttering value judgments just because these are matters of opinion. Rather, they consider most audiences capable, practically if not theoretically and articulately, of defending themselves, in regard to the acceptability of proffered belief. Again, as listeners, they recognize the opinionated nature of the other's conclusion but they generally also recognize the worth of his thinking in other respects, so that while he may not coerce their belief in his value-assertive conclusion, he may attract their consideration to the worth of his view—and that is probably all that experience has led him to expect.

To account for these responses I can only report as best as possible what my observation warrants and invite the reader to see whether it comes close to his own. On that basis, I suggest that we actually are reasonably generous for the most part, possibly even too generous, in our reception of the beliefs of others of which they desire to persuade us, that at the same time we are adequately defensive of the integrity of our own beliefs, and that we remain reasonably alert against the pitfalls of accepting beliefs which we in some sense ought not to believe. I further suggest that we reach this state by virtue of actually carrying out some sort of assessment of value-assertive propositions, even though we do not and cannot test them for truth—that is, test them in ways that are parallel to those we use to test fact-assertive propositions. How we accomplish this will be understandable after we elicit some further information descriptive of value-assertive propositions.

To understand how this may be the case, let us return to the question of why it is that there is no objective test for value-assertive propositions. This is, of course, what we have said when we have said that all value-assertive propositions are matters of opinon. Concerning matters of opinion, in turn, we have said that there is no accessible evidence, no state of affairs within reach of observation, that would serve to supply the test of their truth. Now it has been shown many times over in the literature of ethics that "one cannot get from 'is' to 'ought,'" or, in other words, that no number of facts is going to give logical validity to a conclusion that is an ought-judgment, a statement of how things ought to be. That this is so follows from what I went to some length to demonstrate in chapter three, namely, that the notion of "what is" is quite separate and different from the notion of "what ought to be."

Even in the instances where something that ought to be actually *is,* the two meanings are different. The concepts or ideas are different, and that, of course, is what enters into their logic, even though in some specific state of affairs both *what is* and *what ought to be* are said to be present in a single actuality. "*X* ought to be" logically implies neither "*X* is" nor "*X* is not," but is compatible with both. The same is true for "*X* ought not to be." "Is" does not imply "ought"; granted that "*X* is" (or "*X* exists") is true, "*X* ought to be" and "*X* ought not to be" are both compatible with "*X* is"; neither is implicit in it. Nothing in "*X* is" logically determines either "*X* ought to be" or "*X* ought not to be." Further, "ought to be" (or "ought not to be") by itself implies no more about "is" than it implies about either "*X* will be" or "*X* will not be." To believe otherwise, and particularly to believe that "*X* is" implies "*X* ought to be," is to commit the naturalistic fallacy, as understood by many of the writers who have discussed G. E. Moore's *Principia Ethica,* wherein the phrase was first introduced into philosophical literature. Despite its being a derived version and debatably a correct interpretation of its originator's intent, I shall employ this understanding of the term *naturalistic fallacy* consistently, herein, because of its great usefulness.[3]

Now, is it merely because various theorists differ on what actually is the *quid* of "what ought to be" that the evidence is inaccessible? In other words, is it the lack of agreement about the substance of value, what value *is,* that keeps us unsettled? And may we look with hope to the day when *one* of the substantive theories of the identity of value shall have emerged victorious as the time when the truth about value (an "existing" something called *value*) may become known, *in concreto* and in detail? I think not, because of certain features of the concept of *what ought to be.*

Man evidently generated his language at least in part by assigning words to referent objects, to function as symbols of those respective objects. In this fashion he determined the meanings of the words, in one sense—the referential sense—of the term *meaning.* Once he got the hang of this, he went further. Reacting to the fact that there is another sense of the word *meaning,* namely, conceptual meaning, he devised certain words and invented meanings for them without the presence of any referent objects. This was like inventing the basket or the pail without first deciding what substance was to be carried, but rather deciding and declaring that the new invention was to carry something in, as a container. Words of the sort I now describe might aptly be called *container words.* There may be some important abstract terms among them, such as *perfection, perpetual motion, absolute zero, complete vacuum*—not to mention *Cloud Nine*—whose appropriate referent objects never have been and never can be met concretely in experience. And just as there are container words, I suggest that there are *container concepts,* for of course the concept *perfection* is a different thing from the word *perfection.* For a word to be a container word is for its conceptual meaning to be a container concept, one whose referential content has not been finally settled upon and assigned. The phrase *what ought to be,* which is the key phrase defining value-assertive propositions, symbolizes such a container concept.

Container concepts are by no means rare. Some of them, including some quite familiar ones, are indicated by single words; others are indicated by phrases. They include *perfection, the ideal, infinity, Utopia, El Dorado, total freedom, success, knowledge, happiness, the perfect crime, the absolute, perpetual motion machine, a body persisting in motion in a straight line free of impressed forces, the best way to cook a fresh-caught catfish, the best way to invest my savings.* For some young man, *my future wife* is a container concept, having no specific referent; but after his engagement, the expression *my future wife* becomes "filled" and joins the ranks of expressions that have both conceptual and concrete or actual referential meaning. The list of names of container concepts surely should include many phrases beginning with *whatever,* in familiar uses: "whatever it takes to be popular," "whatever it takes to get rich," "whatever appeals to the buyers of 45-rpm records," and so on. In fact, the word *whatever* may be taken as a sign of a container concept (except in its purely intensifying or emphatic use, and possibly even then, as in "None whatever!"). The fact that the users of the language have evidently developed a catch-all word to serve the purpose of identifying container concepts of all sorts (any container concept whatever!) confirms that their use is quite ordinary and taken for granted in everyday language. Other locutions also signal explicitly the employment of container concepts, such as "anything that . . .," "something that . . .," and the like.

Container concepts function in a way in which we make use of them with ease in fact-assertive propositions. We readily understand or originate such locutions as "Aristotle denies that there is *a real infinite*," "Young people today believe they can have *total freedom* with total release from responsibility," *"Whatever you may want out of life,* you will be certain to get some *things you do not expect."* It is evident that the concepts summoned up in the mind by the italicized phrases in these instances are fully meaningful conceptually, while they in fact have no determinate referents.

One of the most common and useful forms of the container concept occurs in questions. In fact, a well-formed question is in effect a collection of terms used to establish a container concept, to enable the originator to think this concept and to induce it accurately in the mind of a receiver. "What are you going to buy in the city today?" Clearly the reply will be a specification of the referent object of the concept *What you are going to buy in the city today.* Many questions are not phrased for a recipient but for keeping one's own thinking clear—that is, for the questioner's own benefit. A disciplined investigator in any field works at the task of settling upon a good phrasing of his problem, a phrasing from which the kind of answer desired can easily be seen, a phrasing sufficiently clear that if the answer were found, its aptness for fulfilling the container concept expressed in the formulation of the problem would be evident. The investigator may even be more interested in achieving an appropriate formulation than in finding all possible referents for his concept; this will be especially likely if he has reason to believe that the solution to the problem is beyond his own limitations or even those of his whole generation of investigators.

What it is that identifies a container word or a container concept is not a requirement that the filling, the content, be never encountered at all (as we suppose is the case with *perfection*), but rather, that the concept or the term indicating it be in fact employed by users who do not actually have specific referent objects in mind as they use the term. Its being a container concept is relative to its user—its originator, or its recipient, or both. The samples listed above were container concepts relative to everyone or nearly everyone, but that was simply for convenience of exposition, to make the absence of a specified referent obvious. The young man who speaks of "my future wife" at a time when he has not made any marriage proposals is probably reasonably sure of the existence of the referential content of his container concept, but awaits its specification. Surely there are many container concepts whose status is of very short duration, like *what I am to have for dinner tonight*. The framing of many problems is aided greatly by our formation of container concepts, such as *what to have for dinner, which girl to ask to marry me, which wine to take to my host and hostess, what foreign policy to adopt toward the nations of Asia, as cold as it can get, absolute zero, a just settlement in the Near East*. A container concept is virtually a predicate without a subject, at least a permanent subject. But when a referent becomes permanently determined, then the concept no longer functions as a container concept.

On this showing, we can see that container concepts, like other concepts, may vary considerably in degree of complexity, from the simplest conceivable to the most complex of those concepts we are likely ever to construct. The suggestion also emerges that they are instruments extremely useful for solving problems, and probably this is the essential fact about them. Finally, in that they are concepts, they are rational instruments, that is to say, instruments by which we enable ourselves to reason about the situations in which our problems arise and are recognized, and in which we set about solving them. As a means of conceptualizing, they are means of applying intellectual processes to the world in our endeavor to understand it, adapt to it, modify it, and bring its features into the service of our own purposes. More narrowly, they are instruments helping us to deal with the unknown, by enabling us to anticipate conceptually what the facts yet to develop may be, and what values could be envisioned with respect to them. All this being seen, it is now easy to discern that *what ought to be* is a phrase indicating one very general concept among the whole collection of container concepts, which along with other concepts are in turn rational instruments for dealing with the world.

It is widely acknowledged that different people fill the container concept for *value* or *values* in different and often contradictory ways, according to the diversity of human purposes and their relation to human limitations. For example, while very many of us regard world peace as a value, a state of affairs which ought to be, and while we who espouse this value tend to assume that everyone else agrees in espousing it, we must recognize that it is actually false that everyone does espouse it. Rather, there are large numbers of persons who espouse war as a value. While one group says, "Worldwide peace is what ought always to be the case," another group says something like, "My nation ought to undertake war under certain conditions," or "My nation ought to undertake war when that is the only (or best or most likely) means for it to get what it wants," or "My class of society ought to undertake war when necessary to get what it wants." At the present writing, Americans seem nearly evenly divided on the issue of abortion: About half are saying, "Abortion ought to be available and ought to be used whenever a woman has an unwanted pregnancy," while the other half are saying, "Abortion is wrong in general and ought not to be used unless necessary to save a mother's life." In the arts, one critic may say, "That work is excellent" (i.e., it is like what a work of art in that medium or style or genre ought to be), while another may say of the same object, "That work is abominable" (i.e., it is nothing like what a work in that medium, style, genre, ought to be).[4] The list of samples of differences of view such as these can be extended as long as man lives. It seems a fair summary to say that two people can survey the very same field of fact and, upon completion of the survey, come to quite opposite, or at least very different, judgments about what ought to be, with respect to that field of fact. A frequently attempted way to resolve such differences is for each disputant to expose to the view of the other still more factual matter so that his opponent will be supplied with something new to think about, which would presumably bring him to the same judgment as the protagonist. However, so long as there is a dispute, the new matter that would potentially compel a single judgment on the data by all those who judge is not actually in view, and in that sense it is inaccessible. Hence the issue is a matter of opinion for just that long. And we may gather from some of the unended controversies that all the human ingenuity that may ever be brought to bear may yet fail to uncover such controversy-quenching factual matter. Thus our container concepts have great usefulness to us insofar as they are necessary instruments for expressing our differences of opinion. For this reason we will no doubt always preserve them as a device, even though when opinion crystallizes on certain matters the former container concepts used in discussing those matters will become filled and will no longer function as container concepts.

Their practical utility say, "It would be good to have a fence around the garden," or "It would be good to fence in the whole property," or "Perhaps I should put up a 'No Trespassing' sign," or "Perhaps I should post myself·on watch and turn the trespassers back when they start across my place," or "Perhaps I ought to have an officer of the law show himself a time or two to discourage the trespassers." Normally, we survey all the conceivable proposals, without any of them first being made physically actual, and judge in favor of one or more of them; thus *we are deciding upon what, specifically, ought to be.* What an *experiment* is, is a realization "in the flesh," in physical actuality, of a concept of a possible state of affairs, and as such is the filling of its content.

A third circumstance that inclines us to maintain container concepts as a device is the short life of some of the states of affairs that we judge ought to be the case. We can say and intend quite literally, "What I ought to do or have today is not what I ought to do or have tomorrow." Many a person, especially among those who cook for themselves or their families, has a constantly recurring problem expressed in the container concept "what to have for dinner." The container somehow gets filled daily, but also recurs daily, so that people are heard to say, "What to have for dinner—it's the biggest problem of my whole life!" While the referent varies as it is filled in now for one day and now for another, the concept endures perennially as a container concept. We need it to function as variable, fillable in various ways, longer than we need to assign to it any one referent, or, using it as a grammatical predicate, to attach it to any one subject.

The uses of container concepts in phrasing questions and framing and solving problems suggest to us one way of understanding our affirmation that the settled filling of a container concept does not take place because the evidence that would persuade in favor of a given referent is inaccessible. In the example of the garden, it is only in the future that the effect of any one of the proposed measures could be ascertained in actuality, although predictions with varying degrees of probability for each may be made in a given present moment. Fencing the garden, fencing the whole property, posting a "No Trespassing" sign, standing guard, or stationing an officer could be tried, and once the designated future time comes, we could then determine factually, "That was (or was not) effective in accomplishing its purpose." But first of all, as of a given moment, one cannot read the temporal features of the future perceptually; one can read only the temporal features of the present moment. Thus, right now while pondering my problem I cannot watch it happening, that an officer turns away a would-be trespasser. Moreover, some of the possible solutions for many problems exclude others, at least practically if not logically. If I post a "No Trespassing" sign and find that it is effective, then at the given moment when I was considering my problem, the solution of posting a sign was future, but the solution of fencing the property was only potential, not future at all. As something that was not even future but only potential, it lends itself not at all, not even in prospect, to being tested by the perception of actual happenings in experience. Thus it is, to be sure, evidence that is systematically inaccessible for supporting the value-assertive proposition, "It would be good to (or I ought to) fence in the whole property."

Again, we know too well that sometimes there is a vast gap between human intent and earthly outcomes, not to mention errors of judgment in executing plans. Hence, while envisioning the solution adopted and its expected effects, we cannot actually *prove* that these effects will come about; we cannot *prove* that the course of action once begun will match our vision of the solution; we cannot prove that the effects of the solution will be as predicted. It could happen that we try all the envisioned solutions to our problem one after another, or even simultaneously, and discover that we do not succeed in creating the condition that we affirm, in advance, ought to be the case. The fence falls down; the sign is washed away; I fall ill and am confined indoors; the officer malingers. Thus the value-assertive propositions motivating each of these attempted solutions fail to receive their empirical tests—the evidence remains inaccessible.

Yet the major bar to the testing of ways of filling the concept, "what I ought to do about the trespassers who cross my garden," remains that other kind of inaccessibility of the evidence, the logical barrier arising from the fact of the simple difference between "what does happen" and "what ought to happen." Even the effectiveness of a method of deterring the trespassers, which might be observed once the method has been put into effect, does not itself establish the *oughtness* of what then does happen. For example, I might put into effect the measure of hiring a private guard to turn away trespassers, and the measure might be thoroughly effective; and it would be through empirical observation that I should know it to be effective. But that does not test another measure, such as putting up the fence; and perhaps though each method would be quite effective, the thing that I "really ought to do" is put up the fence, not hire the guard. It may be, for example, that there should be less cost for the fence than for the guard. And while we pretty automatically let the cost factor settle such decisions, once again we have only pushed the criterion of value a step further away: Why *ought* I to do that which costs the less? I don't solve all my problems by always adopting the option that costs less. We see that the logical difference between "what is" and "what ought to be" is still not one that is transcended by empirical means.

We have now seen some reasons for the endless differences, and no prospect of a simple resolution of them, with respect to value-assertive propositions. Value-assertive propositions fundamentally employ the container concept of *what ought to be*. The concept can be filled in within a particular scope, or with a scope that is broad enough to encompass all human action. It is usual in moral theory to fill it in with some thoroughly general principle, such as "One ought to do that which will maximize pleasure and minimize pain for all who are affected," and by simple syllogistic reasoning to subsume particular actions under the general principle ("Everyone will be happier in the long run if I put a stop to this trespassing across my garden, even if the culprits will be unhappy at first"). But no convention of either language or substance has unequivocally filled in referential content (such as "actions that maximize pleasure and minimize pain for all who are affected") for this concept or for its symbolizations in language. Therefore, thus far in history, at any rate, every speaker is free to fill it in as he deems best. Theorists, assuming that there *are* values, that there is a *quid* from which they are abstracting and generalizing, have filled it in with their own best estimates of what it is that all values have in common. The practical man does not worry much about abstracting and generalizing, so as to have a tidy means of unifying his various value judgments, but rather, fills in the container concept with now this and now that external referent as what he intends by *value* or *good* from time to time. Perhaps the future history of the phrase and the concept will be different—will see a specific referent become settled upon, to be conventionally adopted as the referential meaning of the phrase and the concept. However, up to the present time this has not happened.

I believe that it has not happened, and that it will not happen, for more than adequate reasons. The usefulness of the phrase *what ought to be* lies in its special meaning as a container concept. If it were to be filled in permanently, its essential usefulness would disappear. We fundamentally need this concept (no matter by what words we happen to know it); we need its variable applicability for our applications of the *ought* in "what ought to be." Thus *our needs determine that the referential evidence for the ought-proposition in general must remain inaccessible;* that is, we must always maintain a concept for a pattern of expression in which a predicate is invoked but the subject for it, the referent of a naming term for its bearer, does *not* become agreed upon or conventionalized.

However, it is not any empirical fact that finally justifies our assertion that there is no objective way to test value-assertive propositions. Reasons that community opinion has not settled down are not proof that it shall never settle down, although they are very good grounds for supposing it likely that it shall not. Rather, there is a logical fact, one that is based on a principle that is necessarily an assumption rather than an established truth, that provides the justification for this belief. Thus, to the extent that we find the assumption acceptable, the conclusion following the basing of this logical fact upon it is equally acceptable.

The assumption is simply that of an external world. Although the possibility is always present that only oneself exists and that all the appearances of anything exterior to oneself are self-generated illusions having no counterpart whatever in an external reality, the inductive evidence against this solipsistic view is, for practical purposes, overwhelming. Hence, I should say that for purposes of practice, of conduct, we may legitimately believe that there is a world around us, a *given* world, a given exterior or environment, with which we interact and to which therefore we are in relation. The external world may or may not nicely match the apparent world that our perceptions show us, and epistemological criticism has shown us the difficulties of establishing whether or to what extent perception matches what may be the reality independent of that reality being perceived. However, whether it is distorted by perception and interpretation or not, we assume confidently that there is a given of *some* sort, with which we interact *somehow*. It is this external world that is apparent to us through our perceptions, that we believe exists and affects us, and that we call, for purposes of conduct, the world or realm of what *is*, the realm of existence, the realm of actuality, or the world of *fact*. These phrases arise from our interaction with that world before we have subjected our knowledge of it to epistemological criticism; however, we continue to know it by those terms in our practice, even after we have warned ourselves critically against considering that to be certain knowledge, which at bottom is uncertified assumption.

Now we move on to our logical fact: It is that our general concept of *what ought to be* is something that we generate in comparison and contrast to the *realm of the given*, the realm of fact, existence, or actuality. This concept of *what ought to be* is totally mind-generated, not generated at all by abstraction or generalization from perceptions of the particulars of a corresponding external given. There is no given of the value realm. Rather, the concept of *what ought to be refers always to a non-given realm*, by virtue of its genesis—by definition, as it were. This is the ultimate underlying theoretical reason that there is no objective means of testing value-assertions. This is why we cannot take them to be something that *is*, even if it "is" only in consciousness, and come away with demonstrated knowledge as to whether they match or do not match.

Certain consequences issue from this conception of the nature of value-assertive sentences and propositions. We have noticed that they may be of a great range of specificity, from particular or singular propositions ("Mary is the girl I ought to marry") to universal ones ("All persons ought to exercise a responsibility to maintain world peace"), and comprehensive propositions that may be singular grammatically but are all-embracing in thought ("The world ought to be such that there is no poverty"). They may employ the grammatical tenses, but very typically will employ the atemporal present (like the three samples just given). Those that do not express the *ought*-nature of things present in actuality (as do "Paula sings well"; "Anderson is not a good lawyer") characteristically express propositions about objects that are present to consciousness as future objects or potential objects or non-existent objects, relative to their equivalents in other modes of appearing ("It would be good to have a curtain here to keep the sun out").

Even when a value-assertion is a report of an affirmative and favorable value judgment, such as "Paula's singing is just the way it ought to be for that Lied," or "Paula's rendition of that song is excellent," it is the logical predicate concept that conveys the valuation, the container concept, which, before the judgment is made, functions for us as though it is a predicate without a subject. While we do make a judgment upon an actual object or event that is to provide the grammatical subject of any sentence reporting the judgment, and while that sentence-subject may refer to an actuality or an existent, the independence of the valuative expression from reference in the sentence is maintained. The sentence is still structured as though "the way she ought to sing" refers to an entity, but the predicate evaluating Paula's singing has been brought into being in the mode of thought or conception only, not in the realm of the actuality (such as the physical performance of a song). And of course, for the negative or unfavorable value-assertions, there is no question whether the object or event that is judged has a positive counterpart in the value realm. "Paula *doesn't* sing the song the way she ought" does not imply that there *is* in the physical realm a physical singing that is the way Paula doesn't sing the song but ought to. Though perhaps Mme. Schumann-Heinck once did sing the song the way it ought to be sung, such an event is not implicit in what was said about Paula, and may, but need not, have occurred. We can consider the example of a unique object of judgment. Let us say that a unique event takes place, for example, the assassination of President Kennedy. We still understand anyone who says "The assassination of President Kennedy was a bad thing," and to do so we do not have first to construct somehow a notion of what would have constituted a *good* assassination of President Kennedy, and then to cross it out.

With this origin of the basic concept of valuation in mind, let us consider some simple instances of arriving at value judgments. Suppose that Smith is tasting ice cream for the first time. He responds to it by saying, "That's good." It is the ice cream that is a *given* here. A simplistic analysis might tell us that Smith has responded to the goodness of the ice cream, and that the goodness was also a given; this analysis calls for the identification of the predicate *good* as either a component or an attribute of the ice cream. However, the experience, we now see, need not take place that way. If Smith had said, "That is as I imagined it would be," we would not say that "the way I imagined it would be" was a given attribute or component of the ice cream, for Smith could not have gotten from an object, by perception, a response from an object that he had never before experienced. Again, if Smith said, "That is the first ice cream I have ever tasted," we would not attribute the "firstness" of the ice cream to the ice cream as a characteristic or component of it, and if we were to taste the ice cream ourselves, we would be very unlikely to say, "That tastes like the first ice cream that Smith ever tasted." Rather, we now analyze the event by saying that Smith has *brought* the concept to the ice cream and found that the ice cream has fulfilled his concept (either the concept "as I imagined it would be" or the concept "good ice cream"). The taste or texture or temperature or other characteristic or combination of characteristics of the ice cream are, to be sure, givens of the ice cream, but the judgment that these things are what *ought* to be characteristics of the ice cream is not given with nor a characteristic of the ice cream. Thus a value-assertion is fundamentally different, logically, from a report of a perception. It does not say "That object out there has characteristics in common with other objects out there that I have also experienced," though that may be true. Rather, it says something about a relation of that object "out there" to a concept or a conception "in here," a function of the judge rather than the object.

When an object is given that we judge to be good, or as it ought to be, the possibility remains that we still can conceive that the outcome of the judgment could have been different or, in other words, that the judgment would be that the intellectually conceived possibility could have been unlike the given. Quite commonly, those who sample coffee or beer for the first time are not pleased with them and judge that the beverage is not good, and only later develop an acquired taste for it. This shows not only that we can change our minds, but also that we do not need to suppose that there is an *object,* in the old and puzzling sense, which is the not-good-ness of coffee or beer that the judge in making a negative or unfavorable judgment is perceiving in the coffee or beer that he has sampled, or that there is another object, the goodness, which he somehow knows about and finds to be lacking even though he has never previously tasted coffee or beer. We can avoid these perplexities through use of our framework of modes of appearing in consciousness. We can acknowledge the "existence" of the not-good-ness of coffee by saying that coffee, and with it certain flavors, textures, warmth, and other characteristics, may appear in consciousness in the way of potential, expected appearances, or remembered appearances of other beverages, and so on, and that the event of having these appearances in mind can occur while sampling actual coffee, physical coffee, and finding that the actual coffee does not resemble the mentally appearing object. The report of the *value judgment,* which is no part of the coffee but becomes logically posterior to sampling the coffee, may inform us that the person doing the sampling regards the coffee as therefore differing from the way coffee ought to be—ought to appear in perceptions of it as a physical object.

Thus the essential underlying idea of value judging is the idea of the *possibility of difference from the given,* and that idea enables us to build our concept of *what ought to be,* which must necessarily then be a container concept, having had its origin in something that could not be directly abstracted from a given presentation.

There is a parallel case of this kind of logical fact that has long been recognized. We construct a concept of *nonbeing,* although we never encounter or perceive nonbeing, as such, and hence we cannot abstract to nonbeing from separate perceived instances of nonbeing. It is in a similar way that we construct *what ought to be* also on the basis of a difference from the given, encountered being. It is a logical construct, not an empirical abstraction. Failure to realize this is the reason we have had "naturalistic" ethical theories, and is also the reason they cannot be made convincing.

At this juncture, it becomes a most interesting question: "What is it that value-assertive propositions actually assert?" It appears clearly from the facts surveyed in the present chapter that they do *not* assert facts about existing states of affairs. Even those that concern present states or events ("Paula sings well") are "about" actualities or events (the way Paula does actually sing), but they place the actuality or event mentioned under the heading of the concept *the way things ought to be*, and we have seen that that concept in itself neither requires nor excludes the existent. It becomes secondary then, in respect to whether or not the assertion being expressed asserts that the apparent actuality does match the expressed *ought*, for the opposite assertion is also a report of a valuation. Of course, in "Paula sings well," the assertion that the way Paula does sing matches the way Paula ought to sing is the whole burden and purpose of the locution, but the locution would still be a value-assertion if it were "Paula does not sing well." Thus we have an interesting linguistic situation. Our value-expressive language symbolizes a conception that we have and places that conception under the heading *ought*. This is much like the situation for the existential proposition, which symbolizes a conception that we have and places it under *is* or *exists*. An existential proposition essentially expresses our belief as to what exists or whether some particular or collection of particulars exists. A valuative proposition essentially expresses our belief as to what ought to be or whether some particular or collection of particulars ought to be.

Existence is not a predicate of objects.[5] Whatever else it may be or do, it functions as a principle of classification, so that we may produce a "yes" or "no" answer for any object when the question is asked of that object, "Does it exist?" And we make it a general rule that if the object can be encountered in the physical-object mode, we say "yes," it exists. If no mode of existence is specified in the question, we ordinarily assume that the question is asked with respect to the physical-object mode of appearing. For other modes—a point that is generally ignored—our answer may be governed by whether there is an indication in the question of a different mode of appearing or existence. Someone may ask whether, for example, the *concept of negative role-models* exists; an answer, "yes" or "no," will be made, relative to the conceptual mode of appearing. Again, the question might be raised, "Is there a character who is a chimney sweep in Dickens's *Oliver Twist?*" A reader familiar with the work will readily answer "yes" or "no," consciously or unconsciously replying in terms of the fictional mode of appearing. In this fashion, the concept *existence* is a principle of classification, and we can see that in order for the response to be correct and thus for the function to be useful, it is advisable that either the question or the classifying proposition indicate a relation to a given mode of appearing.

Just as Kant has cautioned us against assuming that the external real world is exactly matched by our perceptions of it, or even is actually there, we must be cautious also about assuming that the realm of what ought to be is likewise exactly matched by our propositions about it—or even is actually there. We realize now that there is far less of a guarantee in the case of the value-assertions than in the case of the fact-assertions. Kant's criticism of the reigning Aristotelian theory of knowledge eventually brought about a shift in the empirical canon from objectivity to intersubjectivity. This shift induced us to consider truth as a scientific ideal rather than as even partially or provisionally an actuality in the sciences. It caused us to be more aware that a science is a constructed body of belief rather than a perfect photograph of all existence. Our everyday experience with valuation, valuings, and value-assertive propositions leads us to infer that value structures, too, most assuredly are constructions, rather than snapshots perfectly resembling a segment of existence, and indeed that with them intersubjectivity attaining to the near-unanimity of the most recent and best science is simply not to be had. The truth-model for empirical, scientific knowledge is that of the expression of perceptions of competent observers, the agreement among their reports approaching 100 percent. But since it is the case that there are for values no comparable or parallel perceptions, then it is clear that we must not apply this kind of truth-model in order to establish an alleged truth of value-assertive propositions. Therefore we either should expunge the term *true* from descriptions of value-assertions entirely, or else we should draw up an appropriate new definition to give recognition to what sort of thing people could be alleging when they allege a value-assertion to be true. As there are separate kinds of truth already for synthetic and analytic statements, there is precedent for establishing a new kind of truth for value-assertions. In the next chapter I shall attempt to examine further the nature of concepts, in order to gain further understanding of the container concepts; thereafter, I shall go on to investigate what tests of "truth," if any, might be applicable to value-assertive propositions.

5

Concepts

Concepts, like many other things, are clear and familiar before examination but become indefinite and mysterious when we are forced to examine them rather than merely using them. They are indispensable to the philosophical enterprise, as is evidenced by the frequent mention in philosophical works of various concepts on a wide spectrum of relative generality. They are perhaps still more heavily depended on in discourses in other disciplines, where scientific principles, psychological tendencies, legal interpretations, all sorts of things are freely called concepts. Yet there is surprisingly little philosophical inquiry into what "concepts" actually are. The summation of the literature seems to be something like "Concepts are indispensable tools of thought, but they really do not exist."

In order to understand container concepts, we need to understand concepts themselves; most especially, we must be able to reconcile two widely employed notions: that for some of our purposes concepts function as static and fixed, as "ideal objects," while for other purposes they function as developmental, changing, and dynamic. Thus far my treatment of concepts has assumed the convenient view, long established in the history of philosophy, that a concept is a *something,* an entity. But if a concept is indeed an entity, what entity is it? If it is developed over a period of time, what is it that is developed? Is a concept perhaps not an entity but an event? If so, what event, and then how is it that a concept remains unto us from moment to moment, even from generation to generation and age to age? Let us occupy ourselves now, and for purposes of a preliminary to our principal inquiry, with the problem of just what these things are, with which we have been explaining other things.

There is certainly a body of convincing reasons supporting the view that a concept should be treated as an entity. It was so convincing to Plato that he generated the whole doctrine of eternal ideas on the thesis that an idea (which we may for present purposes equate to a concept) is what it is, once for all, indestructible by the influences of those forces that erode and obliterate the objects in the world of appearances. An idea could not be destroyed, though it might be forgotten; a new generation could *re*discover an idea, such as the essence of justice, even if a given people had strayed so far as to have lost the thought of justice entirely. *Justice itself* would have remained unchanging; any changes would have been in the proclivities of the human beings rather than in the overarching reality within which they had their being. Plato extended his view to assert that ideas are not only indestructible and unchanging but also uncreated, hence perfectly eternal, that is, completely unaffected in their being by the dimension of time or of things that have their being within the dimension of time. Truly it does still seem plausible to us that ideas such as the ideas of quantities and geometric figures are by their own nature ever-enduring and unchangeable. We say of *seven* that the quantity, seven, as an idea, will forever be seven, not six and not eight, regardless of the passage of time and regardless whether it is remembered or forgotten—that the *word* "seven" may change, but that what it means, conceptually, will *be*, without alteration and regardless of the passage of time. Thus an idea or a concept has the semblance of an entity, and a remarkable one at that. Just as an action requires an agent to do the acting— so we seem to reason—it requires a *thing* to be unchanging; to be passed from moment to moment or age to age; hence a concept must be an entity. Further, our language embodies the concept in terms that apply to entities: A concept, we conventionally say, may be discovered, may be built, may be examined, remembered or forgotten, communicated, may be a symbol or token or counter for a physical thing. Thus our usage confirms two things that are frequently inconsistent, both that concepts are entities and that they are enduring, unchanging intangibles.

On the other hand, there are problems in regarding concepts as entities. Taking it as assured for a moment that the term "concept" refers to something rather than nothing, to what does it refer? Can we find some samples? We can first of all discount the possibility of finding samples in the physical-object world along with the tables and chairs; that is not where the reference of "concept" lies. In the mind, then? This seems more promising. For certain terms referring to entities of the mind, I can easily summon up in my mind the things to which the term refers: the look of an oak leaf; the light greenness of the needles at the tip of a redwood twig, and the contrasting dark greenness of the older needles on the same twig; the recoil of a gun when fired; the smell of cognac; the sweetness of a favorite dessert—in other words, *images* of all sorts. When I am invited to convey to someone else an individual concept rather than an image, my first tendency is to summon up an image if there is one, then generate a description based on the image. If the object of inquiry is not tangible and therefore does not give rise to an image, I find myself making statements largely of a fact-assertive nature, using the term contained in the inquirer's question as the subject of my statements. However, in this circumstance, I am not at all conscious of there being a picturable or recollectable or reproducible *thing* corresponding to that term. And while there are certain things that I can say about images *as* images, such as that they are of the same nature as the sense perceptions to which they relate, are somehow fainter, are of varying vividness, or are inherently pleasant to hold in mind, when it comes to concepts I cannot say these or similar things about them *as concepts,* but rather, I speak of particular things, this or that, of which I "think the concept," at a given moment. I am in fact hard put to find any occurrences of concepts that I can identify with confidence. Like Hume's self or ego, they seem to vanish upon the attempt to examine them in their own right, and the search yields only this or that particular notion, not a body of data—concepts—that can become objects of study.

How can it be, then, that we know and use concepts, and thus become so certain that we indeed possess them? It is ordinarily by words or phrases that we identify them: "the concept of justice," "the juvenile offender's self-concept," "the concept of mind," "the concept of law." However, neither does it appear that simply every noun is the name of a concept, nor that all concepts have words or phrases that identify them—not all concepts have names. Again, to use a word or phrase as the name of a concept risks the pitfall against which Gorgias warned in the days before Plato: To talk of a chariot running on the sea does not ensure that there be one. To talk of concepts by using a label or name is not to ensure that there is a quiddity that, like a little freight car loaded with its specific cargo, goes shunting about here and there on the tracks of the mind's freightyard. In brief, the name of a concept is itself like a container—perhaps an empty container. However, it is not by virtue of this circumstance meaningless. Rather, begging the question for a moment, we know that the term "concept" possesses at least a conceptual meaning, if not referential meaning, for much can be said about "concepts." Some of what I take to be commonly acknowledged under this heading is presented in the following pages.

The nature and the processes of abstraction and concept formation are still controversial subjects in psychology.[1] Sometimes the meanings of these two terms are treated as different, sometimes identical. When they are taken as different, sometimes the one, sometimes the other, is placed first as the necessary precondition of the other—which works out to say, "as the explanation of the other." Psychological science is largely committed to the method of the study of behavior, hence it is not surprising that it should have considerable difficulty in requiting the interest it takes in concepts. While the method depends upon events—actions, behavior, responses—to deliver information, yet the very terms *abstraction* (in the application *an* abstraction, an abstract idea) and *concept formation* implicitly treat the concept as an entity. The investigators' usage still suggests that a concept may be something like a penny, which, once minted, passes intact from hand to hand or rests in a secret place available for use; or that it is like the log cabin that the young frontiersman must learn to make by his own interaction with the environment in which it will be set. There are correct and incorrect versions; he must obtain a correct one as his final product, which he will then use unchanged throughout the rest of his life. The psychologists appear to accept the view that certain kinds of behavior will be accurate signs that the possession of such an entity has been attained or its formation completed. I am inclined to suggest that their inquiry is on a wrong footing, coupling a method appropriate to one kind of evidence with a goal the evidence of whose attainment would be of a different kind.

A possible alternative of the view that a concept is an entity is the view of a concept as a dispositional property of the person "possessing" it. The concept becomes not a treasure one stealthily shelters within, but a collection of actions, a behavior pattern: If I possess concept *C*, then I do behave in certain supposedly *C*-influenced ways; lacking that concept, I do not (except at random) act in those ways. The objectivity of concept *C*, so regarded, is the similarity of behavior patterns among the individuals "possessing" concept *C* as a dispositional characteristic when occasions for performing *C*-behavior have arisen. Evidence of my possession of this abstract concept (that is to say, evidence that I discern element *e*, of which concept *C* "is the concept," on objects O_1, O_2, . . .O_n consists in the fact that in some respect I respond to O_1, O_2, . . .O_n all in the same way, and in a different way from objects lacking *e*. My treating these objects in this way is, operationally speaking, the possession and use of the concept of the element *e*. If, for example, I consistently treat others "equitably," this behavior is said to constitute my possession of the concept of *equity*. It is the behavioral reality, observable overtly, and may as well be considered as what the concept consists of. In this fashion the explanation of a concept may be to call it a dispositional property of myself.

But this account does not ring true to the experience of those who have much traffic with concepts. Surely the very utility of a concept is that it is precisely *not* behavior, not a collection of doings or actions, but largely rather the surrogate for actions which for myriad reasons may be unfeasible or inadvisable. To make a concept to be nothing but a set of behavior sequences peculiar to the conceiving of the particular conceived object is to put it in the same predicament as *thought*, under that explanation that takes thought to be subvocal speech, rather than speech to be vocalized thought. The *explicans* and *explicata* are made to trade places. Finally, to make the concept be the behavior (the behavior that is explained by the possession of the concept in question!) is to deny or ignore the reality of thought, including conceptualizing, as internal, a move that seems merely to blink the facts to those of us, at any rate, whose work is largely done by use of conceptualizing rather than by performance of overt behavior.

Again, neither is a concept a universal. A universal *term* is the name of an object or characteristic that is encountered more than once; and the universal as somehow a *thing*, the referent of the universal term, is such an object or character. Various philosophic schemes have taken different kinds of things as universals (such as Plato's essences, Husserl's essences, physical properties, intangible properties), and the long history of the attempt in Western philosophy to sort out the signs and their referents, if any, and establish the ontic status of the latter, is well known. The element opposite to the universal is the unique. But as I understand ordinary usage, I see nothing unidiomatic in speaking of a concept of something unique, and I see no reason not to suppose that a person may have a concept of a single object. There can be a unique concept; it is a concept of the uniquely experienced, the thing one encounters only once. A single, relatively simple perception can be remembered and thought about, taken as mental content into thought as well as into remembered imagery, and it is a concept to the extent that it is thought rather than only remembered in the form of an image. I am sure that each of us has been able to conceptualize for himself unique experiences such as the specific feelings of illnesses suffered only once, or the specific fear of a danger in a situation in which we have been only once, or even simply the look of this or that object that we have seen only once. Incidentally, any theory of abstraction that insists that a concept, as an abstraction, must be a universal runs into trouble in attempting to account for the unique, for if the formation of a concept requires plural occurrence of its object, and if there are occurrences that are unique, we would be unable to form a concept of the unique things and presumably could then neither know nor tell others about these singular occurrences. We would be hard put even to generate the concept *uniqueness*.

An abstraction has as its defining characteristic, especially if we are to take etymology seriously (and the theories seem never to succeed in getting very far away from the etymological meaning of the word), not in being a universal but in being detached in thought from the collection of other elements with which it occurs in experience. An abstract concept is a conceiving-of-an-object whose object is taken as discontinuous from those other elements. *To abstract* (the verb) is to do this separative conceiving. Granted, the process is aided immensely by plural occurrence of that which is thought as separate, but the abstraction need not arise solely under that fortunate circumstance. I can encounter a physical object of a hue I have never seen before, and can thereafter conceive of that hue separately from conceiving of the object. What requires plurality of occurrence is not the conceiving, but the naming of the property by a universal term, when the recipient of a communication about it has not himself encountered this specific hue. Even there, I can actually name the property, say, by coining a new name, and can make my listener understand that the new term refers to a unique hue of which I am thinking (but which he cannot specifically think, having no image to help him); but this is simply an instance of a communication that is not fully successful. It does not convey to him the whole of what I have in mind, because he has experienced nothing to associate with my coined term as the referent of that term. There is a way, however, of conveying to him the nature of the specific hue in question other than through naming it. That consists in forming and stating to the recipient a number of propositions about the unique object referring to experiences familiar to him, on the basis that we are summoning up images that are *nearly* like our unique property, and inviting him to imagine or think of something *nearly* like what we mention. The new, coined term may take on for him the conceptual meaning of this collection of propositions, until he can actually encounter the object in his experience and thenceforward can designate what he then encounters as the referential meaning of the term. In this fashion, by using concepts, we can supply for him partial knowledge of something for which he has no image.

Now we have three clues that will come together to suggest how it is that we have an acquaintance with concepts and handle them, and what it is that a concept "is," or better put, what is the ontic status of the concept. The first clue is that the genesis and history of a concept is developmental—ordinarily, when one comes into being, it does not spring fullgrown from Zeus's or anybody else's brow but rather is worked up over a period of time. The second is that concepts, unlike images, are not known by direct confrontation nor remembered in a single, reproducible package, but rather are normally known simply by terms serving as their names, terms that often are also the names of their referent objects. The third is that when we wish to explicate or clarify, or especially to define, concepts, what we resort to in order to accomplish this is propositions. In taking stock of these three clues, we can, I believe, arrive at an adequate understanding, for the purpose of our inquiry into valuation, of the nature of concepts.

Concerning concepts and language, the cultural belief is that our concepts can be true to the world as it is, and, further, that by carefully selecting elements from our language we can communicate our concepts. Thus we believe that it is possible to tell the truth—communicate accurately to others—about the world as we believe it to be, by rational and linguistic means. We tend to forget that we ourselves are the inventors of these means for attaining adequacy to the project. We—our species—devised concepts and language, intending them to be adequate to the objects of our world, and we pretty much beg the question whether they are. We do indeed operate successfully with them on great numbers of occasions, and accept this success as proof of their adequacy to the world. However, our proofs of any sort of truth-claim essentially embody a circularity. The very circularity—and the very *possibility* of a claim that a set of propositions is logically circular—rests upon the inventions in question. Fundamentally, our devotion to consistency is a part of a willed commitment to be rational,[2] a deliberate adoption of those devices that employ consistency with themselves as one of their means of achieving success in understanding the world and communicating about it.

In the pages ahead, I shall try to enlist the aid of the method used in chapter two for clarifying the proposition—that is, to list the everyday beliefs that we preserve (what we "know" before critical reflection) about concepts, then to ask the question, "In just what ways does this object of inquiry, the concept, enter into human consciousness?" then to see whether answers to that question will add to our knowledge. The everyday beliefs may steer us toward a consistent and acceptable view of their object once we examine the facts that have given rise to them.

The list of items that we "know" about concepts in our everyday, un-critical grasp of them is a much longer one than the similar list for proposi-tions. Not all items of the list are completely consistent with one another. I submit that the following are statements that, as we use concepts in our investigations of and explanations for other things, we generally take to be true of concepts.

(1) Concepts relate in some way to objects. This is expressed in our customary phrasing, "the concept of x," where x is an object. However, "object" may, and frequently does, mean other sorts of object than physical objects. While we readily refer to concepts of physical objects, the usefulness of the word "concept" probably inheres considerably in the fact that it enables us conveniently to speak of things that are not physical. These too are "objects" for the present purpose.

(2) Concepts are public, intersubjective.

(3) Concepts are fixed, and may be used as yardsticks or criteria to correct individuals' subjective impressions or beliefs.

(4) Concepts can be objects of attention and of thought.

(5) Concepts can be subjects of predicates, and can be predicates of subjects.

(6) Concepts can be communicated.

(7) Concepts have a relation to perception: "Concepts without percepts are empty; percepts without concepts are blind."

(8) There is some sort of transition from perception to concept, for neither one is identical with the other or a mere further development *per se* of the other, without any augmentation.

(9) The purpose of communicating a concept ordinarily is to convey a description of some appearance or aspect of our world or some part of it.

(10) Concepts are related to ideas, and in fact may be in some sense identical with ideas.

(11) Concepts are related to thinking or thoughts, but whereas a thought is transitory, a concept is enduring, in some sense permanent. (Our phrasing, "thinking the concept of *x*," takes the thinking as temporary but the concept as fixed rather than transitory, so that the concept is an object of attention, and is not the attending itself.)

(12) Concepts are somehow the stuff of knowledge, and are the basis of truth, or at least of one kind of truth [although the phrases "true concept" (of *x*) and "false concept" are by no means as frequent in usage as "true belief" and "false belief," or equivalent expressions].

(13) Although concepts are fixed and permanent, the learning of a concept by the individual is a process often achieved in stages.

(14) Similarly, the coming to full awareness or knowledge of various concepts by humankind has a history of stages, rather than always occurring in one fell swoop.

(15) Concepts are explanatory; they help us to understand the world.

(16) We speak of a concept as something to be *reached* by an effort, like the peak of a mountain we are climbing, so that with each step or stage we have partially attained what we seek. But we also speak on some occasions as though we can *build* a concept, part by part.

(17) We regard concepts as teachable, and speak of teaching children concepts (such as number concepts and social concepts).

(18) Concepts are abstract. Some concepts are "more abstract" than others.

(19) Both the philosopher and the psychologist have a technical interest in concepts.

(20) The concept has a counterpart mental operation that we call "conceiving" or "conceiving of."

(21) Concept formation in the individual depends upon our memory of earlier events.

(22) A concept is substantive, an entity.

(23) A concept is a surrogate for its external object, and, when thinking it occurs, the manipulation of it is often substituted for the manipulation of its external object. To have concepts short-cuts the necessity of dealing physically with things in the world. It enables us to select certain actions and perform those only, within the physical setting, rather than physically to carry out every action we can think of. (All this is also thought to be true of the symbol; probably there is confusion here, in our uncriticized views, between the concept and the symbol—which suggests that concepts are strongly related to or associated with symbols.)

(24) A concept is something about which statements can be made.

(25) A concept does not have a name of its own. We identify concepts with phrases, usually in a conventional but sometimes in a quite *ad hoc* way: "the concept of justice," "the concept of justice presented in Plato's *Republic*," "the concept of gravity," "the Founding Fathers' concept of liberty," "the concept of one-man-one-vote," "the total concept of the mind that Gilbert Ryle builds in his work *The Concept of Mind.*"

(26) A concept can be a part of another, "larger" or broader concept, or can contain a "smaller," narrower concept.

It is not now our purpose to decide wherein the items of the above list are inconsistent and how the inconsistencies might be reconciled. Rather, we should ascertain how concepts actually do enter into conscious human experience, and attempt from that information to arrive at an understanding of the ontic status of the concept sufficient to ground our distinctions among kinds of concepts. This understanding should enable us to clarify items on the list and to account to a great extent for their presence there.

One thing that we may be quite sure of with respect to our encountering of concepts is that it is in discourse (including inner discourse) that we encounter them. Just as with propositions, the intrusion of a concept into discourse often has as its sign the mention of a particular concept—that is, the use of the word "concept" in a particular connection—by a participant in the discourse. Upon remarking this, we of course set ourselves on guard against the word-magician's assumption that whatever has a name exists. Accordingly, when we are interested in tracking down concepts, we might challenge the user of the term *concept* in some such fashion as in the following episode. He mentions "the concept of equity." We ask him to tell what he is talking about. He responds, naturally enough, by making some statements about equity. We then rejoin, "But don't tell us about equity, or give us examples of that. For we are well aware that there is a difference between equity itself and the *concept* of equity. Please just focus on the *concept* of equity, and tell us what *that* is."

In the encounter just narrated, we may notice several features. First, we who are being critics need not assume that we are ourselves in possession of the concept of equity, regardless of our having spoken of it. We shall not be the victims of our own word magic. We are asking our colleague to produce for us that to which the phrase *concept of equity* refers, so that we ourselves then can correctly assign the phrase to its proper object, not some other—or possibly so that we can expose the belief in the concept as the belief in something nonexistent. We have made it clear to our fellow speaker that we and he both recognize a difference between the concept of equity and equity itself. *We* do not assert that such a concept exists (and the issue is not whether equity itself exists, for that is conceded). We are in the position either of talking about something that is at the moment entering our experience that we cannot recognize and of which we have little awareness and knowledge (this "something" is of course what we wish to study in the present chapter), or else of talking about something that does not exist, hence does not enter our experience, and about which, therefore, our colleague must be mistaken on both counts.

One rejoinder our friend might make is that what is different about the concept of equity is its content, and that except for that feature, the concept is like all other concepts, and therefore to find out what a concept is, we may refer to something like the list of items above. He may plead excuse for answering our challenge by making statements about equity, not about the *concept* of equity, since he thought us already familiar with the characteristics of concepts in general.

Yet, on this showing, we are no further in our attempt to get at the nature or ontic status of a concept, for other than the statement that a concept is substantive, an entity, there is nothing on the list that really tells us the ontic status of the concept. We "know" that concepts are related to thoughts and to ideas, yet we also "know" that they are not exactly thoughts or ideas. We "know" that concepts are public, but we "know" that a thought (e.g., my thought at a given moment) is not public but private. And to tell us that a concept is substantive and an entity is an incomplete description, for we will wish to know how or wherein it is substantive, what kind of an entity it is, how it is different from other entities. So our questioning and our friend's reply, while reasonable enough in an ordinary discussion such as one on equity, has apparently not advanced our inquiry into the ontic status of the *concept* of equity—or of any concept *per se*.

Another direction in which our friend's explanation might go is to say that the concept *is* a thought, your thought or his own thought, or similarly that it is an idea, held by one or a collection of individuals; that the word *concept*, like most words, is ambiguous, and that these are some of its several meanings. Thus, this explanation might continue, there is nothing odd about the inconsistencies, for the various meanings of many individual ambiguous words are inconsistent with one another. Without such inconsistency there would never be any humor in ambiguity. However, this line of argument does not explain why there should be any separate word, *concept*, as well as the words *idea* and *thought*, or why we do not indifferently use now one and now the other. Moreover, it does not account for the much stronger connotation of intersubjectivity of *concept* over *thought*, even though the latter has especially that connotation in such phrases as "twentieth-century thought" or "early Greek thought." The prevalence of the word *concept*, along with other related (but not unquestionably equivalent) words, is presumptive evidence that indeed something does enter our experience different from the objects of reference of those other terms—something to which we are prone to give a name, the name *concept*. And finally, our intuitions tell us that when our friend is talking about the *concept* of equity, as distinct from equity itself, he is somehow talking about something rather than nothing.

Could it be the case that the word *concept* or the phrase *the concept of* is merely an intensifying device, used by individuals to place special emphasis on what they are speaking about, so that *equity* and *the concept of equity* mean the same thing, though the latter is more emphatic? If this were so, then it would not be surprising that statements about the concept of equity should reduce to statements about equity itself. Here, however, the account does not accord with experience. We have the intuitive impression, as mentioned above, that there is something separate from equity itself that enters our friend's consciousness and presses him to use the phrase *the concept of equity* rather than simply *equity* alone. This seems to be our own situation also when we ourselves are induced to use the word. And clearly when the burden of the discussion is not an intangible like equity but a physical object, to reduce the concept to the object itself is absurd. I can carry my concept of an elephant about with me, but I can hardly carry an elephant about with me. And there is no discernible difference in kind, though of course there is a difference in specific substance, that distinguishes concepts of physical objects from concepts of things of other sorts. We appear to encounter all concepts, and to deal with them all, in largely the same way.

Yet it appears that in a discourse in which there is mention of concepts, it does in fact happen that the phrases embodying the word *concept* do achieve special emphasis. However, we can see that the special emphasis is divided. Some of it goes to the object referred to. When the speaker mentions the *concept* of equity, he draw our attention rather formally to *equity*, in such a fashion that from then on in that discussion we tend to be especially aware of the nature of equity, to heed the differences between equity and similar things such as justice, to think carefully rather than casually about equity. In this respect, the concept now begins to sound to us like the precision device that we found the proposition to be. The other direction in which our attention may be directed with special emphasis is that of the concept itself. While this is not nearly so prominent in experience and perhaps not so important to the outcome of the discussion of equity, it does happen occasionally that we speak of the endeavor to "sharpen up our concept" of equity, to "clarify the concept," perhaps "to transfer the concept to a new application." Thus, in these two emphases, the language behavior of an individual employing the word *concept* includes, at least partially, some control over the degree and care of attention of the company in which he is speaking. To this extent, evidently the concept is, like the proposition, both a precision device and a control over behavior. Yet there remains confusion as to what we are making precise: How is it that making the *concept* precise happens by virtue of attention to *equity,* something that is not a concept? And how does this happen without changing *equity?* Or could it be that the latter is being made more precise—more narrow, more closely delimited—by undergoing a reworking? For equity is not a physical object, but a human intellectual constructon, an abstraction.

Is it the case, then, that part of the meaning of the word *concept* is certain correlative behavior? And are there rules that we apply when concepts come under direct attention in consciousness—that is to say, correlative with the introduction by speakers of the word *concept* or with their employment of concepts even if done without mention of the term *concept?* Yes, this is indeed the case, although the matter is far from being as clear-cut as it is with the proposition.

To see what occurs under this head, and before eliciting rules from concept-behavior, we must look at another aspect of the appearance of concepts in our experience. The word *concept* is much more colloquial, broader in popular usage, and obviously needed on far more frequent occasions than the word *proposition.* Occurrences of the term *concept* are embedded in a set of circumstances much more complex than those surrounding the term *proposition.* Evidence for this is the greater length of the list of pre-reflective understandings of the nature of concepts, not to mention the internal contradictions of that list when its items are taken in everyday form rather than made precise by technical philosophical handling. We learn something more if we select out of the total list certain statements that often receive the focus of discussions of concepts themselves. I see special significance in these. Concepts seem to be produced by the process of abstraction, for they are related to percepts or intuitions and they are abstract. They relate to ideas to the extent that we sometimes have the impression that a speaker uses the term simply as a more dignified synonym for the word *idea,* which may have lost force in its long history. A concept must have something to do with intuition, in a sense of that word soon to be set forth (below p. 100); and especially when we consider physical objects or properties we seem to believe that we get our concepts by abstracting from collections of intuitions (some essential, some incidental) of physical things. Concepts are affirmed emphatically to be public, and sometimes this characteristic seems to be the most important thing about them, yet concepts are harbored in minds, and must *ipso facto* be private mental possessions. We are quite ready to speak as though Einstein first privately conceived of special and general relativity, then in his writings made these concepts public. When he arrived at their notions privately, then at least in that guise they must have been subjective and relative to one person—a far cry from Platonic ideas that are eternally unchanging and wholly objective. Is there any element in experience that we can seize, upon which to fasten an explanation of concepts that renders all these suggestions about concepts understandable, perhaps even reconcilable?

There is one additional factor to be elicited about the concept, already evident in our episode concerning *equity*, in which the challenge to the term *concept* occurred. That is the characteristic proneness of the speaker introducing the word to describe the *referent object* when he is asked for information about the *concept*. To be sure, he recognized the difference, when it was pointed out, between the object and the concept, but the fact is that he was too hasty in desisting from supplying propositions about the object on that account. We were misled in asking him to confine his attention to the concept, and he was misled in modifying his response accordingly, because both of us were too ready to believe that if he were talking about the object he was ignoring our request for the concept. Actually, what he was doing was just what we had asked him to do, although neither he nor we were fully aware in ontic terms that he was doing it, nor how he was doing it. His reply, supplying us with propositions about equity, is different from what we anticipated to be a proper answer to our request, for it is *part* of the thing we were asking to have exhibited to us, the *concept* of *equity;* and our friend would no doubt, if left uninterrupted, have continued to oblige us by going on supplying descriptive statements as long as he had something to say. Thus he would be supplying to us all the parts of what we were asking for, in an *ostensive* definition of the concept of equity. For *a concept is simply a collection of sentences or propositions,* clustered together about some element such as an image, an idea, a word or a phrase (in this case, the word *equity*), something that is not a proposition. I shall call this element the *organizing idea* of the concept. Nonverbally, our respondent knew this, and was replying to us in the only way feasible for him, which was to exhibit the concept, part by part.

It is as statements—that is to say, sentences and propositions in a collection—that concepts enter our experience. They may come all at once, or piecemeal, one or a few at a time. For each individual at a given time, the collection may be complete or incomplete. Further, we may in fact produce some concepts ourselves, such as the concepts of things we invent or of things already existing concerning which we are doing pioneering research; and we probably produce the concepts of these things a little at a time, so that only after a stage well along in our project are we willing to say something like "I am now at last beginning to get the concept of this thing" (the object we are researching or inventing). This description of concepts, I believe, not only is experientially true, but is sufficient to establish the ontic status of the concept as a collection of statements (sentences or propositions) gathered around an organizing idea. It should also serve largely to explain the various items on the list of notions of our pre-reflective understanding of concepts.

Just as a proposition is founded on a sentence, *is* a sentence treated in a certain way, and thus has a physical constituent, the concept has a physical constituent. It is that collection of all the sentences, expressed in physical form (speech, writing, alignment of molecules on magnetic tape, or whatnot), which go to make up the total collection. Of course, no one ever directly experiences the total of the physical sentences basing a widely known concept. We content ourselves with our impressions of what is typical of the whole collection, or if we are not content with that, we strive to learn more of what has been said on the matter. And in such striving, as well as in other actions that we undertake in relation to a concept as such, we are performing the behavior that, taken together with the physical expressions, constitutes the concept.

Again, just as not every sentence is a proposition, not every collection of sentences unites with conceptual behavior to comprise a concept. Some collections of sentences are random, and others are collections made up on some other plan than those that comprise a concept (an example is the short story). Obviously the principle according to which a concept is collected is pertinence to that object of the thought which the concept concerns (which is to say, that which its component statements concern in common), the object of conception of those conceiving it. Thus it is an easy thing for any speaker to identify the concept he is entertaining by using a phrase beginning with the words *concept of.* It is his way of announcing what he is concerned with, in his present discourse. Others who join in the discourse agree tacitly to be concerned with the same thing, although the agreement does not restrict them to that topic only. The case as to what behavior is appropriate in respect to concepts is not by any means as strictly determinate as with respect to propositions.

Just as with *proposition,* there is correlative behavior associated with the word *concept* and making up part of its meaning. That behavior may take more than one form, but performance in one form is sufficient to constitute a concept. The behavior includes either *naming* a concept that one introduces or acknowledges, *collecting* propositions that in their integration will comprise a concept, or else *accepting* as a concept a collection already brought together, or a mixture of more than one of these (which is represented, for example, when someone accepts in some part a preexisting concept of something in which he is interested but revises it after accepting it). When a participant in discourse does any one of these, singly or in company with others, a concept, and explicitly the concept of that which his collection of propositions concerns, is present in his experience. And while our entrée to the recognition of the nature of the concept was through incidents in which the word *concept* itself was employed in discussion, we can now recognize that the presence of the word *concept* is not itself a requisite. When the above described events take place, namely, the building or the utilizing of a collection of sentences of this sort, regardless whether the word *concept* occurs, the concept itself is present to those who are concerning themselves with its conceived object.

However, because concepts themselves are much more open to diversity and variation than individual propositions are, the rules implicit in and regularizing concept-behavior are much broader and less specific than those for proposition-behavior. Those who participate in it have many more legitimate options and much more freedom with respect to the controlling element, the concept, than when performing according to the Rules of Propositionality.

The First Rule of Conceptuality is:

> Consider a plurality of statements (sentences or propositions, or both) as each relating to a single object of conception.

This rule does not command the *collecting* of a plurality of statements, for one acting according to the behavior of using concepts could simply accept a previously assembled collection as a group of statements each of which relates to the object of conception. As well as collecting by himself, either another individual or social convention (most especially including linguistic convention) could place the collection before him. The recipient could of course discover or deem that among the propositions there is one that does not relate to the object of conception or belong with its fellows in a consistent structure, and he could expunge it privately, in his own conception, or could advocate its rejection publicly, that is, advocate that it be expunged in the public version of the concept. The essential thing about the user's observance of this rule is that he regard the cluster of features portrayed in their respective statements as unified in the being of the conceived object, and unlike the case with propositions, he may do this uncritically. Although it has to some extent a precision function, a concept, unlike a proposition, is more a convenience for practical intellectual operation than it is a precision device.

The Second Rule of Conceptuality is:

> When collecting statements for a concept, bring within the collection only statements that relate, apparently always, to the object of conception.

This rule does not specify the nature of relation to the object that the introduced statement has or may have. That is left to the judgment of the collector, the builder of the concept. The collector may of course be a single inquirer or a group of any size up to and including the mass of speakers of all languages in which the concept is ever used or discussed.

The Third Rule of Conceptuality is:

> Treat the collection of statements as having existence in an atemporal or time-free mode of existence.

Thus, even though Agamemnon's throne has long since perished, the concept of it is still extant and, as more and more is learned about the Mycenaean culture, is still growing and changing. It is our ability to perform according to this rule that accounts for the permanence, the eternal unchangingness of concepts (or of ideas in the Platonic sense) and makes them serve as lasting tokens, counters, for things that change. This feature especially, among the features of concepts, makes container concepts possible and useful.

The Fourth Rule of Conceptuality is:

> Gather the statements belonging to a concept around an organizing idea.

An organizing idea may be a symbol of the object of conception (usually a word or phrase designating it), or an image of it, a memory of it, or anything else that it is possible to think and communicate as related in thought to the object of conception. The term *organizing idea* in this formulation of the rule is used to preserve the recognition that there may be a difference between the realm, whatever it is, in which the silent thinker manipulates propositions and concepts, and the realm in which he carries out the activity of manipulating the objects of conception. It is appropriate in whatever way the terms *concept* and *proposition* are appropriate, and does not beg the question of mentalistic explanation any more than they do.

The Fourth Rule completes the list, so far as I am aware. Concepts—lists of statements about something in common—can be assembled in so many ways, on so many specific principles, for so many human purposes, that it seems to me unlikely that there is any additional practice that their collecting has in common, from which our observation could derive any further rules.

The force of these rules, like those of propositionality, is not primarily legislative. Rather, to state in the form of rules the principles that we can observe in actual application by persons busily engaged with concepts is a device for saving considerable space and time in exposition. I am averring that speakers do behave in obedience to these rules, more or less well according to their perceptions and skills, when speaking of concepts or using the word *concept*. Thus my account is descriptive, with respect to actual practice of serious participants in discussion, and, moreover, it is a recommendation—advice on how to understand such discussion in its underlying principles. I hardly need add a Stevensonian "Do so, yourself!" for it is hard for me to see how someone discussing a concept could very far disobey them without making havoc of his listeners' attempt to understand him.

From this survey of the basic ontic nature of an important feature of the means of knowing and communicating, the concept, I suggest that, in practice, concepts generally are not the perfect eternal entities that logic requires them to be. We do indeed *treat* some of them as such, and we succeed very well in doing so, but human volition enters into viewing them *as though* they are eternal, whereas with respect to the personal experience of any one of us, surely they are developmental and growing, continually changing for better or worse.

To acknowledge that concepts have a history and may for some purposes be treated as developing while for other purposes they may be treated as eternal and unchanging, yields better understanding of our world than does the specious idealization of the efficacy of our own inventions. That is, on the lower of the two planes, in effect we say, "I want to understand the things of the world as they evidently produce appearances in my consciousness, so I will make *concepts* by means of which to do it, and thus I will do it. And I want to communicate this understanding to others, so I will make *terms*—words and phrases—with which to do that, and the terms will communicate my concepts. The concepts will each accurately reflect some element of the apparent world, and the terms will summon up those concepts in the mind of the listener when I speak." On the higher plane, we accept the concepts as though they are perfected, as therefore ideal in their being and in their quality; and we study them to gain full knowledge of them. "What are the properties of the square?" we ask, or "What is justice?" But if in fact we have not first perfected the concepts in question, then obviously they are not thus ideal, and we fail through our own lack of knowledge of the nature of what we have done to arrive at a geometrically ideal knowledge of such imperfect things—as encountered in practice—as justice.

The mind is capable of some pretty ingenious manipulations; perhaps doublethink (thinking that *A* both is and is not *B*) is one of them. I am sure that there are some legitimate forms of doublethink and that, in a way, the use of concepts is one legitimate form. I take man to be a natural being, both in a neutral and in a somehow honorific sense of the word *natural*. I have been suggesting that his inventions of concepts and language are artificial, are artifices, and of course there is a sense in which the artificial is not natural. That sense must apply to these artificial objects as well as to any others. But there is another sense in which the artificial *is* natural, the sense that reminds us that it is natural for man to make inventions in order to survive and improve his lot. I therefore seek to learn when it is more helpful to admit the artificiality, on the one hand, of the unchanging eternal ideas with which man does his calculating and some of his understanding, and when on the other hand to regard man's activity as continuous with the world and thus as natural, thus as changing and developmental just as is the growth of living beings, of species, and of humankind.

Seeing man as a natural being in his natural setting, I conjecture that within his experience, the stuff that concepts are ultimately made of is continuous with man's living nature. Concepts must then be developmental. A man is a temporal being. All his elements—his form, his organs, his brain, his culture, his mind—are developmental, either progressively or retrogressively. He is a living, changing being, not an eternally static one. That the mind shares this nature strikes us as true when we designate its operation as thinking and its stuff as thoughts. It is only after we hypostatize, making "thoughts" into the generic "thought," or into the singular, "a thought," that we begin taking the dynamic and making it into—or treating it as—the unchanging and eternal.

The consequence of taking this approach is that we can account in a consistent sketch for our concepts, container concepts among them, to the extent that our problem about the nature of value demands. We can regard concepts as practically functioning in such a way that they can be built up element by element; in this sense they are generated developmentally. One might speculate that they are built the way a brickmason develops a wall or an archway from individual bricks; but this is not a satisfactory model, for the solidity of finished masonry belies the changeability of concepts. Are they then built as a boy uses a construction set to build a truck to play with? That is a better analogy, for it allows that the complex structure can be revised or even dismantled in the passage of time. Yet the pieces themselves are rigid and static. Rather, what appears to me to be a nearly satisfactory analogy is the living grass roof of a Norwegian peasant house. The matter of which it is composed includes much that is alive and changing. It is put into position section by section when it is being built; it lives and grows while in use; it is capable of being augmented or of being repaired if parts of it should fail. Above the peasant's head, something constantly lives and undergoes its own organic functions, while he thinks of it simply as a roof, single and unitary, a rigid, static object in the respect of serving its purpose, namely, keeping the rain and melting snow from coming through onto the floor beneath. This is something like the use we make of concepts. They must indeed be of the living stuff, because of their origins, but *we treat them as* fixed, unchanging and eternal; and so long as they are confined within certain limits of change, they can function and serve their purposes quite satisfactorily in the way in which we artificially treat them.

In viewing concepts under two aspects, then, we can perform an acceptable process of doublethink. Their usefulness depends considerably upon their fixedness, at least in many contexts, but their occurrence, their genesis, depends upon and can be explained by natural development. To understand them in both these ways is better, I suggest, than to regard them Platonically, solely as fixed and eternal, and then to marvel at their inexplicable, metaphysically absolute nature. Further, their adequacy for the purposes of somehow matching up with the real world is more acceptably explained by heeding their developmental origin, rather than by heeding the way we treat them once we have them (meaning, to heed them as fixed), for *it is from our treatment of them*, not from their objects of conception in the world or in our consciousness, that they get their fixedness. If the concepts are late stages of the same series of processes of which perceptions are early stages, it becomes less mysterious how man might ever become so lucky as to have his ideas match reality to some extent. By thinking a concept, an individual may mentally refer to an object. Thus, thinking a concept is closely associated with the other sort of reference, the reference of a linguistic unit to its object. Reference as *developmental* thus grows out of life situations in which the various objects of reference are encountered; reference as *logical*, as relations of fixed and unchanging and perhaps eternal ideas to the things to which they refer, accomplishes our apprehending and understanding of, and our reasoning about, these things; and reference as *linguistic* enables us to convey our concepts and other sorts of experiencings of these objects to others.[3]

The description of the concept set forth in the first part of this chapter treats the concept as the public object that we normally regard it to be. Although my chief interest in the concept is in noticing how a completely developed concept enters experience, it may repay us also to glimpse its typical genesis. Mrs. Langer defines the concept of an object as that which all adequate conceptions of an object have in common.[4] The genesis of a concept undoubtedly begins with an individual's private conception, a remembered thought or image of something important to him. The remembered thought in turn is probably a fragment of the whole of some moment's consciousness, a fragment that does not change significantly or obviously during that short period of its occurrence which is later remembered. Practically speaking, then, it "may as well be" unchanging as changing, and we can more readily handle it if it is unchanging. The compulsion that the idea exercises upon the assent of the rational mind thus is natural and not remarkable when seen from this point of view. It is not the separate metaphysical nature of the idea, but the nature of intellection, in treating the changing as stable, that compels the mind; and the idea is no less respectable for that than it is when it is taken to be the very building-stuff of thought, or even, as by idealists, of the whole universe in all its aspects.

There is a function that we know by practical acquaintance, which is called by the phrase *to conceive of*, and possibly also by the phrase *to abstract from*. I disclaim the ability as well as the responsibility to describe this function in detail. It is a process that actually takes place; it is therefore in the purview of some science, I suppose of psychology. However, I can describe it in respect to some of the features that we know it has or must have, on account of the products that it yields to us. I use with confidence a certain general vocabulary that: (1) assigns the term *intuiting* or *intuition* to the earliest stage of this process, the first apprehension of or reaction by the knowing mind to its object, or the first interaction (as the case may be) with its object; (2) assigns *perceiving* or *perception* to an early but not the earliest stage of this process, to acknowledge the role of the psychological processess of the subject in delivering to that subject something objective that he comes to cognize; (3) assigns *knowledge* or *knowing* to the function that is the gainful result of performance of the process (while acknowledging that this may in turn simply be a part of the process or continuous with it); (4) assigns *conceiving of* or *conception* to a kind of mental handling of the specific awareness of objects and includes the *of* as the sign of the objectivity (the status of being an object of consciousness) of the object of which there is awareness; (5) assigns *abstracting from* or *abstraction* to the function of rearranging noted items into an order different from that in which they originally occur in current experience, such as the drawing-off of an appearance property, say, grayness or squareness, from one or more objects exhibiting that and other properties. This last function, abstraction, is so apparently necessary to the previously mentioned one, conception, that it may indeed prove to be part and parcel of it. The two, at any rate, function surely with far more complexity than this survey of everyday terms suggests. In these processes, the possibility of the subject's generating propositions about his object of attention emerges.

What is the stuff that concepts are ultimately made of? This is a question that psychology is answering in its characteristic way, and perhaps the question will be answered in that framework. My own framework is different. I am, so to speak, attempting to set forth some things that must be logically true, logically descriptive rather than empirically descriptive even though based partly on empirical descriptions. I am admittedly conceptualizing about conceptualizing. My endeavor is intended to provide new or revised concepts (that is, newly better-understood concepts), a philosophical enterprise, rather than the empirical enterprise of seeing whether some existing concepts are fulfilled. I suggest, then, that concepts grow from conceptions, and that the stuff that conceptions are made of at base includes at least the intuitions of the senses, which are the initial mode of interaction of the organism with the environment and his own physical being, and also the life urge that drives the organism onward through its developmental stages and through its assortment of activities, of purposes and achievements. But I am convinced that the human being is something more than an organism, at least as organisms are ordinarily defined and described. What more the human is, is probably best to be understood through the principle of development rather than that of miracle or that of accident. The next ingredient for conception making is the perception, which supplies interpreted empirical matter to the concept. It is already implicit in our description that we find humanity, *supra* the organism, at this level, for we ordinarily employ the term *perception* with the connotation of interpretation, of processing the data rather than of merely absorbing raw data. The transition from intuitions of sense to perceptions is no doubt a passage through a margin, rather than a step across a line; it is of the nature of growing through a foot of height, rather than of putting on stilts. Insofar as we can be said to know what we perceive, from perception we arrive at knowledge, and already are able to form relevant propositions even if only simple ones. Through our surveys of perceptions of immediate and remembered experiences, we can flesh out our earliest proposition by the addition of others, thus building our conception, our private parallel to the concept. And we can make the important choice between whether *this* experience is to be classed as unique, so that this conception applies to it only, or whether this experience is to be placed with others, so that this one helps build the general conception including it and others—an abstract conception. Thus, I suggest, a brief episode of experience contributes to our knowledge a conception of what it contains. To the extent that in building its conception we incorporate shared propositional beliefs and preexisting concepts, we depend upon the earlier experience of our culture.

In considering that concepts probably grow from the materials supplied by perceptual processes, I am led to suppose that the starting-point for the concept, in man's early intellectual history and probably in the biography of the individual, is the image, and that the concept was gradually worked up from the remembered or interpreted, modified image as its beginning. As the mind matures in its ability to handle the intangible as well as the physical, words or phrases replace the image as the organizing idea of the concept around which beliefs, gradually expressed more and more articulately in sentences, then in propositions, are gathered. Reflection becomes an important source, alongside perception, as contributor of materials for the concept. When a concept is fairly well stabilized, people who discuss or employ it know it by a suitable phrase beginning "the concept of . . . ," which is as much of a name as it ever attains. Thus in some instances the name and the organizing idea coincide, but knowing concepts by names has not been so necessary as to have brought about a universal single practice for designating them.

An example will instance much of what has now been said. Someone asks me the question "What is the concept of the Cape Cod cottage?" In considering what to reply, I first of all picture to myself a Cape Cod cottage, then describe to my interrogator the characteristics that distinguish my image of the Cape Cod cottage from those of other dwellings, say the country manse or the Dutch Colonial house. Thus I adduce the following propositions and impart them to my questioner: "A Cape Cod cottage is a small one-family dwelling. It has a rectangular plan, with two rooms. It has a central fireplace structure of masonry, which not only provides heating for each of the rooms by having fireplaces on opposite sides, but which also serves as support for the ends of beams holding up the walls, ceiling, and roof. The front or facade has a door in the middle, with windows on left and right for each of the rooms. The front and back walls are of only one story in height. One slope of the roof rises from the front wall at an angle of forty-five degrees from the horizontal, and another roof slope rises similarly from the back wall. The end walls are gabled, extending in height to the ridge of the roof. The material of the exterior is unpainted cedar shingle." So much I gain from my image of the

Cape Cod cottage, which is compounded out of memory of instances seen, photographs, and printed descriptions encountered in books. Now I might add, going beyond what my recalled image alone supplies to me: "The place of origin of this architectural genre is Cape Cod, Massachusetts. Many fine examples are still to be seen there, and many others exist throughout that state. Modern adaptations often substitute another material for the cedar shingles of the exterior, and even on some of the original specimens the ravages of time have made it necessary to refurbish the exterior. These were good dwellings, secure against storms, and some that still exist are well over 200 years old." And so on, as I shift from the image which first supplied my propositions to additional beliefs that constitute part of my knowledge of the Cape Cod cottage but do not spring from or cannot be incorporated into the visual image. In other words, in the second phase I am imparting that part of my concept of the Cape Cod cottage that I retain only verbally in statements associated with that phrase, rather than in my visual impression of it, expressed propositionally as I "read off" propositions from the image in mind.

Of the foregoing, much belongs to a public concept of the Cape Cod cottage, and, on the other hand, perhaps some may be sufficiently variable that it does not have an assured place in that concept. For example, it is probably allowable, in terms of the conventional concept, that the exterior of a given specimen is of painted clapboard rather than of weathered cedar shingle. But it is *not* allowable that the roof rise from a second story rather than from the ceiling-height of the ground floor. Perhaps it is nowadays debatable whether the central fireplaces and chimney must be present for the specimen to be a Cape Cod cottage "properly speaking." This was an essential structural feature upon which the originals depended for strength against winter gales, but if one were today to order from an architect a plan for a Cape Cod cottage, the strength-giving role of this masonry might be sacrificed, or some other heat source might be supplied, while the result could still ("properly"?—at least idiomatically) be called by the name *Cape Cod cottage*. Together with my propositional beliefs, which I am sure are part of the public concept of the building, I preserve certain "connotations" in the literary sense: I associate with it snugness, coziness, warmth and shelter, ease of access, simplicity, the sharpness of smoke from a fireplace fire, and similar affective qualities. For each of these there is, of course, a corresponding proposition: "During a storm one feels secure here," "One is impressed by its simple comfort," and so on. Thus anything expressible in natural language can be made a component of my conception, by being put in stae of it serves to restore some part of the image to my memory.

We can see how each of our clues is represented in the above account. The concept under discussion is known by its name, the phrase *the concept of the Cape Cod cottage,* and the latter three words taken as a phrase serve as the nuclear idea. The concept was built up over a period of time as the type of architecture in question developed; it may yet gain new features (such as being designed by an architect); it may lose old ones (the central fireplace). And so far as it consists in anything, and especially in anything publicly knowable, it consists in the sentences by means of which we impart it to one another. Since these are thought through with care, it is proper to term them propositions. The propositions, of course, are not *about* the concept. They are, rather, about the objects of conception, Cape Cod cottages, and together they *comprise* the concept. We can readily see that the means people have of gaining possession in common of features of each other's conceptions is communication through propositions. True to this usage, I can say meaningfully that the weathered cedar shingles are part of my conception of a Cape Cod cottage (perhaps a "proper" one, by *my* standards) but not necessarily part of the public idea, or the concept, of one. I can also say that those connotations that I associate with the Cape Cod cottage are part of my conception of this object, but probably not of the public concept, "the true concept," for indeed some of these connotations may be quite private with me.

Thus concepts, compounded of the common features of individuals' conceptions, are collections of propositions that have become clustered together, virtually agglutinated, through conventional usage. They originate with individuals' intuitions, especially but by no means solely their sense intuitions, which merge into their perceptions of these objects of attention, and acquire associations with other intuitions and perceptions. The perceptions with such interpretations and judgments as may be addressed to them emerge in concrete form (that is, in spoken or written language) as statements. When a particular cluster of statements has, through social manipulation, become familiar and recognizable among a group of persons who concern themselves with it, we may say that it has become a concept. The concept known by a term thus constitutes the public conceptual meaning, as distinguished from the referential meaning, of that term.

This view of the concept has the convenient advantage that, although there might be controversy about whether concepts exist and about what they are, statements—declarative sentences, including propositions—without doubt have concrete existence in the language, in the form of the written or spoken words with which they are stated. People assuredly do speak and write sentences. These are the material constituents of the concept. The physical events, the actions of speaking or writing those sentences, are the concrete behavioral constituents of that concept. (These, of course, are separate actions from those actions that bestow concept status upon the collection of statements, for these are the behavioral acts of affirming this or that predication about the object of conception). Concepts, like the propositions comprising them, may be of very great duration. We are, for example, still building upon Aristotle's concept of *eudaemonia* (happiness), examining propositions he wrote in connection with it twenty-three centuries ago and adding interpretive propositions of our own.

Both logic and attention to cognitive experience will show us that a mind can be occupied with more than one concept at a given time or within a given very short period of time. We shall keep ourselves clear on such matters if we acknowledge that, although many concepts can in some sense be present simultaneously, there is a difference between the taking up of a concept constructively and attentively as a focus of the organizing of ongoing experience, and the mere remembering of a concept. While I am joining with a friend in an attempt to purify and articulate our concept of *equity,* there may well be many other concepts providing a kind of background for my thinking. However, unless I begin to examine these with a view to analysis, revision, systematic application, or the like, they are *remembered* concepts, not concepts *essentially occurring* with immediacy in my experience. Of course one can draw too fine a line here, and there can be many episodes of experience in which it could be very puzzling to attempt to point out exactly when a certain concept is no longer being merely remembered, from earlier experience, but has passed over into the stage of being actively worked up cognitively. There are also times, of course, when we are working up not one but two or even more concepts simultaneously. However, as we are occupied with one reflective project, most of our concepts are not called under examination even if there are some that receive a second-level reexamination while we are submitting one or a few, more conspicuous in our attention at the moment, to the processes of examination and assembly of propositions that constitute them as concepts. And while it is important to understand the concept through examining it as it occurs in experience, it is also important to recognize that the concept occurring and the concept as remembered is the same object of thought and of investigation. The difference is a psychological difference, relative to individuals at given times, not a fundamental difference making a remembered concept a separate kind of thing ontically from an occurring concept. Perhaps one reason we have had difficulty in isolating concepts for inquiry is that the collections of propositions that, once collected, constitute concepts are far more often merely remembered as such than actually engaged in our conscious deliberation in the manner I have been describing.

But it is of course extremely useful that we can summon up concepts in memory readily, just as other remembered things are useful. This is not only to say that we need not create or re-create a concept anew each time we need it, but is also to explain how it is that concepts, even the most complex and ramified ones, can contribute fruitfully and easily to our thinking. While a concept is a collection of statements, it may itself be designated by a single brief term and may be predicated about, or applied as predicate to a subject, or may figure in other ways in new sentences and propositions that extend our reasoning involving it. Thus we need merely mention the word *equity* to one who is informed about equity in order to summon up in his mind a complex ethical and legal concept; and by warranted predication we can add to society's knowledge about equity, thus augmenting that concept. In some cases, the proposition we produce in this way may become part of the public concept of equity; in others, of one's own conception only.

What I have intended in previous chapters in referring to the conceptual meaning of a term is this collection of statements. It simply is not the same thing as referential or denotative meaning. In fact, a concept itself may have a referent, which is the object conceived of by users of the concept. However, unlike the case with the referential term, the *raison d'être* of the concept is not reference, but conceiving. It is the mode of knowledge, not merely the pointer that indicates what a thinker or speaker is thinking about.

We have by now a fairly complex set of logical and semantic relationships in which the concept is involved. We are considering several separate things— the concept, the object of conception, the organizing idea of the concept, the name of the object of conception, and the name of the concept. Among these, only the object itself never has a reference relationship to something else (excepting, of course, if it happens to be of that class of objects that are signs or symbols). The Cape Cod cottage does not refer to Cape Cod cottages—it simply *is* one of them. But the phrase *Cape Cod cottage* refers to these physical objects, the Cape Cod cottages, and in that role it may be considered a noun phrase naming such an object. However, that noun phrase also may, and generally does, act as the organizing idea for our concept of Cape Cod cottages. As such, it is, so to speak, a hook on which statements about Cape Cod cottages may be hung; being a referential word or phrase is one of the possible ways in which something might be an organizing idea, but it is not the only one, another common sort being the image. And it is a not usual idiom to say that an image of an object *refers to* that object, though we readily call it an image *of* the object. Hence, reference is not essential to the role of the item that is an organizing idea, although it may *per accidens* be a feature of it. Once a concept is formed, we may say that the concept refers to the conceived object (e.g., our concept of the Cape Cod cottage refers to Cape Cod cottages). We rarely have occasion to speak in this way, but it is idiomatic rather than strange to do so.[5] It is the whole cluster of statements making up the concept that does this referring, for not all of the individual statements themselves need have the Cape Cod cottage as their grammatical subject or other part. Some might make predictions only of parts of the cottages; others might indicate relations among elements of the experiencing of Cape Cod cottages, and so on. Finally, we have the name of the concept, which has the reference relation to the concept itself: *the concept of the Cape Cod cottage*. The referent of this phrase is a cluster of statements, not a collection of buildings. These are statements in a particular collection, which, *as statements*, may include physical objects or events, may be printed in various places or spoken by various persons to others, and so on, and may also include the statements that are carried in mind and not overtly realized in physical form, the statements that people think when they evoke for themselves their concepts of Cape Cod cottages.

It is time to remind ourselves that not every naming phrase has a physical referent, but rather that some may have as their referents objects having quite other ways of appearing—for concepts are especially useful in dealing with intangible objects. It is worth suggesting in this connection that for some things, the name of the intangible object of conception is also the name of the concept, for we hear exchanges such as that in which one person mentions equity, and another may respond, "Tell me what you know about that concept." This in turn suggests that possibly everything intangible, everything that can be a referent but yet is not a physical referent object, may perhaps be a concept. I should not like at this time to have to explore that possibility, for it would be a long byway indeed. Could it be that the so-called ideal objects, like circles, squares, and triangles, have their whole existence in being concepts? In having been generated or posited by virtue of having been abstracted from physically appearing objects and then attracting descriptive propositions to themselves? Letting that be as it may, I shall bring this sketch to a close by remarking that referent objects, whether physical or intangible, comprise the referential meanings of their naming words or phrases; that the clusters of statements concerning the conceived objects comprise the conceptual meanings of the same naming words or phrases; and that the same set of symbols may be sometimes the one, sometimes the other, depending upon the employment being made of it.

Someone might object to the above explanation of concepts by asserting that the mind simply does not perform all these operations, such as summoning up in a situation certain concepts for specially considered acceptance, augmentation, or revision, attending to other germane concepts as aids or as background for reflection upon the first one mentioned, and remembering countless others as discussion proceeds. That would seem to require us to have a thousand propositions all in mind at once, while we are making the most ordinary statements about equity or whatever else it may be that concerns us. Yet I think that a protest on these grounds undersells the human mind. While we are discussing equity, we probably are indeed not conscious of a thousand propositions, but these propositions nevertheless are at our command. I cannot explain memory, but I need not, if for no other reason than simply because without it my reader would not have arrived at the present page. However, it is obvious that we do remember much that we can state propositionally if we but have the time and the wish, and that though perhaps we do not remember concepts primarily in propositional form, as clear-cut collections of propositions, we seem to do pretty well in remembering the symbols of our ordinary language, then at forming these into propositional accounts of what we remember, whenever and to whatever extent our needs determine. This form of knowledge contributes greatly to dis-our needs determine. This form of knowledge contributes greatly to discourse even while somehow remaining "out of sight." It pretty obviously depends heavily not only upon memory but upon symbol and the human gift of symbolizing. That fact is consonant with the individual's tendency to remember a concept by the term having the respective conceptual or referential meaning, naming the object of conception, and while answering questions about that object correctly, to be unaware that he remembers the concept as a collection of statements, or that that is the way in which it functions for him.

It is a reinforcement of the point just stated to notice that not only is the concept a cluster of statements but that statements in turn are, in a way of their own, collections of concepts. In philosophy, for purposes of analysis we tend to focus attention upon the object and the predicate concept of a proposition, and upon determining whether these are the same or different. We screen out meanings on a secondary level, and substitute simple letter symbols for terms that are laden with a multiplicity of meanings. But in practical situations, this is only a beginning, for every word of an ordinary twenty-word sentence summons up a concept of its own. Some of the concepts, as meanings of the words that appear, control and shape others, so that a grammatical predicate of perhaps eighteen words might convey only a single logical predicate, with which we deal as a single concept without noticing that its unique conceptual meaning is compounded of numerous other concepts that enter with certain words that are present, and is narrowed down, concentrated, and made specific by other carefully selected words. It is as though every discussion of a concept shuffles cards and deals them out as bridge hands, but without any set number of cards in each hand, and with an infinitely large deck to start with. Each card has a place in a hand, and also soon has a place in a trick—and eventually is returned to the deck and reshuffled. In this day of attention to linguistic and logical structures, none of this is any novelty. That being the case, it should no more be a wonder that the mind possesses and manipulates concepts readily, probably as readily as symbols, somehow knowing without constantly mentally rehearsing everything that they contain.[6] One may feel a dissatisfaction at my saying that concepts consist in collections of statements, while at the same time statements (as collections of words), word by word, present many concepts. This is, however, an expression of the fact that as we begin to philosophize we must start, as Augustine pointed out, in the middle of the thing. We do not begin with a total innocence of eye with which to look out on the world or to look within upon thought. We have been involved in building the structures, inarticulately, long before we come to the stage of analyzing them reflectively and verbally.

Images are sometimes mentioned in connection with concepts, often as the origins of concepts through the process of abstraction. An image, so far as we need to consider it here, I take to be simply a remembered sense impression or a sensual construct from remembered sense impressions. There appears to be a contingent, though not necessary, relation between an image and a concept. Just as an immediate sense impression may summon up a concept in a given person's experience, an image also may evoke an appropriate concept. Thus, not only symbols but immediate stimuli and their remembered images may have associated concepts—that is, may serve as the organizing idea around which a concept clusters—and the memory for concepts is aided by memory either of symbols or of sensory stimuli and the images in which they result. However, of these latter, I venture that there are few nameless images that occur to most of us roughly alike and that thereby summon up their respective concepts uniformly for most of us. The image tends to remain the vehicle for discourse whose purposes are more dominantly affective than cognitive. Hence, while the statements comprising a concept can cluster around things other than linguistic symbols as the organizing idea, this occurrence is probably rarely important to deliberation and serious practical discourse.

The fact that concepts are what conceptions have in common suggests what sort of thing it is that actually determines the settled nature of those concepts that are public. The conceptions that various individuals have of some object x of which all of them are aware will tend to converge, so that the propositions they will have originated upon having experience with x will tend to be the same propositions, or at least to comprise a large concentration of propositions that all of them in common believe of x. All will also have had largely the same sort of interest in x, so that the propositions will tend to cluster around those aspects of x that we call its important features. Processes of naming and in some cases of defining x will aid in the assembling of their agreed propositions, although they will tend to divert attention from the collecting *per se* of the concept since they must focus strongly on x itself. Thus while they effect the reification of the *concept of x*, they tend to mask the concept itself, the conceptual quality of our set of propositions, in order to direct our attention to the object x—and thus they assist in creating the mystery of the nature of the being of concepts.

A public list of accepted beliefs about x will naturally accrue. This is the concept of x. Many of the individuals concerned may know additional incidental information about x, but they will be little disposed to attempt to attach the propositions reporting incidental information to the public concept, first, because they know that many individuals who are aware of x "for what it is," in terms of the existing public concept, are not aware of the fact involved and by its introduction would only be hampered, not helped, in their efforts to communicate through using the concept of x; and second, because they also know what general sort of interest in x most people take and consequently what sort of thing people will disregard as a potential part of the concept of x even though that item might happen to be true of all x. People generally are aware of what is esssential, and it is no accident that *essential* means both "important" and "related to the governing or defining characteristic."

It begins to sound as though "the concept of *x*" means simply "the existing public knowledge of *x*, expressed in propositions." That is not accurate. The employment of the word *concept* does not beg the question usually assumed in the application of the word *knowledge*. That is, we accept a list of propositions as the public concept of some object, whether they are true or not, and we grant that the state of knowledge may be imperfect, whereas we apply the word *knowledge* to a proposition or set of propositions with the assumption (usually, though there is a movement to break down this convention) that those propositions are *true* and that we would not apply the word *knowledge* if they were either untrue or unknown as to truth-sign. Further, with respect to *concept*, we admit as two stages of inquiry the settling, first, of the concept of an object, and second, the determination whether the object fulfills the concept as so determined, whereas we reserve the word *knowledge* for the occasions that are determined objectively rather than by preliminary decisions of our own with respect to what we think we might possibly discover. Hence while some concepts may in fact be wholly knowledge, not all concepts are knowledge and it is not a requisite for a concept as such that all of its component statements be knowledge, i.e., be true. This is consistent with the circumstance that some of them may be value-assertive.

Concepts relate to objects because individuals are interested in objects, and users of language establish objects and bring propositions together to express their knowledge of those objects. It is fundamentally through their component propositions, and because of what people are interested in, that concepts relate to objects. Concepts are for the most part fixed, and the more a term is familiar to users and the more frequently it occurs in their language, the more closely and strongly the associated concept is attached to that term, and the more firmly it is fixed there by the force of convention. Probably no concept is immune to aberration, but, on the whole, people find that there is an advantage in a concept being fixed rather than variable (with important exceptions, shortly to be examined), so in general they keep them that way. Some concepts, such as the numbers and the geometric figures, are so firmly fixed by usage and convention, and so advantageous in that fixedness, that it is reasonable to call them eternal. It has long seemed to many who have been struck by this feature that their immutability bespoke their metaphysical reality independent of a relationship to minds; they comprised an eternal part of the very world in which individual humans are but temporary residents.

Concepts can be communicated, and are the stuff of knowledge, simply because what they essentially consist in is propositions, of which these things are true. Of course they are explanatory; all knowledge or belief (even mistaken belief) is explanatory so long as we remain content with the explanations. If we begin to doubt their truth, or their explanatory power (which may not be the same thing), we set about replacing them with others. That is the form taken by much of our revision of concepts.

Of course individuals come to a full awareness of concepts by stages, as they are taught, or as they discover, step-by-step or simultaneously, the beliefs comprising a concept. Civilizations do the same thing. To communicate or to teach a concept is to build it in the recipient's mind in that fashion, step by step, proposition by proposition.

Concepts are surrogates for objects in our dealings with the physical world, since they are linguistic in form, and perhaps the greatest function of language as a symbol system is exactly to free us from the constraints and restraints of the immediate physical situation.

According to our preconception of it before examination, a concept is an entity. We now see that, in addition to the organizing idea around which it gathers, a carefully clarified concept is that entity consisting of all the sentences that have been made propositions by proposition-behavior in relation to a particular topic of concern, the conceived object (which is usually readily identifiable by consideration of the organizing idea, since that is most often a word or phrase naming or otherwise identifying the concept in question).

As to the view that a concept is a dispositional property of a subject or person or mind, it appears more legitimate to interpret a conception in this fashion than a concept. It has been my endeavor to break down the internal-external dichotomy to some extent and put in its place a continuity. Once this is done, we see that sentences (hence propositions, hence concepts) have their being both abroad (in a language and in the society whence we as individuals derive our language) and within (in our heeded stimuli, imagination, belief, memory, and the like—all the things that privately seem to us to be our life of the mind). Since part of the entity that makes up a concept of such a thing, say, as equity, lies outside my own mind, it seems a little odd to claim that the concept *equity* is a dispositional property of *myself.* Mrs. Langer's description[7] uses the word *adequate,* implying that there is a standard of adequacy that makes the one into the other, the conceptions (ordinarily of a plurality of minds) into a concept (which is one, regardless of the number of conceptions). This standard of adequacy, I suggest, is to be found in the exigencies of communication and is probably to be tested by general agreement, or consensus, among critics of the concept concerned. Thus, even though a case could perhaps be made to the effect that the possessor of a concept (such as, let us say, the concept of religious salvation) exhibits behavior of a kind distinctive to possessors of that concept, I should rather accord to each such individual the possession of his own conception. Then I should associate any distinctive behavior with that conception of his, serving as the sign of his disposition to worship in a certain way, and the like, even though he acquired his conception of salvation entirely from others rather than from any proposition collecting of his own.

We should notice a fact parallel to one concerning the proposition. The behavior that supplies part of the meaning of the word *concept* is the necessary condition for the subject matter of the discussion to *be* a concept. It is not behavior determined by the specific nature of the subject matter itself. In other words, although there may be different correlative behavioral meaning distinguishing the concept of *equity* from the concept *salvation*, there is other correlative behavior, hence different correlative behavioral meaning, which occurs when we are treating *any* concept *as a concept*, and this latter behavioral meaning travels with the word *concept* rather than with the word *equity* or *salvation*, and rather than with the speaker who talks of equity or salvation. Thus when distinctive behavior is observed when a specific concept enters into a deliberative discussion, the behavior relating to the specific concept may be considered a dispositional property of the subject taking part, but the behavior relating to the fact that the discourse involves examining or explicating a *concept* is the correlative behavioral meaning of any word or phrase indicating the concept (not necessarily the conceived object) that is crucial in the discussion. It is in this way that concepts are related to behavior.

In order to account fully for the way in which container concepts work and fully to understand their logic, we must further note certain kinds of proposition that the user of a symbol or a concept must believe in order to use the symbol or concept successfully. In the studies of language in the past century, it has been customary to attribute certain relations to the symbol. The referential symbol, it is said, has two (if not more) kinds of meaning; various authors have called these denotative and connotative, or extension and intension, or referent and reference, or object and concept, or nominatum and sense. Believing that *referent* is the most widely used term for the one, I have spoken of *referents* and *referential meaning* for the relata and relation, respectively, of the symbol in that direction. For somewhat less reason with respect to settled practice, I have spoken of the other terminus of the relation as *conceptual meaning*. In turn I have affirmed that concepts are collections of statements gathered about an organizing idea, and that a term may itself be the organizing idea (although other things also sometimes serve). Now it becomes apparent that our sketch of symbolization is not yet complete. What we are attempting is to lay bare a part of the logic whereby linguistic symbols function for us, and in our use of statements for the purpose of making them function, there are certain statements that express operative beliefs that are not purely the property, so to speak, of the sense or conceptual meaning of the symbol, nor yet of the referential meaning, but nevertheless are peculiar to the use of *that* symbol and *that* meaning. These are propositions that state relations of the three elements of the symbol relationship—symbol, concept, and referent object. Each expresses a relation between two of the three elements. Letting the letters S, C, and R stand for symbol, concept, and referent object respectively, we see that there are three possible combinations: S and R, S and C, and C and R. The propositions are to the effect, "S indicates R (or, R is indicated by S)"; "S summons up C (or, C is summoned up by S)"; and "C applies to R (or, R is what C applies to)." These are the propositions that one learns and comes to believe when one is learning vocabulary, whether in a foreign tongue or one's own. However, in practice they are so unproblematic that one's continued belief in and use of them is quite taken for granted, so much so that though they are fundamental to symbolization they seem to have escaped analyses of meaning and do not appear in the classifications of kinds or components of meaning. We need a name for them, as we shall refer to them again, and may as well call them *semantic couplings*, so that these propositions are respectively the *symbol-referent coupling*, the *symbol-concept coupling*, and the *concept-referent coupling*.

Now the case with a container concept is simply that both the symbol-referent coupling and the concept-referent coupling are lacking as items of belief of the user of the term identifying the container concept. A container concept is a set of propositions such that either there is no referent in the appropriate way of appearing, or at least that the user of the container concept has no positive belief that links a possible referent to the term for the container concept. Rather, he employs the concept either in a search for its referent, or as a guide to realizing the referent through action, or in some other useful way. When, for example, the young man is contemplating his concept of *the girl I ought to marry*, he is affirming to himself that the lady would have this and that quality, but he is not yet ready to specify the referent of the concept. However, when he has finally decided for himself that "Mary is the girl I ought to marry," then his concept is no longer a container concept. When a theorist is searching for a designatum for the expression *good*, he asks himself what he would require of any proposed designatum for that concept. He may propose that it is something, for example, which all persons of sound mind seek. In so doing, he is building his concept of *good*, and to the extent that that is what he is occupied with, his concept is a container concept. When, however, he reaches the stage of affirming such a proposition as "Pleasure is the good," then his concept is no longer a container concept; he has now, as it were, not only built the container but has also filled it. Now he has a belief of the pattern, "x is the referent of my symbol S, which has the conceptual meaning C; and the referent object that C applies to is x." He has supplied the previously missing semantic couplings.

So long as controversy still goes on about the nature of *good*, then the general and public concept of *good*, held by those who do not regard the controversy as settled, remains a container concept.[8] Each disputant who favors one or another theory of the good advocates his own concept ("Protagoras's concept of the good" or "Aristotle's concept of the good," etc.) as that concept that in his opinion disputants and spectators alike ought to accept as the public concept, thus filling in the public container concept. Thus the fully public concept of *the good* remains a container concept, but there is also a public concept that we call *Protagoras's concept of the good*, which, since we understand it publicly and since it has specified reference, is not a container concept; and presumably, it is a match of the *conception* of the good that Protagoras actually had, minus whatever wholly private connotations it had also for Protagoras that he did not impart to others in making his conception known. Controversy among advocates of rival concepts commonly involves not only selecting and identifying the referent object for the anticipated public concept but also debating which propositions properly belong to the concept that the public should finally accept as its own adopted belief.

In some of the explicit treatment of concepts in the philosophical literature, the term *concept* is described as an undefined word that authors may employ *ad libitum* for whatever notion they happen to wish to elevate to the dignity of that name. It is virtually just a pronoun, not a noun at all, not a name of a collection of things, not a universal that designates particulars having something in common. But when an author wishes to make his conception of an object into a concept known to and used by others, surely he actually does it by setting before them the relevant propositions that relay it to them. The understanding of the concept present in the current chapter may admit that loose sort of application of the term. The utility of having such an indefinite, if not undefined, instrument need not prevent us from having a doctrine as to the ontic nature and status of the concept, for we always do better to understand the instruments that we employ. In this case, the benefit will be a fuller understanding of value and value-assertive propositions.

In our present inquiry, the organizing idea for our topic is simply the word *value*. This is the term by which value theorists know their subject of inquiry. It is because the cluster of statements accompanying this term is not a settled concept, so that different individuals are by default left free to bring various conceptions to mind with the term, that a study of the concept is needed. Such a study could have two kinds of outcome. First, it could exhibit actual propositions that are part of the commonly held concept of value that is associated with the term *value* more or less as the individuals involved entertain that organizing idea. This result would be a fact-assertive description. Questions whether it had been successful, whether its resulting description were accurate, would be questions of fact. Second, the study could arrive at a recommendatory result. The investigator, after surveying various facts, could recommend to others concerned with the problem that they ought to adopt such-and-such a concept of value, and lay aside any conceptions that they term *value* that are incompatible with that concept. That, of course, would be a value-assertive result. The methods of gaining acceptance for the recommendation would be methods of justifying value-assertions, and these are topics of subsequent chapters of this work.

6

Reference and Objects of Consciousness

In the tradition of Western philosophy, the question of the metaphysical status of value or the good is fundamental to the inquiry into a theory of value. "Is value (or the good) a reality? Does value really exist?" Few have denied that value is a reality of some description, but there have been divergent opinions whether it exists as a predicate or as a relation. As a predicate, it has been called a property of things in the senses of the pleasant or pleasurable, of the satisfying, of interest we may have in an object, of that which is conducive to survival, and so on; and it has been ascribed not only to any and all sorts of objects, but also to experience itself. ("Only experience, or *an* experience, can be good, can be valuable.") Again, value has been located in relations such as those between various objects and the experiencing subjects who are inclined to appraise them, or between various objects and other objects ("ultimate values" and "instrumental values," "intrinsic" and "extrinsic" values). One of the most persistent views is that which sees value as a real property intuitable and known in no other way. The people who attack this view rejoin that "no such thing exists." Obviously the view of the sort of reality in which value partakes is an important element of the way in which value is understood.

Yet we cannot wait until this, the metaphysical problem *par excellence,* is solved before going on to other matters, particularly those of ethics and the practical. I therefore am attempting, for the purposes of the present study, to write within a framework that could be consonant with a variety of metaphysical doctrines, allowing each reader to understand my proposals within his own metaphysical framework and hoping not to presuppose anything totally inadmissible to one or another of the major metaphysical schools of thought. This is why my basic assumption for exposition is consciousness, not the external world. In this chapter I shall more fully set forth the features of that framework. I take it that consciousness is a process of the mind, the human subject, and that the collection of objects of which a human mind is aware in many gradations of awareness are termed the "objects of consciousness," comprising the "content of consciousness." By this device, I do not at all wish to make something mystical out of consciousness. I merely wish to set aside questions such as "When I see what I take to be a squirrel in the driveway, can I know that a real squirrel is there? Can I have adequate knowledge of the truth of the claim that what I perceive is the same as what is real?" My device is not intended to answer the question about the transcendent reality of the contents of consciousness, but rather, merely to enable me to talk understandably about those contents. Nor do I want to be seen as adopting the metaphysic of *esse est percipi*, to be is to be perceived. I should, however, say that to be perceived is one form of being, even if it is to be a delusion, and yet that there may indeed *be* things that are not perceived.

In order to speak more fully about the contents of consciousness, I have to acknowledge that they are of various sorts, and (borrowing a clue from phenomenological philosophers) I shall refer to the objects of consciousness as having characteristic *ways* or *modes of appearing in consciousness* (or, synonymously, *ways* or *modes of appearing in experience*). While it is perhaps true that the origin of at least some of the ways of appearing is largely within myself as subject, I shall use as the criterion of difference between ways of appearing simply the fact that I, the subject, can tell the differences among them—for in the present study of value, one would go too far afield if one were to attempt a taxonomy of all the ways of appearing. I shall even go so far as occasionally to refer to the ways or modes of appearing as *modes of existing*, merely for convenience, omitting the proviso "apparent." Since I disclaim the purpose of doing a metaphysic of existents, I intend by this terminology only that it *appears to us* that a given item exist in that mode under which I subsume it, and I do not suppose that its classification there instead of elsewhere will be controversial. Thus I treat metaphysical propositions as *devices of classification* and am here interested in them only in respect to that function, no matter what other functions they may have.

The most obvious way that things have of appearing in consciousness is that of appearing as a physical object, the spatiotemporal way of appearing. This is the type-form, the paradigm mode of appearing. However, it is far from the only one. The list is long, and since some of its members are determined by the powers of the subject, which I take to be free and endlessly variable, there is probably no possibility of systematic completeness for it. Other ways that items have of appearing in consciousness include appearing as sense impressions; as images (some of which are reproduced sense impressions, others not); as perceptions (by which I intend processed or partially or fully interpreted sense impressions in more or less complex structures); as abstract objects or "ideal objects" (such as numbers, geometric figures, and general qualities like virtue or color—color itself, not specific colors); as propositions; as concepts; as hallucinations, or hallucinated objects; as fictions, fictional objects, whole fictional states of affairs; as atemporal objects; as dreams, or as dreamed objects; as fantasies, fantasized objects, daydreams, or daydreamed objects; as plans or projects; as purposes or intentions; as pretended objects; as words and units of language; as symbols; as referent objects of terms; as supposed or conceived objects (either abstract or concrete).

Concerning the natures of these objects, it must be noted that some of them are characteristic of whole mental dispositions, or "frames of mind," while others are not. Some, like the objects of a typical dream, are embedded in a context consisting wholly of objects of that way of appearing. One's way of apprehending a dream is such that a dream is a distinctive way of appearing, and one may sometimes know that one is dreaming even while one is dreaming. But other objects of consciousness are discrete in their character from the context in which they are embedded. A symbol, such as a word or a checkered flag or a cross, has its being as such within a situational context that substantially is not symbolic, and functions successfully because of that fact. Of course, although a single word, as a symbol, normally appears with other words, which also are symbols, a whole text, while symbolic in nature, is perceived and known against a background that is not itself exclusively symbols but rather contains objects of other modes of appearing. What we may say to summarize, then, is that there are some modes of consciousness, such as dreaming, daydreaming, reflecting upon abstractions, and perhaps some episodes of artistic creation, that give their nature to the whole stream of objects of that consciousness, while there are other modes of consciousness, most notably that of everyday waking alertness, the normal or usual relation with one's world, in which various simultaneously appearing objects may distinguishably have their own different ways of appearing. And there may be combinations of the two, as when one dreams of artistic creation or when a symbol appears *as* a symbol in a dream.

Now I must stipulate a few meanings for terms used in the present study, meanings more restricted than those of everyday occurrence. I have already employed some of them; they include *real, exist, existence, be,* and *being. Real* may have its basic metaphysical meaning, though I shall rarely use it. I shall, however, export *exist* over into consciousness, so that I may follow everyday usage to say of something that it exists (say, as a dream, or as a character in a novel) while it "actually" is not real. Thus I am defining *to exist* as meaning *to appear in consciousness,* not as *to be real.* This usage is not at all uncommon, notwithstanding that our paradigm of existence is the physical object, and that in our natural attitude we regard physical objects as real or as among the realities. However, locutions like the following are quite idiomatic. "The child Timmy plays with isn't real but exists only in Timmy's imagination"; "Of course there never really was a Jim Hawkins although there certainly exists such a character in Stevenson's novel"; "She was a convincing Peter Pan on the stage even though there never really was and never could be such a child"; or "That is the only work of this famous portraitist whose model never existed." These locutions show us two things: one, that we do indeed take physical existence as the type-form of existence, and the other, that we concede other forms of existence also, even though we hedge the concession about with qualifications.

There are ways other than the physical in which an object can *be*. The chair created in a painter's picture is not a three-dimensional chair in the physical sense, that could be sat in, and is therefore in the physical sense nonexistent, although it certainly does exist in the mode of being a pictured object, and in that mode it clearly can and does *be* a chair, not something else. A chair may exist in the mode of a designer's project before it is drawn, or of the designer's concept of it, or even of an image in his mind before it is ever manufactured and could, by being physical, give sense images to other persons. A child may exist in the daydream of an adolescent girl or a newly married soldier without there being as yet any such physical child or precursor of one. The kindergartner can play with an imaginary child, who necessarily must "be" a child in order to be the docile and congenial playmate. The novelist can create a fictional child; the actress can "be" a child on the stage; there are many modes of *being* in which a child can *be*, be a child and not something else, without having to be physically actual.

Thus *to be* is to be the object of consciousness in some way of appearing, some *mode of existence*. Any way of coming within the purview of a mind is a way of "being." It is a way of being the bearer of at least one predicate, for it is the bearer of the predicate that characterizes the way of appearing that is involved. "Tommy is Timmy's imaginary playmate": Tommy exists as a pretended child, an object in the way of appearing of a pretended physical object. Other predicates also can be credited to Tommy. He is of a certain age, he likes Timmy, and so on. Very importantly, he is the referent object of the name that Timmy has given him; his name is, in a sense, one of his predicates; he has that way of appearing of being the referent object of a linguistic symbol (his name) *as well as* having the way of appearing of a pretended object. Thus the pretended child, Tommy, while not physical, exists in at least two ways in consciousness.

To get the full benefit of the framework we have adopted, let us look more fully into the matter of linguistic reference. It appears that just as the physical is the paradigm for our concepts of reality and of objects of consciousness, it is also the paradigm for referent objects of linguistic symbols. When we want to explain how words function, we distinguish between the desk or the table and the words *desk* and *table*, and we attest that the words *refer* (better, that speakers refer) to the actual desk or table by employing (by *using* rather than merely *mentioning*) the words *desk* and *table* respectively.

Now the fundamental assumptions of that sketch of reference include not only the physical object as the typical referent object but also the present tense and a pretty uncomplicated statement (of the order of complexity of "The cat is on the mat"). Yet if we observe the use of referential symbols a bit more fully, noticing that they are embedded in a matrix containing many other forms of verbal functions, we discover that no neat theory of reference quite suffices to describe language as it actually operates. I shall work from the position that there is indeed a symbolic function for words and phrases in language, and that the explanation through the principle of reference is at least a part of a full explanation of it, and I do not believe that this stand shall prejudice my eventual description of value. However, I shall point out that some of the gaps and features of our use of referential terms give us clues as to how it is that we speak intelligibly of values and express value judgments.

Reference, however, is joined by assertion as a fundamental function of language. And for the two to operate together, the consequence is that certain indeterminacies enter into communications between persons and into the sentences that comprise them. To instance this, let us take under consideration for a few moments the familiar figure:

&

which is of course called an *ampersand.* And let us look at some sample sentences that use the name for that design.

(1) The ampersand is a sign for the word *and.*
(2) Reader, there is an ampersand printed on page 119 of your copy of *Value, Language, and Life.*
(3) There is an ampersand printed on page 119 of *Value, Language, and Life.*
(4) If you want to make your firm's name more memorable on your placard, you can do in by putting in an ampersand instead of the word *and* between the names of the partners.
(5) The ampersand should be used for a reason rather than for no reason.

Now as we apply the principle of reference, the word *ampersand* may be said to refer to the distinctive design that is printed on page 119 of this volume; but it also may be said to refer to each and all instances of that design, wherever they are to be found. In fact, it refers to all past instances of it that may have been erased or destroyed, to all future instances of it that are yet to be brought into being, and, oddly enough, even to nonexistent instances of it, so long as it is that specific design of which they are (nonexistent) instances, and not something else. We must return to the last-mentioned matter in a few moments, but for the present, let us look at the sample sentences.

We might formulate one of our problems in the question "What are these sentences about?" but I should rather formulate it in a fashion that is more practical, more obviously connected to everyday life: "What is the speaker talking about when he employs the word *ampersand* in each of these sentences?" For it is speakers who have meanings, and to say that sentences have meanings, or exhibit "about-ness," is merely a brief way of saying that it is persons, minds, that determine these. We must not let ourselves lose sight of these facts when our purpose is explanation of usages in contexts.

In the case of sentence (1), the speaker is undoubtedly using the term *ampersand* in the generic singular. That is, he is using it to refer to "the ampersand in general," to *all* ampersands that are, that were, that will be, or even that may be. He is literally "referring" to all actual and possible ampersands. No matter what instance you might present to him, he is prepared to say of it, "Yes, that one too is a sign for the word *and*." *Reference* is in fact understood as universal in scope; an occurrence of an individual class term *refers to* all members, actual or possible or even nonexistent, of the class involved. And it remains undetermined in many cases whether a particular reference is a reference to members that are currently nonexistent but shall in future exist, or to members now nonexistent that definitely shall never exist, or to members that are now nonexistent of which it is unknown and perhaps unknowable whether they ever shall exist or not. Yet the speaker of sentence (1) is happy to affirm his statement about *whatever* his key class term might now or later comprehend.

Language is sufficiently flexible that a speaker with a message in mind is by no means bound to assert it about the entirety of a class that he is thinking of. Sentence (2) narrows down the subject of his communication to a single instance, namely, the ampersand contained in a single copy of the book of the title given. Reasonable interpretation of the wording would have it that a single reader is addressed, and therefore a single copy identified, thus an individual ampersand singled out. There remains the universality of reference of *ampersand* as considered alone, but the qualifying expressions cause the *assertion* to concern only one member of its class. While so far as the word *ampersand* alone is considered, the same indeterminacies pertain to the occurrence of that class term, the speaker has removed indeterminacy from his assertion and has made quite clear which member of the referent class it offers information about.

There are differences worth noticing between sentences (2) and (3), which outwardly appear to say much the same thing. We can readily state for either one of them that the speaker has let his recipient know the scope of his assertion by controlling the wording of his entire sentence. In sentence (2) only one ampersand is the subject of his statement but in sentence (3) more than one is the subject. Sentence (3) is simpler in structure and thus less completely qualified than sentence (2). This fact is coordinate with the fact that the number of ampersands "covered" by sentence (3) is indefinite rather than definite, at least to anyone who does not know how many copies of *Value, Language, and Life* were included in its press run. There is an indeterminacy here in the scope of predication. Yet any person familiar with English will know at once, upon reading or hearing it, what sentence (3) means, and, moreover, if he is a reader of this book, he will know that it is true, by his own observation of page 119. The indeterminacy interferes neither with the meaning, with the occurrence of assertion, nor with the truth of the sentence containing or creating it. We have now found indeterminacies both in respect to *reference* and in respect to the subject of an *assertion*.

Sentence (4) has an interesting twist in terms of the indeterminacy of assertion. Sentence (4), as we usually interpret our words, is actually about a nonexistent ampersand! That is, we usually use the word *exist* to signify physical-object existence. Yet no one is disturbed by the notion that a term, namely, the word *ampersand* here, refers to a nonexistent object, and no one who is acquainted with English has any doubts about the meaning of the sentence. In fact, knowledge of the relative frequency of ampersands and of instances of the word *and* may prompt a recipient of sentence (4) to give it the truth-sign *true* without further quibble. And since our speaker here is talking about a *nonexistent* ampersand, it hardly can be a meaningful question to ask *which* nonexistent ampersand the business partner will paint into his sign. So far as there is an idea of an ampersand at all here, it is not determined, but that does not matter to the success of the function of sentence (4).[1]

With sentence (5) we seem to have another universal statement, that is, one applying to all members of the class whose name is *ampersand*. But a second look shows the matter not to be quite clear-cut. The uses of ampersands are instances of their occurring, so that the sentence after all seems to be aimed at the engagement in a context of a particular ampersand, or possibly of some determined collection of ampersands. Bearing in mind the placard of sentence (4), we could suppose that the speaker of sentence (5) might be in a situation like that of (4), so that he is talking of one or a limited number—yet an indeterminate number—of ampersands, not all of them. Thus the previously noticed indeterminacies still obtain. But the interesting thing about sentence (5) is that it is a value-assertive sort of sentence, not a fact-assertive one. This introduces new problems about assertion. Is the ampersand that is spoken about an existing ampersand? The remark indeed could be made about an existing ampersand, whose rationale has come under question; or else it could be about a potential ampersand, for example, the one that is contemplated by the business partner of sentence (4). Are we to say that provided that the business partner does substitute an ampersand for the *and* in "Smith and Jones," then the sentence was spoken about the ampersand that he *did* insert (making "Smith & Jones"), whereas if he decides against using an ampersand, the ampersand that he does *not* insert is no ampersand in particular? Is that *not* a specific ampersand, the one that he decided not to insert in "Smith and Jones"? Whether it seems much to matter or not, we have here a further and very clear instance of the indeterminacy of assertion. No recipient of sentence (5) is likely to mistake its meaning on account of the indeterminacy, even though (to put it in the extreme) he doesn't know what is being talked about! And again, clearly the principle of reference, if it is it be a principle at all, must cover the nonexistent instances as well as the existent instances, but apparently the indeterminacy of *assertion* allows an assertor to make meaningful true or false statements even when he systematically doesn't know, literally, what he is talking about.

One advantage of the device for exposition that I have adopted in this study, namely, to adopt the framework of consciousness as our structural principle, is that we are enabled by it to speak of things like those nonexistent ampersands with a bit more understanding and a bit less mystical awe than if we were to adopt instead a framework of existence as over against nonexistence. We now can say that the "nonexistent" ampersands of not only sentences (1) to (5) but of the entire reference of *ampersand* are nonexistent in the physical-object mode of appearing, but they obviously are existent in the mode of being of referent objects of referential words. We extend the model of one-word-one-referent (one cat for *cat* in "The cat is on the mat," more apparent in the Latin, which lacks the definite article, something like "Felis in storia est") to serve for reference to designata that exist in only one, not both, of the ways of appearing that we are now concerned with. We understand a speaker who refers with his referential word to instances of a thought object of which it is not (or not yet) known whether or not there are corresponding objects in the physical-object realm. We continue to manipulate the word as a token, so to speak, unmindful whether it is in some respects empty of reference, much as we continue to manipulate dollar bills in a currency backed by a gold standard although in the national treasury there are only a tenth as many dollars'-worth of gold as there are dollars presumably redeemable in gold. We may be vaguely aware that there is not so much gold "backing up" our token as surface appearances suggest, but the awareness does not hinder our manipulation. And we probably would not get along as well linguistically if we did not have this device, just as we would not if we did not have monetary currency, even currency whose backing consists far more in faith than it does in gold.

An important aspect of our manipulation of such things as symbols, but also of images, remembered perceptions, and perhaps other elements among objects of consciousness, is an element that we ourselves contribute to those objects. The particular element that I speak of has no name, so far as I know, but may occasionally be called an interpretation, insofar as interpretation is controlled by the interpreter rather than the interpreted, or may be called a construction, in the sense of construal. I shall speak of it as the process of "seeing as." This is not merely a matter of illusion—of mistaking, as I did one day recently, a seed pod on a bush for a bird perched on a branch of the bush. Rather, it is a case of having under one's attention an item of consciousness in one way of appearing in such a fashion that one can apply to it descriptions that belong to some other item possessing the same way of appearing in consciousness. There are, for example, certain things I could say of the seed pod, either before or after I realized my mistake, that also could apply to the bird, such as certain predicates of color and shape. But "seeing as" need not be thought of as either mistaking or altering what is seen. A clear example is the instance of a church undergoing repair. The worshiper sees the edifice as a church and accordingly behaves reverently within it. The stonemason sees the edifice as the repair job he is working on and behaves toward it just as a stonemason does on any job—perhaps distressing the worshiper with the clatter of his hammer. The church both *is* a house of worship and *is* a stonemason's job.[2] An example closer to the reader is the previously discussed ampersand. If the author's words established for the reader the "set," at least momentarily, of his mind, then the reader first saw the ampersand as a figure, for that is what it was called. Then in a moment, or perhaps simultaneously, the reader saw the ampersand *as* an ampersand (or if he did not call to mind that name, as an "and-sign"). The practice of seeing one thing as another, or, we had better say, of seeing one thing in two different acceptances of it, is common and familiar to us all.

One of the most familiar ways in which "seeing as" functions for us, so familiar that in everyday life we take it completely for granted, and so common of occurrence that our youngest schoolchildren learn to perform it without it ever being articulated to them, is the seeing of written or printed patterns as symbols, as words. Yet even more primitive is the hearing of spoken words as verbal symbols. We hardly remember in our mature life that there ever was a time when these designs on paper "made no sense" to us other than simply as designs—the letters and the combinations of letters that became words. There is still such a thing as encountering an unfamiliar grouping of Roman letters, say "cwm," and failing to see the combination as a word in the English language, although such it is, courtesy of its Welsh ancestry. Moreover, in a non-linguistic context, there are things that may be seen as signs or not, depending upon the construction put upon them by the perceiver. A card player is dealt an ace of spades; he may see it as a valuable trump that will take a trick in his game of bridge—or he may see it as a portent of death. One person sees a Rorschach blot simply as an ink blot; another sees it as a butterfly, or a dragon, as well as its being an ink blot. Almost needless to say, much of art in all the media makes heavy use of the human gift of seeing one thing as another. Not only does the spectator see the cross over a building in a painting as the sign of its being a church; he sees the patches and areas of paint as a picture of a building in the first place, even though he "knows better," knows that it is not a building but a painted area on some canvas.

Since we have the gift of seeing a single object in a number of guises, we are enabled to do much that we could not otherwise do. Perhaps the whole story of symbolization could be laid to this human propensity, if it were more sharply delineated than it is here. However, our purpose for the present is to attempt to explain only what pertains to our account of value. That purpose calls for us then to identify not only linguistic symbols but also many other things as importantly influenced by the "seeing as" process. And an important application of it is our ability to see a common noun, like *cat* or *ampersand*, as having reference even without attributing it to any designatum—in other words, seeing it as a linguistic symbol even when in a given mode of appearing there appears nothing for it to symbolize, nothing to which it can refer. We can see *centaur* as a word, *as though* it referred to something, that is, to actual centaurs as well as possible or nonexistent centaurs, while we may indeed know that in the physical-object world there are no centaurs. There are, of course, paintings of centaurs, tapestries of centaurs, stories of centaurs, philosophical illustrations of centaurs, and concepts of centaurs; centaurs have other ways of appearing besides the physical-object mode, and in those other ways of appearing, centaurs are as real as anything else in those ways. But since we can see *centaur*, the combination of letters, *as though it were* a word with physical-object reference, like the simplest or paradigm cases of reference, we can use and understand the word *centaur* even when we know that no specimens of centaurs ever appear as physical objects.

It is in this fashion then that we speak, meaningfully, and with the capability of achieving truth or falsity, about the supposedly nonexistent, about nonbeing, about unreality. While it may be true, as Parmenides long ago urged, that we cannot *think* nonbeing, we surely can mention it, as he himself must when cautioning us. We can, moreover, make assertions about it by converting many affirmative assertions into negative ones; and since we can make assertions and develop propositions about it, we can have a concept of it, that is, we can *conceive of* it.

But for practical purposes, we may wish to look at other applications of the process of seeing an item as a second thing, such as seeing *cat* as the symbol of a feline animal. The device helps us to have concepts, both of things that are physical and of things that are not. We put the letters c-a-t together in that order to make a printed word, which either itself becomes our organizing idea for the concept of *cat* or else is taken as a sign of a spoken or heard word, a sound, so that it is the sound that becomes our organizing idea for the concept. When we become literate, something that we call "the word *cat*" becomes that organizing idea, regardless of what explanation we may have for what a word is, whether written or spoken or some shadowy underlying entity that somehow is both. Again, it is well to notice that in our pre-literate days, it may very well be an image, perhaps a remembered seen cat or a remembered picture of a cat, that is our organizing idea around which we gather our statements as to what a cat is—our concept of *cat*.

A further and most useful consequence of our ability to see an object of consciousness under either of two guises, as either of two possible entities, has to do with the passage of attention from items of one way of appearing to those of another. It is often important to us to be able to say "The *same thing* may occur in consciousness in more than one way of appearing," or the like. The usual instances, of course, are quite specific, and are exemplified by such ordinary remarks as "That was a dream that actually came true," "I had both an accurate memory image of the end of the race and a good photograph of it," "The same person that I saw before me was the one of whom I had formed a detailed conception through our telephone conversations." What is still more important is that we actually think in the fashion that is expressed by this general statement and its more specific exemplars. What happens is that we adopt the attitude that it expresses toward some organizing idea, usually a word, and treat the word as a symbol of the item that the word symbolizes in *any* of the ways of appearing. That is, I may use the word *armadillo* either to symbolize an actual armadillo that I see beside the highway, or to symbolize my concept of armadillos, or to apply as symbol to a picture of an animal that I can identify as an armadillo, or to apply as symbol to a picture through which I was taught what an armadillo is before I ever saw one, or to symbolize my mental image of an armadillo, or to symbolize the armadillo about which I dream, and so on, indifferent to changes in the way of appearing of one for another. As a result, we can say with no confusion, "The *same thing* may have more than one way of appearing in consciousness." The meaningfulness of the expression is shown by the fact that we could even challenge the affirmation that item a_2 were actually a second appearance of item a_1 in a different mode of appearing, and claim that it was instead not a at all but a different item. That would be a factual question, but the configuration that I have exhibited is a part of the theoretical framework that makes it possible to speak about the fact. The "thing" that is "the *same* thing" is no one thing, but is simply whatever we are treating as or seeing as the referent object of our word, *armadillo*, that serves as our organizing idea. It can be any one or more of the "kinds of armadillo" just listed, which, more accurately, is to say it can be an item in any of the ways of appearing and identifiable in its respective way as "an armadillo." As it were, for a moment at least, it is nothing but the referent object of the term *armadillo* and need not be anything else in any mode of appearing in consciousness. The use of the symbol that is serving as our organizing idea enables us to carry in thought from one mode of appearing to another the notion, "whatever is the referent object of the term armadillo," and we successfully manipulate this notion without having to specify it in any other mode of appearing than simply that of the referent object of a symbol.

This application of the function of seeing a given item in first one guise then another presupposes that we control not only the notion of time but also that of the timeless. We speak of eternal ideas or timeless concepts or ideal objects, and we recognize the allegedly atemporal nature of their existence. We know ourselves to be far from eternal in our actual lives, and marvel that the numbers, the geometric figures, and other abstract ideas will "outlive" us, will perdure unchanged through time; rather, we say, they should be described as having no dimension of time for they never change over time. There is no way that they can be eroded by the passage of time. Now whether or not there is a sense in which numbers and triangles are eternal externally to particular minds, there certainly *is* a sense in which they are eternal or atemporal relative to particular minds, and that sense is the sense in which we simply treat them as such. It may be that we recognize an atemporality that is genuine in some metaphysical sense; but quite surely we recognize the advantages of there being certain atemporal things whether there actually are, apart from our consciousness, or whether, on the other hand, they are inventions of our own. While I have given accounts of the proposition and of the concept that are genetic in the respect that they take the origins and presence of these in particular minds into account, I have also pointed out that we benefit greatly from taking the posture that the propositions and concepts are atemporal. Now I can add that although to do so is nonsense in physical, historic terms, we treat symbols themselves as atemporal. As shown in the above discussion of reference, the referent objects of a referential symbol may be past, present, or future, as to their occurrences in consciousness, or in the pertinent mode of appearing they may never appear there at all. Yet we succeed in thinking and communicating about them, through symbolizing them; and this presupposes that the symbol itself be regarded as unlimited in terms of time so that it may remain constant through the shifts from, say, consideration of past to consideration of future time. Of equal importance, the symbol remains constant and unlimited as shifts take place from one way of appearing to another—shifts that are events in time, of course, of a subject's mind. The symbol for x remains the symbol for x when I first consider x as a physical object and later hold x in consciousness simply as a memory, or in some other mode of appearing. This principle, too, is necessary so that I can say that x is "the same thing," first as physically present, then as remembered, and that my organizing idea for its concept, its word or name, remains the same for "the same thing" throughout. There actually is no *thing* that is "the same thing," since a physical object and a memory of it are two quite different things. But we treat the "thing" as "the same." What we are doing in this case is using the "thing" as a putative thing only, and for us it is appearing simply as the referent object of its symbol. We could say, if we like, that in the interim between having x in our consciousness as a present, physical thing and then later having x in our consciousness only as a remembered object, the "thing" x exists, or appears in consciousness, *only* in the way of appearing as the referent object of a symbol.

Thus, all that is required in order for us to assemble a concept is an organizing idea, which may be almost anything in some mode of appearing but which most conveniently is a word or phrase, together with one or more statements that we gather around the organizing idea upon which the statements will center. It does *not* require that there be a prototype in the physical mode of appearing, for us to form a concept. We can now see that we probably form our first concepts around actual physical objects, those most evident of all objects of consciousness, and tend to engender explanations of concepts through our impressions of how it is that we abstract from objects, forming abstractions. To be sure, concepts are abstract, in the sense that they are not themselves physical. They are mental; they are more like thoughts than they are like physical things. But for something to be a concept is not simply the same as for it to be an abstraction. We can and do possess concepts both of concrete objects and of abstractions. Since there is no law of nature that requires us to start from a physical object, we need not infer that the concept of *value* is abstracted from some external entity, some physical or natural object in our surrounding world.

The container concept, it will now be seen, fits into this scheme of objects of consciousness very readily. It gathers statements around its organizing idea, which is probably a word or phrase. The concept and its name and organizing idea are treated as atemporal. The holder of a container concept necessarily has pertinent objects within his consciousness, which will certainly include the statements (propositions, in the case of a well-refined container concept) that gather about the organizing idea. The objects may also include images (such as images of pictures, models, sketches, or diagrams), remembered narratives as illustrations or examples, and other items in various appropriate ways of appearing. What the concept will lack, however, are the symbol-referent and concept-referent couplings, linking symbol and concept to some object in the most pertinent mode of appearing, saying "*This* is the referent object itself; *this* is specifically that to which the concept applies."

What *Ought* Means:
The Pure, Simple *Ought*

The concept indicated by the term *ought* is so fundamental to our thinking that it is difficult to discuss. It is tempting to suggest that *ought* is a primitive term. Perhaps its closeness to this status has helped to foster the modern schools of intuitionism, which have in effect enshrined the difficulty here mentioned into a semblance of positive doctrine. If *that which ought* were a simple cognizable property, then *ought* could function as a primitive term. In turn, if *ought* were a primitive term, we would find it useful for explaining other things, but so well known in and of itself that to explain it by the use of other terms or concepts would be to explain the familiar in terms of the unfamiliar, the reverse of the normal process of explanation. This effort then would hardly be effective. But I believe that we can successfully analyze *ought* to an extent highly useful for our purposes in the present inquiry. I shall endeavor now to examine the core idea of that term, calling it the *pure* or *simple* ought, which in general founds the whole field of value. Then, further along, I shall look at important subfields of value under the headings of the *prudential ought,* the *aesthetic ought,* and finally the *ought* of obligation, the *moral ought.*

In the English language, and no doubt in natural languages in general, there are many locutions that commonly express the notion of fact, or of the given, as represented above on page 16. Some are: "the way things are," "the way it is," "how things are," "how it is" (as well as variants in all tenses on these expressions), "reality," "actuality," "what really happens," "what really is so," "what is the case," "the state of affairs," "the actual situation," "the truth," "the true situation," "what in fact occurs," "the facts." The variety of expressions for substantially the same idea shows that the notion of an objective given enters our thinking very frequently, and therewith shows us that the category that defines fact-assertive propositions is very important to us.[1] If there were but one term to express the referent of all these terms and their synonyms, its prominence in our thinking would be readily seen to be great indeed, for the single term would be used so often as to become quite tiresome. I cite these points to show that the framing concept for what we call "statements of fact" is indicated often in language. If we may assume that the dealings with it are normally successful, then we may infer that that concept is widely understood, in the sense that equates understanding to successful responsive action. It is my view that the parallel framing concept, that which functions for value-assertive rather than fact-assertive propositions, is also functionally understood quite as well by all of us who use the language, but that we encounter greater difficulty, and achieve less success, in being articulate about it. The one is partly because of the greater complexity and subtlety of the subject matter itself, and the other is partly because our purposes on most occasions for using language require little precision of description, and therefore little persistence in analyzing what we are describing.

I have asserted[2] the thesis that we employ the concept of *what ought to be* as the framing concept of our value judgments. I have suggested that, essentially, value-assertive propositions have the same linguistic pattern as fact-assertive propositions, and are formed grammatically in the same ways. We tend therefore to postulate a similar objective subject matter for the value-assertive statements, to complete the likeness to fact-assertive statements that the grammatical and syntactical similarities exhibit. But there are important logical and epistemological differences. The most obvious is that many value-assertive propositions are employed to symbolize subject matter having, or potentially having, quite different existential relations or status from those of the factual subject matters of fact-assertive propositions. We have not yet fully explored these differences. What we shall find, when we do so, will further enhance our understanding of what it is that we are doing when we are originating or receiving value-assertive propositions, or accepting or rejecting them, or appraising—evaluating—them. It can also, I believe, enable us to improve our understanding of our orientation with our world. More specifically, we will come to know how the crucial meaning of *ought* may be understood, and what are the relationships of value-assertions to claims of truth.

The first question one thinks of, once the point is suggested that value-assertive propositions symbolize the realm of what ought to be, just as fact-assertive propositions symbolize a factual world, is "How does one know what ought to be?" The very phrasing of the question reinforces the parallelism that we see between the structure of value-assertive and fact-assertive propositions, for it suggests that verification is the first thought when one has been offered a value-assertive statement, just as it is when we receive a fact-assertion of any importance. In general, we believe that we know *how* we know "what *is*"—that is, we know how we test factual statements. We habitually and automatically attempt therefore to take the same stance toward "what ought to be."

The honest answer to the question "How does one know what ought to be?" is, simply, "One never really and finally knows." This is why many, possibly even most, value disputes remain unresolved, so far as the beliefs of the parties are concerned, although when action is called for, compromise actions are often agreed upon. As explained in chapter four, there is a reason for this beyond the indomitability of the disputants. It is just because value-assertive propositions relate to the framework of what *ought to be*, rather than that of what *is*, that there is no objective solution to the question of which of two conflicting claims as to what ought to be is the finally correct one, the "true" one. The search among the givens for such an answer is a logical mistake, no matter how charming and powerful the delusion that leads us into it. As we round out our inquiry, I shall endeavor to state how much we *can* in a sense know about what ought to be, or about how we can come to know what ought to be.

When we speak of "the world as it is," we very likely intend reference either to the actual earth, or to the universe, as a physical world. It seems easier to think about physical things than about abstract ones, and we customarily use the physical as our pattern. However, both world and universe may also be understood as conceptual rather than physical entities. We treat the universe conceptually as all being, all existence, all-that-there-is taken at once. It is this conceived world, of course, rather than simply the physical world (although its concept includes the concept of the physical world) that serves as the frame of reference within which our fact-assertive propositions have their specific conceptual meanings. We ordinarily assume and act as though these concepts have referent objects that are physically existent objects, or other kinds of objects that are equally objective.

On the other hand, "the world as it ought to be" is a phrase whose meaning is basically totally conceptual in nature. We do not, and in some respects *must* not, assume that it has correlates in physical existence. The concept it names probably has its origin—either for the species or for each of us as individuals—in perceptions, and thus in the physical world, but certainly in perceptions modified, perceptions treated in a special way rather than simply accepted or even than as accepted and abstracted. Events such as successes in bringing about changes, and such as comparisons of degrees of pleasures or pains, have perhaps stimulated us to generate in our minds the concept of *how things ought to be* as a fundamental contrast to how things are.[3] I need not presume to attempt to state its actual origination. However, granted that it is here, I can try to describe our ways of employing it.

Situations like the one portrayed in the following sketch probably occur frequently to most of us. I am at work at my desk, with open books and stacks of papers before me and a typewriter on an extension of the desk at my left. I sit in a straight chair with a relatively high seat and firm back. In my work I peruse the open books and papers, and occasionally turn to the typewriter to record or respond to material I have read. Finding that the chair is best fitted for both reading and typing when it is sat in squarely rather than sideways, I turn the chair for the intervals of typing, then turn it back toward the desk when done. Tiring of this distracting activity, I eventually say to myself, "What I ought to have in this study is a swivel chair, not a straight chair."

A glance at the narrative just given will show certain relationships. The expression *straight chair,* for example, is a term for the kind of chair in which I am sitting when I utter the value-assertive statement in which the narrative culminates. That is a physical chair, a specimen of which is actually and currently present. The phrase *this study* has reference also in the physical-object world, and serves to establish the setting of the state of affairs that the judgment concerns. In classifying the chair that I am sitting in as a straight chair, I am thinking a concept that I hold atemporally, under which I subsume the present specimen. However, I cannot indicate a particular specimen of the other class of chair that I mention, for none is present, and no particular specimen is intended. Hence my words symbolize only an unspecified potential member of the class *swivel chairs,* which I also treat as time-free.

I am also treating the verb *to have* as atemporal, as I am considering both present and future applications of it—and indeed, I am using the infinitive form, which is very literally unlimited as to time or tense. The possessing that is symbolized by the wording "What I ought to have . . . is a swivel chair" may be considered to be a member of the class of all possessings, but what member is it? What mode of existence, what way of appearing in consciousness, does it have? Obviously it is now a conceived possessing, but is it also more than that? One possibility is that it may prove to be a future possessing; that is, it may prove in the future that I actually come into physical possession of a swivel chair and place it in my study. But again, it may be solely a conceived possessing, and the mentioned swivel chair only a conceived chair, once for all—in other words, I may never realize the physical state of affairs that the value-assertive proposition symbolizes. In that case my locution should have as part of its meaning no physical, actually existing object of reference, but only a conceptual meaning, the concept of a member of a physical class taken atemporally, the class *swivel chair,* a member that is nonexistent physically now and that remains physically nonexistent for all time; and linked with this concept the concept of physical possession, the physical locating in premises of my own, of such an object, which possession also remains forever only conceptual. As of the moment of my utterance, it remains undetermined whether both, or one only, of these modes of existence are partaken in by the physical object and physical situation referred to. But, almost astonishingly after these indeterminacies have been identified, no one who hears me has any difficulty understanding me, even if neither listener nor speaker knows the mode or modes of existence of the objects symbolized by the key terms of my value-assertive utterance, other than their being the putative referent objects of symbols.

It appears that what I have done is to appraise my situation—my activity of working within my work setting—and have formed an assertion that holds all its features constant as they are, so far as any conceivable changing is concerned, except one, which is singled out for the contemplation of a change. The concept that I adopt, then, of *the world as it ought to be* as the basis of this particular value-assertive utterance, is a concept that in most respects matches my present concept of my study but supplies one variant particular within that total concept. Probably most of our routine problem-solving thinking is on a scale about like this. It is probably most typical, hence most frequent, that we think of a single change in a setting—replacing a chair, putting up new draperies, reading this book instead of that one, planting a leafy ground cover instead of grass, filling an empty tumbler. If this is the case, it is easy to see how we get our ought-judgments and to infer that we have ample instances of them in life from which to abstract and generalize in order to carry out the large proportion of thinking that has to do with arriving at new ought-judgments and new or changed action.

The circumstance that it can remain undetermined which mode of existence is held by the object crucial to the meaning of a value-assertive proposition, and that nevertheless this value-assertion can be readily understood, shows us some further important features of the value-assertive propositions. If it is undetermined which mode of existence is participated in by the particular swivel chair I might eventually obtain, then value-assertive propositions must be capable of bearing meaning regardless of further determination of either the symbolized object or of its mode of existence, its way of appearing in consciousness. The conceptual meaning, once established by convention, is made to slide away from the physical referent objects that were first associated with the terms concerned, so that when the terms are given atemporal application to *indeterminate* objects, they are understood as if they still referred to something of that previous sort, while the new application makes it literally impossible that they actually could do so. But it apparently gives no one any practical difficulty to think the new thought *per impossibile*. And if we cannot determine either the mode of existence of the object or the particular object itself, we obviously cannot examine these for testing purposes, in an effort to ascertain whether the value-assertive proposition is true or false. To assert that a value-assertive proposition is true, then, either is to give a quite different meaning to *true* when so applied than when applied to fact-assertive propositions, or else is to talk meaninglessly. To put this conclusion more forcefully if somewhat oversimply, we may say: *Value-assertive propositions essentially refer to a realm of their own; but since that realm doesn't exist factually, value-assertive propositions cannot be submitted to factual tests for truth.* The modification described here makes it possible to formulate value-assertive propositions, either for affirming that things the way they are, are as they ought to be, or for affirming that things are not the way they ought to be and ought to be changed. In an incident of this sort, in order to arrive at his value-assertion, the originating individual has removed a set of phenomena from their setting, handled them independently of it, and held certain dimensions of their new situation systematically indeterminate. This must be done in order for the value-assertive proposition to be fully meaningful. The fact that this is done breaks down the mechanism on which a naturalistic ethic such as a moral intuitionism depends, and supplies the refutation of those ethical theories that we generally call naturalistic ethics.

It is necessary to acknowledge the use we make of what we might call affirmative existential-content, value-assertive propositions, those the effect of which is to evaluate positively or favorably the way things currently appear, as the way they ought to be: "She is an excellent soprano," "She sang Butterfly just as it ought to be sung," and so on. These are no exception to the principle just stated above. Insofar as the sentence states that the soprano sang Butterfly, it is a fact-assertive statement, can be tested as such, and not only can possess truth or falsity but can be known to be correctly marked by the one truth-sign or the other. However, it is the valuative portion of the sentence that is its *raison d'être,* and insofar as the sentence is *about* the way Butterfly ought to be sung, it is about that value-realm which is not factual. The singing of Butterfly can be proved, but the excellence of the singing of Butterfly is forever left unproved and a potential subject of controversy, a matter of opinion.

The term *ought* is a crucial term in ethical and moral discourses. Normally, it is strongly associated with obligation or duty (its roots in Middle and Old English had meanings of both "to owe" and "to possess"), so strongly that these are sometimes treated as synonymous with *ought* or at least as essential to it. But in fact the concept of obligation is only secondary in the meaning of *ought* when the word stands alone, and can rise to primary importance only when a moral or ethical context determines that it do so. Hence I wish to separate off and leave aside until later (chapter fifteen) the notion of obligation from the concept usually summoned up by *ought.* The obligational use of *ought* is exemplified in such familiar propositions as "Any person ought to pay his freely contracted debts," and "No one ought to lie merely to advance his own selfish purposes." This connotation of obligation is not at all necessary to the success of the word *ought* in communicating. A sensible, communicative sentence can be made on such patterns as:

(1) There ought to be in all nations enough people who insist upon peace that peace will prevail.

This sentence, I suggest, does not involve obligation, even though it touches upon a subject having a moral dimension. We can be sure that it does not involve obligation for two reasons. First, it does not designate, nor even suggest, anyone upon whom any obligation should fall. It merely expresses that the world "ought" to be such that there is a preponderance of a certain kind of person. It does not call upon each individual to make himself such a person, nor allege an obligation upon him to be such. Second, the sentence is understood even though it does not make these claims of obligation and does not depend for its meaning upon such claims being either explicit or implicit. Therefore the assertion is justified that the sentence, including its use of *ought*, is meaningful—that is, it succeeds in communicating through concepts indicated by its terms—without the necessity that its concepts include the concept of obligation.

The sample sentence (1) may at first glance call to the reader's mind another sense of *ought* that is commonly used in a fashion unrelated to valuation, which does not involve the concept of obligation and admittedly does not carry any ethical or moral implication. That is the use exemplified in this new sentence:

(2) He left at seven o'clock this morning; he ought to be in London by now.

This familiar use might well be termed the *inferential* use of *ought*, and is simply a brief way of asserting the inferential relation in "Since he left at seven o'clock this morning, he has had enough time for traveling to London by now, and therefore the inference that he has arrived there seems justified." This employment of *ought* obviously has nothing to do with whether the traveler went to London because of an obligation; nor is he obliged to spend only a reasonable minimum of time in getting there. There is no connotation of obligation in the inferential *ought*. It is simply a different special sense standing on its own, a simple ambiguity of a common word. However, it does invoke the frame of reference of "what ought to be" in an incidental sense, namely, that the world as it ought to be includes the specific reason-ableness of the particular inference expressed; it ought to be such a world that this inference is credible to reasonable persons and sufficiently so to warrant relevant conduct.

Although the inferential use is probably an offspring of the kind of use of *ought* with which we are concerned in our present inquiry, I wish also to leave it out of our ken for the explanation of matters of value. Specifically, I deny that the inferential use is involved in sample sentence (1). Its beginning, "There ought to be enough people . . .," leading to a syntactical *that* or *so that*, a result clause, does not in fact lead to a logical consequent. While this pattern resembles the pattern frequently found with the inferential use of *ought*, sample sentence (1) is not a primarily inferential statement. It is, more accurately speaking, the expression of a wish or an ideal. It is distinctly not an appraisal of a factual situation (like "He left at seven o'clock this morning") leading to an inferential conclusion (like "it is reasonable to infer that he is in London by now"). Thus, while sample sentence (1) does not make use of the concept of obligation in order to be meaningful, neither does it make use of this particular nonethical concept, that is, the concept of inference.

An additional use of *ought* that does not invoke obligation is commonly employed in hypothetical imperatives:

(3) If you want to keep out the winter cold, you ought to use window lights that consist of three layers of glass separated by air.

This sentence, constructed as a hypothetical proposition, embodies what we may designate as the *prudential* use of *ought*. Clearly there is no expression of a moral dimension here. The speaker leaves it to his listener to make the choice whether to do what is suggested, and even in fact the choice whether to adopt the objective (keeping out the winter cold) as a need or a desideratum. If he has this choice, he obviously has no obligation, moral or otherwise, according to the sentence (3) itself in usual contexts. Hence, we have now catalogued three familiar uses of *ought* in which it does not connote obligation. Yet I need further to identify and clarify the non-obligational use of *ought*, separate from these, that I do wish to employ in this inquiry, and in fact find central to it.

Some examples of this sort of employment of the term *ought* and of the concept it summons up are:

(4) The large, dark green and blue areas of this painting ought to be offset by a small area of a bright contrasting color.
(5) Neither students nor faculty members ought to wear frayed bluejeans to class.
(6) The flavor of the nutmeg ought to come through more strongly in the sauce.
(7) Even at age eighteen, a person ought to have a moderate pride as a basic motivation.
(8) The pace of life ought to be slower than it is for us in this decade.
(9) The Orioles play baseball the way it ought to be played.

It is my claim that each of these sentences asserts a conceived state of affairs that we would call a value, or, put another way, there is an assertion about a state of affairs as to how it would be well for that state of affairs to be; yet at the same time there is no claim that there is an obligation on the part of anyone to bring about the condition as asserted. Thus an application of *ought* is made in each case that does not assert a moral or other obligation, much less announce an inferential conclusion or a hypothesis for obtaining an indicated result. All that is said is that things ought to *be* thus-and-so. This is the fundamental, essential sense of the word *ought*, the sense I shall call the *simple ought* or *pure ought*.

One of the clearest examples of this non-obligational, simple application of *ought* is in a passage by Bertrand Russell. He wrote, "To explain what we mean by Good and Bad, we may say that a thing is good when on its own account it ought to exist, and bad when on its own account it ought not to exist."[4] Though I cannot accept some of the implications of this proposition, I can certainly comprehend it and can point it out to my reader as containing two clear instances of *ought* in the sense that affirms value but does not affirm obligation, the sense that is basic to all value-assertive statements and propositions. We can understand the difference between a thing's existence and its nonexistence, and we can further understand what is meant when someone says of a thing that it ought to exist rather than not.

I have said that the essential employment of *ought* in the present exposition of its simple use is to express a condition of that state of affairs which is symbolized by the terms of the value-assertive proposition that contains it. I have indicated that what condition this is, is best conveyed by holding in mind the contrast with *is* in the pair of phrases, *what ought to be* and *what is*. I have implied and now further assert that the condition of the mentioned state of affairs is known and held in mind by two parties when those two parties are engaged in controversy over a specific situation that one of them claims, and the other denies, ought to be—such as when one of them asserts that there ought to be capital punishment, special consideration for youthful entrants in the labor market, or publicly financed political campaigns, and the other asserts that there ought not to be capital punishment, special consideration for youthful entrants in the labor market, or publicly financed political campaigns. By communicating successfully with each other on the point on which they disagree, they demonstrate their *like* understanding of the condition symbolized by *ought* in their common language.

I believe that what actually happens in the experience of individuals, as their linguistic facility grows, is a progression in the opposite direction from that in which I have sketched my explanation. First, the individual encounters the use of the word *ought* in many instances, some with moral connotation and others without. From these he builds a conception of "that which ought to be," and this conception has its moral and nonmoral branches. By means of these conceptions, modified by the public concepts to the extent that he learns and heeds them, and although he does not generally remain explicitly conscious of or attentive to these conceptions, he comes to understand the value-assertive statements that enter his experience as expressions of what (morally or not) ought to be. Finally, and perhaps only with explicit teaching by others or instruction through reading, he becomes sufficiently sophisticated to abstract still further so as to be able to recognize in many value-assertive sentences a pattern that they have in common and that we express in the formula "X is good."

It is important to note in this sketch of typical experience that it begins in the full and rich fabric of the life situation and progresses toward the ever more abstract. When the young mind first hears "ought," it will be in a situation freighted with concrete detail including specific human relationships and human feelings. Yet it is not long until the developing intellect can meaningfully, successfully employ expressions (in listening sooner than in speaking) as general and as abstract as "That's the way it ought to be." The conjecture that our linguistic learning moves in this direction is borne out somewhat by a fact to which all of us can readily attest, namely, that in a controversy over a value such as a social moral value, our language becomes less particular and concrete and more general and abstract when it is the principle, rather than the application, to which we attach the greater importance. We incline to say "Abortion ought (or ought not) to be permitted" when discussing the matter of abortion as an issue in human rights; but we say "South Carolina ought (or ought not) to pass a law permitting abortion" when the point discussed is whether something should be available in South Carolina that is already available in a nearby state. There is a descending degree of abstractness in the expressions, "It ought to be that way," "Somebody ought to make it that way," "*You* ought to make it that way." In these examples, the element of claimed obligation enters only in the last, the most particular. The kind of *ought* above termed the *simple ought* in fact is more abstract than the *moral ought*, and may have an ancestral line to the *moral ought*, which has been effaced through increasing abstraction in our reflections upon issues of principle. Consistent with this conjecture is the fact that on many occasions we first conceive abstractly of states of affairs that will resolve our issues of principle, then we conceive of measures that could bring about those states of affairs, then, finally, we fix the responsibility upon certain parties to undertake those measures. Parliamentary and corporate bodies often are quite explicit in this order of procedure.

Thus it is clear that the expression *what ought to be* and its variants have one central conceptual meaning, that of the *pure ought*, the framing concept of our value-assertions, and that to this there may be added in different contexts one or more of a variety of secondary conceptual meanings. Some of these are apparent in some of the sample statements (4) through (9) above (p. 135). Not all *oughts* are moral *oughts*, although a great many of them in life situations are. The concept that makes *ought* moral in a given context is, therefore, a secondary rather than the primary or essential meaning that is always present in the conventional applications of the word. Other *oughts* are aesthetic; others religious; others prudential; still others are something else again, for which we may or may not have terms. When one hears an ought-judgment and then asks "Why?" he readily understands the answers "Because of moral considerations," or "For aesthetic reasons," and so on. Thus the simple *ought* was primary and was understood, and it was the secondary conceptual meaning for which inquiry was made. These usages argue for the primacy and greater simplicity of the pure *ought*, which is consistent with providing the frame of reference for all the different sorts of value-assertive propositions.

The elements contributing to the concept of the simple *ought* include a notion of similarities and differences that can apply across the various ways of appearing, and also a notion of the resultant of the operation of will. The first is probably operative, for the ordinary man in the street, as a notion of the difference between existence and nonexistence of an entity whose attributes he holds to be "the same" in either case. Of a physical object that he evaluates positively, he will say "It's good" and "It should be kept just the way it is," affirming by that language that the entity in question is as it ought to be. Of an entity that he would replace, he will say "It isn't good," or "It's bad," and "We should eliminate that and put something else there instead" (for example, "We should take out that AM radio and put an FM radio there instead"). Thus he is saying that the present entity is not as it ought to be, or is less as it ought to be than something else in its place would be. In our nomenclature in the present inquiry, we would explain that he is (for the latter case) comparing a present object in the physical mode with a potential object that he holds only in the mode of concept or of referent, or both. The objects are similar in the sense that one of them, say, a standard amplitude-modulation radio, which is physically present, is being compared to a radio having frequency-modulation reception, which is not physically present and exists for him only, as yet, in the mode of a radio of which he possesses the concept and the term. The two objects mentioned are similar in being radios, but they differ not only in construction but also in that one is appearing as a physical object and the other is appearing only as a concept and as the putative referent of the phrase that names it. They are different in that the physically present radio receives on amplitude-modulation bands, but the conceived of and potential radio, which may in fact not physically exist, receives on frequency-modulation bands. The crucial point for our examination of the value-assertion is the originator's ability to compare and contrast entities across the boundaries of the ways of appearing in consciousness. For all the value judgments that tend toward change rather than retention of what is already in place, that difference is a logical as well as a practical requisite.

Even in the case of a judgment that tends to favor the *status quo*, to the extent that the judgment is a complete one, not expressed before the thing being evaluated is compared with other items of the kind, there must be the comparing and contrasting across the boundaries of the ways of appearing. Let us consider an opera lover who says of a soprano, "She sang the role exactly as she ought" (or "She sang the role brilliantly," or "impeccably," or the like). Here the speaker is conceiving of two different things. One is the role as actually sung; the other is an interpretation or a collection of interpretations of the role other than as the speaker has heard it sung by the singer in question. In making his evaluation, the speaker is conceiving of the actual rendition, which is a physical-object entity occurring in space at a certain time, and of other possible renditions (as well perhaps as previous actual renditions of which he is aware). He recognizes a difference between the two, for he must in order to yield up his value judgment. Thus, even in the cases where the judgment comes out in favor of what has been actual or of what is the case, as contrasted with some non-actual entity, the ability to recognize similarities and differences across the modes of appearing is presupposed by the process of arriving at a value judgment and expressing it in a value-assertion.

The other ingredient required for the simple *ought* is the resultant of the operation of will. In the case of the opera lover, he might well say, "If I could have it my way, sopranos would always sing that role exactly as Madame has just now performed it." This is consonant with his value-assertion, and explains one aspect of it. On the other hand, the person who judges that an AM radio should be replaced by an FM radio is indicating, "If I could have it my way, there would be an FM radio in that place instead of the AM radio that is there now." Each of these speeches indicates what would be the result if it were the speaker's will and that will alone that influenced the state of affairs. Throughout our lives we have ample instances of successful and unsuccessful operations of the will. To perform our value judging, we project onto an envisioned state of affairs a quality that we take from the sort of experience in which the result of the operation of our will is realized.

This is not to say that every value assertion simply expresses a wish. There are, for example, times when a person speaks in this vein: "That is the way that it ought to be, and that is the way I would have it be, if it were up to me, but I will not lift a finger to make it so." There are, in other words, times when factors enter consciousness that would in practice offset the desire of the individual to realize his own ought-judgment. One such occasion might be when the envisioned state of affairs would be enormously costly in some respect. Another might be when he is considering the state of affairs in the abstract, aware that he is not relating it to conditions actually obtaining. Again, there are value-assertions whose originator qualifies them on account of his own limitations of knowledge or some other factor. He would say, in effect, "So far as I know what the pertinent conditions are, I judge that *X* ought to be the case, but I am open, upon becoming better informed, to believe otherwise." Therefore we cannot say that in every value-assertion an *actual* element of the originator's will is a part of the total expression, the value-assertion.[5] He may wish to have it understood that his value-assertion is not unqualified. However, the notion of the result of the will is part of the conceptual *meaning* of his assertion, even if his actual will itself is not asserted. As such, it is necessary to the understanding of the *ought*, for if that element were lacking, we should have no indication that the envisioned difference would make a difference—that it would be important or meaningful in human terms.

Further, it is timely to point out that just as a valuation is not essentially the expression of a wish, neither is it the affirmation of a liking. We do often evaluate positively, and highly, things that we like, but neither the events nor the meanings are the same. One's assertion that one likes something is a psychological report. It is empirical, and it may be verified, normally with a fairly high degree of accuracy. But our assertions of what ought to be the case occasionally fly in the face of our assertions of what we like. I like doing what makes me weigh 200 pounds—I like eating large quantities of delicious foods; but I ought to do what will make me weigh 170 pounds—I ought to eat sparingly. Everyone has had experiences that have led him to say, "What I like to do and what I ought to do are two different things."

The basic factor in the meaning of *ought*, then, is the *pure* or *simple ought*, which is the framing idea for all ought-assertions of any kind. We say of *x* that it is good, meaning that it ought to exist rather than not, or that specimens of the type within which *x* falls ought to be more like *x* than not. This is the common strand that runs through all the favorable valuative judgments, and whose negative runs through all the unfavorable valuative judgments. I shall endeavor now to show how, by applying the *pure ought*, we go on to create from the world of the actual a different, non-actual or only partly actual, conceptual, and ideal or idealized realm, the realm of value, the world as it ought to be.

This simple concept can be held in mind by such phrasing as *that which ought to exist or to take place, thought independently of that which does exist or take place.* What this concept clearly relates to is change and action; for of anything that *is*, it is the belief of the originator of a value judgment upon it either that this thing is as it ought to be and ought not to be changed, or else that it is *not* as it ought to be and hence ought to be changed. Thus value judgments may be applied to anything and everything whatsoever; the idea of the *ought* is therefore just as inclusive as the idea of existence. Like the idea of existence, it is a signal, not of a property of some thing, but rather of our stance toward it, our categorization of it. Now we readily categorize things as existing or not existing, in one or another mode of existence. We are almost as quick to classify things as belonging to what ought to be or to what ought not to be. *To say this is mainly to say that we acknowledge and react to what we encounter in our experience.*

It is appropriate to seek in a childhood situation for an instance of the pure *ought*, since by the time we are mature, we devote most of our time to specific activities of complex purposes, and we are habituated to perform, even in moments of idleness, acts having connections with the fields in which the special kinds of ought-judgment are characteristic.

Consider the following situation. One winter's day, Wilbur, returning home from school, notices that the fall of melting snow from the garage roof has tipped a stick of kindling wood so that one end sticks up rather than lying flat on the stack of firewood beside the garage. Upon contemplating it, Wilbur says to himself, "I ought to see whether I can knock it down with a snowball."

Now as I conceive this incident of child's play, there is surely no moral reason for throwing a snowball, but equally, unless a person or piece of property is endangered, there is no moral reason prohibiting it. The boy sees how things are, envisions something else that might be, and simply is curious about whether it *could* be and what it would be like to make it so. Or perhaps he is charmed, so to speak, by his intuitions of how it is and of how it could be, as he sees the one before him and imagines the other. He may be aware that if he succeeds in hitting the stick with a snowball he will experience pleasure from doing so. His reasons for trying perhaps include this; but they may also be balanced by awareness that so long as he fails, he has occasion to continue throwing and will continue to feel the enjoyment of throwing snowballs. At any rate, Wilbur's activity exhibits two important features. First, it exhibits the ought in very pure form, unmixed with moral, prudential, or other factors. Second, it is like much child's play in that the individual has an *action* as the object of his judgment, not a static situation. It appears to the child in play not so much that a state of affairs ought to *be*, but that there is something that ought to be *done* (for children surely are more interested in activity than in states of rest).

For children younger than Wilbur, much play is imitative; the action consists in imitating the father and mother as the child "plays house," or enacts other roles. These children know what ought to be done because they have seen their adult models do it. As for children older than Wilbur, no longer preoccupied with snowball throwing for its own sake, play may have the form of engaging in hobbies, in which there is an interaction between free choice and observation of rules in the form of "directions" or "instructions." While no doubt many an unfinished model ship or plane owes its incompletion to failure of perseverance of the young maker, I am sure that an additional large number owes its lapse simply to the fact that as activity draws to a close, there is no longer the object of fascination—the performance of the activity—that brought about the undertaking. Engagement in sports, which in large part replaces other forms of play for most adolescents and adults, is further instance of the action itself being the object of the judgment as to what ought to be (that is, ought to be taking place).

It is in adult life that we are more apt to think in terms of what states of affairs more permanently ought to *be*. However, this usually is thought in relation to the enabling of one or more actions, often of repeated actions. In planning the house, we say, "There ought to be a door in the kitchen wall leading into the garage." Once the plan is executed, then the state of affairs is that there *be* such a door; but it is there, it exists, for the sake of countless goings to and comings from the garage protected from the weather. Similarly, the state and the act might be expressed in the inverse order. "I ought to go and buy a blender and put it in my kitchen" expresses an act as the object of an ought-judgment such that the act would come about—"exist"—for the sake of the state of affairs (which in turn would exist for the sake of other, different acts, and so on). Thus it is possible for either an act or a state of affairs to be the object of an ought-judgment.

A conclusion that is reinforced by these observations is that the *ought* concept, equally applicable to actions or to states of affairs, admits no metaphysical superiority or inferiority to the one or the other, and hence no priority in the generating of value judgments. It is interesting that there has been an issue originating with Moore and Ross as to whether *good* (of things) or *right* (of actions) is primary, or whether both are independently real so that neither alone suffices to found ethical theory. In chapter nine I shall offer objections to the intuitionism of the proponents of these; beyond that, I find my remaining interest in the issue to be in the niceties of our language that the controversy exposes, rather than in metaphysical claims about these as reals, or in epistemological claims about them as the objects of moral intuitions. Prichard has stated, "The word 'ought' refers to actions, and actions alone."[6] I must contradict, not by affirming that *ought* refers to states of affairs alone, but rather by asserting that it may refer both to actions and to states. In "What this study ought to have is a swivel chair," a state of affairs is the object of the ought-judgment; in "I ought to go out and get a swivel chair for this study," an action is its object. The important feature of their difference is not that one is a state and the other an action, though related to it. Rather, it is the assignment of an agent, in the expression through action, where agency has been left undetermined in the expression through a state of affairs. That addition is crucial to the origin of moral judgment, and will be examined later (chapter fifteen).

Further considering the concepts *value* and *existence* and their relations, we may fruitfully ask, in parallel fashion to the well-known problem concerning existence, "Is value a predicate?" It is obvious that the answer, if by *predicate* we mean "property exhibited by an object," is no. *Value too, like existence, is a principle of classification.* In the same way as has been done with existence, *value* can be thought of as a universalization of the innumerable instances of value, the discrete "values," encountered in human life. However, there is the fundamental difference that these instances of value are themselves not mere existents, but rather include the judgings upon existents and nonexistents by which humans respond to the existents that they encounter. Every valuing, every act of value judgment, has some existent as an object of judgment, in *some* mode if not the physical-object mode of existence; and this circumstance has led many to assert that value is existential and real and factual. However, those existents by themselves are not values; they are, as it were, *envaluated;* they have value imposed upon them by value-judges. In one sense, a world without rational minds would be a world without value, for no value judging would occur to constitute anything a value. In another sense, of course, if the world were otherwise the same but there were no rational beings, it would still contain other things that in fact we, who do now exist, do value; and one of our usages permits us to call those things values, effacing from our own sight the function that our own value judging has had in constituting them values. One might idiomatically say, "Even in a world without human beings, gold would still be more valuable than iron," but the tortuous attempt to qualify the statement to make it plausible would bring forth more clearly what is already visible in the statement itself, that it is the relation to the human being that is essential to the idea of the valuable.

Having asked whether value is a predicate, as we have long ago done for existence, we cannot sidestep the next question, suggested by our answer: "Are there modes of value, just as there are modes of existence?" Here, things are different. *Prima facie,* we may be tempted to answer yes, for we know of various kinds of value—utilitarian value, aesthetic value, moral value. But these kinds of value are not modes of value in the same way as certain modes are modes of existence, and this is in the nature of the case. The modes of existence are, as it were, kinds of existence that various things may possess— kinds of ways of appearing within which we may classify things we encounter in consciousness. But the functionally important, and in that sense basic, question about the existence of *x* is whether *x* exists *in a certain specified mode* of existence. Otherwise the question answers itself by the mention of *x; x* exists in some mode of existence, just by virtue of its being mentioned, though that normally is not what makes the question "Does *x* exist?" interesting to the questioner. However, it is not a basic question whether a value exists as utilitarian and not aesthetic or moral, or as moral but not aesthetic or utilitarian, and the like. An *x* does not pass from one mode of value to another, or spread out over a number of modes, in the way that an *x* with respect to its existence may inhabit one or more than one mode of existence, or pass (for example) from physical object to memory, or from dream to concept, or the like. An *x* that is valued may be classified in more than one field of value, *not* with respect to its existence, but rather with respect to the action or inaction for which it is the incentive. We may of course ask these questions, but in doing so we are not questioning what is fundamental to the notion of value. What is fundamental is the pure oughtness applied to the existence of an object that is valuated. Thus, *what is required in the way of modes for value are not separate modes of value, but are modes of existence,* and these are of course the very same modes of existence that obtain with respect to the objects of existence, of "what is." We may inquire of an object, whether it exists as a physical object, or in concept, or in imagination, or as a dream, and so on; and of the very same object, we may inquire whether it *ought to* exist as a physical object, or ought to exist in concept, or ought to exist in imagination or as a dream. One may say, for example, that poverty ought to exist only in the minds of planners and legislators whose tasks are to see that society avoids it, and that it ought not to exist in the physical mode of being. In a loose way we might say that values do not have modes of their own because the same modes of existence suffice for values just as they do for existence. This description of the rationale of values with respect to modes of existence reinforces our suggestion that value is not a property of existing things but rather is a way we have of looking at existing and non-existing things. And this peculiarity in which values are different from factually existing things, in not having modes of their own, is what makes it possible that values and facts may interact, for that is something they do not do externally but do in human consciousness.

We use the idea that we call *existence* to help frame our thinking, to respond to and register the objects that occur in our consciousness as having a given mode or modes of occurrence, and not others. Now it can be seen that we use the idea of *value* in the same way, adding to the belief reached about existence a further belief about the oughtness of that existence.

Let us look back on our snowball thrower to recapitulate some kinds of ought-judgment. In the simple fact that he judges "I ought to see whether I can knock the stick down with a snowball," Wilbur judges with the pure *ought*. This is not even a prudential *ought*, for it envisions no particular subsequent benefit from the action. If also he envisions the tumble of the struck stick as itself satisfying, Wilbur's ought-judgment to that extent may contain the aesthetic *ought*. If he throws partly from thinking that throwing will be fun, pleasure, then to that extent it will also be an egoistic, hedonic *ought*. If in this boy's culture, when snow is on the ground any apparent target that may be upset is simply always thrown at, then his judgment contains the *ought* of tradition. And so on. But if I remember or observe childhood well, I am justified in suggesting that for our lad simply the pure *ought* dominates among these motives. He throws simply to *real*-ize what it would be to knock down the stick. And this exemplifies a fundamental human tendency, the tendency we have to be in action except when usefully resting ourselves. It is considerably from this tendency, I daresay, that the thinking that generates the pure *ought* derives.

A fulfillment or a satisfaction is the result, or actually the corollary, of any action and accompanies any activity, even idle or pointless activity. Over and above such fulfillment there may be a resultant pain or pleasure; and anticipation that it will be pleasure rather than pain is an added motive to perform the activity. It is, I take it, a psychological principle that (since it is man's nature to act, be active, to undertake behavior rather than remain passive) the very carrying out of activity is accompanied by satisfaction. That satisfaction is the logical corollary of the activity carried out; psychologically, other things being balanced out, it is *felt* as a satisfaction.

Now let us go further into the scene involving Wilbur and try in our description of it to reach the level of the brush-stroke. The things that are incentives to our curious boy are pretty simple elements of the world as it is and as it might be. One is the very oddness of the stick's being tipped up. The boy's generalized belief about sticks is that they lie flat. This exceptional stick stimulates a notion that *this* stick *could* lie flat like the others, hence could conform to the generalization rather than being out of line. Further, the presence of snow tends to be a pretty constant subliminal feature of consciousness for children, and impressions of the texture and weight of snow, its compressibility and pliancy, give intuitions of satisfying feelings, a consciousness of control over this pleasant feature of nature, as one shapes snow into a snowball. The kinetic and kinaesthetic tones of the act of throwing are attractive, are, so to speak, worth trying out. The idea of subduing something that can be regarded as an obstacle (the upstart stick) at a single stroke assists in making a concept of oneself, one's powers and abilities, that one would enjoy. Simply to have interacted with the environment, then above that to have changed it without oneself in the process becoming detrimentally changed, is pleasant to experience and to know.

While there might have been other activities and projects with which Wilbur might have chosen to fill the same stretch of time, I am not now trying to account for the choice of this activity over another. I am attempting to show on a fundamental level the things that serve the boy as incentives. They are factual, particular qualities of his environment and his experiential activity—his perceiving, his memory, his interpreting, his projecting of possibilities for the future. They all blend together rather than occurring in atomistic isolation. They exhibit to him not only simple qualities, but qualities in relation to one another, then qualities (of a new level) of the relations so apprehended. All of these make up for him a total structure of qualities, compounded of the actual and also the potential. Within the structure some of the qualities apprehended are incentives, *values;* these incentives are, or may be, either the factual current situation wholly seen as a structure of values, to be preserved; or else they may be rearrangements of the experienced things, into conceived or imagined rather than physically existent objects, the things in rearrangement being seen as values, as what ought to be. Since this young human is inclined to act somehow anyway, these rearranged qualities beckon to his tendency to act, and he "follows suit," as it were, to act as they invite.

There are obvious differences in the sketch of how a youngster is spurred to activity by the sort of incentive that appeals to him and the sort of thing done by an adult in the process of daily life. Wilbur's slight escapade demonstrates for us the play of incentives free from the cares of the moral relationships and even of the prudential, practical relationships of mature life. We will eventually look at the sorts of incentive that come into operation when we make decisions and choices in those more demanding realms. Before that, however, in the next chapters let us review the ways by which it has been proposed, in the tradition in value theory, that we have grounded our value judgments and arrived at our value-assertive propositions.

8

How We Ground Value Judgments
I. Authority, Irrationality, Emotion

We have seen that there is no separate realm containing a body of existents or events of its own, to supply us with what, if we may mince words for a moment, would be called "value-facts," by means of which to test the correspondence of our value-assertive statements to something real. Yet this circumstance does not lead us to skepticism, for not only would that conclusion fail to show us the basis of our day-to-day acts of valuation; it would also be so far from according with the facts of our lives as we experience them that we should find it unacceptable. For we *do* have value experience, we *do* make evaluations, and we *do* arrive at satisfaction that our valuations have been both rational and adequately based on what we take to be real. Further, skepticism is not the sole possible outcome of our reasoning concerning statements involving the concept of value. Consequently, our next task is to see what other possibilities may appear and to discover whether some other possibility is more plausible than a skeptical result.

The approach to the assessment of values, hence origination of value judgments, need not be solely through the question "How can we know what ought to be?" Rather, we may approach it from the point of view of the quality of judging, itself—of the circumstance that some of the persons we know do a better job of making value judgments and constructing scales of values than other persons we know. If we accept that generalization as true, we can find some useful implications in it. I for one am glad to accept it as true, for I have known some persons whom I have greatly respected for their ability to respond to events from a point of view within what I would call a wisely selected set of values, to be guided by these in their decisions, and to be active not only in exemplifying them but in constantly reappraising and improving the array of values that they espouse. Further, we all have the experience of improving upon our own value judgments from time to time, as we gather moral experience, develop in our aesthetic tastes, and the like. This to me is in itself adequate evidence that it is not the case that one value judgment is as good as another, that valuations are nothing but subjective, incorrigible caprice. Evidently there is some basis for ranking value judgments themselves as good or poor, better or worse.

The implications are two. First, the very possibility that I discern the higher quality of Smith's value judgments over Jones's argues the possibility, not the impossibility, of there being valuations of valuations themselves, of there being some solutions that are better than others to the problem of which value-assertions to believe. Second, the fact that I recognize the superiority of Smith's valuing activity presupposes that I can and do perform significant valuation of valuations; I can find it in my experience that I do so. That being the case, I probably can discover when it is that I do so; therefore, perhaps I can discover *how* I do so.

In these few paragraphs I have, I think, employed the terms *value, scale of values, array of values* in quite ordinary English that successfully communicates. But I believe that other expressions I have heretofore used are truer to the situation as regards values, and I shall continue employing that other set of usages rather than to speak of values as though I were speaking of something substantive. The term *value* translates, I believe, into something like "objects of attention (not to imply objects of any other sort of reality) of an originator of statements when he is originating value-assertive statements." This is a more cautious position than that taken by a speaker or writer who confidently uses *values* as though there were referent objects in external reality for his term. (We hear and read of "Christian values," "American values," "the values of Western civilization," "values one could fight and die for," "the values of primitive as contrasted with civilized societies.") Thus to say that one "espouses such-and-such a value" is said with stricter accuracy in the words "attaches belief to such-and-such a value-assertive proposition." To say that someone "compares values," such as comparing the values of the capitalist and the communist, or of the Christian and the Buddhist, or of the suburbanite and the ghetto dweller, is better said in words like "compares the value-assertive propositions which the parties holding them, respectively, believe." To say that Smith holds a better set of values than Jones is more accurately said in such words as "Smith believes value-assertive propositions P, Q, and R, whereas Jones believes value-assertive propositions S, T, and V; and furthermore, I who originate the present judgment believe the value-assertive proposition that Smith's structure of beliefs in this regard is better than that of Jones."

Several points must be met at once. It may appear that little is accomplished by setting up my own valuations as superior to Smith's and Jones's, which I seem to be doing when I arrogate to myself the function of judging theirs either individually or comparatively. For how do I either justify Smith's valuations vis-à-vis those of Jones, or my own vis-à-vis those of either Smith or Jones? Again, do I think that I have removed some of the mystery from the idea of the process of valuation by rephrasing it in terms of believing value-assertive propositions? Is not the process of fixing belief likely to prove just as mysterious as the process of valuation?

To address the latter point first, I state that the purpose of the rephrasing is to defer until later the question of the substantiality or definability of *value*, and rather to reach it through a mode of procedure we have already found fruitful, namely, the study of the ways in which rational humans use language. We need not believe value to be an entity in order to study it, and indeed we ought not, for to believe it so is to beg a question that has been hotly controverted. Rather, when we study the ways in which humans do use language, we are studying an actuality substantial enough to be called objective, and on which numerous, diverse observers can agree; and the success already enjoyed beckons us to strive for further success through this means. In the present case, the rephrasing shows that *to espouse a value* may be expressed as to hold a certain kind of belief, something that I presume every reader will grant, at least for the sake of following the argument of these pages. This expression produces the advantage of showing that the originator of the judgment of comparison is not and cannot be a neutral observer, like the ideal laboratory scientist, but is a participant in the same process as that which he is studying—a fact too easily forgotten. Further, whereas the logic of value is as yet its infancy and handles controversial matters in perhaps controversial ways, the logic of propositions, of potential beliefs, is fairly well understood and relatively uncontroversial. We may as well see how far it will take us.

We are now led back to the earlier point, the question of my justifying *my own* judgment when I make my claim that Smith's collection of beliefs in the form of value-assertive propositions on some topic is superior to Jones's collection of the same sort. The explanation for this point is by its nature required to be a much longer one. It will occupy us, off and on, throughout the remainder of this book.

Granting that valuations are in fact made, which is to say that people do come to attach belief to certain value-assertive propositions as against others, traditional discussions suggest that the possibilities for their grounds include these:

(1) The attachment of belief to a value-assertive proposition arises from the conditioning of the subject by his social peers or leaders, such as parents, teachers, friends, figures he emulates, governmental or military or religous superiors, or others. This basis for valuations is *authority*. This basis may function in a given case more as a cause than as a reason—that is, it may be determinative upon the subject without reflection by him, rather than as a result of his deliberative choice of whether to yield to authority, or of which authority to follow.

(2) The attachment of belief to a value-assertive proposition is simply *irrational*, and not to be explained by causes or reasons.

(3) The attachment of belief to a value-assertive proposition arises from the emotion dominating, or from the resultant of the various emotions present, in a situation at the time when the subject fixes his belief. This is a basis for valuations in *emotion*.

(4) The attachment of belief to a value-assertive proposition arises from the intuitive recognition of a quality in a state of affairs, such as the goodness of a good object or the rightness of a right act, and the value-assertive proposition arises as the expression of this intuitive recognition; it is the meaning of the value-assertive proposition. This is a basis for valuations in an experiential *intuition*.

(5) The attachment of belief to a value-assertive proposition arises from a reasoned projection of the relationships, such as causal consequences, of a state of affairs or of a change that is imagined or conceived, or from other actual, anticipated, or potential facts. This is a *rational* basis for valuation.

A simplistic way of seeing the problem of value would lead an inquirer, after surveying a list such as this, to ask, "Well, now, which of the five is it?" The assumption would be that if one of these five were the basis for valuation, it must therefore not be any of the other four. However, in my endeavor to describe experience as it actually occurs, I will in the sequel support the position that not simply one or another but, in actual fact, *all of these* are in one way or another origins of value-assertive propositions. That sequel may, however, also be expected to lead us to a valuation upon that state of affairs itself. In other words, while people do actually ground their value judgments in all of these ways, we need not infer that it is not open to us to select certain ones among them over others, nor that there is no proper and reasonable basis upon which we may do so.

The first thing to do is to acknowledge the first suggestion, that belief is sometimes adopted upon authority, then dismiss it from the list. Each of us is probably willing to concede that some of his valuative beliefs at some stage of his life have been reached on the basis of sheer authority. The child absorbs valuations from his parents and siblings long before he is able to articulate his own deliberations or otherwise to arrive at original valuative beliefs. Some of us are willing to admit that we continue doing this to some extent throughout life, either because we accord adequate justification to the authority to whom we turn,[1] or because it is simply easier or more convenient to yield to another, or because a given valuation is not important enough to warrant investing one's time or energies. But the same thing is true of the method of authority in fixing valuations as is true of that method as a basis for factual knowledge, namely, that it does not suffice as a basis, because it merely pushes the question a step further along in the inquiry. Upon what foundation does the authority base *his* value-assertive propositions?

Each of the four items remaining on the list provides instruction for us, as we look more closely at it. I appeal to the reader's knowledge of life and his experience of people to seek his concurrence that in fact individuals do base belief in value-assertive propositions upon each of these four possible grounds. My personal experience, sometimes most plainly that of childhood, provides me with examples. Some readers will agree that their experience does also. In addition, we will need to acknowledge that total structures of value-beliefs are highly complex indeed, and that therefore it should not be surprising that the four bases are sometimes intermixed, the value-beliefs of individuals or groups are sometimes mutually inconsistent, the structures are incomplete, and any exhaustive description of the entirety is a practical impossibility.

Some readers may reply that it is true, to be sure, that people *do* use more than one of the bases listed, to arrive at valuation; but that in doing so they are using spurious bases and therefore are arriving at fallacious beliefs. I believe I shall eventually meet this objection *passim* and on the whole, by presenting a more plausible alternative view of valuation than that presented in any one of the items on the list above. I shall undertake to do so from the viewpoint of a renunciation of the position mentioned, that there is but one right or genuine basis for valuation. This renunciation in turn springs from abandonment of the model already cited, the assumption that there are actual "value-facts" to which correct value-assertions correspond, just as there are presumably actual molecules to which chemistry's descriptions of molecules correspond, or baseball games to which sportscasters' play-by-play narrations correspond. The burden of proof for "value-facts" is on those who claim their existence, or who assume the model of correspondence; and in the history of value theory they have yet to prove their claim. My description of the value process makes it essentially a different kind of process, with different origins and motivations, than descriptive processes. Implicit in it is the view that values are not real entities on a plane with physical entities that are simply given in experience. A corollary is that there are not separate value-intuitions (which would have as their objects of intuition the "value-facts," if such existed), but that value-beliefs are generated from no special sort of intuitions. If the term *intuition* is correctly applied in certain ways in any sort of epistemological inquiry, it will be correctly applied in the same way in inquiries that investigate value belief, rather than differently from the way in which it is applied in investigations of factual belief.

We shall now look at each of the remaining four possible bases of valuation. When we are candid with ourselves, most of us willingly identify some value-assertive belief that we have fixed upon without knowing a reason, or possibly even having no reason. Some will affirm that this is necessarily what happens. It is alleged that freedom (especially the dreadful freedom asserted by the existentialist), by nature, makes value judging necessarily irrational, for to judge thus-and-so for a *reason* is a failure of freedom. One who judges by such a criterion, it is argued, is not free but bound. The existentialist affirms that freedom to choose is at once man's ultimate nature and the condition of the continuing absurdity of his world; that the world is absurd and without rational pattern is offered as a descriptive truth. To be true to his nature, then, the authentic man must be choosing, but it must be the case with his choosing that he is *freely* choosing; another way of saying what this comes to is that he is freely choosing but it must not matter what he chooses. Now, probably only a portion (and I shall not attempt to guess what portion) of those who confess to irrationally based value choices will profess that it is because they believe the existentialist description to be true that they have done so. Nevertheless, if the irrationalist position on founding value choices is to be defended—that is, if a value-assertive proposition favoring belief in it is to be urged—the existentialist's is probably the only ground on which the defense can be taken seriously, for this is an irrationalist defense, as much, I think, as anything can be a genuinely irrationalist defense.

I believe that to the extent that the irrationalist position is an argument favoring the irrational way of founding value judgments, it can be set aside. Presumably nothing could be more futile than arguing with a thoroughgoing irrationalist and offering *reasons* for him to change his position. However, if there is a thoroughgoing irrationalist, he is undoubtedly enjoying (or suffering) his position rather than bothering to defend it. The person for whom one should be concerned in this matter is the one who, though not an irrationalist himself, is asking whether the irrationalist principle is descriptively true and whether the consequence therefore is that he might be forced to believe it although he should prefer otherwise. But we can assure this person that the irrationalist position has no merit. Most of us—the radical irrationalists being the exceptions—who are willing to grant that at some time we have *without reason* invested belief in any proposition, whether value-assertive or fact-assertive, are, as it were, philosophically shamefaced about it. Thus, we have already attached belief to the value-assertive proposition that it is better to be rational than irrational in fixing our beliefs. In keeping with this commitment or similar ones, we probably also believe it is better to believe that things are *as* they are rather than to believe otherwise. This is why we are open to the *possibility* that the irrationalist principle truly describes the value-judging situation. Thus the irrationalist who would try to persuade us to accept that description as factual—and some irrationalists admit that they are given over to flights of reason at times, even though they decline to be bound by them—is using not his own position but *our* position to attempt to win us to *his* position. Insofar as he attempts to persuade us, then, exactly that far his instruments of choice and decision are by nature defective relative to *his* purpose and beliefs, and are incapable of achieving the result that he declares follows from them. On this ground we can decline to accept the view that since some value judgments are arrived at irrationally, we should believe either that all of them are or else that all of them ought to be.

But further, let us look at the substance of the irrationalist position on the foundation of value judging. That the position is shallow is, I think, shown as follows. I deny that to judge thus-and-so for a reason is a failure of freedom, a lapse into being determined by the reason and therefore into being un-free. Rather, I should point out that when I exercise my freedom, usually I do not exercise it in the absolute but rather in a limited set of circumstances, in a situation such that I have actually two or three or some larger, but finite, number of choices set before me. I am, let us say, grading a student's work of a semester. There are a limited number of marks I can give; the whole alphabet is not at my disposal. Or I am planning to purchase a boat; I cannot buy a battleship or a ferryboat because I can command only so much money and am therefore limited in my selection to vessels of, say, up to thirty feet in length and no more. Or an even more stringent example: I am a member of a jury sitting in judgment of a criminal case. I may vote either "guilty" or "not guilty," and have no other options than these. In the last of these examples—which is the most convenient to use, although the same points will apply to the others—I am *free* to choose to say either "guilty" or "not guilty." I do *not* lose my freedom if I say "guilty" on grounds of the evidence or "not guilty" on grounds that I do not find the evidence sufficient to support a verdict of "guilty." I am no less free to choose either vote simply because I have a reason for my vote, for I would equally have had a reason for the other vote, if it had been the other vote that I had chosen.

But, the reply is made, no matter which one you chose for your vote, you were not free. Say you chose the verdict "guilty"; you were compelled by the weight of evidence. Say instead that you had chosen "not guilty"; you were compelled by the lack of evidence. Either way you were compelled.

This rebuttal does not hold. One way of countering it is to treat it as a dilemma and supply a counter-dilemma: I chose "guilty" because I was free to consider the evidence sufficient rather than insufficient; or else I chose "not guilty" because I was free to regard the evidence as insufficient rather than convincing. In this riposte the two disputants stand on equally good or bad ground, the rebuttal and the counter-rebuttal being, as it were, made of the same stuff, so that my opponent has no better argument than I do.

However, I think the pattern of the conclusive argument is better shown by taking an example in which the reason supporting one option is not simply the negation of the reason supporting the other. I was once picking out a shirt in a store. I had narrowed my choice to two (thus performing already, of course, an act of considerable freedom). One shirt had a light tone, the other a dark tone, of the same color. I could have chosen the first, which matched my eyes, or I could have chosen the second, which was more fashionable. I now report that I freely chose one of them. If I actually did choose the lighter shirt, I chose it for the reason that it matched my eyes; but if I actually did choose the darker, my choosing was for the reason that it was more in style. In either case, I freely chose the shirt that I selected, and also in whichever case was the actual one, my choosing was for a reason. Thus I not only chose a shirt; I also, simultaneously, *chose a reason* to realize, in the act of choosing a shirt. Prior to my choosing, it was simply a fact that the lighter tone matched my eyes and simply another fact that the dark tone was fashionable. By my choice, I not only selected a shirt; I also treated one of the two aforesaid facts in a different way from the way I treated the other. I *constituted* one of the facts the *reason* I did what I actually did; and *my so constituting it was a free act of my own.*

I do not want my point to be mistaken. I am not arguing all over again the issue of freedom versus determinism. I am of course espousing the side of free choice, but so is the irrationalist. I deny what he asserts, however, that if it is to prove the freedom of the free choice, one's choosing must make no sense. I deny that freedom of choice must be defined only as choice for no reason, rather than as choice (which he then claims is no free choice) for a reason. Rather, I affirm that I am as free as he is, but further that my freedom includes the freedom to choose among reasons as well as the freedom to choose among actions or beliefs. Hence, if there has been an occasion on which I have fixed my belief with *no* reason, I know that I have not done as much as I can do in the situation in order to arrive at the best available belief. I should therefore judge myself adversely upon that occasion and charge myself in the future to do better.

This inquiry into the irrationalist ground for fixing valuative belief gives us a principle that is very important for our eventual description of the valuative process, our developed response to the question "How do you know what ought to be?" The principle is that we are free not only in the choices we make on a given level, but we are also free in the choices on the level of reasons for the choices of the first-mentioned level. A fact, a principle, or whatever it might be, is a reason because we *treat it as* a reason, and we are free to treat it so or not.

The survey of the irrational as the ground of value-judging thus shows us that in fact some value-judging does take place on irrational bases, but also that most persons—indeed, all persons to the extent that they are rational— adversely judge the practice of so founding them. Most persons so judge implicitly, even though on a few occasions or in connection with a few issues singled out for special attention a few proclaim that they judge independently of a rational ground. Most persons evidently presuppose that it is false that the only free choice is the choice that is made without a reason; they regard it as open to themselves to choose reasons as well as—and anterior to or simultaneously with—choosing actions and beliefs. I am among those who so regard it, and I shall soon invite the reader to follow a discussion of grounds for arriving at a different preference from that of the irrationalist, among the possible bases of fixing belief upon value-assertive propositions.

Some of us occasionally confess to having adopted a value-belief "for no reason" when a moment's reflection shows that we should more accurately have said "for an emotional reason," or still more strictly, "by virtue of an emotional cause." For example, someone may believe of himself that he had attached belief to a given value-assertive proposition "for no reason," when in fact he had been caused to believe it by being told it by a person with whom he was in love. That this sort of thing can readily happen shows us how little we know or heed our own states or activities of mind, and perhaps also how little we watch epistemological relations when we are attempting to establish our knowledge. However, cases of this sort are quite common and, as we say, quite human. This is another instance in which the person who identifies for us the nature of the ground of his belief (in this case mistakenly, until we persuade him to seek further) has already committed himself to one or more of the possible bases of fixation of belief, and actually against one or more of them also. He certainly prefers some basis other than the irrational; the sign of this preference is that he feels or reports it a confession of shortcoming that he has established a particular belief "for no reason." Thus the usage in the context tends to bear out the impression that typically a person confessing to occasonal lapses into irrationality does not in fact prefer that basis as his general basis for value judging, although he does occasionally (inconsistently with his usual practice) employ it.

Two linguistic points briefly considered will be instructive here. To elicit the first, let us suppose that a friend reports one of his value judgments to us and adds the remark, "I believe this for no reason," or "I had no reason—I just chose to believe it." Let us say further that he has actually accepted the judgment because he simply derived a pleasure from affirming to himself that he judged so. This is a frequent and typical kind of case, which explains various fads and popular movements. Now, strictly speaking, it may be accurate for our friend to say that he had arrived at his judgment for no *reason*, but that is not to say that he arrived at it without grounds. His ground was an immediate emotion. Our friend's explicit statement is that the ground was not a reason, and since we distinguish between reasons and causes, it is easy to suggest that the remark shows that the judgment was not reached for a reason but rather through a cause—that is, that it was indeed not a free judgment. Judgments, as we have shown above, may be made freely yet with reasons or for reasons; by contrast, judgments may also be made by virtue of causes, but if they are so made, they are not made freely and are not "autonomous judgments," or judgments made by the autonomous individual as such, exercising his autonomy.

Our friend, if he were candid, would probably concur about his remission of autonomy. However, this concurrence does not refute the proposition that value judgments may be made—value-assertive beliefs may be chosen—freely. Rather, it merely reminds us that our freedom is a thing won hard and over a period of time. We have little of it as infants, more in youth, and the greatest amount in our intellectual maturity. (Perhaps the same sequence also holds for societies and for the species on the whole.) It is our experience that there are times when we *are* in fact caused in some of our mental events such as judgments and decisions. However, also in our experience there are other occasions when we do make judgments and decisions quite freely. One of the best demonstrations of the latter is those experiences that occur to all of us in which we overturn a belief or judgment that originally was caused or determined externally to our own minds, and put in its place a belief or judgment that we have arrived at after deliberate reflection in which we do choose reasons and choose an outcome freely. All of us have had occasion to say something like "I see now that when I was young I believed that statement only because my father did. When I thought it over for myself, I came to believe quite differently." Again, one may recognize an early cause for a belief (such as the child's unquestioning acceptance of what he is told, when he is told that a benevolent God exists and watches over him), which he gives up as his ground for believing, *while yet holding on to the same belief for a more recently chosen reason* (such as his consideration and intellectual acceptance of the ontological proof for the existence of God).

Our second linguistic point is brought out by language that might be used by the same friend who gave us the first, and in the same situation. With slightly greater accuracy he might have said, as people often do, "I had no reason for choosing that. I just felt like it." The addition of the latter statement indicates a further general view of some importance to us. It shows that persons generally downgrade emotions as a ground for arriving at a belief, setting them below reasons proper, below what is called a *reason* in contrast to what one "just feels like." Here our idiom shows, I think, that most of us do in fact rate reasons higher than emotional causes as determining grounds for belief. This is easily accounted for by the very fact that most of us highly value freedom, and valuing on grounds of reasons is a more free thing than valuing by virtue of emotional causes. Surely the man in the street is well aware of this distinction, even if not articulate about it, and is accurately reflecting his attitudes in the language that he uses. It cannot be claimed that he on *no* occasions adopts value-assertions (or other beliefs) on emotional grounds; none but the least perceptive of us could affirm that. But it does show that, whatever the frequency of his employment of the one or the other might be, he does attach higher value to judging freely than to judging by unchosen determinations, which, although it is a way of fixing belief, strictly speaking is not judging at all. Moreover, the man in the street does evidently attach higher value to judging for reasons than to judging for "no reason" except the feeling of the moment.

However, we ought not dismiss the emotionalist basis as emphatically or as completely as we did the irrationalist basis. First of all, we admit that an emotion is something rather than nothing, and as such deserves to be taken

into account. Relative to a given person, an emotion is a class of his particular feeling-events, including those of the past, those extending across the
present moment, and those of the future. Fear, for example, is the total
collection of occasions on which an individual has been afraid together with
the projections he makes for his own future in which he conceives that on
one or more occasions he may be afraid again. The fact that emotions and
even specific feelings on particular occasions may be predicted gives us a
second reason to treat emotion quite seriously as a ground of fixing belief. A
future feeling-event is an object of knowledge in the same way that any other
predicted event is an object of knowledge. We take into account and give
much importance to the way we expect to feel in connection with whatever is
expected to happen, including the adoption of a prospective belief. Thus to
reason about what emotions the future may contain for us is not at all the
same thing as to adopt a belief by virtue of an emotional cause. Rather, it is
one of the kinds of application of *reason* to the adoption of belief. Thus, in a
specially qualified way, namely, as causal consequence, emotion is a legitimate ground often involved in freely choosing beliefs.

Before we can dismiss emotion in general as a proper ground directly
determining valuative belief, we must treat some important positions that
have been taken in this regard. Many will credit a thesis that has been stated
very persuasively by William James,[2] that as between two beliefs where other
things do not determine, where choice is unavoidable and important, and
where each belief has some *prima facie* appeal, one is entitled as a reasonable
person to fasten his belief upon the proposition to which his passions determine him. In fact, however, under those circumstances one could hardly
do anything else. To the extent that one is in a situation in which all of
James's qualifications are realized, I should acknowledge that to fix belief by
this means is indeed reasonable, especially since (by James's hypothesis) full,
deliberate exercise of reason has disclosed no third possibility. But it would
be extremely rare that a person would find himself actually in a situation
possessing in exact balance all the features of James's "genuine option,"
certainly not frequently enough for the principle to be capable of explaining
valuation in general.

Two other positions adopted by philosophers and others attach a great
role to the emotions in the general business of living, and in the nearly as
general business of arriving at value-assertive propositions, will occupy us for
a few moments. I shall treat the first of these under the loose-fitting label of
romanticism, and the second under that of the proponents of emotive meaning as the characteristic sort of meaning of value-assertive propositions.

Romanticism I understand to be many things, including an emphasis in
one's life outlook as well as a movement in literature and the arts. My use of
the term here is highly abstract, for I intend by it only the romantic's stress
upon the reality and the maximum significance of human emotions as decisive factors both in selection of actions and in fixing upon beliefs. The

romantic tendency seems to move in counter-action to the intellectualistic tendency, and often to counterbalance its effects. This pattern is to be seen for example in the German *Sturm und Drang* as a reaction to the rationalism of Leibniz, Wolff, and Baumgarten; in the English romantic writers as a reaction to the English and Continental Enlightenment; and in the twentieth century in the reaction of the Counterculture to the Establishment. Although we have a historic period in Western civilization known as the Romantic Period, there have been romantics in my sense in every era of past history. Moreover, romanticism is to be seen in the lives of individuals as well as movements of the culture. There are in all times some persons who are dominated by and champions of emotionality, just as there are others who are dominated by and champions of rationality.

The significance of a romanticizing tendency as a basis for fixing beliefs in value-assertive propositions is simple: It demonstrates to us how important such an emotional basis is. A trend that motivates entire schools of poets, dramatists, and visual and musical artists is not to be slighted. However, romanticism is essentially an emphasis, not a substantive philosophy in itself. As such an emphasis, it is an expression of an aspect of life so fundamental that it is to be found in all of us, and is by no means the same thing as either a departure from rationality or a separation in theory of some beliefs from others. Persons who are of the romantic tendency can have quite opposite beliefs among themselves, and can share virtually the same body of beliefs with representatives of other movements or temperaments outside the romantic. One way in which the romantic can teach us is his insistence that emotions and feelings are realities, and as such are worthy to be taken into full account along with abstractions, syllogistic conclusions, statistics, nuts and bolts, and other "realities." The more extreme romantics will insist that nothing is more important than feeling as a means of fixing belief. Indeed, some of our young people in the second half of the twentieth century seem to be specializing in insisting upon such a view. Nevertheless they demonstrate, regardless of what they may at the moment be saying, that one cannot exclusively, or even mainly, fix belief by the passions. There may be some propositions in prominent places within their belief structures that are chosen with conspicuous passion, but these on the whole, while important, are relatively few. For their less prominent valuational and other beliefs—the impressive multitude of them—the current young romantics employ a basis of belief that is just about the same as that of anyone else in the culture.

The holders of beliefs grounded in the emotions are fully entitled to hold them. Some of the great passional characters of history and literature are highly admirable. If a life dominated by passional attachment of belief to specific valuations is satisfactory to them, then it *is* satisfactory to them, and we have little reason or right to attempt to make them believe otherwise; and, because their ground is what it is, there is little prospect of succeeding if we make the attempt. To induce one of them to abandon a particular valuational belief, we would probably have to stir him with some overriding emotion other than the one that had determined him to the belief we were contesting. Our recourse, in other words, would be simply to the passions that are operative in fixing his whole structure of valuational beliefs. Those of us who ourselves employ the passions as the only or the best grounds for fixing belief will freely do this, so that if the passional structures of motives coincide, agreement will probably be reached, but if they do not coincide, the ensuing clash will be a battle of the passions. Such clashes are usually futile. Others who do not regard the passions as the ultimate best determinants of belief will sense themselves at a disadvantage in such a contest, for a question of conscience will arise for them. Is it acceptable, while not believing in the propriety of the passions as sole arbiters of belief, to manipulate the passions of one whom they wish to convince? To use their own weapon, reason, is to invite the opponent to turn to that in which he places his own confidence, the passions, and will at the outset prejudice the outcome adversely to the subscribers to reason. Yet if they believe in it, it is what they believe they ought to use. What I think actually happens over a large number of cases is that the reasoners do attempt through reason to induce the passionate believers to modify their opinions, perhaps only by a little at a time, and frequently this is the eventual outcome. Although man's passions are strong and tend often to blind him, in the long run his rational nature wins out. It seems to me that there is perceptible if snail-paced progress in rationality over a long period of time.

Some who could be characterized as "romantic" in the sense used herein are hardly much more so than not, while others are completely devoted to passional grounds for belief. But regardless of the extent of adherence to it by individuals, it appears to me that the romantic position is a limited one. Despite the customary high valuation that the romantic urges for freedom, romanticism is not as free a position as that of the one who does not make emotion his most important ground for value-fixing. This is because it is essentially an attitude of yielding to events (emotional events) and being determined by them, rather than of holding insistently to the function of self-determination independently of, often in spite of, the emotional events that occur to one. That individuals allow the immediate emotion to dominate and often to be entirely determinative is shown in expressions of our language that portray this. We are "caught up" in the moment's feeling, "transported" by it, "wrought upon" by it, and even "overwrought," "carried along" by our emotions or by one of them, and so on. These are expressions we apply to this mode of arriving at valuations in crucial moments. We do not apply these expressions to moments of deliberation and reasoning. Even when the romantic is extolling freedom, as he often does, his dominating consciousness is consciousness of the joyous *feeling* of freedom, not of its logical presuppositions or factual preconditions. I should furthermore concede (though not in keeping with usual romantic views on emotions) that emotions can be both controlled and cultivated, as by disciplined practitioners of aesthetic activity or of moral action, so that one can both enlarge one's disposition to be subject to certain emotions and minimize the disposition to be subject to others. But nevertheless, at the moment of being affected, one is still being determined by something that is not wholly, directly, and immediately one's own choice. Thus, to whatever extent an individual is a romantic under the conception here stipulated, he is being determined by a narrower range of factors than the broadest available range, and in fact by factors among which he can make no on-the-spot selection. He has, by his commitment to the romantic position, excluded himself from having access to the broader available range of options of possible influences on his judgment. Thus his position is more limited than what is possible.

We now look toward the position of those who claim that value-assertive propositions bear emotive meaning as their distinguishing sign. The logical positivists divided meaning into two kinds, cognitive and emotive. Their explanation of value judgments was that in sentences that express value judgments, the kind of meaning that is present is emotive meaning, whereas in sentences giving scientific descriptions, the kind of meaning present is descriptive or cognitive meaning. The present inquiry is not the place to survey in detail the criticisms of the emotivist position, its dichotomy of meanings, and its doctrine in particular about value judgments and emotive meaning. I should like, however, to state briefly why I cannot accept the view of logical positivism upon the nature of value judgments.

It is surely true that language bears both cognitive or descriptive meaning and expressions having emotive origins and effects. We can agree in general with the positivists' view that cognitive meaning is of two kinds, the empirical (verified by observation) and the tautological or analytical (verified by logical procedures). Using empirical sentences as our example, we further explain that the sentence achieves communication through reference to a particular (Frege's *Bedeutung*) and predication (Frege's *Sinn*).[3] Symbols enable us to understand these, and their definition is accomplished substantially ostensively—by pointing. For tautological sentences in natural language, the truth of the sentence arises out of the definitions adopted; for empirical sentences, their truth is ascertained by observation. In natural languages the same symbols may express now one, now the other sort of cognitive meaning.

To symbolize, then, was to employ an arbitrary linguistic symbol for either a particular or a predicate, and there was not much practical difference between saying "The sentence *S* means. . ." and "The speaker, when he speaks sentence *S*, means . . .," for the speaker's correct selection of symbols from the word-stock of his language would assure that the meaning would be communicated. But when the positivists introduced "emotive meaning," they broadened the public concept belonging to *meaning* so that now it included something that the words of the sentence *S* did not symbolize, at least in the same sense in which referents and predicates or relations are symbolized.

While the positivists acknowledged that the same words might be utilized, they indicated that the whole effect of the speaker's selection of words now was simply to signal what feeling he was undergoing toward an object to which his words referred. Thus the notion of the burden of a word now included something that the term *meaning* had not before included. *Meaning* now has become the behavior, or an aspect of it, of the user of the words rather than a cognition he is symbolizing. The meaning of the entire sentence became a signal of a feeling, not an assertion of a possible item of knowledge. And the influencing of conduct and of belief were the purposes of such a signal, not the achieving of a body of knowledge except perhaps incidentally.

Critics of the positivist theory of emotive meaning and of Stevenson's adaptation of it have asked important questions about the emotion involved. Is emotive meaning that emotion which stimulates the speaker, or is it rather that which his words evoke in the listener? Or is it somehow that which each of these has in common? It seems to me that one of these possibilities, even the more sophisticated third one, is acceptable, for none seems to jibe with the facts of our cognitive and emotional lives. We can summon up concepts at will when we are contemplating and forming assertions; and when we hear speech or read we can readily respond by reviewing in our minds our conceptions of those things that are symbolized by the words of the speaker. But emotions do not behave so obediently. Even the most consummate literary art does not in fact move us to feel "genuine" emotions in response to humor or pathos presented in the literary work. We do not lose control of ourselves that easily. Children and naïve readers or listeners do indeed sometimes cry tears; but everyday value judgments, that the positivist view is intended to explain, hardly approximate to the quality of presentations of humor or pathos in literary art. Even the person who used to cry over "Hänsel and Gretel" as a child does not as an adult feel emotion that is genuine in that sense, upon hearing the story anew. Rather, when the adult hears either a fearsome children's story or an ordinary value assertion like "He pitches well, but he is the league's worst batter," he responds in a fashion that I suggest is almost entirely cognitive—or at most, that is little more emotional than the reception he gives to information like "He has won seven games and lost two. His batting average this season is .027." Surely in our mature lives it is more accurate to affirm not that we always respond emotionally to value judgments, but rather that we almost always entertain them cognitively; we acquire knowledge when we apprehend them, although some of the knowledge we acquire may be about emotional experience. The same, *mutatis mutandis,* must be true of the originators of the value judgments. Baseball enthusiasts surely often utter judgments like "He pitches well, but he is the league's worst batter" without being swept into doing so by emotional fervor. I grant that one *may* make a statement like that in a welling-over of feeling, but for most such utterances, they do not coincide with such a transport.

All this leads me to conclude that the handling of both value judgments in verbal communication, and emotion in literary art of either the juvenile or the adult level, is actually done importantly and often exclusively by the mediation of knowledge, not by the actual evocation of the emotion concerned. This can be put otherwise, very simply: Discourse that significantly communicates emotions has its success by virtue of *symbolizing* concepts of emotions, not by signalling the existence or occurrence of the emotions themselves in the speaker or author at a given time, and not by stimulating those emotions themselves in the listener or reader.

But this conclusion at least partially confounds the emotivist's doctrine of a simple cognitive-emotive dichotomy, for it makes actual emotive *meaning* a kind of cognitive meaning, namely, that part of cognitive meaning which deals with emotions through symbols of concepts of these emotions. Emotive meaning, in the sense of conceptual or referential meaning that travels with the word in the word's function as a symbol rather than being an event in the life of a speaker or his interpreter, is thus a form of descriptive or cognitive meaning. Or if it be denied that cognitive meaning is meaning that depends for its success either upon the reference to items occurring in experience or else upon the symbolization of concepts of these, the alternative would seem to be that cognitive meaning is not to be known by its method but rather by its subject matter, hence its nature is to express the things of experience—objects, events, states of affairs. However, emotions and feelings are certainly events or states of affairs, even objects in a legitimate sense (that of objects of attention or of consciousness). Again we must conclude that there is no separate emotive meaning useful for subtle and discriminate communication, but that these events are communicated in ordinary life in the same way as batting averages and boiling points, and that there is little justification to assert a radical dichotomy establishing emotive meaning as a separate category of meaning rather than a branch of cognitive meaning. This is why Ayer does not ring true when claiming "If I . . . say, 'stealing money is wrong,' I produce a sentence which has no factual meaning . . . . It is as if I had written 'Stealing money!!'—where the shape and thickness of the exclamation marks show, by a suitable convention, that a special sort of moral disapproval is the feeling which is being expressed."[4] This is also why no matter how highly expressive of emotion a sentence may be, it is nevertheless a compound of cognitive meaning about emotion and other sorts of cognitive meaning. Nothing can be pure emotive meaning and at the same time be a *sentence,* for a sentence is a cognitive instrument.

In the ordinary origination of value judgments, it seems to me quite unlikely that what operates most decisively is always, or even generally, an emotion—whether at the flood, or sublimated. Rather, both emotions and concepts are importantly involved in the formation and understanding of both fact-assertive and value-assertive statements. Although the conclusion drawn in the two stages of the preceding argument is that classifying emotive meaning as a discrete kind of meaning on a level with cognitive meaning is not warranted, I am glad to grant that experience with language exhibits something that may warrantably be called emotive meaning. However, it does not coincide in its presence or its application with the occurrence of value-assertive statements as distinct from factual statements. The early positivists may have assumed that value judgments are about nothing tangible since they are notoriously unprovable, then found emotive meaning as an account for this condition of value judgments, rather than moving in the opposite order—first discovering emotive meaning, then finding its function. Surely the function of emotive meaning, granted that there is such a thing, is broader than the expressing of value judgments.

A later form of emotivist doctrine is that of Stevenson in his well-known *Ethics and Language*.[5] Stevenson suggests that "This is good" is equivalent to a combination of a report and an imperative: "I approve of this; [you] do so as well!" Stevenson has rightly discerned that there is something more, and something more subtle, about value judgments than the simple expression of emotional response. However, as it appears to me, his first element, the report of approval, falls under the same account that is made of the earlier use of emotive meaning by the logical positivists—it reduces to a report of an event, which is perhaps an emotional event (though I do not yield to Stevenson that it is *necessarily* emotional, any more than I yield the point to the earlier positivists). If it is a report of an event, it depends on that kind of meaning which is employed in reporting any kind of event, and is distinguished only by its subject matter and not by a kind of meaning it employs, which is to say not by the distinct method of linguistic communication that the speaker or writer uses.

Stevenson's assertion that there is present in a value judgment a second element, the imperative with which the listener is commanded to approve also of that which the speaker approves, seems to me empirically inaccurate. Many a value judgment is communicated, many a "This is good" is uttered, in situations in which the speaker does not at all attempt or intend to command the agreement of any listener. I suspect in fact that this is true of most occasions of the stating of value judgments, in speaking or in writing. Hence it seems to me unjustified to claim that the element of command is so characteristic of the value judgment as to serve along with another element as one of two elements comprising the defining characteristic of the value judgment. There are other things that one might see as readily in the value-assertive sentence as uttered in life situations, such as an expression of a wish: "I wish you would approve of it too," or "I wish most people approved of it," or even "I wish I weren't the only one who did." The wish in fact need not relate to approval: "I wish this happened more often." And so on. The point may be raised that Stevenson is not attempting to tell an empirical truth about every value judgment, but rather to account for the structure of value judgments by taking a clue from a feature that is prominent in some of them. But this point may be met by pointing out that the purpose Stevenson has is to account (whether genetically or in some other way) for *all* value judgments, and the presence of a feature that is present in some only, perhaps a minority at that, will not do the task when that feature is not present *necessarily* and may indeed yield to some other feature on some occasions, and to no corresponding feature on others. The force of a criticism of Stevenson's interpretation may depend on the force that we expect a theory of value judgment to have; if it is to be a theory that is characterized by necessary truth, then we must not arrive at it by surveying experience and amassing instances. If, on the other hand, it is to be an empirical theory, then we must generalize from a sufficiently great proportion of the instances to warrant drawing the generalization, and we will prefer to accept a theory drawn from the most complete collection of instances, rather than from a lesser number that may amount even to merely a minority. Under practical circumstances, I for one choose the latter alternative, and I do not find among the value-assertive propositions that I encounter even a majority that arguably contain the imperative element.

9

How We Ground Value Judgments
II. Intuition and Reason

There remain two items for us to consider from our list of possible grounds for valuative judgments, namely, intuition and reason. To face these is to cringe, for the greatest philosophical minds have been exercised over them and the greatest problems have been assaulted, in the campaigns and wars of theory of knowledge. Following the counsel of boldness rather than caution, I shall desert orderliness and attempt to consider these two together rather than separately. For it is surely not mere coincidence that Descartes, the father of modern rationalism, appealed to intuition as well as to rule of reason; that British empiricism gave rise to moral sense and sense-of-beauty theories of valuation as a response to rationalism on the Continent; and that when anyone attempts to defend the one fully at the expense of the other, what he is defending ultimately seems to vanish into nothingness. Those moments when I have found the intuitionist position to be at its most convincing have been when the inadequacies of reason alone are most apparent, so that intuitionism seems, then, to win out by default as the only possible alternative. Or again, when I find the role of reason apparently the strongest, it is when the intuitionist, in attempting to exhibit the *je ne sais quoi* that is intuited, is made to realize that in saying "I know not what" he has just confessed his ignorance, the bankruptcy of his method taken by itself. In what is presented in this chapter I hope to show the reader a reconciliation of these two thrusts, which gives each its due.

The term *intuition* has been applied as the name of the process of apprehending all sorts of things—essences (under various definitions), goodness, rightness, beauty, the evil, the ugly, the sublime, the ridiculous, identity, logical consistency, future events, distant or otherwise inaccessible events or facts, objects in realms of being that are normally inaccessible (such as Heaven), qualities of objects in "this" realm of being (such as colors and shapes), truths, conditions (such as the love present in another person), and the Divine. The operation, or alleged operation, of intuition with respect to most of these remains pretty mysterious. However, once an inquirer has resolved somehow to go beyond it to other things, accepting the process of intuition as a reality even without adequate explanation, sometimes he is able to get along rather well. Even logicians have been moved to take refuge in "an intuitive proof," where a rigorous and strict proof is difficult to originate or to follow, and, when pressed, they appear willing to grant a role to intuition in the simple steps of deductive argumentation. Yet, explaining intuition is not one of the tasks of logic—a fact for which logicians are probably grateful. The companion object of investigation—reason—is explained, and with considerable success, by the logicians. However, insofar as the explanatory principle to which they ultimately move after surveying the specifically logical principles is *intuition*, we can see why one might be unable to adopt reason alone as the basic ground for value assertions, and why it becomes convenient to treat intuition and reason together in our inquiry into value judging and value-assertions.

Concerning intuition in general, it seems that what different intuitions have in common is a belief that may be expressed in a pattern that they all exhibit, even though the nature of the object of intuition differs. The general formulation exhibiting the common pattern of intuitions may be put thus:

It is of the nature of our process of apprehending X that X is there, that we encounter X, it confronts us and we address it, and by virtue of its confronting us and our addressing it, and without the intervention of any intermediate process, object, agent, or vehicle, we apprehend and thus come to know X.

In this fashion, it has been alleged, we are made aware of the rightness of right acts, of the goodness of good objects, of the beauty of beautiful works of art, of the truth of certain propositions, and the like. But through this formulation, the weakness of intuitionism becomes apparent: It is an explanation that is no explanation. It begs the question that X is there. How do we know X is there? By intuition. How do we know intuition? (That is, how do we know it to exist or to operate?) The answer is, "By addressing ourselves to—when we are confronted by—X. By the simultaneous presence together of X and the observer." But that is just the same thing again. However, from the emphasis in this circular return, we begin to see a linguistic side to the intuitionist position. If one were to become able to state *how* the process operates, then it would cease to be a process of "intuition," for then we would begin calling it a process of vision, or of acoustics, or whatever it were then understood to be. Intuitionism is thus, linguistically at least, a position to be occupied by those who have no categories of explanation—which boils down to a theory for those who have no theory.

But in similar terms, reason is not much better. What is reason but a position for those to occupy who do have categories of explanation? Having these, they are at liberty to juggle and shuffle concepts, arrange and rearrange classes and relations and elements and operations, while systematically excluding the metaphysical or ontological problems regarding the existence of members of the classes, or objects of the operations, and so on—and ultimately voicing an appeal to *intuition* ("logical intuition") when hard pressed for explanations as to just how rational validity is achieved or claims of it justified. The advantage reason enjoys in this contest is not superior grounds in reality, but rather simply the immeasurably vaster number of experiences we have with it whose success as acts of reasoning is obvious to us, as compared to the small number of experiences we have in which it is evident that we have depended upon the intuitive grasp of some important thing and enjoyed a successful outcome.

In the eighteenth century, the hypothesis that value is intuited took the form of belief in the moral sense and the sense of beauty. The human being was endowed, so it seemed, with an inner sense, analogous to the physical senses, that detected the moral and the beautiful, just as the eye detected light and color. In the twentieth century, the notion was renewed in the intuitionism of G. E. Moore and W. D. Ross. Moore's famous analogy of *good* with *yellow* as a simple, indefinable quality provided the pattern for the whole movement of twentieth-century intuitionism. Moral philosophers, even those who reject the views of Moore and Ross, still find useful the reference to "our moral intuitions" as somehow basic and explanatory.

The proposition that good and right are intuited does indeed reach us precisely by analogy. We are satisfied that patches of yellow and other sensible things become known in the way that the formulation of intuition just given (page 165) describes—that is, that we grasp them directly when they are before us and we heed them. Hence, when we discover that we are aware of other things whose presence in consciousness cannot be accounted for in other ways, we draw the analogy and declare them to be intuited also. However, analogies are not proofs. Once speculation, through conceiving an analogy, has provided a hypothesis, it is for the proponent to confirm the hypothesis by his own and others' experience, and this is what has not been successfully done by the moral intuitionist.

It is obvious that value is not an additional quality of things, similar to color or shape, intuited like these qualities in simple intuitions, and eventually known conceptually by the same sorts of processes as those by which we apprehend a certain pale-yellowish surface and transform our perceptual knowledge of it into the proposition, "The color patch is *very pale yellow* in the system of the Inter-Society Color Council and National Bureau of Standards."[1] It seems likely that if value were on all fours with yellow, the few among us who are value intuitionists would have little difficulty in causing the remainder of us to receive the same intuitions of it that they claim to obtain. That should be as easy as replicating experiences of yellow. The world would be teeming with *goods* or *rights*, patches and flashes, as it were, of value crowding in from all sides. All of us would have had a plethora of practice in intuiting it by the time we were learning a basic vocabulary. But these things do not at all seem to be the case; here is where the value-intuitionists still bear the burden of proof, and have yet to supply the preponderance of evidence in general experience.

The intuitionists have not, in fact, treated *good* or other value-objects as though these do abound on the landscape with the preponderance that I have attributed to color patches and other elements that are, I should concede, objects of our actual intuitions. Rather, they speak of value or good as though value is one and simple even as it is present in such a thing as a right act, or a good condition that is to be brought about. The rightness of such an act as one of rescue, they say, is somehow spread all over the act, rather than being inherent only in the throwing aside of the jacket and shoes; or the plunge into the water; or the swimming; or the getting of a grip upon the victim; or the hard transport back to shore; or the emergence from the water; or, finally, the administering of artificial respiration. It is *simply* there, we are usually told. Yet I submit that an act of this sort, like an action that is an event in a work of art upon the stage or in a film, is itself perceptually far more complex than is a painting or a sculpture. It has movement, and the temporal dimension as well as the spatial. In fact, it is more complex than the same sort of episode on film, for it involves the real investment of emotions in what is directly lived, rather than the solely aesthetic involvement of them, and involves further the conceptual factors of that which is physically and morally practical in terms of what the situation is and what the rescuer ought to do.

Someone might now remark, "Possibly you have been looking for the wrong kind of an intuition. A long-honored application of the term *intuition* is to intellectual objects, and the value-intuitionist does not mean an intuition that is *physically* like yellow at all, therefore, not one that has any object in the physical-object world as its content. Rather, he means that the rightness of the right act or the goodness of the good state of affairs is intellectually intuited,[2] like a sum, or like a congruency of figures in plane geometry."

This suggestion, if creditable, accomplishes one thing: it points out that the analogy with yellow is unfortunately chosen. However, I do not believe that it removes the objection I have raised, for that objection can apply, *mutatis mutandis*, to intellectual objects as readily as to physical objects. True, we do not have systematic, articulate acquaintance with intellectual objects—with concepts and their relations—at as early an age as we do with colors, shapes, and sounds. However, we start learning these as we learn words, counting, simple arithmetic, and simple reasoning. As our acquaintance with them increases, we come to know them for what they are, at least to the point that we can succeed very well in naming, handling, conceptualizing, and applying them. Our learned ability to grasp concepts and relationships supplies to us intuitions proceeding from these concepts and relationships, so that we become able to demonstrate for ourselves or others the actuality of the functioning of geometric intuition, mathematical intuition, and logical intuition. I concede that individuals do have the experience of achieving improved ethical knowledge and moral conduct with the advance of time during their lives, but unlike the case with mathematical or geometric problems, there are no demonstrations that are sufficiently replicable that it could be argued that they clearly demonstrate the operation of an intellectual intuition for the moral or aesthetic quality, and arrive at results to which may be attributed a certainty as great as that of mathematical or geometrical results.

Again, there are artistic intuitions, through which we cooperate with poets, musicians, writers, and dramatists to construct what we come to know as their poems, musical compositions, stories, and dramatic works. There are analyses—though I must concede that some of them are wordless, as, for example, the film of Pablo Casals instructing young cellists simply by playing phrases to them until they can repeat the phrases perfectly—which adequately amplify the operation of the various forms of artistic or aesthetic intuition. While it may seem to some moral intuitionists that the alleged moral intuition is most similar to these artistic intuitions rather than to other sorts, yet once again there is insufficient demonstration and replication to provide a convincing body of evidence that such an intuition actually operates. As we move ahead, especially after our chapter on aesthetic ought-judgments, this will become more and more apparent.

Are we to believe that there are no intuitions through which a higher level of morality may be achieved, or children trained, or adults improved in their actions? Is there no good to be achieved? Is there no rightness of right acts, and do right acts consist simply in the mechanical movements, linked in a series, which comprise them? If there are no ethical or moral intuitions to account for our acquaintance with the moral side of experience, what is left to account for it?

First, there are no demonstrable value-intuitions *per se*. Rather, the intuitions that do function, those particular intuitions of the sorts that I have already introduced above, those that do disclose the yellows and reds, the tones and thumps, the tickles and shivers, have a role in the moral aspect of experience just as they have in cognitive and other aspects of it; and I shall endeavor in the next few chapters to describe how they function. Further, I suggest that the notions that have absorbed the attention of ethicists, such as *good* and *right* and *virtue*, are not simple essences of a Platonic sort, apprehended by direct and simple intuition or abstracted from objects as simple properties, but rather are only to be understood as highly complex structures. We do not simply find value among the yellows and reds and rectangles and circles of the world, any more than we find paintings and quartets floating freely, without human intervention. Rather, we find that we humans build these things. We probably have arrived at the capability of constructing them only at a very recent evolutionary stage.

Conscious of the greatness of the problem area and of the great number of its branches, I can but sketch a few suggestions by way of arriving at a *modus operandi*, with hopes that it may, like good *modi operandi*, be self-correcting in the long run and may eventually help us to attain knowledge about the nature of both reason and intuition adequate to our task regarding value assertions.

Since it is possible for an inquiring mind to slip back and forth between intuition and reason in such a manner that each seems to explain the other, a first suggestion is that the two are better regarded as in some way a continuity rather than a dichotomy.

My next suggestion is that as we investigate this sort of thing we find more and more that the role of language in the development of knowledge is of cardinal importance. One sign of this is the usefulness of the method of "ordinary language philosophy," which assumes that the objects people encounter have molded their language to a significant extent, and hence that features of our language may give signs of the nature of the objects.

These first two suggestions taken together yield a third, namely, that the difference between intuition and reason may be a difference hinging upon language. Of course the first suggestion above, to regard intuition and reason as continuous rather than discrete, does not preclude that there is a difference between them. Just as there is a continuity from black to white, through successive shades of gray, in the same way, there could be continuity from intuition to reason, while the two remain different things. Thus, it may be the case that an intuition is an unlettered piece of reasoning, or that a reasoned argument is an articulated intuition. We experience intuitions, of course, and we experience instances of reasoning. Just as we apply terms to these events, these experiences, we manipulate them mentally in understandings that are or may be somewhat artificial. The apparent purity of the concepts of *intuition* and *reason* may be spurious, suggested to us and then crystallized because of our having established some fixed terms for them, in the customary way that rationality has of treating dynamic concepts as fixed, rather than because of our having encountered them in a pure, fixed state. Just exactly what an intuition is, I am not sure. I suspect that uncertainty about the matter has contributed greatly to the inability of a doctrine of intuitionism to become successfully established in epistemology, aesthetics, or ethics even though some sort of experience properly named intuition surely does occur. Aesthetic experience probably shows this most convincingly, because characteristically it is disinterested and hence not biased by goal-directed thinking and practical concerns. Thus, instances of intuition stand out in spectator or creative experience.

Intuition seems to connote something more definitely intellectual than *feeling*, although these two terms evidently mean things that are greatly similar in that in their specific natures they are largely determined for the subject rather than being engendered by oneself, whereas chains of reasoning may be initiated by oneself. Again, in some of our epistemological discussions we do not seem to differentiate greatly—though we do differentiate—between intuition and feeling. If we are familiar with the word *intuition* in its epistemological context, we may say that we have an intuition of pain almost as readily as we say we have a feeling of pain. Without unduly fracturing English idiom, we might go further and say that our intuitions include the feeling of pain. The difference between the words seems to be in the connotation of greater nearness of pain to the body and of intuition to the mind; we seem to require intuition to lie somewhere between the physical event and the conceptualization of it by its subject.

At this juncture one might remark, "Well, we have always known that intuition and reason are *psychologically* continuous, but what is important in philosophy is that *concepts* are discrete. Intuition and reason when *philosophically* considered are discrete."

That may well be so—which is to say that in many applications it may well be the best way to regard them. However, since we are indeed free to generate concepts, we may do better to set new sorts of concepts alongside the old ones in order to give ourselves new models to supply explanations for us; and a concept of intuition and of reason that places them on a continuum, even for logic, may prove fruitful for explanations where previously we have not had satisfactory explanations.

It is worth noticing that in the history of logic the essence of justification has been in the identity of things that are the same and the differentness of things that are different, the tacit assumption being made that what justifies claiming two items to be the same is that they *are* the same, and what justifies claiming them to be different is that they are *not* the same. The traditional laws of thought, the various sets of axioms, and even everyday argumentation and debate exhibit evidence of this principle. This primary pattern of justification will prove suggestive for our further progress.

Finally, we often remark that language is arbitrary, in the sense that a given referent may be either "chair," or "chaise," or "Stuhl," or "silla," and so on; it doesn't *have to be* any one of these. Nothing in the nature of the referent cited or of the concept symbolized necessitates any particular linguistic formation in connection with it. Our linguistic culture is free to voice either the referent or the concept in whatever way it may.

Bearing in mind the suggestions just enumerated, I make some proposals for explanation, intending them not as ultimate truth but rather as offered for testing by use. I first propose that in fact some instances of intuition that are seriously claimed to be such *are* indeed instances of the mind's grasping that which confronts it and to which it addresses itself (although in some cases, of course, the claim may be mistakenly made). In other words, there actually are instances of intuition. Further, it does happen sometimes that when someone labels an occurrence of an instance of the apprehension of X by intuition, this labeling is indeed the sign of an instance of the apprehension of X (not of something else, or of nothing); and that furthermore it is an instance of the inarticulateness of the apprehender in his attempt to handle rationally his apprehension of X. He has no words for his mode of apprehension, or else he has no developed conceptual scheme into which his apprehension fits (a conceptual scheme depending importantly, in turn, upon words), or else he has neither words nor concept but he simply *has* X, immediately. It is not surprising that even the sense impressions of ordinary physical qualia are in some contexts called intuitions, for at base (so far as our knowing of them is concerned) they are sheer graspings, sheer content for consciousness on-the-spot. Now if these simplest contents of consciousness at the moment of their generation as consciousness are indeed raw data apprehended, for which we do not as yet have either concepts or terms and about which we have not as yet discursively reasoned, then it seems possible that many things of other sorts (love, God, right, good, the whole previously given list), with which we perplex ourselves in the various branches of philosophy, could answer to the same description. However, we are not entitled merely by some sort of awareness of these to make the identification and call them intuitions or objects of intuition, for that yet remains to be shown. (Our inarticulateness about them does not alone suffice to prove the intuitionist's claim!) But there does occur at least one group, I propose, of things allegedly apprehended "by intuition," consisting of things that are apprehended immediately, by a direct addressing and grasping of them when they confront us. In other words, I am on this point accepting it that some claimed intuitions are in fact veracious, although it is a separate and difficult question which ones they are.

Much clarification remains to be accomplished, as to which items comprise this class of things actually intuitively grasped, among the many items and groupings of items that are asserted by various claimants to be so apprehended. The items within the class concerned must bear at least one hallmark, namely, that an item of the class is known during two moments: One is the moment of unarticulated immediate confrontation, in which the subject *has* the given; the second is the moment of discursively handling that which is given, by language or conception or both, which is to say, by reason. When anyone claims that X, Y, and so on, are among the intuitables, the burden is on him to establish the certainty or plausibility that the first moment actually takes place, in which X or Y confronts us and we address ourselves to it and directly apprehend it, not merely the second moment, in which we talk about it.

One of the ways of discharging this burden is, of course, simple exhibition. Let him who claims that there is a mouse in the corner point, and let his questioner look, and the questioner either does or does not see the mouse in the corner. When one claims that rightness, for example, is an integral property of an action labeled charitable, let him point, somehow; and let his questioner examine; and the questioner either does or does not discern the integral rightness. It is quite possible that there might even be those who deny seeing the mouse in the corner under circumstances in which most of us would not deny it. We normally accept the preponderance of evidence, however, and the evidence includes not only our own discernment of the mouse when the claimant points and we look, but it includes also the corroboration of others, the aforementioned "most of us" or an adequate representation of them. That preponderance of evidence is precisely what is lacking to the claimant who insists that there is integral rightness in the act of charity. The questioner not only examines the act and fails to find the rightness (as his counterpart examines the corner and fails to find the mouse), but he also learns that most of us also fail to find the rightness upon examining the act. It is the lack of a preponderance of evidence in the form of the concurrence of others that has rendered the ethical intuitionist's claim implausible, despite his report on his own behalf. (Of course, cases have been known in which an actual entity has been discerned only by a minority even when other percipients were present to it. The arts attest to this.)

A second way of supporting the claim of the existence of an intuitable, when that claim is challenged by questioners, is by the discovery and subsequent exhibition of additional intuitables that are coordinate, concurrent, or concomitant with the first one claimed. Thurber's character, after claiming that there was a unicorn in the garden, assured his wife that it was eating a rose. Very well, if the wife couldn't actually see the unicorn, she could perhaps see the rose disappearing. Of course she might make a counterclaim (if she were patient enough, which apparently she wasn't) that the rose was indeed disappearing but that this phenomenon was due to other causes. Thus the controversy might continue until the successful claimant for the intuitable entity were able to amass a preponderance of evidence in the form of additional intuitables concomitant with the first one claimed, so that the whole seemed beyond doubt to make an ordered pattern. This seeking of additional qualities that can be perceived is a standard laboratory method for verifying the presence of an entity whose presence is not sufficiently confirmed by the occurrence in a context of one phenomenon alone.

One point relating to our becoming articulate about what we intuit may be readily illustrated by the instance of ordinary qualia, for example, a pair of color patches. If one color patch is red and the other blue, plainly they are not the same in hue, and we are satisfied that the grounds of our *claim* that they are not the same is the *fact* that they are not the same. Yet, how will we rationally communicate this? Shall we say "This one is red and that one is blue"? To understand, our hearer will have to know the meanings of *red* and *blue*. To teach these meanings to him, normally (and on the assumptions that he genuinely does not know, is not faking, is merely ignorant though capable otherwise of manipulating our language) we point to something red to illustrate *red*, and to something blue to illustrate *blue*. But if this is our means of communicating meaning, we find we have done so precisely by fulfilling our definition of *intuition*, that is, by setting up a circumstance in which our listener apprehends something by addressing himself to it when it confronts him.

However, when are we sure that we have succeeded in instructing our pupil? What we wanted to do was to justify our claim to him that the red patch and the blue patch are not the same. How shall we make sure that we have not merely taught him *red* and *blue* but further have achieved his concurrence that, on the basis of the actual situation, these are "not the same"? Suppose he says, "This one is red, and that one is blue, and they are the same," intending in his assertion of their sameness to convey to us that the two patches are both patches *of color*, or are both *shapes*, or have some other characteristic in common. Our task then becomes somehow to illustrate or convey to him the meaning of *same* and/or *not the same*. To do this, must we not have recourse to some other presentation that will once again set up the conditions for another intuition?

To clarify this method of proceeding, suppose that we are looking at a large area of yellow (on a painting, a piece of roadgrading equipment, a dress-shop wall), and we say, "It's yellow at the top, and it's yellow at the bottom, but they are not the same yellow." What, now, is "the same yellow"? When are two yellows "the same," and when are they not? They are the same in their being yellow but they are different in—what? Slight shadings of the brightness? Differences as to the thinness, milkiness, or the like, of the specific color quality? Actual variations in the hue, toward orange for the one and toward green for the other?

What I elicit from these considerations is that whether we are for the moment concerned with gross differences like that between red and blue, or fine ones like that between very light purple and very pale purple in the system of the Inter-Society Color Council and National Bureau of Standards,[3] there is indeed arbitrariness in the application of the word *same*. What matters is not only that it is the case that red and blue are not the same with respect to hue, but that they *are* the same in respect to their both being colors. That much is conventional with our language. But it is by our own free act of will—it is "arbitrary"—that we choose to speak of hue on some occasions, and choose to speak of color rather than shape on others; and this is important to our ultimate understanding of reason, for we justify rational conclusions on the basis of the principle of sameness, whose application is free or arbitrary.

Further, it is the case that very pale purple and very light purple are the same with respect to hue (purple), but different with respect to saturation ("light" being closer to "vivid" than is "pale"). On a shop wall or the side of a road grader, these differences are likely to be insufficient to occasion remark, but in a work of art they might have importance. The means by which they have become expressible with accuracy and understanding internationally is itself evidence that it is by acts of decision that *X*'s, intuitable upon confrontation in the physical object world, become labeled linguistically *and* become available as concepts, *through having propositions formed about them;* so that any individual may proceed from the stark apprehension in a confrontation to the conceptualizing of the intuitable and now intuited items *X*. In the case of the illustration through color, the *X*'s are color samples of slight differences of coloration. They are labeled linguistically through agreed standardization of the samples (specified by means of instruments), and of the terms to be applied to varying samples. The terms *very pale purple* and *very light purple*, once the decisions are made to assign them to specific colorations represented by standardized samples, now symbolize concepts that become communicable by means of these terms whether or not color samples are present to those communicating—concepts whose features are arbitrarily fixed by those taking part in making the many decisions that constitute the process of setting up the system of nomenclature and of selecting standardized samples to which to give names. The concepts can thus be considered verifiable by reference to the officially adopted color samples—but only a person who freely consents to use the terms in a standardized way is likely to consider that an agreed standard is what constitutes correctness in the use of the terms or of the thinking of the concepts of the specified samples to which those terms refer.

Those of us to whom the ISCC-NBS scheme is not a familiar operative framework probably have been at a loss on some occasion to express, because of being at a loss to conceptualize, a fine difference in color intuitions. The illustration of these two colors not only exhibits the continuity of the progression from intuition to conceptualization, hence to amenability to rational manipulation, but also exhibits both *that* and *why* language is arbitrary. It is by free acts of will, of individuals or of groups, that elements in experience are made the same or different, or made the same in one respect and different in another (for example, hue—"purple"—and brightness—"pale"), and hence are made to fit into our general pattern of justification through sameness. Our logical ideal is that a claim of identity is justified if the subject and predicate elements *are* the same; and they *are* sufficiently the same for purposes of justification if by a decision—an act of will—we *treat them as* the same regardless whether objectively they are or are not the same, and as long as in our operation we remain within the limitations of argument that we accept as our rules for justification. In practice we do treat them as the same as long as they do not make for us what William James termed a practical difference.

It appears to follow speciously that we can commit absurdities like asserting that blue and yellow are the same in hue, simply because we can say "they are the same." This *is* absurd, however, because it takes into account only the subjective factor, whereas in most of our inquiries we are actually investigating the physical object world, and, accordingly, we determine our concepts in conformity with it, not as we ourselves whimsically or captiously decide. The difference between blue and yellow is important enough to most of us that we do model the two concepts in correspondence with their perceived difference. On the other hand, the difference between very pale purple and very light purple may be so inconsequential that we either pay it no attention or else call them ("for all practical purposes") "the same." Rather than the rejection of this pattern as captious and whimsical, what follows is that we freely and by choice engage to determine our concepts according to actually perceived or intuited differences to the extent that we think these have any importance, so that we tend in our specific selections of differentiations to follow determinations jointly controlled by what actually arises independently of ourselves and by our abilities to perceive differences in the experientially given.

This making, this manufacture, of *sameness* must be understood as fully as possible, for it underlies our proofs and justifications of reason. Of course I do not mean that someone who neglects the actual difference between very pale purple and very light purple thereby causally achieves an effect in the world of light and optics. Rather, I mean that he achieves an effect among concepts. Sameness, that which is symbolized by the adjective *same*, is an entity only conceptually, not a referential entity in the physical-object world. Look at the yellow shop wall, of which it may be truly said that the yellow at the top is not the same yellow as the yellow at the bottom because of differences in the lighting from different light sources. Let us suppose that at the top, where white light is strong, the yellow may correctly be called brilliant yellow, but lower, where less white light falls, it is properly named deep yellow. As we look at the wall and concentrate in different small areas, we can see at eye level two areas, left and right, of which we are willing to say "they are the same yellow," and two areas, one high up at the level of the brilliant yellow and one lower at the level of the deep yellow, of which we say "they are not the same." But what it is that we visually see—that to which our words refer—is the areas of yellow, not the sameness or difference. What is physically referential here is what came out of a paint can; what is conceptual is our way of handling it mentally, an understanding of it that we impose upon it, namely, the sameness or difference that *we impute* to the relation between selected areas. We do not see the sameness or the not-the-sameness, in the same sense of *see* as that in which we see the color of yellow on the wall. This is why—or at least this is consonant with the fact that—we are free to consider two areas of the wall as the "same" and two other areas as "different" even though their covering came out of a single uniformly mixed can of paint, and even though under uniform conditions of lighting we would change our designations and term all the areas "the same" as to color. I intend with this to show that sameness is actually arbitrary, and is responsive to the human will, through an adjustment by the will of the operative concept (*sameness* in some respect) at a given time, whereas the yellowness of the wall is objective, and is not in the same way amenable to change by virtue of mere physically unassisted acts of will of the onlooker. The underlying principle of this demonstration is the one that is important on those occasions when it becomes obviously necessary to disputants that they must define their terms; the need to define carries with it the admission that term *T* used by disputant

A may not be *the same T* as term *T* as used by disputant B.

What has been accomplished in this chapter thus far is to set forth the proposal that whatever an immediate apprehension is, it may in fact be known (by a process that we call *intuition*), and it may be handled by the mind by naming, conceptualizing, and categorizing (by a process that we call *reason*); and that a fundamental operation in handling apprehensions is the *treating of them* by the mind as *the same*. The imputed sameness never needs to be entire (and indeed it cannot be, for there do not ever occur in experience any genuine indiscernibles), but rather the mind can treat two items as "the same" even when it is fully aware of some of their differentiating characteristics. However, when it finds two items "the same" for its own practical purposes, "the same" with respect to the properties in which it is interested to the exclusion of others, it then can be content with belief in the proposition that "they are the same" and it can base on their alleged sameness logical demonstrations and claims of true conclusions from acceptable premises. This ability of the mind, which is at least part of what we call reason, is undoubtedly an evolutionary product which has developed continuously from the other abilities of the human individual that we regard as distinctly physical abilities (such as seeing). In accordance with this sketch, we can view the relation between intuition and reason as a development along a continuum rather than as the placing of a discrete new building block alongside a preexisting one.

Consistently with this view of the intuition-reason continuum as developmental and as integrated in its action, we can realize that the solidity and stability of concepts such as sameness arise in the mind's ability to recognize the advantages of such solidity and stability, and then to treat its concepts as though they are stable and unchanging, and in this way to make it possible to enjoy those advantages. Plato could never disprove that the ideas or forms were eternal, for he constantly and unwittingly treated them as eternal. Indeed, he must and so must we all. But the actual operation of the mind depends not only on the rigid stability of its concepts but also upon the mobile, flexible, and dynamic intellection that makes use of these. The situation is analogous to that of the laborer who prefers to carry water in a sturdy, rigid pail rather than in a flexible and elastic plastic sack.

10

The Roles of Intuition and Concepts in Establishing Value: The Prudential Ought-Judgment

I have been maintaining herein that what is essential to value-assertive propositions is that, in a neutral sense of *ought*, they express or reflect ought-judgments, that is, judgments as to what characteristics conceived states of affairs or actions ought to possess, or what component elements ought to comprise them. Philosophical concern has been concentrated on ought-judgments chiefly in two fields of human activity, namely, ethics and aesthetics; it has devoted virtually no attention to what is probably the most common kind of ought-judgment, the prudential. All three are alike insofar as they are ought-judgments, but each applies in a distinct field of action and each has a distinct character added to the pure *ought* that makes its kind of ought-judgment fitting for that field. In a separate chapter for each of these distinct characters of ought-judgment, I shall try to show their origins in and relations to experience.

The view that rather than being disparate processes, intuition and reason belong to a continuity extending from physical sense impression, through perceptual interpretation and cognitive processes, to belief, has implications important to a description of valuation. It can help to explain what use we actually make of intuition as a base of valuation, why the notion of moral intuition or other direct value intuition has so long seemed plausible, and how value judging is a rational activity. We have had a first look at the processes involved in the illustrations of a boy contemplating whether to throw a snowball, an incident exemplifying the *pure* ought, and of a desk worker contemplating whether to acquire a swivel chair, the latter illustrating the *prudential* ought. Among ought-judgments, the latter is next beyond the pure ought in the progression from simplicity to complexity. It is relatively little controversial, although there may of course be differences of opinion between its maker and someone familiar with its outcome, because by defini-tion (as it were) the prudential ought-judgment is a judgment made solely and simply in the maker's own interest, and he is normally deemed to be the most competent to affirm what that interest is. Although many, probably most, prudential judgments enter the moral sphere through their effects, for convenience of exposition we now give our attention to the prudential ought-judgment whose outcome does not affect others and thus does not enter the moral sphere.

In our two supposititious illustrations, one of a boy planning to throw a snowball and the other of a person deciding to substitute one kind of chair for another, we have seen the interaction of items in both temporal and time-free modes of appearing and in both determinate and indeterminate ways of appearing. We have also seen the implicit phases, components, or aspects of the event: the *intuiting* of the qualities of the objects of consciousness present as the situation arises; the *conceiving* of the things believed about those objects, thus supplying to consciousness new objects (which in this role are themselves concepts); the *grasping of other objects in other ways of appearing*, such as remembered objects, imagined objects, predicted objects, and the like, and relations among all the objects that are now present; *intuiting again* as the knowledge of the qualities of these newly introduced objects of consciousness is accumulated, the attention by now being of the sort that we call problem solving; *conceiving again* as the mind rounds out the significance of the information it is collecting; and finally, *judging* to render a resultant value-judgment as an outcome. Beyond these phases, subsequent to their functioning, we might expect the adopting of a belief or the taking of action as the result of the judgmental process. The relationship in time of either or both of these is clear; it occurs after the judging. However, the phases or aspects of the judgmental process, those that I have just now separated out and emphasized, do not require any specific sequence in time and may indeed go on very much simultaneously, or with such quick alternations from a moment of one to a moment of another that it would be quite meaningless to put them in a sequence that is thought to be temporal rather than logical. Since the whole incident in many practical situations takes place at the electric speed of inarticulate thought, there is little purpose in trying to arrange it in steps. This is not, of course, to deny that with our more complex and baffling problems we may spend hours, days, or years pondering them before coming to a final disposition.

The prudential ought-judgment is that which is an estimate of what is best for the individual making it, with only secondary if any importance granted to the interests of others. However, a question immediately arises: How do we know the nature of that which is in the individual's best interest? This question requires an answer before we can appraise the claim of the purportedly self-interested judgment.

In order to work our way toward the explanation of the prudential ought-judgment, let us begin with the examination of a hypothesis that has long been held by many as a truth—although here it is rejected as an inter-

pretations of the value-concept—namely, the hedonistic proposal that pleasure is the good. If the hedonist's principle were true, then the prudential
ought-judgment would be that judgment as to what action or state of affairs
would bring to the judge the greatest balance of pleasure. While not subscribing to this plausible belief, we will be able to gain some benefit from
considering it tentatively, in arriving at an improved understanding of the
prudential judgment, for by this means we can orient pleasure as a value to
a larger view of value.

Now I have conceded that pleasure in fact is very often a basis for the
judgment of what ought to be brought about or what action ought to be
undertaken. The operativeness of pleasure in determining many, perhaps
most, of our valuations has been so great that it has given to the hedonist the
persuasiveness of his position, a position reached simply by leaping from
"many instances" to "all instances." According to the simple hedonist position, pleasure is the good, and value-assertive propositions are those warranted by the potentiality or the actuality of the production of pleasure. "X
is good" means "X is pleasant," or "X produces pleasure." In the vocabulary
of the present inquiry, "X is good" means "X is the way it ought to be," and
the hedonist would interpret this to state that the way X's always ought to be
is productive of pleasure.

A more sophisticated hedonist, an Epicurean perhaps, reminds us that
there are various kinds of pleasures, and that some have certain relations
with pains that we ought to take into account, and so on. It is certainly an
improvement upon the basic proposition to note that there is a variety of
kinds of pleasure. In fact, if one heeds not only psychology but also literature
and the arts, one becomes convinced that there is a near-infinite variety of
kinds of pleasure, some so vastly different from others that it seems remarkable that they are brought together under the term *pleasure*. This refinement
of the hedonist's doctrine is a greater service to truth than the more simplistic
concept of pleasure. It further shows us what is important, that associated
with many things called pleasures (pursuits, indulgences, anticipations, consummations, experiences great and small) there are qualitative intuitions that
are themselves the actual feelings of pleasure we associate with pursuits
(stamp collecting, for example), indulgences (candy or cigars), anticipations
(being in love), consummations (climbing Mount Everest), or other experiences. The feeling associated with any of these is different from that associated with any other, different not only in intensity but in actual quality. It
is principally in the mode of intuitions that we are aware of the differences
among specific pleasures, and it is in the mode of conceptualization that we
are aware of the similarities. The very headings *pleasure* and *pain* are intellectual achievements, generalizations, ways of treating as the same things that
in our consciousness are actually very different.

I want to focus our attention for a moment on pleasures as intuitions for
there is a further step often taken by the hedonist that deserts the intuitive

and advances to the conceptual—one that I believe is a misleading step. It is the step taken after he has secured consent that a vast number of things are valued because they clearly yield pleasure intuitively, and from there progresses to classify *anything that people do*, even if encountering much pain in the doing, as *de facto* a pleasure. Why does a mother sacrifice her comfort and well-being for that of her child? "Well, that's *her* form of pleasure, as a mother." Why does the youth smitten with acne pick at his sores? "Because he obviously takes pleasure in doing so." Why does the flagellant scourge himself? "Because that's how he derives his pleasure, his satisfaction, in his religion." Most such instances are safely beyond the possibility of being tested factually, and, under the coercion of the general hedonist thesis, they can be made to seem very plausible. One can ascribe all sorts of aberrations to the other fellow's queer hedonic make-up. However, we should not fail to notice that what was in the numerous first group of cases a criterion—namely, the presence of intuitions of pleasure—has now become in the second and less numerous group mere inference. I do not find this convincing. Rather, I know in my own experience and in that of some to whom I am near that some actions are undertaken that do not at all yield intuitions of pleasure either at the moment of action, or in anticipation, or in retrospect. Yet these actions are undertaken freely. In undertaking the actions, the individual is bringing about what he believes ought to be the case, at least for the immediate future. One instance I have in mind involved a young man's submitting to being drafted into military service in a war he believed to be unjust. It seems to me highly suspect to adopt a route by which this can be alleged to have constituted the seeking of pleasure—for that route must in such a case as this be devious indeed.

A possible rejoinder is the reminder that the hedonist usually makes a corollary principle of the avoidance of pain; the basic principles of selecting action, more fully, he says, are to maximize pleasure *and* to avoid or minimize pain. Once again I accept the factual claim that much of the time we do so act, and further I acknowledge that just as there are of pleasures, there are many specific forms of intuitions of pain. However, the same sort of consequence follows, *mutatis mutandis*, as in the above examination of pleasure. It is possible to rationalize in facile fashion the actions of seeking or avoiding on an inferential basis and in the absence of actual intuitions of pain—"He defended the pass (or braved the surf or fed the dog) to avoid the pain of being among his comrades later in the full consciousness that he had not done so." Furthermore, something else stands out: The pain principle is precisely a second sort of factor in arriving at valuational beliefs, and the intuitions of pain, whether current or in anticipation or in retrospect, function so as to provide material for our conceptualization of pain and our reasoning about the world as it ought or ought not to be. In simple experiences, in works in the arts, and in profound problem situations in life, pleasures and pains both can be present in considerable variety, strength, and complexity, acting not as simple determinants of actions but as conflicting factors, often not themselves resolving the question of what to do to solve the problem, but competing with the effort to do so, and sometimes confusing it and hindering its resolution. The simple dichotomy of pleasure and pain as opposite emotions is an artificial construct from greatly diverse data, and is a greatly misleading model for the understanding of our besetting problems, one that does not deserve to be elevated to the rank of governing principle for them.

To endeavor to orient the powerful factor of pleasure into a larger view of man's world and his motivations, let us notice that the very act of basic interaction of man and world itself yields pleasurable intuitions. We like to travel, to tour, simply to "go for a ride," for the sake of the new sights and perceptions it will bring. Times of boredom are characteristically times when we are *not* having new perceptions. "Merely being alive," merely existing with normal anticipation of a future, of continuing to exist, is not neutral as to intuitions of pleasure or pain, but is positively productive of pleasurable intuitions, even if very faint ones. Thus, one of the factors influencing our valuations is the pleasure of perceptual intuitions accompanying interaction with our world, and therefore we incline to make some judgments that "X ought to be," where X is simply something that is an interaction with our world. We do certain things—we bring about a world that is the world in which we are doing those things—"just to see what it's like." This is, to be sure, a kind of pleasure seeking, but not a directed pleasure seeking, not the kind of seeking for specific pleasures that is envisioned in the simpler hedonism. Many of us subscribe to the value-assertive proposition, "It's good to get out and around a little, even if you don't know just why." This exemplifies the attaining of a kind of pleasure that begins to support a more complex view than a mere hedonism, a view in which reasoning processes and imagination are applied to remembered and prospective feeling as well as to current feeling, and begins to move us toward a position that, though it encompasses intuitions of pleasure, is not a hedonism at all.

We have now reached a stage from which we can see that actions are ordinarily undertaken—and hence value-assertive beliefs have been adopted, even if inarticulately—in view of actual or expected specific perceptual intuitions *whatever* these may be. The particular intuitions, including those called pleasures and those called pains, are not all alike in quality, varying only in degree, but furthermore, they occur in a vast variety of qualities. Some even merge into others of their opposite category; we respond to certain events with mixed pleasure and pain. In fact, there are many neural excitations that we find difficult to classify as a feeling either of pleasure or of pain. We should rather think of the pleasure or pain of a specific simple experience as one aspect of the experience, just as paleness or vividness is one aspect of an experience of yellow, while it is inseparable from the quality of the whole experience as given. The two terms *pleasure* and *pain* stand for concepts

formed—abstracted or generalized—from myriad actual instances of pleasurable and painful intuitions in our experience. However, we still distinguish,
in our more deliberate thinking, between the generalized concept and the
specific pleasure or pain, and it is the latter (the particular pleasure- or pain-
qualities as well as other particular qualities intuited at the same level) that
are at the base of those valuations that we make when we do make valuations
upon the basis of feeling. We may on *some* occasions arrive at a value-
assertive belief, and perhaps carry out consonant action, on account of a
generalized notion "This will bring pleasure" or "This will avoid pain." However, on other occasions we go through the course of valuation and action
bearing in mind the *specific* feeling that has once been obtained and is
expected in repetition: "I want to do that again! I want to have *just that*
feeling again!" We usually express this more explicitly: "That was a great
evening at the Stamp Club! I'll go again next month." "This was good tennis.
Let's play again tomorrow!" "I liked that liqueur; I must buy some." Or
again, we adopt our action in order to *experience* a specific feeling that we
do not yet know, "to see what it feels like." When we review the variety of
"pleasures" and "pains," and consider them simply as specific feeling qualities, and realize that there is a broad band where there are innumerable
feeling qualities not clearly classifiable as either pleasure or pain, then we
realize that when feeling functions as an incentive, it is the *specific feeling
quality itself* that is actually the incentive, and not simply whatever it is about
it that makes it classifiable as pleasure—much less that abstraction having
the name *pleasure*.

Coupled closely with the pleasure derived by intuiting as an incentive to
human action, and probably merging into it or emerging from it imper-
ceptibly, is the feeling of pleasure accompanying successful action of any
sort. I refer not to the feeling of the enhanced ego after action is completed,
but rather to the feeling quality of action that is rated successful by its
performer even as he is performing it. This feeling may evidently accrue to
all kinds of agents: the successful car designer and the successful car thief,
the successful writer of love letters and the successful writer of blackmail
letters, to such a person as a forger or an embezzler who disapproves morally
of what he does even as he succeeds at doing it. This, too, is a quality that is
an incentive adding to the motives for undertaking an action that has self-
interest as its principle, as well as the outcomes of other sorts of ought-
judging episodes that we shall examine later. Then again, the foreseen elevation of ego *after* a success is no doubt an incentive also to those who are
contemplating an action in which they envision themselves succeeding.

However, we precisely do *not* make *all* our valuations on the basis of
feeling. This would hardly be always prudent, nor the basis for the best
prudential value-judgments. Rather, we have the ability to override considerations of feeling and enlist other criteria in our deliberations upon what
sort of a world we should will ours to be. There are countless instances in

every day of life. The person who breaks a harmful though pleasure-yielding habit, or discards an innocent though outwardly offensive mannerism, or undergoes the drill of the dentist is acting in this fashion. Examples that are perhaps less pure but very frequent are those of multi-leveled instrumental actions, and instrumental actions of uncertain outcome. We save for prospective utilization a worn-out shirt, or a phonograph cabinet with the works removed, or a piece of pipe or lumber, yet in doing so we do not know whether it will be used or not, much less to what use it will be put. Yet we say, "It's still good." If the underlying principle of the action is simply achieving pleasure or avoiding pain, we do not know what pleasure will be achieved or pain avoided, or in fact whether the result will be more pleasure than pain and nuisance. This sort of example reminds us that we simply do not always act on the anticipation of this or that specific pleasure, nor even upon the knowledge that what the train of cause and effect will eventually bring is pleasure rather than pain. If we eventually use the worn shirt to stop a flow of blood, we count ourselves prudent and resourceful; if we eventually use it to wash a window, we find the occasion less remarkable but nonetheless a sign of the same claimed merits. What these instances illustrate is our capability of interrupting a formulable mechanistic chain of events, a stimulus-response pattern, a single relationship between a feeling event as causal and an action as resultant. Through conceptualizing and reasoning we break free of that sort of thing.

Now let us look in greater detail at the processes and deliverances of intuition as they enter into the making of prudential judgments. Again we will find it convenient to consider intuition and reason together, for the subject matter warrants keeping them united, and, as we have seen, their separation by analysis can tend to prevent our understanding how we actually function in applying our minds to circumstances.

The intuitive processes are employed by all of us moment to moment and with little or no deliberate attention to them. None of us in his less philosophically inquisitive moments, and under the press of the business of life, needs to doubt that he does indeed grasp what is there for him to grasp when he attends to it, especially when the means for grasping it are the more readily identifiable and clearly functioning physical senses. Moreover, most of us are willing to call the products of such intuition *knowledge*, or at least *belief*. However, when considering what seems to be a simple explanation of intuition, as the taking up of *one* datum by *one* function of *one* organic apparatus (an eye, an ear, a finger, or the like)—when speaking in that fashion, we are drastically simplifying by analysis something that in ordinary life is exceedingly complex and that in some activities of life may be bafflingly so.

We must give the mind due credit. It is capable of instantaneously apprehending thousands of diverse data, such as the thousands of shapes of color patches or brushmarks of a painting, the two dozen or so different colors of the painter's palette and their variants in saturation and lightness, the effects achieved by different combinations of these in the oftentimes quite numerous regions of the painting (such as the depictions of diverse pictured objects), the cognitive interpretations of these (such as the seeing of them as the parts of a person's body and clothing, or as the furniture of a room, or as the waves of the sea), and in many aspects the total effect of the whole. Yet we know that those who are accustomed to looking at paintings can, through well-functioning perceptual and other sorts of intuition, take all this in and come to an appropriate aesthetic response to the painting with just a moment's look. The human mind is obviously capable of grasping, storing, comparing, knowing, and acting upon a virtually limitless number of intuitions simultaneously.

Human capability does not stop there, impressive though that sort of intuitive apprehension is. Just as the taking in of the earth by the earthworm requires not only the earth but the activity of the worm, any percipient must be active in order to continue as a percipient. Any spectator of a work of art must maintain an active attention to it or the moments at which he really sees the work soon pass, and though his eye may still be aimed in the right direction, his thoughts go to other things and his flow of direct intuitions diminishes. However, the observer who continues in his attention to scan the work of art continues to gain new intuitions of it; he sees new relationships, rearranges his previous perceptions into new combinations—he is to some extent making the picture that the artist has placed within his experience. Some of the famous works of the *trompe-l'oeil* art, and dual effect pictures, illustrate this well. A simple instance of the spectator's contribution to the picture is seeing "the man in the moon." In his well-known textbook, *The Arts and Man*, Raymond Stites has demonstrated this by including a picture that may be seen either as a beautiful woman or a hag (Stites, while attributing the difference to the observer, captions the picture "Dual aspect of art").[1] In this way we ourselves contribute constantly to the constitution not only of artworks but of our world, receiving the given and adding to what we come to know of it by seeing not only the shapes and color patches of pictures as persons and pieces of furniture, but also intuiting the other shapes and color patches and perceptibles of the "real" world, the whole environment, and constituting them into the "things"—the "real" persons, pieces of furniture, and other objects of the world as we know it.

In some fashion also, and fortunately for us, we obtain not only physically perceptual intuitions but intellectual intuitions as well—that is, intuitions of intellectual or mental objects. Thus we may and do regard the intellectual realm as also real and intuitable, as it should be, since it is continuous with the other. Relationships among ideas and concepts become part of the world as it is presented to us; logic is in this fashion objective. Intuition for the intellectual as well as the physical realm remains a dependable means of coming to knowledge of just what our world is—just what its features and relationships are, in their whole range from the most concrete to the most abstract appearances and "ideal objects" within our experience, and from the public, external world to the private, inner world. Under our formulation of its pattern (p. 165), intuition remains the instrument for becoming aware of how our world *is*, that is to say, how it is *given* to us, of the actualities with which we are surrounded and, in fact, some portion of which we ourselves comprise.

Now there arises the formidable problem of "going from *is* to *ought.*" If value-assertive propositions take their meaning by virtue of relationship to the world as it *ought* to be, and intuitions inform us of the world as it appears or *is* given, then it would seem that there must be an unbridgeable bifurcation between intuition and value. And indeed, this is so, although we have yet to look at what may seem to be evidence to the contrary. So long as there are *ideas*[2] *about* the world as it ought to be—ideas that include but are not confined to propositions as to what ought to be—then intuition of the logical sort can make us dependably aware of these *ideas and their relations.* For example, it can be my idea that there ought to be two prize-winning poems, and further that I ought to be the author of these poems; logical intuition discloses to me that the number of poetry prizes I should then possess must be at least two, a description that is true of the ideal structure but far from accurate of the actual world. All of us occasionally entertain thoughts of the ideal. We frequently suggest such ideas as that the world ought to have an orderly international organization, that all nations ought always to be at peace, that crime ought to be known in theory but never in actuality, that poverty ought to be abolished, that disease ought to be conquered, that old age ought always to be pleasant and in no way painful, that no person ought to go unloved—and much more of the sort. Now, these are ideas that are in fact presently unfulfilled and unrealized in the physical-object world, every single one of them. In other words, the material content of these propositions is future, potential, or nonexistent, with respect to the appropriate (the physical-object) mode of appearing. However, insofar as we are speaking of the ideas as *existing* ideas, images, concepts, or other mental contents, then the relations between them are existing relations, and the rational intuition concerned is an intuition not of nonexistent relations between nonexistent entities but of an actual relation between certain actual entities—namely, certain actual ideas, present in consciousness. Thus, it is still consistent with the usage employed in this inquiry to state that intuitions disclose to us the world of what does appear in consciousness, the actual or real world, including conceptions of the mind, and among them conceptions of the possible, potential, or future; and these intuitions are *not* of the world as it ought to be in respects in which that differs from the actual. The qualities borne by objects among these appearances are existing qualities in that respect (although, of course, being present only as conceived or imagined, they are not existent in the physical-object world) and intuitions of such qualities (e.g., what it "would be" like to stroke the fur of an imagined cat) are "real intuitions," existent intuitions. The relations among these ideas of the mind, the relations that are logical relations and are known to the rational intuition, are relations that are in fact in existence, that is, present to consciousness, because the relations actually hold between the now-existing *ideas of* these counter-to-fact conditions. Thus we see that not merely in reference to the nonexistent, some ideas of the "nonexistent" are existent, for the practical purposes of thinking and planning, and the logical relations between them are existent, hence intuitions of those logical relations *are by nature intuitions of what is*, and are not by nature intuitions of what ought to be. They are as valid as logical relations attributed through inference to any other existent things.

Moreover, while it is the case that we are able to summon to our minds at will items having the ways of appearing of concepts and conceptions, imaginings, memories, fantasies, and so on, among which logical relations can be and are intuited, it is also the case that we are able to intuit the qualities of these relations, just as we are able to intuit the qualities of relations among entities of the physical-object world. We can intuit the quality of a relationship between, say, a truck and a garage such that the garage looks too small for the truck, whereas when the garage is not in relation to that truck it does not look excessively small; and we can reconstruct this episode in memory and once again intuit the nature of the relationship. We can intuit the quality of the relationship between a woman in the room and another woman who has just entered the room, such that we can say we like each woman individually but that they have a too-familiar (or too distant, or conflicting, etc.) relationship to each other, that we do not like. This relation, too, can be intuited when we remember or conceptualize the incident—or even when we imagine it, inventing it from the whole cloth. And again, when we have summoned up items whose relations we intuit, such as a memory of a feared place, we *involuntarily* apprehend the quality of that item and the relations into which it enters even though we initiated the recall of it voluntarily.[3] The qualities intuited, in other words, are not manufactured by ourselves at will; they are responses to what *is*, what is presented, in our consciousness as it appears or exists in its respective way of appearing. A conclusive example of this is the very real fear we can feel of a previously unknown figure or situation in a dream.

However, since we explain the intuitions not only of physical objects but of mental contents as intuitions of existents, we seem to give ourselves all over again the necessity of having to confess, after all, that it is impossible to have intuitions of what ought to be. And if it is impossible to become directly acquainted with what ought to be, then, we must further ask, how can we ever have any dependable value-assertive propositions? Are we going to have to abandon the view that we can have value-assertive propositions that are true?

I will indeed abandon the view that we can have value-assertive proposi-tions with the property *truth* as usually understood. However, I shall by no means abandon the notion that we can have *dependable* or *sound* value-assertive propositions. All wisdom depends upon our having them—and it is surely to be believed that some wisdom in fact exists. Let the reader retain from his own self-awareness his satisfaction upon that point!

Now it becomes apparent what we actually know, and what we actually judge, with respect to the world as it ought to be. We obviously cannot and do not intuit the absolute with respect to ideal worlds. We have no access to any such thing, although, of course, if we did our intuitions would operate at a rate that would be something wonderful indeed. That which we can intuit, and which we do in fact intuit, when we are faced with a problem as to what change we ought to bring about, is the nature of one or more con-ceivable sets of circumstances ("worlds" on a small scale, the scale on which we ourselves are major figures in it) that we take to be possible, as well as the world that is actual. Here is where rationality has an extensive opportunity to operate, if we but bring it to bear. We go at the matter in any of the available appropriate ways for solving problems. We survey factual infor-mation, interpret it, apply principles of the world of nature and of logic to it, and assess the probabilities of potential outcomes that we extrapolate from the present situation, gather intuitions from these potential outcomes, inter-pret them, and compare the outcomes on their basis. If we are adept at it, we manage to forecast with success the future events or states of affairs emerging from a selected train of actions. This is a sign of the systematic application of rationality. The upshot is that we make a more or less accurate prediction of what outcome there will be if we initiate certain patterns of conduct leading to different states of affairs (*A*, *B*, or *C*). These mental processes represent our endeavor to apply rationality to the situation from which we desire that a wise value judgment shall issue, such as a judgment on the best, most prudent state of affairs to attempt to bring about by the action we shall perform as a result of the current situation.

Moreover, by ordinary and familiar processes of inductive and deductive reasoning, we can infer from current circumstances and trends what the events of the future are likely to be, both including and apart from those in which we ourselves will participate, and in reaching our estimates of these we pay special attention, of course, to those events in which we ourselves expect to perform an influencing role. Knowing what is likely to happen and what we ourselves are likely to bring about, we then can know with high prob-ability what our intuitions *would* most likely be if the world were as we expect it to become when we apply our efforts toward our goal. That is, we can say fairly dependably what such an altered world will be like, and how such a world, when and if realized, would affect us—what intuitions, or at least what sorts of intuitions, it would be likely to give us.

An extremely important aspect of our whole performance is our stock-taking of the feelings that we envision as pertaining to either of the outcomes *A*, *B*, or *C*. We may, for example, predict that if outcome *A* were to be brought about, we would experience the pleasure accompanying a small increase of our wealth; if outcome *B* were to be brought about, bringing a much greater increase of wealth, we would experience extreme embarrassment because we would be exposed as having profited at the expense of a friend; and if outcome *C* were to be brought about, we would experience no embarrassment and no pleasure with reference to our wealth, but would experience a deserved opinion that our personal moral worth had been tested and found acceptable, and a pleasure of pride in the entirely private knowledge that that were so. Thus we would be adjudging from the presence in our consciousness of the conceptions of the outcomes *A*, *B*, and *C* what our feelings would be likely to be in the case that either *A*, *B*, or *C* were to become an actual outcome resulting from action (or deliberated inaction) of our own. And we would have been gathering our determining intuitions, not from another world, but from those envisionings that we had made actual in *this* world, our own world of the mind.

We must face squarely the question of what it is that leads us to select one or another of the outcomes *A*, *B*, or *C*, hence electing to put into action the train of events leading to that outcome. We re-echo the question we have heard before, "How do we know what ought to be?" A first rephrasing of that question, of which we have made use, was, "How do we know what is in the best interest of an individual who faces a problem of choosing an action?" (Above, p. 178.) But now we are in a position to relate the question more closely to our actual situation by rephrasing it, "How do we know which train of actions to choose, and how do we know which outcome to select, as the one that 'really' ought to be brought about?" This question cannot be answered simply, and to attempt to answer it here would be premature. But we can work through a next step in moving toward its answer.

We can see that greater ability to make accurate predictions of future events makes the likelihood greater that an individual can make the best prudential ought-judgments. He will benefit from a knowledge of cause and effect in the physical-object world, which enables him to choose the most efficacious actions for bringing about the physical conditions he values highest. He will benefit further if he can accurately forecast what his own feelings will be upon the occurrences of certain sorts of events, such as the bringing about, respectively, of outcomes *A*, *B*, and *C*. Those of us who simply know what our own feeling is *now* upon regarding a current situation, and do not allow for possible changes in it or in our own responsiveness, so that we fail to take into account factors that may make us feel different by the time the anticipated outcome were to come about, are at a disadvantage and may draw down unintended evils upon ourselves. (For example, a youth who judges now that he will never want to be hampered by a spouse may be misjudging whether he would desire a life companion as he approaches old age.) The person making a prudential decision will benefit also from the ability to predict accurately what the feelings of other persons will be as a result of a contemplated action; he will know whether his relations with others will be improved or injured by prospective actions. Since these abilities are present in widely varying degree among individuals, obviously there emerges a wide range of degrees of excellence even among prudential ought-judgments, one of the simplest kinds. (When a person deliberating upon a prudential judgment enjoys the ability to predict physical consequences and others' feeling responses, he is then able to see when his judgment affects the well-being of others and takes on the moral dimension, something to which many persons are occasionally or even habitually blind.) It is plain, when we consider the simple prudential ought-judgments, that the judgments we call "better" or "best" deserve those terms, not by the presence of any one characteristic or relation, but by virtue of their aptness to fulfill the valuative judgment, the judgment as to what, for a variety of reasons, ought to be the case.

Thus we see that the judgments that we form about the world as it ought to be are in the first place judgments upon a world that *is* in thought, not a world in the inaccessible reaches of the as yet unattained ought-to-be. We might be mistaken about what *is*, as, for example, when we make a logical error; but that in itself is not a mistake about what ought to be. Further, these judgments are on the whole comparative, at least comparing the world that *actually is*, to the extent that we know it, against the world that we envision under the rubric "as it ought to be" or, in the cases in which we can envision more than one possible outcome, comparing the world that actually is against each of those potential worlds that we can envision, and most significantly the one among them that we have adjudged to be the most nearly as it ought to be. If this favored world (or, of course, set of circumstances within the great world) is adjudged as better than the current factual world, that means that we judge that it is the world that ought to be; but if the best of the envisioned worlds is less good than the world as we believe it currently to be in actuality, what that means is that we adjudge the present world to be as it ought to be, decline to undertake measures to change it, and may, if such appears necessary, undertake measures to maintain it. Finally, the judgments of which we speak are judgments upon "envisioned" states of affairs, states of affairs that are of the ways of appearing of imaginings or concepts, or conceptions private with ourselves, or projections or extrapolations or predictions, or any other modes that we may be able usefully to bring to bear. The richness of the selection and the wisdom with which we select among the possibilities will depend upon our individual abilities, our intelligence, and our sensitivity to coarser and finer differences among situations that we can envision or conceive. In respect to these things, value judging is an art indeed.

On this showing, we can have a considerable amount of knowledge, or at least belief, about the conception of the world that we have selected to be designated as "the world as it ought to be." That knowledge will have higher or lower probability, depending upon two principal bodies of the input that went into the determination of its features. One body of that input is all the information and supposition, handled with the processes of inference and projection that we have used, to attempt to predict accurately what will happen once the train of actions apparently required to realize it is completed. The other body of input is our body of belief about what qualities we will intuit from the world that becomes actual during our train of actions and after it is completed. Thus we never know with certainty "how the world ought to be." Rather, we may have highly or weakly supportable belief about what a set of circumstances will be like, once a train of actions initiated with certain purposes has run its course. This total body of "knowledge"—of belief—about "the world as it ought to be" in a specified respect, is just so good as the accuracy with which the value judge is able to assess potential sets of circumstances as to their effects in terms of feelings and other respects, is able to select the train of actions that will bring about the chosen set of circumstances, is able successfully to perform both in assessing the competing states of affairs and in applying method to realize a selected state of affairs, and is an accurate assessor of the effects that the desired state of affairs, once realized, will have upon him and others. Obviously, the better endowed this individual is with a variety of intellectual abilities—such as reasoning, imagination, and memory—the better he is able to acquire this sort of acquaintance with the world as it ought to be. Not clairvoyance, but simply intelligence is what is required.

We must notice at this point how our assumption that there might be "true" value-assertive propositions or "knowledge" of how things ought to be has already undergone two fundamental qualifications and now faces a third. First of all, we have at the outset recognized the apparent epistemological impossibility of *knowing that we know* exactly what the objects of the *real* environing world are like or whether there are any such objects; we took seriously Kant's cautions against believing that human knowledge rests on a guarantee, rather than an assumption, that our perceptions match the external world. (This is why we adopted *consciousness*, not *the world*, as our basic frame of reference.) This qualification must bear upon our impression of the degree of certainty of empirical statements of any sort. Second, we have also acknowledged all the additional cautions that pertain when attempting to know not the present, but rather a future, state of affairs. We cannot directly intuit the future. The scientist, the space technologist, even the meteorologist manages pretty successfully to predict future events, but does so not at all by direct observation of them but rather by observing things that are temporally past and present, then extrapolating to a future period or moment. He qualifies his prediction by an estimate of its probability—and concedes that this is but an estimate, itself a proposition having some degree of probability rather than the certainty of direct report of the observed. However, our situation in the case of a problem of what to do, even when solely a prudential matter not having a moral dimension, is beset with complicating factors that cannot be wholly removed or isolated. For not only is it true that estimates of future feeling-qualities may be much more difficult to make with accuracy than estimates of epidemics, trajectories, or precipitation, but the field within which the predicted events lie is at a second remove from the intuitable and the observable. The first remove is from present experience to external posited reality, the realm that we assume matches our perceptions but is never known to do so. The transition is made to that realm through interpretation of intuitions of the given, by means of which we posit for ourselves a standpoint as though we are in the world of external posited reality. Then we return, as it were, to the actuality of the experience of the mind—which knows that it never was beyond the boundary after all. But now it posits and steps hypothetically into a new field for the events of the valuatively described state of affairs, the field that we have been calling "the world as it ought to be," or "the realm of value." This is an "unreal" world, a world whose reality, like that of the external "real" world, we are systematically always unable to examine directly and hence always unable to prove by direct observation. It is little wonder that descriptions of the world as it ought to be, value-assertive propositions, are always and systematically matters of opinion. The descriptions—value-assertive propositions—of the world of what ought to be therefore suffer not only the limitations upon knowledge of any posited rather than intuited world, but also those applying to the posited "real" external world since the world of value is generated only from and is dependent for its positing upon that "real" world we cognize with our fact-assertive statements.

From the above survey of cautions applying to the value-assertive descriptions, we can see that a grammatical qualification also follows. We must think of our familiar phrase, "The world as it ought to be," and its equivalents, as being couched in the generic singular, not the determinative singular. For there can be no *one* world as it ought to be, at least within the knowledge of humans. Rather, there can be as many versions of "how the world ought to be" as there are multiple possibilities seen and judged as worth bringing about by the millions of minds of rational agents who are value judges. While there may be grounds in what we might call anthropological similarity among these rational agents for arriving at consensus on the ideal, there is no factual basis to compel that agreement, in the way that two competent observers in a science agree on the assessments they make of their replications of an experiment. The limitations of human experience, if not the metaphysical nature of the universe, determine a value pluralism for mankind rather than an absolute of values.

11

Judgment

The term *intuition* has been used in many ways. Some of its users make it a kind of reasoning, as when a person solves a problem or makes a correct prediction of activity in the stock market and is said "not to know how he has done it," but to have "just done it by intuition." Other users make it a part of a creative process, as when a painter is said to paint not by rules but by intuition, or a teacher is said to be intuitively a good teacher. Similarly, the word *judgment* has had a variety of applications. A widespread use is that which makes judgment synonymous with *common sense* or *wisdom*. Another makes it skill at solving problems involving persons. Still another is that of finding truth (Frege, in his essay on "Thoughts," defines judgment as "the acknowledgement of the truth of a thought").[1] Now these usages are sometimes applied within the realm of fact, rather than that of value, and we probably have no reason to attempt to drum them out of it. However, we can see that aside from those usages that are understood strictly with respect to fact, those that may be idiomatically applied within the realm of value need some further exploration and qualification.

First of all, we must leave behind the nineteenth-century usage of *judgment* as *a* judgment, a proposition that is offered as true, for if there is to be any such thing as value judging (and surely there is), and if we have shown the grounds why value-assertive sentences and propositions can never attain to truth, then we can have no use in value theory for this sense of the word *judgment*. Again, we may admit of the notion that *judgment* or *good judgment* (judgment judged!) may be synonymous with wisdom and with skill at solving problems involving persons, but we can disclaim the attempt to explicate the term in these applications, for they are complex, and if we succeed in laying a basis for *judgment* in simple steps and instances, then the applications to these more complex contexts can be worked out.

The understanding of the term *judgment* in respect to value which has been implicit thus far in the present work is "the process of identifying that which ought to be." We can think of this as choosing, but without the implication of the word *choosing* that choice is actually to be consummated—for we may make value judgments, decide upon something that ought to be the case, while having no opportunity or inclination to bring it about. Now in the expression "identifying that which ought to be," I wish to apply strictly the *pure ought,* so that the phrase *to judge* may apply in cases in which the pure ought alone comes into play, as well as cases in which we make aesthetic, moral, or other special kinds of ought-judgments. Now this process of identifying that which ought to be has long been mysterious, and is still so; while I believe I can shed some small amount of light on it, I am not at all sure that I can supply a total description or narration of it, or that anybody ever can. It is recondite and seems often to slip out of reach. But one thing we have accomplished, at least, is to separate off from it the idea and term *intuition,* for we have admitted to the meaning of that latter term a different process, and we have removed from the meaning of *judgment* the notion that it could be, in an admissible sense, a process of intuition, that is, a process of "reading off" from a given some characteristic or predicate of that given which we call "value" or "the good."

Let us look again at an illustrative prudential act of ought-judging, in order to attempt to elicit just exactly wherein such an event contains *judging,* or judgment. Let us work once more with the proposition, "What I ought to have in this study is a swivel chair, not a straight chair." Evidently, from the previous development of our argument, I cannot *know* that what I ought to have in my study is a swivel chair. How, then, can I *judge* so, and *believe* so, while having *no* basis for thinking that it is the *truth?*

Toward the goal of answering that question, let me first notice what kind of circumstance I am conceiving in order to produce my value-assertive proposition. I am surely thinking of my study as it *is,* and in its actuality it includes no swivel chair but rather a straight chair. What is important to understanding the value-assertion is to notice ways in which the reference of the value-assertive proposition is different from the reference in the actual world to the features of the study. The relatively constant features of the study, including its floor, walls, ceiling, closet, door, windows, desk, rug, and bookcases, will remain in the same status, for purposes of our understanding of the value judgment, regardless of whether they are referred to in a fact-assertive or a value-assertive proposition. They will provide a setting, a situational context, within which the value-assertive proposition is to be understood. Without my being specific about them, then, these things are indeed referred to in the proposition simply by the comprehensive noun phrase, "this study." These things are not at issue.

Does my value-assertive proposition refer to the straight chair that is now also a component of my study? Yes, although not as definitely as it would if it contained the words, "The chair now in my study is a straight chair." Rather, it refers to the particular chair as a member of the class, straight chairs, for the wording actually used is "a straight chair." The speaker, in using the indefinite article *a* instead of the definite *the,* is not indicating the dubiousness of the existence of *this* straight chair, but rather the unsatisfactoriness not only of this but of any straight chair. The speaker is thus filling in one indeterminacy of the reference of the term *straight chair*, whose concept he indicates and whose concept is on such occasions summoned up with certain relations left undetermined, such as whether a specimen or a class, a future or an eternally nonexistent chair, is indicated through the thinking of the concept. It is a secondary function of the proposition to report that the study does contain a straight chair. But the chief function of the proposition is to assert that the study *ought not* to contain it, but rather something else, at least as the primary chair of the study. The allegation of its presence surely is a reference to it. What the denial of its oughtness amounts to will become clearer shortly.

The proposition under examination obviously refers to a swivel chair, but to what swivel chair? To an existing one or a nonexistent one? The fact that this sort of question does not bother the man in the street when speaking of such things suggests that the language, in its use as an instrument of human thought and action, already somehow contains the answer. There seems to be no bar, in the conventions governing the practice in language that we know by the terms *refer* and *reference*, to applying referential words to nonexistent as well as existent objects. We may say, then, that a word may *refer* to either of two sorts of things—either to an object that is existent in some specifiable mode of existence (most commonly the mode of physical-object actuality), or else to an object that, relative to the moment of application of the word, is not in existence in the mode concerned but is in existence at least in concept or in some other solely mental way of appearing. That is, *chair* may refer to a chair that is presently existent in concept only, not in physical-object actuality. We are, after all, not referring to a nonexistent *concept* with our term *chair*, but are employing and expressing an existent concept of a nonexistent chair. Either one—the existent concept of the physically nonexistent chair or the existent chair when one exists physically—may be known by the word *chair*, the former being known as a concept, not as an entity in the physical-object world. It seems well further to note that when we employ *refer* we predicate it either of words or of concepts; thus, while a swivel chair exists in my study, my words "swivel chair in my study" refer to that chair; but while *no* swivel chair exists physically in my study, my words "swivel chair in my study" summon up a certain concept, and that concept may idiomatically be said to refer to a chair in some other mode of existence—that of a future physically existent object, or of a potentially though not actually existent physical object, or of an externally nonexistent (although thought about) physical object. And it is of course correct in English to know any one of these by the word *chair*, not by separate words respectively for the object in each of its modes of existence.

What happens when I am deliberating about the equipment of my study (and this may indeed happen pretty subliminally, as I go about other functions that I carry on in my study) is that I am conceiving two contrasting states of affairs. One of them is the state of affairs as it *is* in the physical-object world—walls, ceiling, and so on, desk and a straight chair in which I am actually sitting. The other is a state of affairs that is in every way just the same except for the nature of the chair in which, if that were the physically actual state of affairs, I would be sitting. That conceived but not physically present chair is a swivel chair rather than a straight chair. I compare the two conceptions, the conception of the actual and the conception of the specified possible but not actual state of affairs. Comparing them, I judge them; I judge the specified possible situation to be a better one than the actual, and I couch my decision in this judgment in the value-assertive proposition, "What I ought to have in this study is a swivel chair, not a straight chair." So much has been evident in our previous sketches of judging situations; our analysis must now get down to the details that more fully explain such situations in all the richness of their variety.

First of all, let it be noted in passing that with either outcome, the situation sketched remains a judgmental situation. That is, if I were to have judged that what the study ought to have is the straight chair and not a swivel chair, the situation would have been every bit as much a judgmental situation as with the other outcome. Since the study is in fact furnished already with a straight chair, the situation simply would be less likely to have attracted my attention, and surely would be unlikely to stimulate any chair-procuring action. Nevertheless, something would have happened, something probably forever inaccessible to behavioristic identification, observation, and analysis. That event would have been an instance in which the realm of what ought to be had been judged, in one respect, and judged to match the world as it is. If the inducement to consider the matter whether a different chair would somehow improve the functions of the occupant of the study suffices to constitute the situation a problem situation, then it was equally a problem situation whichever way it turned out, and a consequence is that it does not necessarily require behavior to identify a problem situation as such.

Next, let us notice that from the viewpoint of the practical man, there was an equal possibility of choosing the one or the other state of affairs. Here the issue of freedom enters. The existentialist insists that the assertion that the agent is free is true; persons with deterministic philosophies insist that it is false. We do not need to decide that issue here; rather, whatever explanation the deterministically inclined interpreter of the situation ordinarily uses to explain the appearance of freedom will apply equally well for him in judgmental situations as they do wherever he applies that explanation. My own position is simply that persons are free to come to judgmental decisions different from those that they actually do reach. (See above, p. 153.)

A question that the above comment may appear to raise is "Very well, granting that you were free to choose either way, what was it that made you choose *this* way?" Well, of course, that phrasing betrays either some illogic or a deliberate trap. I should answer it by insisting, "Nothing *made* me choose this way (favoring the swivel chair), but I can, and happily will, exhibit to you the reasons for my choice." In other words, as explained earlier, my freedom extends not only to choosing situation S rather than S'; it extends also to treating certain things as reasons for choosing S. To these I now proceed.

When I am actually at work in my room, I become aware that I am often changing my position so as to use first the desk surface, where some papers rest, then the typewriter, which is placed not on the desk top alongside the papers but on a leaf extending from the desk, lower than its top surface, to my left. I have sometimes sat with the straight chair fully facing the desk, while perusing the papers, then turned both myself and the chair so as to face the typewriter at my left when I became ready to write. The necessary lifting of the chair constitutes a small amount of welcome exercise, but the lifting has to be done sufficiently carefully that the chair legs, in passing over the edge of the rug, do not disturb and cause wrinkling in the rug. The use of such care interrupts the train of thought involved in doing the work. I have experimented with turning the chair at an angle so that I can either read by facing the desk or type by turning my body a quarter-turn to the left, but to do this causes me either to sit in a strained posture while reading, or else to type in a strained posture in order to keep my left arm clear of the chair back. A thought that with almost instantaneous speed follows my articulation to myself of these difficulties tells me, "A swivel chair would turn with you exactly as you wish to turn, without its base having to be moved at all." Ergo, what I ought to have in my study is a swivel chair.

This second narration, however, is still an incomplete sketch, not the entire story. It still makes sense to say, "You have told us that a swivel chair would be easily turned, whereas the straight chair is turned only with difficulty so great that it interferes with your work. However, to say that a swivel chair would be easily turned is not the same thing as to say that there ought to be a swivel chair in the study. How do you get from the first of these to the second?"

The challenge is both a fair and a crucial one. For the instance given, it puts succinctly the whole question of the theory of valuation. It requires me to answer first in terms of the illustrative instance, then to extend the answer so that it will cover other kinds of cases.

As I am actively working at my desk, I have already made a great number of valuational judgments that have launched me into this activity at this given time. My value judging while performing my desk work is in some respects related to this activity, and the one concerning the chair is of that sort. Since it is made with respect to the equipment used for this activity, the judgment is made on the basis of criteria selected in the light of fostering the main activity. That is normal, and not at all strange. While carrying on my desk work, I am at the outset not conscious of the limitations of my chair, for at the outset I am simply perusing my papers, not typing at all. After a period of work, however, I have used the typewriter several times and have turned away from it again. Now I discover that my chair is teetering unsteadily. One of its legs is off of the thick rug, hanging over the bare floor. Evidently I have failed to keep all four legs on the rug while turning the chair. Now in order to continue to work efficiently without the distraction of teetering, I must get up, lift the chair, and replace it with all four legs on the rug. In doing these things I receive sensory intuitions springing from these acts, though my mind is still principally occupied with the ongoing mental work. The intuitions, becoming interpreted, act so as to incite me to assert to myself that I have a physical problem. These were intuitions arising in muscular activity connected with lifting and replacing the chair, of fretfulness at having to interrupt my work, of satisfaction with the smooth functioning of my typewriter, of progress in the work and including pleasure felt in the recognition of that progress, of irritation at having to take care in moving the chair not to mark or damage the floor, and no doubt others. Those intuitions were reflections of what was actual in the situation. I also had intuitions of the conceived, non-actual situation: of the aptness of a swivel chair to turn easily merely from the pressure of the occupant's body motion, of the greater comfort usually associated with a swivel chair, and of the adjustability of height of such a chair. However, I also had intuitions of the heavy caster marks that I have seen on floors where swivel chairs had been used, which, however, can be prevented by the placement of a protective hard-surfaced pad so that such marks might be avoided. Finally, I intuited the smoothness of the continuing work that I predicted would result from the introduction of a swivel chair.

It is important to recognize that some of these intuitions were collected from the conceived swivel chair as a possible object that could be made physically actual by action; and further, that at the same time some of the intuitions were collected from memories of past, actual swivel chairs in previous experience, no one of which would or could be the one that might be introduced into the present actual situation as the solution to its problem. This demonstrates to us again that intuitions may come from conceptions, concepts, propositions, memories, and other sorts of content of consciousness, not solely from physical actuality.

Moreover, the entertaining of intuitions is not the only process taking place in this swiftly passing interlude. Some reasoning also has taken place. I had intuitions that were simply visual, like those of caster marks on the floor under various previously seen swivel chairs, and further intuitions that I think may properly be called aesthetic, of the ugliness of such caster marks. However, I also had visual intuitions of plastic-glass pads that could be placed on a floor or rug to serve as a hard surface on which swivel chairs may be placed, and found myself reasoning something like "I have seen protectors for these; hence protectors for them exist physically. If protectors for them exist, I can obtain such a protector. If I obtain such a protector, I shall not mark my floor in an unsightly fashion by introducing a swivel chair into the study. And if there is a way to avoid marking the floor, then whether or not a swivel chair would mark the floor is not a factor in deciding whether or not there ought to be a swivel chair in this study." This argument was of course shorter than, and merely ancillary to, the main piece of reasoning which read off its own particular premises from the intuitions I had of the existing straight chair and of the conceived swivel chair. The main argument runs, in effect, "This straight chair has the disadvantage of poor mobility. Since it has that disadvantage, my work is interrupted. I should prefer that my work not be interrupted. If there is a kind of chair that does not have the disadvantage of poor mobility, then presumably my possession and use of such a chair would bring it about that my work would not be interrupted. If such a chair does not possess other disadvantages such as to interfere with my work, then my possession of such a chair *would* bring it about that my work would not be interfered with. A swivel chair is such a chair. Thus my possession of a swivel chair would bring it about that my work would not be interfered with. And since I have adjudged in the past, and am acting upon the judgment, that my work should be going on, then the way things ought to be is that my work not be interfered with. Therefore what this study ought to have is a swivel chair."

In an incident of the above sort in a usual setting, we normally do not at all deliberate in such detail as the narrative here has given. Most if not all of the thinking is subarticulate. However, we do occasionally articulate such thoughts, on two sorts of occasions: to communicate and explain our conclusions to others, and to formulate them for ourselves in order to be able to apply criticism to them. Thus such an extended narrative as this of a moment's thinking may indeed sound labored, but it is not an unrealistic reproduction of such a familiar kind of thinking.

In the illustration of the study chair, then, we can come to a result with confidence. Upon surveying (at probably the speed of an electric current in a nerve) the intuitions yielded by both the actual and the conceived state of affairs, and reasoning to the pertinent conclusions so as to acquire beliefs about the probable outcomes of changes in the actual state of affairs, I judged that the world that contains a study for me equipped with a swivel chair is better than the world containing a study with a straight chair. I treated my desire that my work should flow with as little interruption as possible as a reason for so judging. I treated my awareness of the possible ugly caster marks as *not* a reason against such a judgment. In so selecting, I maintained my belief in the soundness of my earlier judgment to the effect that my work indeed ought to be carried out rather than abandoned or postponed, and again, in so selecting, I treated the judgment about the chair as subservient to the judgment about the work activity itself. My awareness of all the sensory intuitions I hold in mind treated the assumed objects of these intuitions as facts in the world, to be taken account of by a being who occupies a place in the world. (See above, p. 191.) My desire that the work should flow with little interruption was also treated as a fact, as of this moment a given. My knowledge that I had earlier judged that my work ought to be carried on was also treated as a fact. There once had been a time when it was not such a fact but was rather the issue involved in a process of judging—another process of judging such as this one—but now it was a fact, a given along with the other givens. The treating of my desire to work uninterrupted as a fact does *not* mean that judging is simply the carrying out of a psychological desire, for there were numerous other desires I had that I was *not* carrying out. Rather, it means that I was selecting one desire and treating it as a reason, while not even raising the question whether to treat many other desires—to play some tennis, to do some pleasure reading—as reasons for a new judgment. The treating of a former judging process, a valuation, as now a *fact*, is especially significant. It could of course be reexamined, even reversed; but for now it is not; it is itself an established fact treated as a reason in the whole cluster of reasons bringing me to a new ought-judgment. If we will be careful to keep our definitions firmly in mind, we may now say that values turn into facts, at least temporarily and on sufferance, when we reinforce them by treating them anew as reasons for additional value judgments. Thus a judgment-in-the-making is a creature of not only the facts that are given to us that we cannot affect, but of the facts that we ourselves have been responsible for and that have been shaped by our own acts, first of judging, then of doing, of thus realizing our valuative judgments. As human identities—as persons—we are what we are not only because of our accidents of birth and surroundings but because of our network of accomplished and of ongoing value judgments.

We may note that all of this can be expressed in the vocabulary of "better," which may be our most favored route to value judgments. (See above, p. 52.) The judgment that was preliminary to the episode described was to the effect that it is "better" for my work to be carried out than not. The judgment about the chair was to the effect that it is "better" for my study to contain a swivel chair than for it to contain a straight chair. The treatment of the intuitions and reasoning about caster marks is to the effect that it is "better" to introduce nothing into the study that will cause ugly markings, or that it is or might be "worse" to have a swivel chair accompanied by ugly markings. One proposition implicit in the judging about markings is, "It is better to have an unmarked floor than to have a floor showing caster marks." The "better" and "worse" expressed in these rephrasings are very little abstract; rather, they relate very explicitly to the particulars of the actual and of the conceived situation. These phrasings in terms of "better" and "worse" strongly suggest that it is from our everyday comparisons resulting in judgments of better and worse—*A* is better than *B*, *B* is worse than *A*—that we generate our concept of the pure or simple *ought*, of *what ought to be*—that which, among the conceivable possibilities, we should will to bring about. Moreover, the readiness with which we couch our value judgments in terms of "better" and "worse" is consistent with the general fact that we make our value judgments in the flow of action and life, for the most part. We ordinarily take circumstances as they come, interrupt that flow as little as possible, adopt the obviously better of alternatives, and pause to reflect upon or to articulate those judgments only on occasions of unusual importance or perplexity.

The act of comparative judging probably originates when its objects are within the same mode of existence, most likely the physical-object mode. Between two chairs that are both physically present, one can easily judge which is the higher, which is the lighter in color, which is the most refined in shape, and so on; similarly, treating certain propositions as the reasons for judging in a certain way, one can readily judge which of the two physically present chairs is better according to the selected criteria. But with memory, imagination, and conception to aid us, we also can judge very readily on such points when it is necessary to make the comparison across the boundary line dividing two modes of existence. We can compare the color of a physically present chair with the color of a remembered chair, and judge that the one or the other is of the lighter color. We can compare a remembered chair with a conceived chair, and judge whether it matches or does not match our conception in certain respects. We find no obstacle in the fact that we are comparing across the boundaries of modes of appearing in consciousness. Though we may need to be deliberate about summoning up a clear memory or conception, we do not need to "shift gears" to make any adjustment to our way of thinking, or to adopt any difference of outlook toward the one or the other so far as the making of the judgment is concerned. We need not even be put to the trouble to remind ourselves that the two things judged have different modes of existence, though the point may be very necessary to bear in mind for other reasons on some occasion when in fact there is such a difference.

Other variations upon the form of the objects of judgment also occur. In the example, another judgment simultaneous with the judgment upon the particular, physically present straight chair is made, namely, a judgment upon the entire class of straight chairs: ". . . not *a* straight chair." The exemplar and the entire class are adjudged unsatisfactory. But it is to be noted that though the class is invoked, it is as exemplars that the members of the class are judged unsatisfactory. On the other hand, it is possible to judge a class *as a class*, a kind of judgment that one supposes belongs to methodology. For example, how shall a community apportion its parcels of real estate? Should they be classed as either residential or commercial? A legislator for the community might decide against using those classes on the grounds that together they did not include all the parcels of land that might be taxed, or on the grounds that some parcels are both residential and commercial, and so on. How shall the available automobiles in the existing market be classified? Should one of the classes be, for example, "economy compact cars"? One might decide (as some have) that that class is good, or, in other words, that there ought to be such a class, and that in his concerns (buying a new car, renting cars out for profit, or whatnot) that class is suitable; or he might decide that the term *compact* originally referred to size, and that consistent with the advantages first gained by introducing the term, all the classes of cars should be established with reference to size and not with reference to economy. This is the pattern of judging a class as a class, strictly speaking, rather than of judging its members as exemplars. It seems especially fitting that since classes are devised by man and are instruments for his purposes, he should be able to judge their suitability and to control them fully.

Classes themselves are types of concepts, and we can extend the statements made about judging them to concepts in general. Man generates concepts for his own purposes, and we may idiomatically speak of trying to find a good concept to define a word or phrase on which some perplexity centers. One can criticize—evaluate—concepts that he himself holds, or those held by others. As to other modes of existence, their objects can be judged as well. The evaluation of dreams is quite familiar. There can be good imaginings (perhaps those that result in works of art, or inventions for man's use), and bad ones (those that take too much of one's time without producing anything, or those that produce mistaken beliefs). One probably judges that all hallucinations are bad, but even then we judge some as worse than others. As the list is extended, it appears that any object in any mode of existence may be an object of valuation, judged better or worse than another object in the same or a different mode.

It appears to me to be crucially important in this description to note that, although all kinds of entities appearing in consciousness (thus "existing," according to the usage of this volume) can give rise to intuitions, and although all kinds of those entities can be the objects of judgment, *to intuit them and to judge them is not the same thing.* The two processes may indeed occur simultaneously, but it also can be the case that one can intuit an object without judging, and one can judge an object without first collecting all possible intuitions from it. The fewer intuitions one collects before judging, the more likely we are to label such a judgment a hasty judgment, and hasty judgments certainly do occur. (Incidentally, to label them so expresses one of our forms of evaluating evaluations themselves.) Now, to intuit is to gather whatever the object has to offer upon confronting us and our heeding it. However, judging it evaluatively is to render a response to it based not solely on its nature but importantly on the nature and functioning of the judge. The sweetness of a cherry is, in one sense, a combined property of the cherry that stays with the fruit as my mouth passes from the cherry to a forkful of sauerkraut; but whether the sweetness is as it ought to be is a judgment I freely render in response to the taste, the sweet flavor, of the cherry. Two of us can disagree on the judgment, and often do. With the example of cherries, we are not likely to controvert so general a problem as "Is the sweetness of the cherries good or bad?" although it would not be out of the question to do so. Rather, we are more apt to consult one another by asking, "Are these cherries sweet enough to serve? Or do they need to ripen a bit more?" This is a clear instance of asking, in more particular language, whether the cherries are as they ought to be.

The importance of the separateness of judging from intuiting is great. In the first place, it separates mechanistic principle from theory of value and valuation. If the *ought*ness were on the object as a property of the object, then valuing would not be free, but rather mechanistically- determined. Value judging would be automatic to those possessing the apparatus of value-intuition, and the situation would yield a tendency for there to be far, far fewer disagreements upon value matters than there actually are. The description of the state of affairs that says that value itself is intuited is inaccurate, being untrue to our full experience of values carefully observed. A further significance of the separateness of judging from intuiting is that judging may be free whereas the intuiting of what we *do* intuit is determinate. The freedom of judging has its further all-important consequence, namely, that when we are undertaking to do our judging we are free to select our criteria—free to treat anything we find, or invent, as a reason. The sort of justifying we do upon being asked to justify a judgment is the exhibiting of these reasons that we have selected. It is in this way that judging can be and is a rational activity, and that the branches of valuation, most importantly ethics, are rational pursuits.

The judgment about the chair in one's study is of course far from being an ethical judgment. It is merely a prudential judgment. To apply the ancient explanations for human action, such as the hedonist's, is to offer an explanation that is always unsatisfactory, because it is always partial. To be sure, man often does select the expectation of pleasure as the functioning reason for his selection of a given activity. Yet (as already shown, p. 153) the mind is free to employ a different reason, any reason. It can only be affirmed inductively, statistically, that man is motivated by pleasure (or sex, or self-interest, or economic need, or any factor to which human choices are commonly attributed). And it is common knowledge that as the activity shifts from one sphere to another, the general trends of the selection of reasons change. One does things for certain reasons when the sphere of activity is economic, for different reasons when the sphere of activity is religious, and for still different reasons in areas of activity that are aesthetic, not to mention areas of personal relations, family activity, and many others.

So what is the process of judging as to what ought to be? It is no simple thing like holding a paint chip up to a wall and telling whether it matches or not; it is no mere "yes or no" deliverance. It cannot be, for the realm to which it applies, the posited realm of values, is generated from the world that we posit for reality. This posited value world is a new world, a private world, with which we are made acquainted by rearranging our intuitions. Each of us judges in any value-judging situation according to criteria, and the criteria applied vary immensely from one to another of us even for the same situation, much less for different situations. Fundamentally, the process of value judging is the process of affirming (or denying) to ourselves that a certain state of affairs, either actual or potential, fulfills criteria that we apply to it, or that actions we contemplate undertaking are justified by the reasons that we have freely chosen—are justified by statements that we believe and that we treat as reasons for action.

Often, and for the less important affairs, the value judgment is simple indeed. We undertake an action because of a mere liking, or because of a preference of this anticipated consequence over that one, or because to perform the action is pleasant in nature, or because its result is expected to be pleasurable, or because it is an action that we approve as contrasted with an action that we disapprove.[2] This sort of reference to a reason is probably long since habitual rather than deliberate for most ordinary, frequently recurring actions. It is not difficult to treat expected pleasure or a tested preference as a reason.

However, we have said that the simple stimulus-response pattern can be interrupted through the use of reason. What, we may ask, is the nature of judging when reason interferes with, say, a habitual application as a reason of a well-established preference, or with a recognition that a great amount of pleasure would be a highly probable result ensuing from an anticipated action? In such a case, are we not simply substituting one pleasure for another, a pleasure more difficult to recognize, or further off in time, but expected to be more heartily enjoyed, once attained?

Yes, to some extent, and in some cases, this is true. It was recognized with Epicurus that to substitute a later and longer-lasting pleasure for an immediate intense but short-lived pleasure would usually result in the greatest balance of pleasure, and so on. This is one of the bases on which some ought-judgments are made. And it is an instance of the use of reasoning. However, reason contains within itself some criteria to offer, some principles available to be treated as reasons, apart from whatever might be the feeling content of the intuitions of a situation in which a prudential or other ought-judgment is being made. These involve the commitment to rationality rather than the straying from it. However, it is more appropriate to discuss them in our chapter on the moral ought-judgment. They are most readily illustrated as well as most important in ethical contexts. I shall therefore defer their consideration until that later discussion.

We can, however, point out a feature of judgment that is present in the pure ought-judgment and all its variations, which explains much about its basic nature. That is the very fact of the constant connection of any specified ought-judgment with those expected to come after it and those that have preceded it in the life of the individual judging. Any single ought-judgment, such as that favoring the replacement of the straight chair by a swivel chair, happens at the given stage of life, knowledge, and activity of its judge. He in turn has behind him a long history of actions, cognitions, and judgments. He has observed the effects of various judgments that he and others have made. He has aimed at many goals, among which the choices have been made on account of pleasures and likings and also on other grounds. He has developed from the life of that little self-conscious animal, the human infant, to that of a highly self-conscious being as a mature person. His intuitions, the "looks" and "feelings" that things have had for him, have been strong as his incentives in early life, and may remain so, but have from time to time been joined by other incentives arising out of new commitments as he becomes able freely to make commitments, new responsibilities as he becomes able to recognize or undertake responsibilities, and new voluntary projects and challenges as his abilities wax and he is encouraged to respond to them. He never enters into a judgmental situation that is in a vacuum, for even though its elements may be few and simple, he brings with him, into it, his whole biography of past experiences and judgments, and his whole structure of expectations, projections, and forecasts. For any ordinary person, these are greatly diverse and innumerable. They are the resources available to him according to which he may exercise his judgment, either consciously or unconsciously, articulately or inarticulately. To our recognition of all these influences, we must add our awareness of his freedom in judging. When all this is before us, we see that there are a great many things that he may choose freely to treat as reasons, as well as a background of personal history within which his imagination and conception may work in order to suggest hypotheses. His judging is thus no simple thing, no "yes or no" answer to a simplifying or simplistic question like "Is it useful?" or "Does it achieve the greater balance of pleasure over pain?" or "Does intuition detect rightness spread over this act?" Rather, his judging is like the placing of one more tessera at the leading edge of a great mosaic, that, starting at his birth, moves across the plane of his existence ever forward to an unseen and indefinitely distant end. Each piece set in place relates to every previous piece, and potentially relates to every future piece that shall be fastened into the whole. Judging, in other words, requires no one touchstone, but a new element chosen for its ability to fill an as yet unfilled position in a whole that comprises the past and future life of the judge, and that will both shape and be shaped by every other element of his entire life. Or, in another figure, each judgment made is like a knot in a great seine, a vast net painstakingly put together one node at a time, so that a tug on any previously tied knot will pull on the one being made, the more weakly, the more remote, but never without influence. Every belief that we have treated as a reason for an action in the past has helped also to pull us in this direction or that as we select the reasons for the judgments underlying the valuative beliefs, with their consequent actions, that we adopt today.

12

Value in Works of Art and Their Criticism

One might suppose that since aesthetics as a realm of inquiry is a highly specialized and sophisticated study of value, we should treat it last of all. However, convenience dictates doing otherwise. Because the work of the artist is more purely an observation of the environing world and a response to it than is the ethical life, our view of the role of value in moral life and ethics will be best understood by first seeing it in aesthetic experience, not the other way around.

The treatment of value in this volume holds it to be substantially conceptual; this view is therefore describable as an intellectual or perhaps even rationalistic view. None of that sort of implication needs now to be retracted. In understanding the work of the artist and the product that he sets forth, we can readily apply our view of value to the situation and activity of the arts. The result, while not founding an excessively intellectual view of artistic activity, is in keeping both with our view of value and with acknowledged facts of aesthetics.

Our society has many ways of regarding the artist. He has been seen as an inspired genius whom the rest of us do not understand; as the dirty-handed craftsman whose work is ornamental but of no social use (unlike that of other superior but nonetheless dirty-handed craftsmen); as a starving person who prefers hardship to honest labor so that he can indulge in whimsically chosen activities; as the transmitter and interpreter of the culture; as one who invents new ideas and contributes them to the culture; as one who does what the rest of us wish we could do but for which we lack the talent or time; as one who is the spokesman of emotions and beliefs for the rest of us; as one who lives a racy, immoral life but is excused for that because his other ways are so odd that there seems little possibility of reforming him; as a cheat who profits immensely from defrauding customers about the worth of the nonsense he creates; and as one of the few truly honest souls among us. No doubt there is some artist, somewhere, who fits each of these stereotypes. In the present treament, I shall view the artist as a person who uses his human freedom to bring into being something that without him does not exist in our world.

There are numerous studies, and testimonials by artists themselves, of how the artist works; and numerous theories have been drawn from these or similar sources. As one becomes acquainted with greater numbers of these theories, perhaps the impression emerges that nothing final, or broadly true, can be said about artists' ways of working, because there are so many ways and they differ so markedly. The same artist will work in different ways from time to time, sometimes according to periods in his development but at other times for causes or reasons unrelated to anything so obvious. One might generalize to the conclusion that this is something about which one cannot safely generalize. The reason for this diversity, I believe, is offered in the main thesis and subordinate propositions of this book.

The one thing that is common to all artists, and by virtue of which we label them *artist*, is that the activity they engage in is of the sort that we call *creative*, and consists in changing something that is given in experience in the fashion that we style *creatively*. The artist engages in activity that produces a work or a performance, and it is of course clear that before he has carried out this activity, the existent or event that he produces did not exist in that mode of existence in which his activity has eventually realized it. In the physical-object mode, the painter transforms paints and canvas into a painting, the sculptor transforms stone into a figure, a writer transforms typewriter ribbon and paper into a novel, and so on. More significantly, we may say that each of these transforms his own experience into something that others may experience, and in a way that is on a level above the simple and obvious. No one, so far as I know, collects old typewriter ribbons once used by Sinclair Lewis; but people do collect snatches of his biography—that is, his experience—and seek to see significance in them for his artistic output. I am suggesting that the artist characteristically is a person who uses means that he controls more readily than most of us, and who uses givens of his experience that may or may not be similar to givens in the experience of most of us, in order to bring into the world things that he believes ought to be in the world. In this fashion, all art is criticism of the world, all art is criticism of Creation. The rest of us, in bestowing upon the initiator of this change the title *artist*, acknowledge that we value what he does.

Whatever else the work of art is or may be alleged to be, it is something whose creator believed of it that it ought to exist. The world would be better, he has judged, if the work existed in it than if not (or the world would be better if he were making the work, or performing the performance, than if he were not). One who walks through Frogner Park in Oslo and sees the hundreds of bulky, striving nude figures by the sculptor Vigeland, figures of both sexes, all ages and (so far as one may surmise without evidence of costume) stations, one is surely impressed that the sculptor felt, if nothing else, that there *should* be such people. In a few acres he has given us a world to see, a world of teeming human vitality. If we think of nothing else, we transfer our thought of the vitality of the figures to that of the sculptor, and wonder at the urge that made him bring all these human figures into a monumental existence. While initially his may seem to us a strange world, after a few minutes, when our ability to identify with it has been heightened by actually walking through it, around and among the figures, and thus participating in it, we are ready to accept his world, to give our consent to it even though we yet find much in it to stir questions within us. The world of the artwork, and within it the work of art itself, intrinsically and entire, is thus a value. It is a value to the artist in that he affirms that it ought to exist and in fact he realizes it in physical existence. It is a value to others insofar as they concur that it ought to come into being and to exist rather than not.

When we think of a work as complex as *Hamlet* or *The Last Supper* or, on the other hand, one as beautifully simple as Brancusi's *Bird in Space*, to say "That is something such that the artist regarded it better for it to exist than for it not to exist" may seem trivial indeed. However, I should rather call it fundamental. This simple fact about the work of art has significance on many levels and in many respects. Let us look at some of them.

What we must first notice is the general nature of the material the artist is given to work with, from which he will obtain the content of his work— namely, "experience." While there are bewilderingly many things appearing in experience and many ways in which they appear, most can be collected under convenient headings. Most obviously, there are the *sense perceptions* or deliverances of the perceptual senses: visual glimpses of shapes, color patches, motions, and all sorts of combinations and arrangements of these involving spatial relations, distances, and directions; odors and flavors; sounds, vibrations, and reverberations; textures and temperatures, the ways things feel when touched; kinaesthetic sensations, the heft of things lifted or pushed or pulled; and kinetic sensations, the way it feels to move a hand or a leg, to swing or to seesaw, or rise or descend in an elevator, or to run, jump, or dance. These are the kinds of appearances in experience to which I have regularly applied the verb *intuit* and the noun *intuition*, and to which I believe that our notion of intuitive awareness is applicable.

But with the sensory perceptions we have only begun to suggest the ways in which things appear in experience. We may progress at once from what we see or hear or smell to what we imagine. That is, we can (some of us more easily than others) summon up images to our minds on our own initiative rather than awaiting stimuli from outside: what a gnome would look like, what a tunnel might smell like, how a tornado—or the music of the spheres—would sound. Further, we acknowledge that we dream, and we notice that some personages in our dreams have apparently perfect verisimilitude although the events are not mere repetitions of what has occurred in waking hours. Other dream figures are modified from the familiar or else are not recognizable at all, are apparently quite novel even though dream theory suggests to us that they are compounds of things already experienced. There are hallucinations, seeming receptions of stimuli that in physical fact cannot be found. Not only are there the images that we do not knowingly engender; there are also those we deliberately induce for ourselves. We daydream. Our imagination responds when reading a poem or narrative. Or we visualize something—what our brother's fiancee might look like, or the scene we will participate in when we report for a new job. We visually plan how something will appear in the future—we mentally rearrange our furniture and imagine the result, or we invent a mechanical device for letting the dog in and out, or for putting a man on a satellite of Saturn, or we image in advance what the next picture we intend to paint shall look like. These non-veridical ways things have of appearing in our experience can conveniently be called *sense-dependent*. They are not directly read from objects of the environment, but they appear in consciousness *as if* they were or could have been presented to us directly by our senses.

We have now made a good beginning, but there is yet a long way to go. Additional elements in experience that are closely akin to the sense perceptions but discernibly separate from them are the *feelings*,[1] and parallel to the sense-dependent elements of experience are the *feeling-dependent* elements, which bear a similar relation to feelings as that of sense-dependent elements to sense perceptions. The particular feelings start as inner, rather than external, perceptions. Most of the *feeling*-elements of experience are thoroughly familiar to us and are thought about by collecting them under the headings of pleasures and pains. I stress again, though, that every so-called pleasure and pain is a particular event, an incident in time unique to its moment and its subject. Although some common attribute makes us rank many diverse things as pleasures, and others as pains, we readily recognize that there is a great distance in quality between the throb of a headache and the anguish of losing a loved one in the flowering of life. Moreover, so many of the feeling-elements of experience possess an associated pleasure or pain that we tend to overlook the hedonically neutral feelings. These include an abundance of twitches, twinges, tirings of a muscle, pressures of an unnoticed but awkward posture, the pins-and-needles feeling, chills, various muscle tones, being warm, being cool—a list probably as unending as it is pedestrian. Experience moreover presents to us the feeling-dependent items, which are not themselves inner perceptions or feelings *per se* but are of similar nature and effect. I should list with these the sympathetic feelings, which, while actually being feelings themselves, depend upon the feelings of ourselves at earlier times and the feelings of others for their origin (our own actual discomfort when we see another subjected to pain, or our glow when we watch the wedding of someone dear). Beyond the sympathetic feelings, whose reality few of us will deny although we may analyze or articulate them differently, I should add the separate class of feelings vicariously known, not those actual within ourselves but imputed by ourselves to others —the nervousness of the singer at her opera debut (*we* of course are not nervous), or the fear "experienced" by a completely fictional character in a novel, a nonexistent feeling in the sense that the character himself as such is unable to have any inner perceptual feelings at all. These feelings do make their appearance, in their own distinct way, in our experience, and they make it *as* feelings rather than as merely our knowledge of feelings, even though we ourselves do not apprehend them in the same mode as that in which we apprehend our own nervousness or fear.

Already, any one of our lists—that of sense perceptions, that of the sense-dependent elements, that of feelings, or that of the feeling-dependent elements of our experience—has shown us a potentially innumerable set of items that can appear to us. However, there are yet other classes to mention, e.g., those of the *concepts* and of concept-dependent elements. The class of concepts, too, offers innumerable instances for us to experience. To be a concept is itself a mode in which an item can appear in our experience. Already in the foregoing, in chapter five, there has been an indication of what that mode actually is—how the appearing of a concept actually happens. There are other closely related elements appearing in experience, elements that are indicated or named in about the same way as actual concepts are, and do not seem clearly or solely dependent directly on events more basic such as events of the senses or feelings, so that I shall take it for present purposes that these are *concept-dependent* elements. A most important one is the sentence. For a group of elements (words, ideas, whatever one's theory advances) to be taken as a sentence rather than as mere random utterances, or as the mere mention of referents in sequence without organization other than sequence, is a distinctive way in which those elements can appear. Anyone who has tried to teach nonacademically minded youths the meaning of the principle "A sentence is a group of words stating one complete thought" will know what I mean. In turn, a sentence can appear as a fact-assertive report, a hypothesis, a rule, a belief, a wish, a duty, a contrary-to-fact locution, an "idea" (in its several senses), an articulate purpose. All that is verbally known or expressible can appear in this way. But to continue the sampling of concept-dependent elements: Additional closely related ways of appearing include appearing as a negative, appearing as a possibility, appearing as a continuity, or appearing as a disjunct. Some things appear as a structure or pattern, while others do not appear as organized or structured, but rather as disconnected collections. To appear as a number (especially as a high number, not readily transformed into a visual image of objects) or a geometrical figure or other ideal object is a way of appearing; the higher orders of these have no doubt broken free of the visual or otherwise sense-dependent to be solely concept-dependent. These are all elements that can, and from time to time do, enter into experience, and depend for their appearance there upon our having formed certain concepts; they are probably much more often partial rather than full representations of those concepts we possess in our intellectual storehouse.

The example of the concept-dependent elements, since our concepts are characteristically constructed in turn from sensed or felt items, suggests that still additional ways things have of appearing in experience are not strictly classifiable as only one of the foregoing kinds, but comprise a mixture or combination of them. We know, for example, that children must learn to see pictures *as pictures*; while pictures seem primarily to be sense-dependent, this circumstance shows that they are also to some extent concept-dependent. Similarly with a mirror-image: To see it simply as an image is sense-dependent, but for it to appear as a mirror-image, that is, as reversed left-to-right, and related to the objects reflected, is for it to involve us in some sort of conceptualizing even if of a low level. Moreover, there are the illusions—the mirages, the *trompe l'oeil* murals, the dancing drawings—which we can see *as* illusions; we at once discern their ambiguity and are taken in by it in seeing the elements as constituting something not actual. And the artists have found application for this combining process; the works of art call upon us to combine ways of seeing them in order to grasp what the artist has brought into existence. For instance, a certain generous-sized compote with two sturdy handles, which anyone could recognize as worthy to serve the fruits of orchard or vineyard, appears in Western experience[2] as a fine representative of sixth-century black-figure pottery bearing a painting of Dionysos in a boat, a work of art. The object can indeed appear to us not only in perception but also in three other ways: the sense-dependent (as a picture), the feeling-dependent (as associated with gustatory satisfaction), and the concept-dependent (as a representation of a narrative).

The purpose of the present investigation is not to catalogue exhaustively the kinds of elements appearing in experience as such, but rather to survey their field so as to ackowledge much, at any rate, of what it contains, and then exhibit how its typical materials may function at that crucial intersection of the realm of fact with the realm of value, of the actual with the possible, where incentives shape action and the world in which action takes place. We may yet learn that there are some elements of experience that do not serve as incentives or as the background for the realization of other incentives in human action. This, however, seems unlikely. Rather, it seems probable that anything that man can experience (and hence, to which he can respond, in any fashion at all) will on some occasion serve him as a value to be realized, a state of affairs once again to be brought about, or to be brought about in a different mode of being than that in which it first occurred (or as a negative value, to be eliminated, prevented, reacted against). Although I intend the foregoing notes to be merely suggestive of the kinds of infinitely numerous items that experience contains, I do affirm that experience, while it may well include many more kinds of appearances, does include at least these, and they comprise a large part of the fabric of experience. I wish to exhibit how each and all can serve as values to the artist—that is, how each and all of the kinds or classes of elements of experience can lead him to choose that which he produces and causes to exist in the world that the rest of us also inhabit.

Let us begin *in medias res* with something quite familiar, the portrait painting. Painters find certain persons more interesting or attractive to portray than others. Portraitists—some of them at any rate—do indeed select from among their friends and acquaintances persons to serve them as subjects. This practice is evidence perhaps of the motive of doing what is enjoyable or interesting, or difficult and painstaking, but in any case of accomplishing the creation of a product that will yield pleasure upon the seeing. This phrasing of his reason for selection of a subject may or may not be very conscious or articulate on the part of the painter. However, in surveying what he has done after some period of proceeding in this way, he will probably be able to affirm that he prefers to paint such-and-such a kind of subject, and to agree that this is his way of bringing into the physical world something that looks good, pleasing for its own sake, hence an additional good thing that previously was lacking in the realm of what is publicly accessible. The painter's invitation to a subject to be painted may spring from a completely intuitive visual response to that subject and not be at all consciously referred by him to a conceptual framework, or it may be referred simply to the framework of *people I'd like to paint.* But in the fact that the painter has such a category, and in the fact that when either on his own initiative or under questioning by others he articulates the categories of subjects he prefers, or of things (his works) that look good and are pleasing for their own sakes, his endeavors are referred to concepts, and he has for his work an incentive that is concept-dependent. It is worth noticing, of course, that they are not purely such. The intuition that stirs him to ask someone to sit for him is no doubt far more strong an element in his experience than any intellection referring his choices to conceptual frameworks. Nevertheless all the kinds of elements—the sense-perceptions, the sense-dependent elements, the feelings and feeling-dependent elements as well as concept-dependent elements—enter the simple choice issuing in his invitation. Thus all are interwoven in his broad decision, expressed in a single example, that what ought to be taking place is the painting by him of the picture of this particular subject. The value in the case is a projected state of affairs (that is, a state of affairs thought as future but also as realizable in a present), which he conceives and probably also images to himself and reacts to with appropriate feeling responses. This complex is a value in its essential role as an incentive.

We customarily say also that the eventual portrait, itself the physically actual work, is a value or has value. This is the value *as realized.* Before the execution of the painting, the portrait as conceived was the incentive for the painter to work, and that was the ontic status of the value relative to that time—it was a concept or conception (regardless whether a sparse or a richly filled-in one). Now the work has attained reality in the physical-object world and in that form has become public. To call it a value or to say of it that it has value in that form is systematically ambiguous, for once it is executed it can have value of a different kind, of a different ontic status, than it had before it was executed. It now may serve *others* as an incentive; they may be purchasers, gallery visitors, students of painting, or the like. Obviously the kind of value (which is to say, the role the finished work may have *as an incentive*) differs for each of these. In fact, the painting as executed may retain something of the kind of value it originally had for the painter, as when a few years after its completion he says "I still like to look at it," or "Now I can do better than that." However, while the statement "This painting has value" may be meaningful and true from each of these points of view, there is a difference in what its opening phrase "This painting" may mean ontologically. Here is an instance in which persons treat something as a reason for doing as they choose to do, but are not particularly conscious of the freedom of their choice to treat it as such, or of the differences in their own treatment of the object and the treatment of the same object by others, even when all parties are in concurrence to the extent of treating it as a value rather than merely and solely as a fact present on the scene.

Once the decision has been made to make a portrait, the *prima facie* value to be attained or the purpose to be served by a portrait is to show the spectator what the subject of the painting looks like. Especially before the invention of the camera, this affirmation might be taken as obvious. However, many a portraitist has subscribed to the purpose of flattering the subject, and insofar, to show what he does *not* look like. This conception of what the picture of that subject ought to be can be complicated by further motives, such as the desire of receiving maximum pay for doing portraits, or of puffing the ego of the subject as a result in itself, or of idealization by the painter of the subject as a person. But looking like a particular being has many levels. Portraitists typically attempt consciously to portray not mere physical appearance alone but also character. A painting may even become more or less fictional and unrelated to the character of the subject himself as known to the portraitist; both the physical appearance and the inherent character may be modified at the choice of the painter. Still another purpose of some painters is merely to produce something pleasant to see in the guise of a personal portrait, not necessarily an image of this or that specific subject but simply an image to be enjoyed in itself. (The term *portrait* may thus lose applicability, though this condition of the work might not be evident simply from seeing it.) Our list of purposes (incentives to the painter) to be realized by the entirety of the specific work may go on in this fashion indefinitely, just for this one kind of work in but one medium of art. This instance of the portrait illustrates that there is a specific value, or combination of specific values, particular to a given work but applying to it in the entirety rather than to parts or aspects of it only. His conception of these elements envisioned as being realized in future experience are direct and highly immediate incentives for the painter.

Most of the incentives mentioned in the above treatment of the portrait painting are either actual concepts or concept-dependent elements occurring in the consciousness of the painter. The very phrase "what the subject looks like" names a concept, in fact, a container concept in respect to its being fillable with that content which is one of the visual appearances of some chosen subject. The connotation of the concept is strongly vision-oriented, and to that extent sense-dependent, but the concept *what the subject looks like*, or, more generally with respect to pictorial representation, *what someone (or something) looks like*, is itself an abstraction, and the more explicit the painter is in asserting his purpose to be the portrayal of what this person, this subject, looks like, the more consciously he is guided by a concept. By *character* we conceive something like the general nature of that combination of particular components of personality which an individual possesses. We become conscious of character as an entity only after familiarity with enough individuals to be able to know that individuals are indeed not all alike in the components of their personality or in the combinations of such components, and yet are enough alike that we can indeed treat these combinations generally in the same way, that is, *as* what we call character, temperament, or personality. A painter must know what character in general is, before he can meaningfully announce that in his portrait of someone he attempts to portray individual character; and to know what character is, is to possess a pretty solidly constituted concept. Thus concepts and concept-dependent elements may strongly motivate the painter.

While one can imagine that a painter might, through an emotional inclination, unconsciously alter the appearance of someone whom he is painting toward the ideal, a conscious attempt at flattery is surely conceptual or concept-dependent. Another concept-dependent incentive is that of pay or reward, and there may be yet others for the portraitist. However, some of the other incentives we have mentioned move more closely to the sense-dependent and the feeling-dependent. In painting in such a way as to puff the ego of the sitter, the painter may be responding rather directly to a feeling active in himself as he paints, or to a vicarious feeling attributed by him to the sitter. Further, when he is strongly idealizing the subject, such as when he has feelings of love for the sitter, he then no doubt responds very directly to his own feelings and not in that respect to his concepts. Psychologically, the situation may indeed become quite a tangle. Is he remaking the sitter into an ideal that he will confuse with the actual subject? Does he will not only to produce a work of art as something that ought to exist, but also to create an imagined person (whom he likes or loves) who also ought to exist? The portraitist's emotional life is surely involved to some degree in his work, even when not to this extreme. In all these circumstances, he is participating in the bringing into the world in physical form a work that he believes ought to exist rather than not; and incentives based on perceptions, sense-dependent elements of experience, feelings, feeling-dependent elements of experience, and concepts and concept-dependent elements of experience all can join in engendering this belief upon which he acts.

Now we have begun to work rather well away from the concept-dependent incentives toward the others, and as we do so we are tending also to move from the portrait as a whole to its particular parts and details.

It seems highly likely that the medium in which a given artist works is a sign of which of his physical sensitivities are the keenest. That is, we suppose that a musician possesses greater auditory sensitivity than visual, compared to the average in each case, while a painter would presumably have the opposite apportionment. The artist probably naturally falls into work in his own most felicitous and appropriate medium, rather than at an early age saying to himself, "I should like to be an artist; now which medium shall I choose?" And if this is generally the case, then the artists who are most aesthetically successful with their art will tend generally to be those who are capable of having highly discriminate sense intuitions in the perceptual field in which their own work is located. It appears true, so far as one can learn objectively of such things, that the successful practicing artists work largely by intuition at this level rather than by deliberate conceptual steps. So to speak, they work so fast that they do not have time to stop and articulate verbally what it is that they are doing, much less why they have chosen to do just this instead of that.[3]

What this enables us to infer is that in some of the activity within the total process of production of a given work, the artist acts dominantly, even exclusively, on the basis of intuition. While generalizations will inevitably be challenged by numerous exceptions, I venture that the level concerned is ordinarily nearly everything internal to the work itself in the relation of part to whole or of aspect to totality, and probably in some cases it even includes the choice taking and decision making at the level of the whole work, the level discussed above. To illustrate what I mean, I would suggest that, in the instance of a portrait, once the painter is beginning his work, such choices as the choice of the relative position of the sitter to the plane of the canvas (will she be full-face, profile, or something else; seen on her own eye level, or from slightly or greatly below or above?), the choice of the apparent distance to be created as the virtual distance between the prospective spectator and the sitter, the choice of the relative intensity of the light to be represented, the choice of the apparent source of light, its direction, and location with respect to sitter and spectator, the choice of the amount of area of the canvas to be occupied by the sitter—all this sort of thing is most probably, I think, determined as responses of the painter to intuitions he has as he is setting about his work. I should say that these intuitions come not only directly from the sitter—that is, he looks at her to see what appearances she presents to him—but also from imaginings, projections, memories of past appearances of the sitter and perhaps of other persons, and other elements of his current consciousness. No doubt the choice made in one regard often carries with it the simultaneous determination of another open choice, as when the selection of an angle of the axis of the face also fixes the angle of incidence of light upon the plane of the forehead. It has often been pointed out that the process of producing a work of art is a continual process not only of making but also of criticizing. The artist puts an element in place on his canvas, surveys what he has made, and either approves or revises it as he continues with his work. Except of course for the arts that work with words, and there only in a special sense, this process is by no means necessarily or usually verbal, articulate, or even deliberate. There are few artists, particularly since the liberating movements of the nineteenth century, who are so cerebral as to conceptualize constantly and gather their concepts into logical arguments in order to make the decisions that result in their works of art. The whole idea of twentieth-century abstract expressionism is precisely not to do this, to stay as far away from the verbal as possible in order to set free the intuitions and creativity—whatever these may be. But my main point is that when choices are being made within the work instead of concerning the entire work as such, intuitions and responses to them (which may be called intuitive responses) are the chief means employed by the artist. Thus, sense perceptions of the subject, and sense perceptions of what has been already made by the painter upon his canvas, are incentives for the execution of the successive stages of his work.

In still more narrowly specifiable processes of the work of art than those just mentioned, the work, the activity that goes on, is characteristically intuitive; and this extends right down to the minutest detail. When the artist will paint a portrait, he must paint a head; when he paints a head, he must also paint a face; when he will paint a face, he must paint an eye; when he will paint an eye, he must also paint an eyeball; when he must paint an eyeball, he must paint its surface parts such as the pupil, the iris, and the white; when he must paint the white, he must paint a red vein across the white of the eye; and so on. Thus we get to the smallest level of detail with which the painter can be concerned. (More fully, when I say he "must paint" the details seen, such as the red vein, of course I intend that he must make the choice how to represent the eye—either with the vein or not.)

Let us make some suppositions, merely to set up an example. The painter of a certain sitter paints his subject sitting on the floor, her head turned an inch or two to her right and slightly inclined, so that a particularly attractive line of the chin is fully accessible to the spectator's view; her left eye is nearly fully visible but her right eye is partly obscured by its angle and by fainter lighting. Once she is positioned, he first covers the canvas with sketching strokes to block in her whole figure, then he proceeds to render prominent features of the prospective finished painting in their respective areas, and gradually supplies more and more detail to the various parts of the painting. As he does this, each step is influenced by what he has already done, and in turn it takes its place as an influence upon what he does next. The colors, the key of illumination, the thrust of the axes of the parts of the body, the atmosphere of the setting, the expression of the face, all become more and more determinate as he works. The incline of the head strongly affects the shadowing on the planes of the neck; the shadowing affects the key of color for the iris of each of the eyes; the coloration and key of illumination of the eyes affects the expression apparent in the face. The strokes shading the neck must have contours consistent with the line of the chin. The painter's strokes to portray the desired chin line must be consonant with those already in place to suggest the incline of the head. He sees as he paints whether his strokes have achieved this, and he either lets them stand as he continues or else he repaints accordingly. In applying his strokes, he determines their direction by his perceptions of the already applied strokes of the chin, and their key by the brightness he sees himself to have achieved in the area above, and so on, throughout all the detailed work of creating the portrayed woman who will bear the relation of *portrait of* to the physically real woman who sits before him.

The lesson in this, not alone about art but about all fields of endeavor, is now evident. Any one of the discriminable and classifiable elements of experience can be a value. So can any combination of these or relation among them. That is to say, it can be an incentive for a human agent, a value-judging person, who is undertaking action. In serving as an incentive, an element of these sorts may occur in various modes of existence, depending upon the time relative to the value-judging agent. That is, before execution of his act of realization, the value concerned is not actual in the realm in which it will ultimately be realized, such as the physical-object realm. Rather, it is something envisioned, conceived of, or *somehow* foreshadowed in consciousness, by the agent who is about to bring it to realization in its new realm. Even a single brush stroke—let us say, a tiny red line to reproduce a red vein that the painter sees in the eye of his subject—is first somehow held in mind as a potential thing to realize, then is actualized by the brushing of paint onto the canvas. Our language ordinarily does not discriminate between the one stage and the other—the earlier unrealized stage and the later stage of actuality—insofar as what we are speaking about is a *value*; but of course it does make a distinction insofar as it is a brush stroke. In the one case we say that it is a potential or a future brush stroke, and in the other, that it is an actual or real brush stroke. However, it seems virtually incontestable that when the brush stroke is merely potential, just an idea in the painter's mind, it is an incentive to the painter to put it down actually on the canvas, thus realizing the covering of a part of the canvas that will correspond to a vein in the subject's eye. Next, once the brush stroke is actually there on the canvas, it is something that the painter *treats as a reason* for the next thing he does; he either extends it or shortens it; thickens it or thins it; adds a second vein-stroke or paints it out entirely; mixes some of the red paint from which it was made with some flesh-tone paint that is intended for the cheekbone, to unify eye and cheekbone into one visage—and so on. Thus the actual vein brush stroke takes its place as a value[4] (or if the painter decides to omit the vein, the otherwise painted area of the eye where it is absent is a value) because he sees it as a part of the totality that is yet to be fully realized, a part of the pictured woman who is pulling upon him to complete her *picturization*. Finally, when the whole painting is completed, the painter considers it a thing (part of a larger thing, of course) that ought to be, a thing whose existence is better than its nonexistence, one of the items wherein the world of fact (the world of what is) and the world of value (the world of what ought to be) have now been made to coincide.

The same general statement can be made of the entire continuity of states of affairs respecting that painter and his career, starting from the single brush stroke, representing the vein, and going up the whole scale of ever-broader items of the actualized or the yet unrealized influences and incentives that impinge upon him. The brush stroke of the vein ought to exist, he judges; the white of the eye in which it is embedded ought to be there; it ought to be in a depiction of a complete eye that will have much to do with the portrayal of the appearance and character of the person in the portrait; the eye ought to be there in the face, the face in the whole body, the body as the content-matter of this painting; this painting as the current stage in a whole career of paintings; the career as the proper expression and realization of one human life. All of these things ought to be, rather than not—so judges the painter. If he does not say so verbally, certainly his behavior—his work—says it for him.

Yes, one will ask, but what *is* it that makes the painter judge that the red vein (let us say) ought to exist rather than be omitted from the portrait? Why does the red vein "have value" rather than plain white having value at that location in the portrait? Is not—the questioner continues—the whole problem of value just in this, that the one does and the other does not have value, and isn't it the presence of value in the one and its absence in the other that makes the difference? And further, isn't the aesthetic intuitionist correct in saying that the value of the red brush stroke is simply intuited, and that the ability (not to say genius) of the painter consists in discerning it there, and does this not explain the widely acknowledged aesthetic intuition?

The answers to these questions are implicit in the position already taken herein, and no doubt will already be quite evident to the reader. However, the position of the objector is as seriously held as it is familiar, and it deserves as explicit an answer as can be summoned. First, yes, the red vein has value, as explained a few paragraphs above. However, it was ascribed value relative to *this* painting and so judged by *this* painter while at work (and was perhaps never thought of by even the most thorough art scholar who ever looked at his work). I cannot believe that the value-intuitionist will be caught in the position of saying that every portrait ought to have a red vein in the eye, or that every sitter having a red eye-vein is to be portrayed with the red eye-vein, or that every red vein portrayed in every portrait bearing one is value-positive or good. The red vein has value (as assumed in our example) by virtue of everything else that is painted into the portrait, both what has come before it, including not only the laying of pigment on canvas but the setting up of the situation, the posing of the sitter, and so on, and of what came after it, all of which was selected by the painter as consonant with everything else comprising part of the portrait, in the knowledge that anything already in place could indeed be painted out at any time no matter how long it had been on the canvas. Hence the value of the red vein must be conceded to be a relative thing, and any absolutist intuitionism must be ruled out as an explanation of it.

How then can an intuitionism be relativistic? The answer is clear. If it cannot be a quality to which a subject responds, while yet he intuits something that is a reality, then the object intuited must be a relation. In addition to the *relata* that he observes, such as the red vein and the eyewhite against which it appears, and whose qualities he ascertains by the direct read-off we call intuition, he also intuits the relation between the red and white objects, or between the red vein and a certain age and bearing, which the subject of the painting exhibits, or the like. But then must not the claim be true that this relation itself bears or possesses value? No, it must not, by hypothesis, which denies that value itself is a quality amenable to intuition, and that must be the case whether the quality is borne by an object or by a relation between objects. But what is preferable than answering "by hypothesis" is to show what it is to which the subject responds by intuition.

There is a vast literature on the nature of relations, and considerable controversy over whether relations are real or not, and if so, in what sense. It seems obvious to me, however, that one thing that we surely do, regardless of what else we do, is conceive of the relations we talk about, and we both know and describe them through the instrumentality of propositions. The way in which some relations are expressed—for example, "to the left of," "older than"—is so patently lifted from propositional expression as to make this obvious. Throughout this sort of study a value relation such as "better than" will be separately expressed; its origin, ontic status, or metaphysical reality will go unquestioned since all we are doing is logic; and yet the relation is never expressed as "older than and therefore better than," or "more natural looking and therefore better than," or "more idealized and along with that better than." What I challenge is the assertion that a relation has the ability *in itself to have a value property* over and above, or along with and correlative with, its being a non-value relation. I do not deny that a relation can *be* a value—can be an incentive to a painter or other human agent. I do, however, challenge the view that both realities do exist, the relation R itself and a correlative property of relation R, which is the value possessed by R along with being possessed by all other things that possess value. No matter how explicit the investigator can be in describing the red vein, stating ever so fully its relations to the eyewhite, to the coloration of the whole, to the total facial expression, to the tone of the entire painting, he can never name or point to the *quid* that is the *value* of that red vein; for value is not a quid. The evidence of value of the red vein is, first, the fact that the painter saw fit to paint, and did paint, a red vein as part of the portrait. The value of the red vein, thereafter, is seen in the fact that those who see and approve of the painting concur that it belongs there, that it ought to exist there rather than not. In their valuations, these persons affirm that the red vein is as it ought to be and that it should exist in its apparent mode and form rather than not. As to its being a relation, the quality it has as a specific relation is a value; it was that which induced the painter to resolve to use rather than suppress the red vein. But that quality is not an alleged value-quality common to all good or beautiful things and intuited by a fortunate few who are able to detect it. Rather, its quality is its specific quality as just *that* relation, *different* from other relations. Very likely the relation of the red vein is complex, not simple. That is, it is no doubt related not only to the background of white against which it appears, but *also* to the color of the cheekbone and *also* to the apparent age and bearing of the subject of the painting and *also* to other features in the work of art. The perceptive spectator sees more and more relationships, if he should study that particular detail of the painting and judges it good, judges that it is as it ought to be, that there are these numerous interconnected relationships rather than not, or rather than a jumble of disconnected relationships having nothing to do with the painting as a whole and therefore with each other. If there is a satisfaction in the relationships, it is not an existing satisfaction to be collected, like a chop in the icebox waiting to be eaten, but rather it is a satisfaction in the apprehension of the specific relationships themselves, for what they are, and as adjudged good. The number of relationships is good because the continued apprehension of the painting continues to be rewarded with new intuitions, and the very process of collecting intuitions is a satisfying activity. The relations are themselves good, not because they all contain a property called goodness, but because they are specifically related in specific ways, in fact unique ways, that in turn are such that a spectator can say of them, "Those relationships in the portrait are just as they ought to be."

This discussion raises the possibility that the distinctive thing comprising the value of the aesthetic perception of the portrait with the eye detailed right down to the red vein is the pleasure we gain when we apprehend the vein. I am inclined to believe that the aesthetic intuition—which is for the most part acknowledged by theorists, critics, and artists nowadays—is more of this sort than of the nature of that of classical intuitionism. However, I should suggest that it is compounded of this and various other kinds of elements of experience. I should readily grant that some observers of the portrait we have watched in the making would comment upon the vein and would indicate a feeling of pleasure associated with apprehending it. However, simply seeing a red vein in itself is rather less likely to make us have a good feeling than otherwise—some of us at any rate tend a little more to be repelled than attracted by such a feature simply in itself. Nevertheless, we might remark that it was clever of the painter to use the vein in the way he did, or that without it character would be less well portrayed, or the like. Aesthetic intuition, in the sense of a result, the cognition of a work, I am suggesting, is not itself simple but is a product compounded of a great number of things. Rather than assert that one apprehends the good or the value directly, as the eighteenth-century moral sense and sense-of-beauty philosophers and the twentieth-century intuitionists have done, I should affirm that it is a descriptively true psychological principle that sentient beings enjoy the exercise of perception—that they derive a pleasant feeling from it. This lends added implicit meaning to Aristotle's principle, "All men by nature desire to know." Knowing, including knowing at the perceptual level, itself embodies a pleasure. This pleasure in perception itself is, I think, one of the bases of aesthetic intuition, but not the only one. Another, I suggest, is our pleasure concurrent with the performance of our interpretive acts, especially in palpably successful ones, or ones that we can carry out with confidence. Such an act takes place in the simple reception of the red on the canvas as not merely red, not even merely as a red line, but as a vein upon the surface of an eyeball. This is another way in which having sense intuitions, and the interpretive acts (those called perceptions and those above the merely perceptual level) that they set in motion, please him who has them. This as well as the previously mentioned one provide considerable justification for Aquinas's definition of beauty as "That which, upon being seen, pleases." Finally, I venture that the entire cognitive activity of absorbing and responding to an art work on the cognitive level is pleasurable. It may contain many acts of recognition, of decision, of exercise of valuative judgment, of memory, of articulation of that which is presented in nonverbal form—many possible exercises of the intellect. There will of course be much more variety from one observer to another in these cognitive respects than there will be in the perceptual and even in the subcognitive interpretive levels, and to that extent they are less aptly classified as comprising part of the total of the aesthetic intuitive product. Nevertheless, to the extent that the feelings have their objective counterpart in the work as public and seen by many spectators, and to the extent that they are immediate rather than mediated, I consider it appropriate that these responses be considered to make up a great part of the totality of what we call aesthetic intuition.

Moreover, I should not claim that aesthetic intuition is infallible, although the value intuitionists normally appear to regard an intuition of the sort that they believe in to be infallible.[5] Since the aesthetic intuition may be and normally is compound rather than simple, and thus there may be a different response in the make-up of the process from one observer to another, it may be different from one to another in its deliverances. Differences of opinion in evaluating works of art are notorious. However, I should claim that aesthetic intuition is trainable. We know that simply getting more and more experience with works of art of a given medium is a highly educative process, and that taste can to some extent be taught, that a culture can heighten or else decrease the intensity of aesthetic responses to various objects, and the like. What becomes the wonder—and a wonder in which many take pleasure—is the fact that with training a great many individuals' aesthetic judgments come into accord, and a canon of the good works of art gradually becomes recognized, both informally and to some extent formally, because the spectators come to judge their experiences for the most part in the same way. In my vernacular, as set out in this book, this means that they come to see the same things and to regard them as values, right down to the level of the particular brush stroke, the detail of the simple red line having as its counterpart a vein in the sitter's eye. It does not seem to require much explanation that a gallery goer, who doesn't happen himself to paints, gradually comes to see paintings more and more in the way that the painters see paintings. Thus he comes not only to adjudge that the work upon the gallery wall is a value actualized in the physical-object world, but also to understand how its parts or even its entirety when only a conception in the painter's mind could serve the latter as an incentive to paint what he painted, and paint it in just the way in which he did.

The doctrine of aesthetic judgment sketched here may seem to many adjudicators of the arts to be paying too high a price, that of giving up the ability to justify aesthetic judgments with authority. I do not believe that this is sacrificed. The justification of aesthetic judgments has more and more proceeded as a highly expository process, even a process simply of pointing in turn to the several parts or aspects of the artwork, then of asserting certain relations to exist between these (relations varying in their subject matter from relations between things perceptually present in the work to relations among concepts summoned up in the minds of spectators), and finally an assertion (which may even be implicit or achieved by tone rather than expressed overtly in words or propositions) that the work is good, or is of such-and-such a degree of worth, or is better-than these or not-so-good-as those other works in the same medium. I must grant that there often is consensus for a time on the worth, the value, of a work, especially of a "great" work. However, even these go in and out of fashion; we must not distort our conception of the degree of consensus in order to support the argument that the aesthetic intuition is so objectively based that it is valid for all spectators. On the other hand, the fact of the high degree of agreement, even if not complete consensus, is itself a stubborn fact to explain away if one declares that there is *no* objective basis for the deliverances of the aesthetic intuition, either individually or collectively among admirers of the arts.

These facts are consistent with the other facts, and the conclusions and suggestions drawn from them, in this book. As just proposed, I believe that there is a natural objectivity in the basis for aesthetic judgments, namely, the basis of the senses and higher faculties to the extent that humans are endowed alike with these, and are accordingly capable of taking pleasure in the various processes of perceiving, apprehending, interpreting, and conceiving that go into the reception of the work of art. And likewise, the differences of aesthetic judgments are attributable to differences in these. Yet the whole thing is not according to formula, by which calculations could show us the percent of aesthetic acuity or blindness of this or that person, the way the eye-doctor can measure his visual acuity. Another factor, without which there would be no question of justification of aesthetic judgment—because there would be no art nor aesthetic object—enters in. That is the factor of human freedom. And the relevant respect in which it enters is the respect in which the artist is free to treat any conception whatever as a reason to do this or that, to paint the vein in or paint it out, to paint the subject with photographic realism or with grotesque exaggeration, even to paint or to compose music instead. Beauty itself has gone out of fashion; painters and other artists have in the last century chosen to produce the ugly or even the nondescript as works of art (or, what is practically the same thing, they have redefined *beauty* to include the ugly, the nondescript, and any other condition of the conception the artist chooses as a potential aesthetic object). While this trend probably could not have been predicted a half-century before it began, few would attempt now to erase it from the history of art by claiming that it was a determined rather than free activity of those who took part in it.

One cannot, then, justify the deliverance of an aesthetic judgment with absoluteness or universal intersubjective validity; but no one needs therefore to stop judging works of art, or to stop justifying his aesthetic judgments to others or to himself. One may continue to point out the features and relations of a work, and invite others to approve. Those to whom these are pointed out may continue to enjoy the original perceptions they had of the work and now may enjoy the new perceptions (conceptions, interpretations, and so on) made possible by virtue of the discussion supplied by the scholar, critic, or gallery guide. And chances are very good, speaking statistically, that experienced judgments will be seen as acceptable to those on the receiving end. However, to give up that which would be necessary to vouch for aesthetic judgments as absolute or universally justified would be to give up the freedom to make choices among potential incentives to the artist, from the broadest to the most detailed level. Then there would be no art; and that indeed would be too high a price to pay.

The description of the process of aesthetic judgment as sketched herein has dwelt upon the interplay of intuitions of elements in an aesthetic medium (a palette, in the example) as incentive for the acts that, unit by unit, create the aesthetic object or the vehicle for the aesthetic object. This is a view that has been important to the arts in the last century, and represents the result of the discipline of the artist who is devoted to the idea of creating the aesthetic work to be free-standing, as it were, independent of the practical life and of its typical elements. However, earlier art and much that is contemporary still admits elements from the practical life, elements that we may call cognitive knowledge of the depicted subjects, knowledge of history or literature to which the work relates, objects associated with familiar sentiments, knowledge of human nature as it may engage in the interplay of personalities, and the like. While much modern art screens out this sort of thing, quite consciously, and deals so far as possible in pure forms for their own sake, in certain of the arts it is virtually impossible and at any rate exceedingly difficult to eliminate such elements. One can hardly conceive of a stage drama, for example, that expunges all interaction of characters and presents solely a spectacle of human forms in motion and human voices independent of speech. Such a presentation would cease to be drama and would simply metamorphose into dance and song. At best, no amount of effort toward purity by the artist would prevent the spectator from projecting cognitive elements from his own stock onto the work of art.

Therefore, any full consideration of the arts embracing all of them must still include the human cognitive elements, those often and effectively rendered by concepts; and these, as well as sensory appearances, have their respective intuitions and feeling-qualities. Rather than court repetitiveness by rehearsing these in description or illustration, we may as well move on to a consideration of the moral ought-judgment, into which these things enter as living factors, rather than as artifices of the work of art. The reader will be well able to accommodate this sort of material, as exhibited in the moral situation, to the representation of the moral situation in the arts.

13

The Moral *Ought:*
How We Make Moral Judgments

We now come to the most important task of our whole inquiry. That is, connecting the principles of value and of value-related language to the moral life, the most distinctly human aspect of our lives.

It has been my thesis that what is essential to value-assertive propositions, making them what they are and distinguishing them from fact-assertive propositions, is that they express or reflect ought-judgments. The core meaning of an affirmative ought-judgment is that a mentioned state of affairs ought to exist or that a mentioned event ought to be brought about; that it is better if this were so than otherwise. I have spoken of this core meaning as "the *pure* ought" or "the *simple* ought." In the previous chapter I suggested that aesthetic ought-judgments are a special sort of ought-judgment, and are distinguished as such by a special sort of consideration added to the judgment pure and simple. It is now time to assert that moral ought-judgments are another special kind of ought-judgment, bearing one or more additional characteristics absent in the judgments of the neutral, pure *ought*. The propositions that are characteristically moral or ethical propositions are value-assertive propositions reflecting their special property *over and above* the *pure* ought.[1]

In the moral life, the same elements will enter as in other aspects of life, because the moral is continuous with all else. Thus, in a moral experience we may expect sensory and sense-related elements, feelings and feeling-related elements, and concepts and concept-related elements all to be present. Not only will these elements be on hand but there will be all possible sorts of combinations among them, and hence all sorts of relationships of elements to others of their own kind and to elements of different kinds. These elements may be present in any of the modes of existence, and they will be present as objects of many kinds—as past objects (such as remembered items, or supposed past causes of present effects), or as present, future, potential, and perhaps even nonexistent, objects. We have already seen, in chapter twelve, how this rich arrray of the possible kinds of component elements of the moral experience is present in aesthetic experience.

Since the elements entering into moral judgmental situations, that is, the phenomena, perceptions, and conceptions of consciousness, are the same in their basic nature as those in prudential or aesthetic situations, essentially we make moral judgments in the same ways that we make these other value judgments. They have their start at the brush-stroke level, as in the incident in which Wilbur (in chapter seven) judged that he ought to throw a snowball. No moral problem was present to Wilbur's consciousness, and the judgment he arrived at was not especially a moral judgment. However, the question whether to perform an action becomes a moral question—or better said, an action has a moral dimension as well as its other dimensions—when it affects the well-being of persons other than its own agent.[2] The entry of a second person into the field of action, then, suffices to make the choice of action a moral matter. However, nothing in experience is more productive of specific intuitions, of relations among them, of the qualities of those relations, and so on, than another human, a living person. Furthermore, virtually every action we undertake *does* affect the well-being of at least one other person, and often of numerous others. Consequently, in a moral situation the number of elements of experience and their relations becomes exceedingly great, practically infinite, and their organization among themselves and vis-á-vis the moral agent becomes immensely complex.

To approach the matter of how we make moral judgments, let us go back to the incident portraying the presence of the simple *ought*. We have seen that Wilbur, in deciding to throw a snowball, has responded to many elements in the total situation that functioned as his incentive. We may fairly assert that Wilbur received intuitions from the physical objects of his environment; from his perceptions of relations among these; from remembered physical objects not then present, and remembered relations among those; from his own physical presence in the setting and the relationships arising as a consequence of that; and from memories of his presence in previous settings and the relationships he had had with them. He received intuitions from memories of actions he had earlier engaged in, such as the previous throwing of snowballs; and he received intuitions from his imaginings and anticipations of the imminent future throwing of a snowball, and perhaps conceived or imagined alternative actions he might perform instead. The qualities of each of these were compounded into the total resultant quality of a potential experience that might become an incentive to him. He received still additional intuitions from factors of his own psychology—his present feelings, remembered feelings, his expected feelings as when making and throwing a new snowball and also when performing alternative patterns of action. He received intuitions from his knowledge—that is, from beliefs, including not only those based on his own actual experience but also those based on teachings received from others. Thus, already at this stage of Wilbur's activity, the matrix of qualities perceived as borne upon elements of his situation is made up of elements that may number in the hundreds when analyzed. Even for a child it is immensely ramified and complicated. This complex pattern of elements, their qualities, their relations—and *their* qualities, relations of relations, and *their* qualities—is all within Wilbur's cognition but is so difficult to describe in full, detail by detail, that few of us ever venture to do so.

Yet the situation of Wilbur as heretofore sketched is among the simpler of those that we experience in ordinary life. We can easily see this through contrast, by making a simple additional supposition. Let us suppose now that just as Wilbur is about to hurl a large, hard, ice-glazed snowball toward the protruding stick on the woodpile, he hears his mother's voice: "Wilbur! Don't you throw that snowball!"

Now the whole situation becomes tremendously more complicated. Wilbur of course has an intuitive read-off from his own name, as heard in his mother's voice. This most intimate of elements of consciousness has not just one but myriad qualities, intuited and perceived throughout the whole period since early infancy, on innumerable occasions favorable and unfavorable. Further, the unwelcome word "Don't!" has many qualities of its own. Similarly, the remaining words of the heard imperative have distinctive qualities, and the total imperative, heard as a unitary structure rather than as a disjointed collection of verbal elements with whatever relations might arise among a collection of disconnected elements, has its qualities. The heard voice as such has sonal, tonal, and other heard qualities. Beyond that, the relation of the imperative to the originating person, Wilbur's mother, bears qualities some of which are familiar and memory evoking and others are unique to the new situation. The total imperative that is introduced by Wilbur's name has a relation to the speaker, Wilbur's mother, and that relation has its own distinctive quality (anxiety, dominance, humor, authoritativeness—that sort of thing). There is a relationship between the imperative and Wilbur himself that in turn bears some quality or other (Meek acceptance? Testing the authority figure? Automatic, grudging compliance? Occasion of a quarrel?).

But the most important new element in the setting that now has been introduced is the entire, immeasurably complex relationship of Wilbur and his mother. Its elements include much that is recoverable in memory, but also much that has long since been absorbed into Wilbur's patterns of thinking and acting without its being articulated by him in his inner discourse. It includes, of course, the present moment and its relations, whose qualities are now to be constructed by the two agents who enter into it, and it includes the future of the relationship, which in turn may be conceived of (as of this or that sort), imagined, hoped, planned, spoken of, engaged in cooperatively, and so on (or else rejected, derided, brushed aside, forgotten, and so on). Wilbur will receive intuitions of the nature of the relationship with his mother as it is and as it might be, in the short run and in the long run. It is from her voice itself, which is her current mode of appearing in his consciousness, that

Wilbur now has intuitions of her; but because of his familiarity with the whole person whose voice it is, he has ample impressions of the posture, disposition, intentions, and general bearing of this originator of the command that he has heard. He thus fills in places of indeterminacy that are left open by her appearing only as a voice. I cannot attempt here to divide the members of this collection of intuitions into those related to sense, feeling, or concept or their derivatives, but I can point out that certain concept-related elements may come to the fore in Wilbur's consciousness upon hearing this commanding voice. For example, Wilbur may remember an order never to throw snowballs while in the yard or near the garage or the house with its fragile windows, or some other such restriction. If so, he thus bears in mind, in the conceptual mode of appearing, a rule or imperative under which to subsume and judge his potential actions, producing particular judgments intended to apply as rules of conduct at the level of the single act, that may govern his selection of actions. And if the command not to throw the snowball brings sharply back to Wilbur's mind a rule of this sort, and he therefore apprehends immediately upon hearing the command that his anticipated action would violate the rule, then he has indeed used concepts and reasoning to gain a cognition of just how matters stand at the moment, when the planned act either must be performed or must be replaced by some other pattern of conduct.

We can readily perceive that with the entry upon the scene of a second person, the number of elements that comprise the total content of consciousness for one participant in it has become a structure of so many elements in so many combinations and relationships that they are, practically speaking, infinite. It is also apparent that with the entry upon the scene of the second person, guarding other interests than those of Wilbur's immediate pleasure and which may be affected by his actions, the situation has acquired a moral dimension.

In practical human life, we characteristically fasten our conscious attention upon the important indeterminacies, allowing to the cognitions of things that are settled and done a lesser degree of attention. Now that Wilbur hears his mother's voice, he has certain things to ascertain (Is Mother angry? Is she fearful? Has Wilbur previously been given a rule about snowballs that he has forgotten?). While the heart tugs at the narrative to bring both its characters to a happy reconciliation, philosophy enjoins us here to notice that Wilbur's mental questions—even if not so clearly articulated as the above examples—will have their answers in the form of propositions. Some of the propositions that might occur to Wilbur are already among his beliefs; others will have to be tested. Among these latter, some will prove true, and others false; still others might remain undetermined as to their truth-sign. Those that he discovers to be true will be added to his beliefs; they not only employ concepts but may be gathered together under some more general concept. Hence, Wilbur in his endeavor to grapple with a moral problem must obviously carry out a significant amount of reasoning. The significance of propositions as such, as elements in the consciousness of the moral agent, is that they enable him to think most systematically, with his best memory retention, with communication to others, and with the countless benefits of communications from others. Undoubtedly there is thinking and reasoning without propositions; however, introspection shows us that this is a process so covert that we have a hard time catching ourselves at it—whenever we try to verify that we have just performed a piece of nonverbalized thinking, we discover that we exhibit it to ourselves in words! Here we need not attempt to establish the balance between verbal and nonverbal thought, or the necessity of language as a presupposition of morality, but we will do well to honor the role played in valuation and in morality by discursive reasoning and propositional language forms. It is through them, first, that beliefs of others, including the funded wisdom of the culture, become beliefs or candidates for our belief; second, that we articulate our moral problems (literally "come to terms" with them), then carry on reflection, and finally express our decisions and justifications.

It has been useful to illustrate the continuity of elements and of the moral agent's responses to them by using the example of a child, because we benefit from the relative simplicity of the child's world and his relationships. If we were to consider some moral problem of an adult, we would find that the pattern sketched above is applicable, but probably the adult performs reasoning more consciously, performs it more often, and is more fully informed by previous practice and broader knowledge. The adult surely operates within a situation in which he derives all the qualities of all the elements and relations, such as those emerging in the illustration of Wilbur. However, there will come to mind for him a greater number of formal concepts of morality. He will have more to work with of this sort, received from his culture and worked with in his personal past experience. He may or may not be fairly skillful in the handling of these.

Let us imagine an adult who is a member of a union that is anticipating going on strike. In arriving at his decision whether he ought to strike or not, he will consider his *obligations* to his employer by virtue of his job arrangement or contract, his obligations to fellow members of the union, to his family, and the like. He will consider the *rights* of the employee and the employer as such. He will consider the duties of his job, and perhaps relate these to *duty* in general. He may express some of the points of these considerations in the form of rules or commandments, sentences that may occur in various grammatical shapes but have for him the force of imperatives. He may test and choose one or an array of more than one of these and resolve to bear it in mind as applicable. He will consider matters of *equity, justice,* and *fairness,* of *law* and *contract.* He will consider punishment and possible retribution against himself that either the employer or the union may exact, depending on his decision. In his debates with fellow union members, many facets of each of these will be brought out, and each facet of a given concept will yield its feeling-qualities and its concept-related or intellectual qualities. Along with these intuitive responses there will be some number of intellectual responses, such as an ordering of priorities among the concepts themselves or the generating and debating of propositions to which they give rise. Characteristically, in such debate, emotion enters strongly and takes on great importance, for people are unaccustomed to deliberating coldly and unemotionally about concepts intimately relating to their basic needs and psychological tendencies. But at any rate, we readily see that in the case of such a fairly common sort of moral decision as this, even alongside strong feeling, much that is conceptual and intellectual will enter into the process in consciousness of coming to a decision. And also characteristically, events may push the issue to decision before many of the individuals involved believe themselves to have deliberated fully enough to arrive properly at a decision.

The average adult in such a situation as the one sketched is not facile in moral deliberation. If anything were to make the reader reluctant to credit the parallel between the description of the artist making an artwork through a long sequence of minute aesthetic judgments (chapter twelve) and the moral agent arriving at a moral decision, it is probably this difference in the capabilities of the performers. The successful artist performs in his art for the love of it. He has a sustained long-term incentive that is not constantly engaged in intense competition with some other motive to the extent that self-interest constantly competes with the moral incentive. He is endowed with above-average talent to start with. Throughout his lifetime, he gains more and more directed practice in its use. He learns, understands, and augments the discipline of his work. In contrast, the moral agent is not singled out naturally by the endowment of talent but is tossed into the moral arena armed only with whatever assortment of abilities and temperament belong to him by accident of birth. He has little or no love for making moral decisions, but rather, often bewails the occasions necessitating them as problems he should much rather not have. He knows that by their nature moral problems tend to require him to set aside some proportion of what he conceives to be in his self-interest, yet he has little notion of how to arrive at a measure of that share, and is as often in error by giving up too much rather than not enough. (The uncertainty here is enough to make many persons abandon the very attempt and to fall back on self-interest, which others, driven by the same motive, tend to understand and to approve.) In his avoidance, which may readily become habitual, of moral problems, he gains only a minimal amount of practice in exercising moral skills, and that with little motivation for improvement; he certainly does not chafe from disuse and go out to seek moral dilemmas on which to gain practice. As to discipline, perhaps here he is less obviously ill-endowed than in the other aspects of the moral art, for after all he is a generous fellow and tends to have emotional impetus toward giving the other fellow his due, and this may reinforce a bit those of his judgments that call for abnegation. However, the circumstances of life make it easy to be self-serving and difficult to excel in the moral art. It is little wonder that virtuosi of morals are rare indeed.

To explore the sparseness of efficacy of the moral-agent-in-the-street, we may remark that he probably does not distinguish very clearly for himself the difference between emotions that sweep through his consciousness and factual or valuative thoughts that arise within it. He probably does not deliberately take steps to assure that all persons potentially affected are considered, their preferences, interests, and predictable feelings taken into account. He perhaps stands directly in the face of important considerations, yet entirely misses them or places a wrong importance upon them. Yet despite all this, one to whom it pertains nevertheless is inclined to agree that rationality, reasoning, is important to his endeavor, and so far as he understands what it is, tries to live up to its requirements. The desirability of rationality is probably pretty obvious to him, more obvious than the specific forms that rationality for his given moral problem might most fruitfully take.

First of all, rationality as it enters into moral judgments and decision making involves commitment, upon which much has been written. The question "Why should I be rational?" is followed quickly by another, also the subject of much existing literature, "Why should I be moral?" I shall assume that for the reader the issue on these two has already been settled—for otherwise, he would hardly be reading this book. Those of us who are sane and normal do in fact make a commitment to rationality. The commitment requires us to apply rules of reason both in arriving at our judgments and in testing and justifying them. A discussion of rationality in the latter connections will be pursued in later chapters. For now, it is worthwhile to note the place of reason in making moral judgments.

We are actually better aware of what we do in reasoning, in making moral judgments, than we are of what we take up as intuitions from the elements of the situation. Possibly this is because reason is a late comer to the processes involved. Again, it is possibly attributable to the necessity to articulate, in order to reason deliberately, whereas one can collect intuitions and store them in memory without at all assigning words to them as memorial, expressive, or communicative devices. Thus the processes of handling concepts are pretty familiar. They include such things as the examination of various concepts to analyze them, the placement of concepts in relation to one another, the subsumption of an instance under a concept or under a proposition that covers it, the attachment of predicates to objects of consciousness, the alignment of concepts according to degrees of obligation or to priorities of importance, the consideration of effects of conceived acts, the consideration of advantages and disadvantages, the ascription of motives to persons, the listing of rights and obligations, the interpreting of statements of information or opinion received from others, and much, much more of this sort of thing.

When reason enters the forum of moral judgment, the possibilities of what the outcomes will be become tremendously more numerous for it is with the arrival of reason that we are freed from being solely the creatures of our own psychophysical responses. No longer are we mere puppets of pleasure and pain; we can forego a pleasure or thwart a pain by applying reason. This is not merely by reflecting to learn how to avoid an otherwise inevitable pain, or to set in the place of a short-run pleasure a longer-run pleasure. Rather, we become able, through reason, to nullify entirely the usual stimulus-response circuit. We can encounter temptation to pleasure and spurn it; we can observe the threat of pain and avoid the pain rather than incur it, or upon feeling pain we can accept it and endure rather than flinching, or react quickly so as to remove the cause of the pain, in ways that are not possible to the subrational animal world. Once there is reason, there is human freedom. Once we can see more than a single possibility, we have freedom rather than confinement to an externally dictated order of events in our lives.

What does the occurrence of freedom in human reason mean to the moral judgment? It means for one thing that there is more than one possible outcome of a moral decision and the subsequent action. If there were not, the notion of moral judgment hardly would have arisen. But moreover, it means that since man is able to neutralize the psychological causal influences upon his action, he may do so. Thus an incident may turn out to have the result that psychological influences would bring about, but on the other hand it may emerge in a rational result that overrides the psychocausal. Normally, a child will accept an ice cream cone when offered, but on some occasion, he may take thought and decline it, for some conscious reason.

A second result of the freeing influence of reason is that persons may not only choose their acts, but may freely chose their reasons for their acts, and even prior to that (logically speaking) may freely choose the criteria for the reasons offered in support of their acts.[3] This fact is of considerable importance. Some individuals perhaps never would choose to honor fairness as a criterion, and would always honor their own power as reason enough, whenever it will gain advantage for them. But others, even those who are favored with strength and natural advantage, will be able to override personal advantage and bond themselves to a criterion of fairness, freely chosen, as the criterion that *ought* to obtain over their own and others' judgments.

The importance of the introduction of reasoning among the factors contributing to the selection of actions affecting persons cannot be overemphasized, for it is this that creates the moral dimension of human relations.[4] And so it is no accident that reasoning—the employment and manipulation of propositions and concepts—has this importance just where there is the introduction of a second performer of physical action, and where the emphasis shifts to its moral dimension. Instincts are obviously not enough for humans to determine selections of actions. In human evolution, these instincts may have been replaced by or possibly developed into feelings and feeling-dependent elements. However, man is now self-conscious; he knows himself as a rational being; and he is at a stage, or at least in transition to it, in which reason is the function through which he makes his selections of actions. The vehicle for discursive reasoning is the proposition, and on that account in a situation in which a person is fully aware that he has a problem that is particularly moral in nature, he turns to reason and summons up within himself such propositions as are available to him and as he believes will serve his moral purpose, the solution of his moral problem.

The propositions and concepts utilized will of course predominantly include beliefs, although they may also include propositions that are entertained but to which belief is not attached. The concepts may include one or more that have the role of supplying method or model. Most important, no doubt, among the propositions brought to mind will be those that may be called moral principles. Their source might be formal teaching, as in the case of the Ten Commandments, the Golden Rule, or some of the common rules of equity and fair play; or their source might be past experience of the individual himself, articulated, interpreted, and adapted according to his own wisdom. In some cases, law will contribute propositions that function as moral beliefs. Other kinds of principles will also be involved: those of systematic knowledge, such as one's detailed everyday knowledge of one's own work or interests, or those of practical physics, psychology, sociology, or government. These will affect decisions about what acts to perform because in the selection the agent will want to forecast outcomes, hence he will need and use principles of cause and effect, of probability, of tendencies of humans in their behavior, and other such things.

It was affirmed earlier (chapter nine) that reasoning is continuous with the other functions and processes of the life of the mind, not discontinuous with or discrete from them. Experience is the source of this statement, and experience supplies to us acquaintance with some consequences of it. First, just as senses and feelings supply to us intuitions of sense-qualities and feeling-qualities, *intellect and reasoning supply intuitions of qualities* occurring in reasoning-experience. Our felt admiration of intelligence is an example; it is probably a summation of particulars among these. Individual episodes, solutions of problems, rational processes such as comparison, subsumption, addition or subtraction, symbol selection—all have their own "flavor." The differences they afford us are known in intuitions that blend the affective, the feeling-character, with the intellective, the knowledge by acquaintance of them that we gain from operating them.

Second, in their presence or their anticipation, these qualities, too, are motivational. Just as with those elements that are sensory or affective, or sense-dependent or feeling-dependent, the occurrence of the intuitions of these intellective elements is also part of the satisfaction that we gain from life. They function as corollaries of activity as well—mental activity in this case—and thereby as incentives to performance, independently of anticipated achievement of other fulfillments. While the fact of these satisfactions is little noted, evidence of them exists on every hand. Some people play chess for their recreation rather than a physical sport; this game is well known for its appeal to the intellect. Everyday recreational pursuits include such things as crossword puzzles and double acrostics, and adult and children's games that call for prowess in thinking. Even watching spectator sports invokes mental analyses of team strategy. All these are recreations partly if not largely because of the character of the thinking and the problem solving that they involve. Moreover, most persons having a daily occupation have enjoyment in the kind and intensity of intellectual activity it calls for, even if that is a modest amount. "All men by nature desire to know," for the intellectual processes required for gaining knowledge are themselves satisfying; they are fulfillments, whether the knowledge finally attained is itself permanent or temporary, valuable or worthless. Many a scientist—some say, the typical scientist—carries on inquiry not so much for the beneficial results as for the enjoyment of the intellectual pursuit of the goal.

Intellectual activity is often described as "higher" in comparison with physical activity. It becomes more and more evident with advancing science and technology that man can achieve structures of intellect of ever-greater refinement and complexity, each advance yielding new, satisfying qualities. However, it is also evident that the addition of reasoning power and its effects on the physical powers that developed earlier in man's history has brought gigantic increases in man's control over things in his world. The satisfaction and fulfillment of an activity is greater the more control and power it brings to its performer. The rational factors in activity, especially those having to do with planning the activity, predicting its results, correcting and adjusting for unforeseen developments as the activity is carried forward toward the intended results, and finally the survey of its actual results—the rational factors are of an order such that they give man greater powers, powers added to the physical powers that he can enjoy out of the stimuli of senses and feelings only, and that greatly multiply the satisfactions of their pursuit. It is legitimate on this basis to call the satisfaction that accompanies them a "higher" order of satisfaction than those of the earlier stages.

Therefore it is a fulfillment and a satisfaction in itself to be as rationally moral as one can,[5] just as it is a satisfaction to employ the rational capacities for other highly challenging intellectual pursuits. It must remain true that for different rational agents there shall always be divergent judgments, and therefore divergent consequences of moral reflection and reasoning based on divergent judgments; but nevertheless man will always be able to justify to himself his continued effort to be rational in morals. Even though doing one's moral, rational best may from time to time seem to effect little social progress or have little effect on the just outcome of controversies, the satisfaction in having done his rational best will suffice to motivate man to devote his intellect to ever more rational morality. We thus may expect him to tend to do this more and more, in his efforts to solve his moral as well as his other sorts of problems. He can justify the rational activity by the higher nature of the satisfaction that it yields, by a process of justification which itself is an exercise of that capacity, yielding that satisfaction. Thus the very justifying itself yields its own peculiar reward. This sounds like the application of a purely egoistic criterion. So far as it goes, that is true, but there is nothing ignoble about it, since the good results yielded for the self can be made to coincide with good results for society. To bring about the blending into one of these two fields of benefit by one's acts and through one's reflections is an important part of the art of moral conduct.

Thus there is nothing alien to man's nature in the application of intellect to moral difficulties. When, on the other hand, we look back to feeling for the explanation of moral experience, as is done by emotivists and sentimentalists in ethics, we simply overlook the nature of our actual experience in reasoning and its fulfillments. Feeling is strongly present, no doubt, and partly because some of it is yielded up by reasoning; but reason is what makes moral experience self-conscious and capable of the very asking of the question of what its basis is.

The general nature of moral reasoning has been outlined in the literature of ethics many times, and in the compass of a book that must also treat of other things, I cannot do justice to the topic. I will, however, bring up a few salient points that help us to see what is involved in the moral episodes of human experience, and attempt to show the moral bearings of the description of value that I have placed before the reader.

It should first be noted that although the ethical philosophers dwell upon the difficult problems and especially upon those that raise theoretic rather than merely psychological difficulties, the course of true ethical reasoning does run smooth on innumerable occasions in the life of any one of us. There are many decisions every day embodying the pattern of surveying an instance, regarding it as belonging under a certain rule, and acting accordingly. I find a colleague's billfold in the lobby of our building. Do I pocket it and say nothing? Of course not, for it belongs to him, not to me. Here comes a co-worker who has done me a disservice; shall I refuse to answer his cheerful "Good morning"? I do not, for that would not be treating him as a peer and a human being. Should I park in front of my office building door, where the curb is painted yellow? Although I probably could park there without being ticketed, I do not do so, choosing rather to conform to the rule. Syllogistic reasoning of this most ordinary sort does quite well in bringing these daily moral situations to a satisfactory outcome.

But the moral problems that give us psychological difficulties—which is to say, those that we regard as difficult rather than easy, those that give us pain, cause us to worry—tend to be problems in which principles are in conflict. When that happens, it is indeed normal for us to worry, for we have feeling-impressions of a disturbing sort. The presence of the conflict of principles gives rise to whole new sets of intuitions that are absent from the easy cases of the paragraph above. These arise from rational relations apparent among the conflicting principles and their adherent beliefs as well as from sense- and feeling-elements of the consciousness of the episode. For many of us, they often quite overwhelm us and we resolve the moral problem, not wholly rationally, by adopting some action that simply brings to an end the psychological difficulty.[6] Other solutions however do remain possible. One solution is to achieve an ordering of the two conflicting principles so that one of them is set beneath the other (e.g., I decide that my duty to my father on account of his health is a greater obligation than my duty to my friend on account of his pleasure). Another avenue is to search for a third principle, to which the two that are in apparent conflict are both subservient, and examine whether it will serve to point out a solution (i.e., an ordering procedure for the two, or a justification for abrogating of one of them).

Suppose, however, that in facing a specific moral problem one seeks for a third principle to reconcile two conflicting moral principles. Is this to be searched for within morality, or outside it? If we manage to find our third principle within our moral framework—even at its edge—we are fortunate; we then know how to proceed. But if we find none there, is it rational and morally appropriate to let a nonmoral principle be the determining factor in a serious and urgent moral perplexity?

In twentieth-century moral discussion, this question has arisen in relation to another: Whether moral propositions comprise a logically ordered system, like perhaps a branch of mathematics or a set of rules for a game. If that were the case, difficulty arises in finding a grounding for the system that is anything more than arbitrary, like the rules for gin rummy or bridge. A game of bridge may proceed along quite strictly conceived lines, but bridge isn't "about anything," and a violation of one of its rules has no scope nor effect outside the artificial setting of the game itself. Are moral propositions similarly arbitrary, unrelated to the world external to their statement, and hence of no binding force upon persons who disclaim them? Or is it the case that moral propositions do have substantive content but that the relation of the moral proposition to its content cannot be explicated? Is the situation analogous to that of facts, in which a fact of the external world cannot tell itself to us, so that our sentences are forever separated from those qualities and relations that purportedly are their subject matter, and *fact* is ultimately indefinable, facts are ultimately unutterable?[7]

It is sometimes stated that within the moral community we subscribe to a set of principles that establishes the moral framework, and we make our decisions accordingly, but that there are no moral principles to serve as determinants of judgment upon the framework itself. Thus when an ethical principle of the broadest scope is challenged, or two such are forced upon us for a choice, the decision is made on some other basis than an ethical basis—

perhaps personal taste, or convenience, or temperament, or a perception of national priorities or self-interest. The framework of rules or principles serves to harmonize the activities for achieving the purposes of individuals or groups, so long as it does not come under challenge. Such a view, even if accurate, should leave us uneasy, for in life on this globe moral frameworks are constantly undergoing challenges, not only on specific points but in entire principles, and general consensus alone is an unstable and impracticable foundation upon which to found our moral structure.

A reply to the view of moral propositions as a closed system is possible on a number of grounds. Principally, and what I believe suffices, is that it does not square with experience. To be sure, communities and societies do use sets of propositions in systematic ways to communicate about and to agree upon moral rights and wrongs—they do employ rational means for solving moral perplexities. This of course is all to the good. But it does not necessarily validate the model of the ideal logical system. There is a fundamental difference. With an ideal logical system, just as with a work of art, a framing is artificially imposed. Once the opening postulates are set down, boundaries to the system automatically follow. However, that is not the case—at least it is not *practically* the case—with the world in which we carry on our lives. We have proceeded from a natural universe that is to all effects an infinite continuity; while we can in some respects create boundaries to our activity, we cannot achieve a radical bifurcation of our own being from that of the world around us, including especially the other persons cohabiting that world. From this consideration it seems to me that if we but devote adequate attention to the dividing line between the world and the system(s) of moral propositions that we use, we will find that these propositions have somehow sprung from that world, that they are not separated from it by an unbridgeable gap, and that the division is not best represented by a sharp line but rather by a broad margin within which the nonverbal may overlap and interact with the verbal and logical.

The interpretation of the moral beliefs as comprising a closed system of interrelated propositions may be illustrated by the mapping of a forest. If we are within the forest and must map its trees, we may locate every tree by virtue of its spatial relation to some one designated tree that we begin with; further, to serve as the point of origin of our coordinates for mapping, any tree will do. Regardless which tree is chosen as "primitive," the primary reference point, the edge of the forest remains where it is as the boundary of the system. To take the view of a logically closed moral system as the model of morality would in effect say "Do not attempt to look beyond the edge of the forest, for what is there is unlike our trees and will do nothing to relate us to our community—our forest and its trees." But knowledge of the unlike may be as explanatory as knowledge of the like; we need not artificially confine ourselves within our boundaries merely because we cannot, for the present, see the relevance of exterior, apparently nonmoral, furniture of our universe to the moral dimension. Thus there is, beyond the body or bodies of ethical beliefs, a broader framework within which all such systems occur, and that broader framework has not lost all connection with the moral upon giving birth to it. The broader frame, and what appears to be the broadest of all potential frames, is the world we live in, the universe, the totality of all things—of all reals and of all possibles, of all things that there are and all things that could be.

To refer to "the world itself," that which in our consciousness is non-verbal in contrast with that which is verbal, is to shift our attention from the propositions of morality as verbalized to the factors that we distinguish as the objects of consciousness, the items of our external world. Many will strongly object to this shift from propositions in which ethical principles are couched to all sorts of other things that are not propositions. Their objection is based on the arbitrariness of language, from which it appears to follow that the entities of language have no "real connection" with what language is "about," and hence that there is a logical gap between the world and the system of moral (as well as all other) propositions. While this shift is difficult to make and may offer potentially treacherous footing, I do not believe it impossible. Rather, I am sure it can be made, for we have in fact already made its reverse, coming in the other direction, from the "real" world to the articulate intellectual viewpoint that we now occupy. That is to say, morality, ethics, and their propositions arose from within the world, which antedated them. This fact appears to heighten the likelihood that we will be able to succeed in looking within our universe for things not yet articulated that will supply to morality grounds of sufficient breadth for our bodies of moral belief.

The way we have made this shift may be expressed by considering the proposition in its role as *communication.* I am proposing to get a basis for connecting propositions, which may be treated as communications, with something else. If we wanted merely to go from one group of propositions to another, we could readily do it, for we have propositional logic to help us. But the problem I am attempting to delineate, then answer, is to get propositions justifying the broad framing principles of our moral system. But it seems, as we theorize, that these justifications must come only from prior propositions—the axioms or basic truths—and our difficulty seems to be that these are exactly what we lack. But the alternative is that somehow there can be communication from the broader frame to the ethical frame, when the frame external to the ethical frame does *not* consist of propositions, but rather of the world. To answer, I submit that precisely this is happening all the time. The world is constantly originating the intuitions that we "see" or "read off" from it, perceive, report in symbolic form in propositions, and conceive of in clusters of propositions. We apprehend the intuitions, and (since there are so many) we select from them those by which we are consciously influenced. We amass these and combine them into structures; then we single out some of them to be reasons for our actions; then long after, having gained considerable experience in such activity, we form and phrase broad propositions to articulate our principles of action, our moral principles. While all this activity by us and by our environing objects of consciousness is continuous in space and time, through rationality we treat parts and segments of it as discrete and as though detached from time—for we have learned the uses of this device, the device of conceptualizing. In this fashion, our world itself is made to be a framework for our ethical judgments; and for those of us who possess a specifically ethical framework that like a branch of mathematics is a closed system, the world itself is the frame for that system, as well as for other coexistent systems, rational and otherwise.

As individuals, even if we avow that we are operating from within an adequate body of moral belief—and hence effectively within a complete and closed system—*we do in fact* refer outside the framework of that system for more incentives, values, *oughts* to be realized. The environing world is what we take as the "real" to which we refer when we ask what we "really" ought to do or decide. We heed our intuitions and structures of intuitions, from the brush-stroke level upward to levels of great compexity, including not only intuitions from the physical, practical world but also, and most importantly, the intuitions we receive from our abstract rational structures and their relations. From these particulars and structures of particulars, we—our society, our civilization, even our species—generalize to the principles we need: first the narrower maxims for particular actions, then the broader and broader principles for ordering the lesser ones. What improves upon mere consensus to validate the broadest principles actually in use at a given time is the process of moral justification, which we develop rationally along with the development of our body of moral belief.

Moreover, we do not in practice cut off our ethical judgments from the particulars, or leap to a moral decision across a chasm that leaves them all behind. Rather, we weave intricately together all our structures—the non-verbal and the verbal, the material and the rational, the sense-dependent, feeling-dependent, and concept-dependent—to make for ourselves just one life-in-the-world. Not only is a given moral episode tied to what precedes and follows it. In addition, it becomes an element in a larger life that has a tone of its own, which can be characterized verbally to oneself or other observers, which other observers also can characterize verbally, and which has its corollary satisfactions not only as the successful culminations of moral episodes are brought about, but also as they are successfully woven with the other elements of one's life. This life maintains both its satisfactions and its motivations, the latter always including the basic fulfillment of the actions that are the responses to whatever environment one has, within which one moves, and which one seeks to control.

While the description just given may sound more grand than lifelike, not only do some individual lives realize it but we find on the broader scale of the social world a trend that exemplifies it. More and more we see the need to reconcile the cultures of many societies, with their diverse ethical systems; and some actual progress is in fact made toward that end. One societal code calls for maintaining peace even if at great material sacrifice; another calls for action at any price to avenge injuries, regardless whether the peace is shattered by such action. We have seen in the twentieth century an era in which some societal codes call for equality of political and economic rights for each individual, while other codes call for the elevation of one group and the depression of another in these respects. Further, we have seen changes in the latter kinds of relation, so that we may suppose that the method of looking beyond the framework of the code in order to find another principle was applied. What is it that makes two warring nations, whose wars are based on religious beliefs embodying differing moralities, finally make peace and begin to cooperate? Apparently something underlying both, in the name of God or humanity, is found that takes precedence over the prior principles. Thus, not only individuals but nations can grow broader both in the scope of their rationality and in the reach of their moral action.

In this chapter we have seen how it is that in practical situations we actually make moral judgments. We do so from a base of intuitions, from among which we select certain perceived and interpreted intuitions as materials upon which we perform considerable operations of reasoning. Our description of the process whereby we do actually arrive at our moral valuations is by nature a summary and therefore can have only rough accuracy. Since exceptions can be found, it must be assessed by reference to experience, the broadest possible experience. It is, however, descriptive in intent. Once we form a moral ought-judgment, of course, we then have the problem of assessing or testing it. In order to do this, we must necessarily bring in the normative, which is quite a different sort of enterprise than description. To attempt to give adequate treatment to the testing of moral ought-judgments, in the next chapters I shall first treat justification descriptively, then speak of how we ought to make our moral judgments.

How We Test Moral Judgments

I. Reason, Justification, and Consequences

In the ideal situation, the reasons we offer to a critic as justification of a moral judgment or of the act that realizes the moral judgment are exactly the same as the reasons we perform it. Of course, the psychological term *rationalizing* reminds us that it does not always happen so. For rationalizing in this sense, which for my purposes is a pejorative sense, refers to the process of finding reasons after the fact, reasons that one hopes will be acceptable to others or even to one's own conscience, that is to say, a moral criticism of oneself as moral agent. For simplicity of exposition, I shall leave out of this account the processes that masquerade as arriving at moral judgments but are actually instances of rationalizing "to salve one's conscience." I shall also leave out any differences that might relate to the place in the sequence in which justification occurs, relative to the act. That is, I shall call *justification* the process of arriving at the best moral judgment possible through conscious deliberation carried on when the agent is still seeking the most justifiable action, and I shall also call justification the process of supplying statements explaining, after the judgment was reached or after the act took place, why just that judgment or that act was the one selected. In other words, it is indifferent in this discussion whether the justification we are talking about takes place before or after the act justified.

When we conclude that the underlying meaning of the valuative terms of our vocabulary is the general notion, "the way things ought to be," or "the way things ought to happen," we immediately face two important questions: "What is it that ought to be brought about?" or "What is it that ought to be done?" For each such judgment, the justification, if any, or collection of justifications, if there are more than one, supply the answer to that question for that judgment. Insofar as these justifications have features in common, it is possible to sketch out a description of the process of justification in general, as it actually takes place. This important matter is the burden of the present chapter. Later, the project will go beyond stating how we do actually test or justify moral judgments and to make proposals about how we ought to test and justify them. Only with the presentation of that material will the doctrine of the present volume be complete, and even then only as an outline into which investigations of less broad and general problems should be fitted.

Justification is so important to the function and effectiveness of moral ought-judgments that in our minds it tends to combine with or be absorbed into the very generation of them. However, the separateness of the ought-judgment itself and the justification for it is very evident; we have no difficulty in thinking of moral judgments of the form "A ought to perform act X" or "B ought not to bring about situation Y" even when no justification or sanction is expressed or seems to be present in context.

What then of the possibility of justification at all, when choices of what to value—choices of what conditions are those that we assert ought to be brought about and actualized—are totally free choices? Obviously justification is possible, for our actual moral experience shows us that it is indeed carried out, again and again. The issue is not the question whether it is ever desired or attempted, but the success of the attempt. And even in the absence of acknowledged absolute values, there are successful justifications. I shall endeavor to suggest how this is possible.

The practical features of justification are quite familiar. When Smith wants to justify one of his acts to Jones, he states or mentions a justifying principle J in which Smith supposes Jones to believe, and in doing so Smith says "I made my judgment (or selected or performed my action) on account of its being required by (or in accordance with) the justifying principle J." If Jones accepts Smith's justification the matter probably ends. If Jones does not accept the justification, then he can rebut it in a limited number of ways. He can (a) contest or deny subscribing to the justifying principle J, or (b) he can deny that J required or permitted Smith's performing the act in question, or (c) he can affirm that while J may seem to have called for the act, it actually participates with some additional principle in a combination of justifying principles that require a different act by Smith. If Jones denies subscribing to J, this suggests either that Smith did not choose his justifying principle well according to what Jones believes in, or that Jones is inconsistent—has once believed in J but has abandoned belief in it, or is lying about what he believes in, or is simply unreflective in respect to this and perhaps other justifying principles. In any of the latter outcomes, it is fair to say that to the extent that the outcome obtains, Jones has lapsed in his rationality or in his commitment to it. That is to say, he is abandoning the use of reasons, or he is making mistakes in his purported or attempted use of reasons. If Smith unfortunately chose a justifying principle that Jones contradicts or does not subscribe to, then this of course is an attempted justification that has failed, at least relative to Jones. (Smith then may want to try again with a new justifying argument that he can sincerely offer and that, he believes, also supports his decision.)

Then, if Jones were to claim that J does not require Smith's performing the act that Smith is attempting to justify (i.e., if Jones holds to b), this opens up an inquiry in which Smith and Jones examine whether J does indeed logically constitute a reason for performing the act or not, and insofar as it is an examination of the relation between a proposition and a reason for believing the proposition, it is a rational pursuit. It may proceed along well-known logical principles and invoke well-known logical rules. It may also require the reviewing of factual statements for Jones's acceptance or the gathering of more fact-assertive statements. If, on the other hand, Jones can show that although J by itself might call for Smith's chosen act, in connection with an additional principle K it must set that act aside, then this is another rational inquiry which similarly will examine relationships between reasons and envisioned outcomes, reasons and their relations to that proposition that expresses the outcome in propositional form. This, too, is a rational pursuit, and may be carried out according to the methods of logic and sound reasoning.

While there can be endless permutations to actual discussions of the sort just outlined, it does appear that properly successful (not just merely lucky!) justifications are rational structures and that proper criticisms of justifications (such as those attributed above to Jones) are themselves rational discourses, while rejections of justification when they are not based on proper impartial criticism are failures of or escapes from rationality. Thus the attempt to justify requires the commitment to rationality by both the justifier and his critic. In practice, justification is relative precisely to these two parties, the one submitting the justification and the other occupying a position to accept or reject it. And success in justification depends upon the maintenance by both of these parties of their commitment to rationality. Nothing could more fully exemplify the principle that morality is a rational pursuit and that man is rational in his actions to the extent that they are freely chosen, since any genuine choice may be submitted to the demand for rational justification. It thus becomes evident again that man chooses his reasons, as well as his actions undertaken for those reasons.

The apparent possibilities in the justification situation show us that, as in any reasoned discourse, there are questions of both fact and form. The discussion by Smith and Jones of Smith's act may reveal formal flaws or gaps—logical fallacies—in the relations claimed by Smith to hold between his act and its justifying principle; or it may reveal errors of fact such as Jones might introduce in an attempt to show that although the principle J was a worthy one, because of the nature of Smith's act that act was not actually required by J. Thus a fact about the act itself may be brought into question, and if the discussion is completed the question is settled one way or the other. Either party to the discussion expects himself and the other to acknowledge both the factuality of exhibited or demonstrable facts, the soundness of correctly assembled logical structures, and the unsoundness of those structures that are flawed. All of us discover, though not all persons are aware of or articulate about the discovery, that life's purposes are better served by acknowledging fact rather than by fixing belief in spite of fact, and are also better served by acknowledging the soundness of objective logical structures rather than by fixing belief in spite of such logical structures. Therefore the expectation on the part of either Smith or Jones about the other that the other will adhere to rationality, by and large, is not an unrealistic expectation, although through lack of knowledge or expertise one or both may make errors in the steps of exercising rationality.

Thus there lie at the base of the process of justification the fundamental epistemological processes, those of establishing beliefs in accordance with the facts of the natural world that confront us and also of the rational, logical world to which we are committed. But also, presupposed by justification, even as by action, there is human freedom to take into account.

We can with profit make a parallel in reasons for moral conduct to the treatment of value we have already given in the field of aesthetics. The same descriptions apply,[1] though much less simply. One portraitist takes the presence of a red vein in the eye of a sitter as a reason to place a representation of a red vein in the finished portrait; another artist does not regard it so, and does not reproduce the vein. Either would say that his act (or omission) is "on aesthetic grounds." One moral agent takes the presence of a beggar on the doorstep of his office buiding as a reason to withdraw a coin from his pocket; another moral agent does not regard it so. In parallel fashion, either might say that his act or omission was on moral grounds, or for moral reasons. Once each has learned this much of the other's response to the beggar, it is not probable that the two would quarrel and think ill of one another, although they might think ill of the other's act. Each would respect the other's deliberate action, for both persons know not only that the other had a reason but that each is free to choose his own reasons for the state of affairs he realizes. In tolerating the other's position while not subscribing to it, each is acknowledging both that the possibility of having values is a matter of the commitment to rationality, and also that the commitment to rationality demands the attributing of rationality to the other party, and of according to the other the right to do as oneself does, that is, to act in view of one's own selection of reasons. This is acknowledged, even though it is true that the other *must* do anyway that which he has a right to do—choose his own values from among a variety within which the selection of the best is debatable.

The rightness of a value, a situation to be realized, is always relative to the agent who acts to realize it, to others who will be affected in their well-being by the agent's act, and to those who will elect to be critics of the act (some of whom may be directly affected by it, and others of whom may be unaffected observers). And it is too simple a conception of things of this sort to speak as though just one fact normally makes all the difference, one fact chosen as a reason by one agent and rejected as a reason by another (for example, the fact that the beggar is on the doorstep). Similarly, it is too simple a conception that a single act like the giving of a coin is what in itself comprises an entire state of affairs that ought (or in another's view ought not) to be realized. In our thinking, we do oversimplify and reduce contemplated situations to their barest essentials, in order to get clear about them, but life does not ordinarily present them in such simple fashion. The person who on grounds claimed to be ethical declines to give the beggar a coin perhaps attempts to justify his restraint of generous impulse by placing the incident in the larger context of professional beggary, of more systematic and comprehensive methods of dispensing charitable donations, and the like. Perhaps his opponent in the argument is equally farseeing but after acknowledging these arguments offers others counter to their thrust. At any rate, the more important situations are complex and ramified, far-reaching and interrelated rather than small and simple. We recognize this complexity and scale of the real situations of life, and that is why we can readily believe that even though we disagree with an opponent in a discussion of ethical reasons, he too has selected reasons and values rationally rather than irrationally. When we are free to attach value to (that is, to regard as an incentive) any of the possibilities that imagination and reason reveal to us, as available for a total value structure, then the multiplicity of steps in the assembly of a structure of values from reflected-upon conceptions based on factual and other beliefs, makes disagreement readily possible *within* rather than outside the framework of rationality.

How, then, does one actually allocate to a fact or a conception the status of being a reason for one's conduct? Is there a touchstone, to let the perplexed agent know whether he ought or ought not to perform act X, and why? Above the level of taking the intuitive read-off from the brush strokes with which the panorama of the world at a given moment is painted, many methods to justify moral ought-judgments are actually brought into play. One of the most common is the citation of authority. Why should I perform act X? Because God, or the king, or father, or elder brother, or the captain, the drill sergeant, the scoutmaster, or another authority has so commanded. For many a situation this reply to the question is effective justification for the recipient of the ought-judgment, and challenge is put to rest by it. However, while on occasion it is practical and perhaps quite necessary, it is hardly an adequate answer to the question of justification of the moral judgment, since it merely shifts the same question to another addressee as the more appropriate source of an answer.

When the moral agent is unable to shift the burden of justification to some other party as an authority, he is forced to draw on his own resources. Among them (but not wholly comprising them) are the same processes as those that go into making aesthetic judgments. The justifier of an aesthetic judgment proceeds largely by stating descriptions of the artwork, by commanding us to heed this or that feature, by asking us whether we notice one thing or another—in a word, by directing the intuitions of his fellow onlooker to the features of the work of art about which he has indicated his judgment. The situation in the case of the justification of a moral judgment is quite the same in form, but vastly more complex in the number and variety of considerations to be heeded, and vastly more dependent upon the carrying on of rational processes as well as those of sensory and emotional function. Moreover, it is usually carried on under the pressure of time, and the necessity to close off deliberation often forces a decision before the agent is satisfied that his deliberations are complete.

This is a moment that puts the moral agent's commitment to rationality to the test. In addition to drawing attention to features of the problem situation, he must cite reasons that act X ought or ought not to be performed, and if he meets the question head-on rather than finding a psychological escape, he selects one or both of two alternatives. (In theory the alternatives exclude one another, but the practical person unschooled in theoretical ethics is usually not fussy about confining himself to only one of them.) The reasons offered are of two kinds that for many ethical analysts demarcate the two main kinds of ethical theory. That is, the reasons are given either in terms of the consequences of the act—teleological considerations—or in terms of the nature of the act itself—deontological considerations.

In the event that the would-be justifier of a moral judgment turns to reasons in terms of the consequences, he is likely to do so by pointing out that when act X is performed, then conditions A, B, and C will be realized. He does so in the hope that his challenger will react by judging, just as he himself judges, that conditions A, B, and C *ought* to be realized. But perhaps after making this statement he is again challenged, on either or both of two counts: It might be alleged that it is false that when act X is performed these conditions A, B, and C actually will be brought about (a factual matter); or else it might be alleged that if conditions A, B, and C are made to come about, that will not be worth achieving, or ought not be achieved (or, for negative ought-judgments, that the realizing of A, B, and C will not be significantly objectionable, or even that it ought to be achieved). This latter is not a factual but a valuative matter. The critic might challenge the justifier by asking the familiar question, "What's good about that?" Then the justifier will have to continue with his exposition of his reasoning, just as the art critic continues pointing out elements of the artwork and their relations until either his critic is satisfied or the two break off discussion without the critic's being satisfied. In such a discussion, *it is the aim of the justifier to bring the critic to make the same evaluative judgment that he himself makes.*

We have already sketched, in the instance of Wilbur (whose snowball must surely have melted by now), what factors enter into a situation that is identifiable as clearly possessing the moral dimension, containing potential for affecting the well-being of persons. Wilbur's apprehension of the situation as moral is dependent, as we saw, upon carrying on some reasoning as well as upon perceptual and affective processes. That was evident even though we got him only so far through his adventure as to hear his mother's anti-jaculatory command.

Quite likely, Wilbur's next move will be to turn and ask his mother, "Why not?"[2] The inquiry would perhaps resolve some of the questions that went through Wilbur's mind on hearing her voice. Let us suppose that he does so, and let us further hypothesize that this lady spurns the citation of authority, doesn't happen to be a deontologist, and ventures to further Wilbur's moral education by offering reasons. She says, "Because you could easily break the garage window. You would make a dreadful mess of broken glass, both outside and inside the garage, that would have to be cleaned up. You would let the cold air into the garage where your dog sleeps and maybe he'd catch pneumonia. You might hit something else inside the garage with the snowball, or with some of the falling glass. And most of all, it would be dangerous to have broken glass left in the window frame or scattered all over the garage floor or in the snow on the ground outside. Now of course you *might not* break the window throwing the snowball, but the results if you did are just too bad to have you run the risk."

While such a reply merits for Wilbur's mother a prize for being an articulate parent, the thoughts it conveys would be ordinary enough and would probably be present, even if not in neat phrases, in the minds of most parents in such a situation. The speaker now has, in effect, justified the moral ought-judgment, "You ought not to throw that snowball," implicit in her command, "Wilbur! Don't you throw that snowball!"

Many elements, united into a structure of considerable complexity in her consciousness of the moment, give Wilbur's mother her matter for expression, when she is led to judge that Wilbur ought not to throw a snowball toward the garage. As an adult she has a greater background of experience to interpret her own intuitions and perceptions than does Wilbur. As his mother, she has been fully conscious of his being and has been gathering knowledge of him and his relation to her ever since his birth. She is fully aware of the setting, including the yard, the garage, Wilbur with his pitching arm ready to throw, and knowledge of the contents and inhabitant of the garage, her intuitions from these being the immediate ones like Wilbur's and also those from a greater store of memories than Wilbur has. Together with these she possesses much related articulate knowledge of things like snowballs and glass. She intuits the qualities of the wording and of the tone of the words she uses, just as Wilbur does, but adds to them knowledge of Wilbur's reactions on similar occasions of the past, hence of Wilbur's probable physical reaction and feeling response on this occasion. She is conscious of the character of her own momentary feeling (of trepidation, amusement, anger, or whatever) and of her longer-range attitudes toward enterprises of this sort when embarked upon by Wilbur. Thus she is aware of as much in the situation as Wilbur is, and many more elements besides, because of her more numerous years and greater experience and cognitive skills. This much may be said merely insofar as she has observed a scene, and her observation runs parallel to Wilbur's, who responded to the scene by deciding to throw a snowball. Implicit in what we have said is the fact that for her the scene is not literally "the same scene" as it is for Wilbur, because her perception of it includes many more elements than Wilbur's scene. Crucially, her view of the scene includes Wilbur as a potential force for breaking glass, which Wilbur's perception of it did not. Her perception of it therefore includes the knowledge of the contrasting scene, also absent from Wilbur's consciousness, in which a window is broken. This of course would have been expressed, if she had had time to express it, by the proposition, "Wilbur might break the garage window if he throws that snowball." Since the scene is before her eyes in all other respects, she has little use for visual imagination, such as for picturing broken glass, so her interpretation "Wilbur might break the garage window" is probably mostly the result of concepts, not images. However, either or both together—imaging and conceptual thinking—could and regularly do produce such interpretations.

But in considering the process as justification rather than generation of the moral judgment, we have much more to notice, even assuming the ideal condition, that they are a perfect match; for *justifications are articulated with the purpose of their being criticized.* First of all, the justification that was offered is rational rather than irrational or a-rational, in that it was an instance of the offering of reasons, and pertinent reasons, rather than irrelevant reasons or no reasons. Next, with respect to the reasons offered, they were reasons that expressed a potential situation, not (or not yet) realized. The situation expressed was imagined or conceived of, or both, and then that situation was judged adversely by the justifier. Moreover, the causal connection between the present actual elements and the potential situation was arrived at through reasoning of cause and effect based on knowledge of masses and forces, considered mechanically, and of boys, considered psychologically. A probability judgment, at least of a rough sort, was reached by probability reasoning. Every element in the potential situation, like those of the actual situation, yielded its own intuited qualities; many of the relations between these elements yielded intuited qualities; and each step of reasoning involving these elements and relations yielded its own quality or qualities also. Moreover, every relation between the potential and the actual situation also yielded qualities for intuition. Finally, a comparison was made between the potential situation (with broken window) and the actual situation (without broken window), and as the outcome of the comparison a valuative judgment was added, making explicit not only the prior evaluations of the two situations, potential and actual, but also the valuative weight of the probability judgment in relation to the weight of the two conceived situations—that is, a judgment of the relation of the risk to both the undesirability of the potential situation and the preferability of the actual one: "It is better not to take the risk than to take it."

In some of the reasoning that she carries on, Wilbur's mother is aided by available branches and departments of science. Estimates of physical cause and effect, of course, are to some extent governed by scientific laws or rules, and to that extent their formation may be scientifically criticized. Probability judgments also are the subject of a science, although the necessary quantifications to measure the likelihood of Wilbur's striking the window cannot be assigned with exactness and must be estimated only roughly. However, they in fact can be so estimated with tolerable accuracy, with heavy dependence on intuitions, just as seasoned watchers of baseball can estimate rather well from the sight of the batter's swing and the sound of the crack of the bat whether a given hit ball will fall beyond the fence. But the making of the valuative judgment is another matter. Here is where science leaves us, save in those special circumstances where "values"—numbers, quantities—are substituted for qualitatively intuitive elements, as 72° Fahrenheit is assigned as the "ideal"—best—atmospheric temperature. With quantification, "values" can be compared arithmetically, for now they are amenable to addition and subtraction. But quantitative handling of valuations is a convenience that merely diverts the issue from the valuation in the first place. At bottom it is a matter of valuative judgment whether it is 72° that is the ideal temperature, or 71° or 73°.

In Wilbur's mother's set of statements offered as a justification for her judgment upon which her command to Wilbur is based, there are several things to notice. Logic suggests to us that in her set of premises there must be at least one containing an *ought*, in order for her to emerge with a conclusion to her arguments that is phrased in the modality of the *ought*. Yet there are present in these sentences no occurrences of the term *ought* or any synonyms for it. The sentences she offers in justification are all fact-assertive in nature. However, Wilbur's mother is speaking not only in propositions, as we do when we are being deliberate about our thought and expression; she is also speaking in enthymemes, as, again, we do upon such occasions as call for systematic deliberation. By speaking in enthymemes, she is appealing to Wilbur's logical intuition, and implying certain arguments for him to examine and approve. We may exhibit such an argument by taking her first statement. Its pattern will also be the pattern, perhaps with a few complications, for the remainder of her justification. The conclusion of each argument will be the same, namely, "Therefore you ought not to throw that snowball." Her first stated premise, "You could easily break the garage window," is supplemented by the implicit premise, "You ought not to break the garage window." The *ought* enters the argument implicitly, in the enthymematic suppressed premise; but it definitely is there, having been injected into the total communication by the command, "Don't throw that snowball," which is implicitly based on the proposition serving as the conclusion, "You ought not to throw that snowball." The *ought* is present in the omitted premise just as surely as it is evident that, when Wilbur's mother says "Don't throw that snowball," she believes "You ought not to throw that snowball."

Thus we can see that the mother implies, through her explanation to Wilbur, the additional premises to several separate arguments: "You ought not to make a dreadful mess of broken glass. . . ." "You ought not to let the cold air into the garage. . . ." "You ought not to chance hitting something else inside the garage. . . ." "You ought not to create a dangerous situation. . . ." We may note that because of the presence of these arguments, her justifying speech is amenable to criticism according to the rules of logic.

Now it is chiefly here that justification enters into the words of the justifier; let us see how.

Wilbur's mother is offering her statements in order to advance her son's moral education. Rather than merely falling back on her own authority as his parent, or some other temporary or permanent escape from rationality, she is teaching that form of justification which is specifically rational, and which, if anything does, will carry the day in an impartial forum as successful justification. She has done this by making factual statements about what could be the consequences of his throwing the snowball if he were to hit the garage window in doing so. She has called upon him to make an ought-judgment of his own that in each case matches the ought-judgment that is the missing premise of each enthymeme. In order to make these ought-judgments ("I ought not to make a dreadful mess of broken glass," etc.) Wilbur must supply to his own consciousness, in imagination or in conception, the state of affairs that is the subject of each of these judgments—the broken glass strewn about, the chill of air near his dog's bed, the jagged edges of fragments remaining in the window frame, and so on. From these Wilbur gathers new intuitions that previously had not entered his mind. Much of this goes on in Wilbur's consciousness in an inarticulate way, and probably some of it is not at all implanted in Wilbur's mind by his mother's justificatory speech. However, that which goes on inarticulately could probably be brought out in words by Wilbur. (And in fact, mothers, fathers, and teachers often assist young moral critics by providing articulation: "You wouldn't want your dog to catch pneumonia, would you?" "No.") Wilbur thus is brought to share in imagination some of the potential course of events that have been mentally generated by the elder person; by that he is put into a position in which to gather intuitions from that imagined episode, and most importantly, in which to make his own judgment on the basis of these artificially stimulated intuitions. What happens when the one to whom justification is offered genuinely concurs in the justification of the ought-judgment, rather than merely bowing to force or authority, is that *he judges the elements and relations* of the proposed situation *in substantially the same way* as the justifier does. He also *carries on reasoning in substantially the same patterns*, culminating on the one hand in correctly reconstructing the scene that the justifier has created, and coming to the same conclusions as those of the justifier's enthymematic arguments, and on the other hand reasoning further with the propositions now on hand in consciousness, such as in counting up and concluding that there certainly are many of them. The very number of reasons propounded itself will often be a highly persuasive factor, just as it is in fully developed persuasive arguments that make explicit all the premises of each of several bodies of support for a thesis.

From the attempted justification, there may issue either of two sorts of successful result, one that we might call the optimum and the other, the minimum. As the minimum that could be called successful, the justifier exhibits to the other party that he is being rational, that he in fact has reasons to offer for the judgment he has made, rather than being unaware of reasons or without reasons, or rather than having offered the judgment in spite of one or another evident reason to judge otherwise. It is always possible that the critic of a justifier of a moral judgment does not understand the latter's reasons, denies their truth, does not see their relevance, or is otherwise dissatisfied with them; but at least it is valuable to the justifier to show that he is turning to reasons rather than a less supportable form of justification. Often this satisfactorily resolves a dispute, as when we say the parties "agree to disagree." They reach an increased respect for each other's position, as each now understands that the other is relying upon rationality, even though the issue remains in dispute. They may even be optimistic about the outcome, for if each can believe the other to be rational in approach, then each may hope that reason shall eventually prevail, and that the dispute will be solved in a way that must be satisfactory to any rational being who is a party to it.

The other possible outcome, the optimum outcome, is the result already foreshadowed in the incident of Wilbur. It is that in which the challenger of the ought-judgment at issue accepts into his own belief the *substance* of the justification offered. When challenged, the agent or potential agent of a given action first states facts about the situation upon which the judgment has been made. As the challenging critic continues to press him, he finds it necessary to state those value-assertive propositions from among his beliefs that have entered into his judgment. He may find it necessary to state factual, then valuative, statements in a series of steps, to meet new challenges as he disposes of prior ones. In a discussion which is a thorough piece of criticism by the challenger, and a thorough justification by the justifier, the justifier eventually has exhibited pretty much the whole structure of all the factual and valuative beliefs that he possesses that pertain to the judgment at issue. It has been his goal all along to silence the opponent by presenting a body of factual and valuative propositions about the situation that will bring the critic, upon apprehending this body of propositions, to judge in the same fashion as the justifier has first judged. The critic falls silent when there remains no further fact yet to be ascertained that could affect the outcome and no significant controversy over value-assertive beliefs of justifier and critic. In this dialogue, going on so long as material is available, reason is constantly revising its own product and thus is constantly improving our belief about the issue until that belief arrives at the optimum status.

Is this success to be reckoned solely as that for the justifier, and are we to condone those cases in which a persuasive rascal can seemingly justify a bad moral judgment to a beguiled, unsuspecting critic? No, we shall not make it so, either by the easy method of definition or by the difficult method of sticking as best we can to the truth. The success of this successful justification is not to be understood as success merely for the persuasive talker—who may be an insincere fraud. Rather, it is to be understood as success in the forum of rationality, such that regardless of who pleads the case, the eventual judgment by the impartial mind, not a party to the particular interests involved, will concur in the judgment reached. Now before the cry goes up of cultural relativism, or of hopeless sophistry, let us remind ourselves that we are once again discussing an ideal, not necessarily that which is generally met with (although something like this, involving the concept of "the reasonable man," is applied in court). In this ideal setting in which optimum justification occurs, we may legitimately suppose that, first, the best ethical thinking of the ages is accessible and is applied (hardly what was true of a Protagorean relativism); that is no insignificant point in favor of rationality. Again, we may suppose that cultural relativism in the form of the code of one culture versus that of another is outmoded, that the framework of our forum of rationality is global rather than limited to lesser scope, so that the broadest possible framework for judgments that must be relative to human minds, rather than a smaller framework, is the one in which it is set. This eliminates the possible partisanship of one culture contending against another for preferment for its moral code, as it might in other matters. Finally, it appears that the rationality to which persons the world over commit themselves is one that transcends national and cultural boundaries and arches over the various plans of systematic thinking; we would expect and want it to do this, for moral justifications as well as for more characteristically scientific pursuits.

If these conditions for the ideal are acknowledged, then we need not be too fearful about the description of the optimally successful justification of a moral judgment. The fraud shall have been detected and ejected from the court. The interests of competing parties shall have been taken quite seriously but subordinated to the larger interests of society in general. Moreover, the elements and relations in the situation occasioning moral judgment shall have been exhibited so fully and thoroughly that no critic's judgment shall suffer one-sidedness. And in the end, both justifier and critic will have their best interests served, and shall have willed that optimum justification shall have been striven for, because they accept the necessity of subordinating individual interest to the social interest, from which the individual as well as his peers benefits.

Even though the ideal situation is (one supposes) never attained in practice, the description of it is useful as a guide, an incentive for improving our moral deliberations. But the unlikelihood of its being realized is mitigated by the occurrence of the other extreme of successful justification, the minimum outcome of justification. It is not too much, in a community context, to expect individuals to have reasons for their acts rather than to have no reasons. It is not too much to expect them to account for themselves, when others are affected, by stating their reasons. And the stating of one's own reasons for one's own acts (implicitly containing the pertinent moral judgments) has a strong tendency to induce self-criticism; this is evident by the tendency to "rationalize," to assign to one's acts "better" or more socially acceptable reasons than the selfish reasons that—one often knows—actually motivated them. We may therefore expect the moral level of a community to rise higher, accordingly, as justification is more and more expected of its members. And as the moral level is enhanced by the practice of social criticism and self-criticism, we may expect the justification sometimes to move above the minimum and to inch toward the optimum outcome, a favorable tendency for all concerned.

There are still important questions. Granted that two judges of a moral situation may agree, either initially or eventually, after one has justified a judgment to the other, why is it that they agree? Is it not the case that among diverse human beings, there will be many diverse purposes and goals, so that there inevitably will be simply too much disagreement among moral agents, too many open or hidden conflicts, so that in fact they will always be acting at cross-purposes, instead of in conformity with moral rules that one or another has attempted to justify? How can this description of the situation lead to anything but a hopeless relativism of morals? Is this "principle" not really the mere vain hope of a dreamer? And supposing that two moral judges do agree, is it not possible that both are wrong? What of that freedom of which this author has made so much? Will not the reality, the operation, of that freedom bring it about that those to whom justifications are directed will simply be free to reject them, and will do so? Why should they not?

The statement of the principle of optimum justification is not, I insist, merely an encapsulated form of a dreamer's wish. It is a description of what often does happen in human life—although of course we tend to arrest our attention on the instances in which it has not succeeded, rather than those in which it has. It is in fact a description of situations of justification not only of moral but of other sorts of judgments. It applies fully to the justification of aesthetic judgments, and explains why much critical writing in the arts is simply the careful and precise statement of what the evaluator actually finds as he opens his intuitions to the work of art. It should be a source of encouragement to us that anything as open to free variation of critical opinion as the arts does in fact from time to time yield similar judgments by the experienced, and widely approved justifications for the judgments involved— even though sometimes it takes a century or two.

But in the area of human moral action there is better ground for optimism. Here, more often than in connection with the arts, people do acknowledge adequate justification by others, and they do so sufficiently often that it makes a great difference in the lives of moral agents. The difference may be quite specific, as when a certain citizen need not become a soldier and lose his life to a threatening invader, because now two previously disputing nations concur in a moral judgment; or it may be general, as when the upbringing of a child is successful, so that he becomes a morally upright person rather than a socially undesirable one or one who acts merely at whim or from animal or affective motives alone. In the field of the arts, we are beginning to realize that the more we see that critics and spectators operate by developing intuition rather than imposing preconceptions upon artworks, and the more they become experienced in the perception of artworks, the more the resultant judgments arising from their intuitions seem to come to agreement. Even where they do not, those who agree in employing this method of perception tend to be able to live with one another without contumely, and seem satisfied in attributing their differences to temperament and personal make-up.

In this last attribution, many who make it are probably right. Differences of temperament not only emerge in differing judgments; they also account for why it is that some of us are artists, others mathematicians, others ethical theorists, others something else—as well as a few who combine these interests in one personality. We account for differences between conservatives and liberals by invoking temperament. However, the explanation of the success of justifications must be accounted for not by differences but by similarities, and not in a single, simple attribution of an intuited quality but by an analysis adequate to the depth and detail of the situation.

By now it is obvious what it is upon which both the ought-judgment and its justification are based. That is the total complex of experience, including all sense- and sense-dependent elements in it, all feeling- and feeling-dependent elements, all concepts and concept-dependent elements in it, all relations among any and all of these, all relations of relations, and anything else—everything—that may yield to intuition qualities that can be present in consciousness. It is true that man is free to select whatever he will, as a reason, as an incentive, as a condition to be brought about or a state of affairs to be avoided. It is true that there are, therefore, many and various motivations for specific acts. However, it is also true that on the whole, persons do tend to make roughly the same clusters of factors reasons for their acts. They do tend to act to bring about certain things rather than others, as the states of affairs that it is their will should obtain, and they tend to shun certain states of affairs that they will should not obtain. In this sense, justification is based on human nature, and some of the success of justification is explained by the degree to which human nature is uniform.

But the greatest factor in contributing to successful justification, that is, to the like judging by justifier and critic, is the role played by reason. If it were not for that, life would be much more a shambles of chance outcomes than it is. Intuition of component elements alone is not enough to lead to outcomes that are equitable, acceptable to losers as well as winners of advantages, and orderly—in a word, rational. Reason fixes and stabilizes the events of particular consciousnesses, arches across from one person or situation to another, and imposes form and permanence where in nature there is variation and change. Reason acts by apprehending the inconceivably varied flux of separate and always different minutiae, and imposing order upon them—by its basic, functional fiction of *treating them as alike* though they are not alike, treating them as "the same" though they are not the same, treating them as possessing an essence in common, a defining characteristic, though they are separate particulars and cannot share a same substance. Reason imposes the shareable upon the disparate. It appears to recognize the shareable in the like particulars; nevertheless it is at liberty to dwell only upon the disparate and overlook that which in fact it apprehends as "alike," "in common," "shared,"or in the classical and medieval sense, "universal." However, this ability to fictionalize, if that is what it amounts to—to treat differing things as alike—is what makes reason capable of functioning at all. If we did not do this, memory would have no value even if it were possible; conceptual thinking would not take place; inference would have no grounds and would never occur. Where nature presents a never-ending flow, a booming, buzzing confusion, reason creates identity and sameness or equality as the conditions, necessary to itself, that it imposes upon the externals entering consciousness in order to cope with them and to preserve its own identity, that of the human being to whom it belongs.

In the case of simple things like whether Wilbur should chance breaking a garage window by throwing a snowball, the actual reasoning takes place at, presumably, the speed of electricity or light, as electric currents pass through the organism of the thinker. However, when we are faced with a moral perplexity obliging us to reflect, and when moreover we have time to do so, we proceed with deliberate system, articulating our thinking at the speed of our inner dialogue. We apparently have an ability in this process to make the natural stream of thought to subserve the articulated thinking. At any rate, as we are doing verbal thinking, we are able to be critical about it, and this is probably why we do it deliberately. We are able to express in propositions principles that we regard as pertinent. Sometimes we have some propositions ready to hand, such as "I should act toward my child in the way that is best for him in the long run, not just the way that pleases him now," or "I should do unto others as I would have them do unto me," or "I should act in the most loving way," or the like—whatever general moral rules we subscribe to. These principles, some of which may be largely private and others of which are familiar to the general public, are usually brought into any deliberate reflection aimed at solving a moral problem. They enter into the various arguments, often enthymematically, that are weighed for various possible acts. When general principles are fact-assertive, they are criticizable by usual methods applicable to their sort of truth. However, insofar as they are value-assertive, like the three examples above, their believability rests on the criteria that we are now in the process of bringing forward. For the present, the point is that they, too, may enter into moral reflection along with more specific value-assertive propositions that express some of the particular value beliefs for the case at hand, and also along with fact-assertive propositions of a great range of particularity.

Finally, since acts have virtually unending effects, it appears that we will never want for possible things to say in judging a given act. What actually happens is that we simply declare cloture at some stage, saying, "Beyond that point, there is no purpose to examining further, because we already have enough information and enough judgments on potential effects to decide our case." And when both parties to a critical discussion can and do agree that the point of cloture has been reached, if they agree also by that time on the justifiability of the judgment or act being debated, then the justification has been successful. If not, they continue in disagreement, the critic believing that the judgment or act was unjustifiable or at least has not been justified by the method attempted, and the justifier continuing to believe in the justifiability of the judgment or act.

In this chapter, we have first suggested the formulation of the pattern of justification, "I made my judgment (or selected or performed my act) on account of its being required by (or in accordance with) the justifying principle *J*." We then examined the typical alternation of challenge and reply, and elicited the description of a totally successful justification, relative to a given critic: When the justifier has exhibited to his critic the complex of propositions embodying his knowledge of and belief about the situation judged, then the recipient of this body of justifying propositions will evaluatively judge the situation in the same way as the justifier of the original evaluative judgment has evaluated it. Although the moral deliberations of our illustration were expressed in the words of two persons, Wilbur and Wilbur's mother, it is perfectly plain that an individual with a moral decision to make may himself perform both roles. He can be both the proposer-justifier and the challenging critic of possible courses of action, allowing deliberation to rest only when all possible challenges have been disposed of with rationally satisfactory replies. In this light, the metaphor we use of "answering to one's conscience" can take on new and more explicit meaning, less mystical or at least less mystifying than the old one that suggests something like an angel sitting on one's shoulder and whispering into one's ear in times of moral crisis; for the conscience can be seen now simply as one's own mind performing purposely developed and enhanced skills of deliberation.

Our illustration for purposes of producing the typical instance was one using a teleological justification. However, a deontologist might as readily apply the pattern of justification. I am not of the deontological persuasion myself, as I find nothing in my experience to give acts or states of affairs "goodness," "requiredness," or "rightness in themselves" or "intrinsically" or "on their own account," totally irrelevantly to other elements of their situations, such as their relations to moral agents, ensuing results, or persons affected. However, I suppose that if one's principle is, for example, "That act containing the most intrinsic rightness (or, state of affairs containing ultimate and intrinsic goodness) is without question obligatory and is to be performed (or, is to be brought about)," this may stand in the pattern in the place of the justifying principle *J*, leaving to the user of the principle the burden of displaying to his critics the claimed intrinsic rightness or goodness of the act or state in question.

The use of the formulation given need not await the conclusion of the debate over rule-versus-act ethical theories, for it is just as workable for justifying rules as it is for justifying actions. The wording merely needs altering to make the sense of "select this rule" or "justify the selection (or application) of this rule" take the place of reference to acts.

A very important by-product of the outline given here for justification of moral decisions is that it gives a format for the development of skill in the solution of moral problems and, perhaps even more important, for the carrying on of moral education. The understanding that the neutral ought is at the base of all our valuative judgments, that these judgments express how we would have the world be if our will could make it so, that we may adjudge this irrationally but normally judge according to reasons, and that we are free to select our reasons, means that the process of moral education need not assume any particular code of morality, or beg the question of any proposed "good" or "right" being the exclusive or absolute "good" or "right." That in the long run, well-informed judges tend to judge alike but that there is no natural necessity to do so, but rather freedom in judgment, allows us with some confidence to suppose that moral education, not assuming a particular moral viewpoint, could be carried on so as to make individuals better aware of the complexities, the requisites, and the skills of judgment without in the process establishing some moral system that we ourselves cannot approve. For this moral education, without assuming a given religious or other moral code, would exercise its pupils in recognizing facts of a situation, discerning possible actions available to those within the situation in order to bring about change, possible consequences of the actions, possible valuative judgments to make upon those consequent states of affairs, and possible reasons by which to support the valuations made. Much if not all of this could go forward without the necessity of inserting any particular principle in the place of *J* in the formulation. Far from enabling those we regard as our moral adversaries from entrenching themselves against us, this prospect holds much promise of assisting the world in ameliorating its myriad moral issues, for a rational plan of conduct in a consciously chosen moral framework even if a "wrong" one, because it is chosen as and thought to be *moral* rather than merely expedient, would surely bring about a better world than the one in which we find ourselves, in which (it is my impression) persons are little skilled in solving moral problems, and are not even in the habit of reminding themselves of the difference when a problem they have is one with a moral dimension and when it is without moral bearings of any sort. And ongoing deliberations by those who have received this systematic moral education rather than none, or rather than an authoritarian and absolutistic one, would operate with that feature of scientific method that we so much admire, namely, that it tends to be self-correcting and self-improving. If I am wrong in my inference from observation, and it turns out that there *is* an ultimate single, absolute morality, this method should be the most promising pathway for finding it and identifying it; and if I am not wrong, and there is not an absolute morality awaiting discovery but rather there is a world in which a plurality of good reasons for actions is possible and hence a plurality of judgments of what ought to be, or to be done, is justifiable, then this sort of moral education, dwelling upon the sharpness of intuitive perceptions, the acuity of logical reasoning, and the inclusiveness of range of possible selections of judgments and of reasons, will surely lead us to a better world, on the whole, than the one we presently inhabit.

15

Obligation: The Relation of the Moral *Ought* to the Pure *Ought*

Our instance of an adult moral problem, the decision whether a union member should go on strike or not (see chapter thirteen) introduced many standard moral concepts, including *duty, rights, equity, justice, fairness, law, contract, retribution,* and *obligation.* Among these, the concept *obligation* (with its variant, *duty*) has been so important in the development of moral theory that many moralists have regarded defining *obligation* or *duty* as the chief burden of ethics. Its importance alone warrants our taking *obligation* as the epitome of traditional ethics, and hence the most useful concept to elucidate as a factor in ethical reasoning. A second circumstance also bids us give especial attention to *obligation,* namely, that in ethical discussions the constant conjunction of the ideas of *ought* and *obligation* has led to the general understanding, and even the definition, of the term *ought* as the usual and standard expression of obligation. By etymological derivation, *ought* is a variant of the modern word *owed,* which has in almost every occurrence the connotation of obligation though we stretch it a bit in constructions like "Owing to his infirmity, he was inclined to give up his golf." The deontologist both arrives at and later justifies an act by virtue of the obligatory nature of the act. The justifying reason may be supplied in a variety of commonly used phrases: "The act ought to be performed because it is one's duty"; "One ought to perform that act because it is an obligation to do so" (or "because it is obligatory," or "because one is obliged to do so"); or "That is the sort of thing that just ought to be done, that's all"; or "Well, I can just see that that is what ought to be done."

The concept *obligation* is such a sturdy thing that some intuitionist ethicists have made it the object of intuition, affirming that we intuitively detect obligation and thus know by an intuition that an act is one we are obliged to do or refrain from doing, or know that we are bound or not bound by a rule or an imperative. These will have been looking in the account of moral judgments in the preceding chapter for the place there where intuitions of obligation arise. While they may infer from my discussion in chapter nine that I deny that we intuit obligation as an objective entity or property in the external universe, they will have watched for the place where I might have overlooked it. The choices open to them are, first, that obligation is within the moral situation itself (one of the trees of the forest, so to say, or a relation between two of them, or an element of one or more of these—a "look" of obligation that a tree or a relation among the trees might have); or, second, that obligation is in the frame, as one of the constituents of the frame (a rule, perhaps); or, third, that obligation is outside the frame of the forest itself, in the second frame, the frame *beyond*, which I have called the world. As said already, I myself simply do not find that I have intuitions of obligation as any real thing occurring in any one of these places, and believe the burden is on the intuitionist of obligation to point out to me where it is, in the way a painter might point out to me the yellows, or the intentional blurs, or the like, on his canvas. However, it is incumbent upon me to attempt to explain obligation in the sense in which I regard such a thing to exist, and thus to explain what does operate where the intuitionist erroneously claims to find obligation as an object of everyone's intuition.

The notion of obligation is applied, in making or discussing moral decisions, for the purpose of justification. *Obligation*, I maintain, is not the concept (nor its name the name) of a metaphysically real, externally existing entity or property at all, in the way that the deontologists generally appear to understand it to be. Rather, we can conceive that if all moral ought-judgments were automatically carried into effect once they were voiced, there would be no discussion about when obligation arises, about whether certain acts are obligatory or not, or about what is the difference between acts that are duties and those that are not. Yet moral judgments are *not* automatically acted upon, and to incite compliance once they are voiced, their makers frequently invoke obligation as the justification for what they have said and thus as an incitement to performance by those addressed. This is why I conceive of the notion of obligation as primarily one for use in justification, and I suggest that in attributing obligation to an act, many theorists assimilate justification to the act, and regard it as an integral part of the act itself. Indeed it can be made to seem a very convincing, even truistic, allegation that some acts simply in themselves are our duties, and that others simply by their very nature are morally out of the question and not to be performed. This is, I suggest, what has happened to make intuitionists of the act out of some of us. It is nevertheless a mistake, as I hope to show.

So entrenched is the view that the very word "ought" expresses obligation, and nothing else, that for many theorists the whole problem of morality is simply the problem of duty, since duty is seen as always compelling "in itself" or "on its own account"—just precisely because it *is* duty. But I suggest that we should push beyond the language of the judgment or statement that "Act *A* is our duty," and try to discover what in fact is the account of our concept of *obligation*, or more specifically, our view that moral injunctions are obligatory and hence compulsory, rather than simply advisory or suggestive. Prior to philosophical inquiry, men have been prone to seat such a thing in religion or myth, and leave it there unquestioned. However, even if we were to find our rule written in a sacred book or embedded in an oral tradition, we would still be interested in inquiring what is the ground, the theoretical foundation, of its obligatoriness, as distinct from the source of its formulation.

What is the obligatoriness that the moral judgment contains? It is certainly no quality of the perceptible, directly intuitable world, on a par with yellow, red, and blue, triangle, rectangle, and circle, as I was at some pains to show in chapter nine for forms of value in general. Yet it is not nonexistent. We do sometimes acknowledge real obligation, which is to say we do acknowledge that certain external objects of consciousness possess the character of obligatoriness; these are such things as laws, contracts, undertakings to perform what the agent has "given his word" to perform, promises, and some imperatives. We recognize that the obligatoriness of these things is indeed external, not a creature solely of our own subjectivity. And the citation of one of these, witnessed or on record, is generally used to show that obligation is present, or to justify performance of the mentioned act either before or after it is performed. It is surely no accident that the sanction, the force, of the Hebrew morality of the Old Testament was held to be a *covenant* with the Lord. In return for their observance of morality and piety as prescribed, the Hebrews were awarded a promised land in which to prosper. In view of the efficacy of the force of law or contracts, which lend compulsion to the performance as prescribed or engaged, moralists have tended to seek outside the agent (as laws and contracts are outside the agent) for other, perhaps even absolute, elements that can be alleged to supply force to moral judgments. But no intuitions do indeed actually disclose any such external basis of obligation, force of moral rules or prescriptions. Kant's categorical imperative, resting the obligatoriness of duty on a rule of reason, the necessity of conforming to rather than violating the law of non-contradiction, can be seen as an attempt to rest duty on the *logical* intuition, rather than on a moral intuition specially attuned to detect obligation wherever it may exist.

To find the referent object of the concept of obligation, let us look again at language, this time at propositions that express judgments of obligation. Let us consider some varying formulations of a sample value-assertive, moral proposition:

(I) The world ought to be such that no adult ever leaves a small child alone in the presence of great danger.

(II) No adult ought ever to leave a small child alone in the presence of great danger.

(III) Do not leave a small child alone in the presence of great danger.

Of the first two formulations, the second is the more clearly an ethical proposition. It involves action and responsibility for action, and the different degrees of good judgment and of potential efficacy in carrying out acts of will possessed by adults and by children. It can in fact be called a rule of conduct, and has a strong *prima facie* appeal as such—few would dispute it as a general rule of conduct. Hence, to call it a moral principle seems appropriate.

However, the first formulation is not entirely devoid of ethical import. We are aware, as we read it, of the relations of children and adults, and of their different degrees of responsibility and of the differences in efficacy of their action, just as we are as we read the second. Yet we could not call the first formulation a rule, even though it readily suggests a reformulation (namely, version II) that adapts its matter into the guise of a rule. The difference is principally in the framework that proposition (I) summons up; it talks about the world, not this or that individual. This formulation is one in which the pure, simple *ought* is clearly present, for in considering it, we do contrast in our minds the kind of world in which children are left in danger and the kind in which they are not. Although in practical terms it would be trivial to do so, we could reformulate every moral rule into a statement like (I), presenting a concept of an envisioned world, embodying the neutral *ought*. While morals might seem to suffer a deathblow by such a procedure, to do so does at any rate show us that the pure *ought* is present in a proposition reporting an ethical ought-judgment just as it is in other value-assertive propositions.

What is it that has been stripped away in the weaker formulation (I) that has vitiated the suggested moral principle (II)? It is the obligatoriness that the principle connotes when formulated as a rule, a clear ethical ought-judgment, and that it lacks when neutrally formulated. We may meaningfully speak of how the world ought to be, other than as it is or else as in fact it is, but in doing only that we have done nothing in the world to make it reach or maintain that condition. On the other hand, statement (II), having the form of a rule, suggests to its morally mature recipient that action is possible and necessary for realizing the envisioned state of affairs, and indeed makes use of the nearness of this formulation to that of an imperative so as to suggest that he, the recipient, is laid under obligation by this rule. "Do not, yourself," it commands him, "leave any small child alone in the presence of great danger!" Thus the third formulation is generated. The morally self-conscious person reinterprets the statement from the form of a rule (II) to the form of a command (III) addressed to himself when he sees that it is applicable to him.

The principle of obligatoriness, then, has as constituent elements the envisioning of a state of affairs as it ought to be or of an action as one that ought to be done (or, of course, the negatives of these), together with *the placement of a moral agent* in relation to that state of affairs or action. Neither element without the other suffices to bring about the presence of obligation. Yet not just any moral agent within or in contact with a situation about which a pure ought-judgment has been made is automatically under obligation; the small child himself, for example, who is in the presence of great danger is not ordinarily said to be *morally obliged* to remove himself, much though it would be prudent for him to do so. The alternative is easy to suggest, that it is of course the adult, not the child, who has the responsibility to protect the child when danger is present. The rule in question makes this explicit. The formulation as an imperative is in its social context still more explicit, for by using the imperative mode of address it singles out its recipient as the party upon whom obligation is lodged. But still, identifying the prospective person upon whom the *ought* is deemed to fall by the originator of the proposition does not suffice to make the value judgment a moral judgment as we usually think of moral judgments.

A new illustration will help us in seeing what is involved here. A spectator at the theater sends a note to the director of a drama, commending the performance but remarking, "You ought not let the leading lady parade her good looks so flagrantly!" The director upon opening the note reacts by saying, "Why the very point of the scene is that the character considers herself so good looking that she is superior to everybody else present. Besides, who is *he* to tell *me* how to direct *my* play?"

Thus the director has replied to his critic in respect to two separate issues. The first, having to do with the substance of the message, is an aesthetic issue, raised in the value-assertive proposition, "You ought not let the leading lady parade her good looks so flagrantly." Presumably the critical theatergoer had intended this remark as having aesthetic subject matter, and in replying in terms of the content of the drama, the director has treated it as such. He has not seen any moral issue in the content of the message, such as whether the actress is committing the sin of pride; rather, he is saying in effect that the actress is playing the role the way it ought, in his professional judgment, to be played. This is an aesthetic point.

But there is a moral issue also, signaled by the second part of the director's reply. Here he is invoking not so much his function or craft, but his personhood, suggesting by his rhetorical question that it is wrong for the spectator to impose himself upon the director, as it were taking for himself some of the latter's territory. Well taken or not, this point clearly raises a *moral* issue, an issue of the relations between the spectator and director, two moral agents, who are in a position to benefit or harm each other, to affect each other's well-being. The moral issue arises from the fact that one of these agents, as suggested above, has assigned responsibility to the other: The spectator has enjoined an *ought* upon the director. There is therefore a moral issue, but it is *not* the issue raised by the substance of the communication. The moral relation involved is one between the originator of the value assertion and the individual to whom it assigns responsibility. This of course is not at all the same as the issue raised by the aesthetic substance of the communication.

Thus the illustration shows us two separate burdens of ought-judgments conveyed by the utterance by one moral agent to another of a single proposition stating what the latter ought to do. One of these is implicit: "You ought to do as I say, for I am telling you what your obligation is." The other is the explicit content of the ought-judgment that was actually delivered in words. Although in the illustration the explicit ought-judgment is aesthetic, far more commonly the content of an ought-judgment explicitly delivered by one agent to another is moral.

Let us suppose now that the spectator further seeks out the leading lady herself at a reception and without preamble says to her, "You ought not to parade your good looks so flagrantly!" She is likely—unless she takes the remark as flattery—to react with aversion to both "oughts," explicit and implicit, of the judgment she has heard; and now both will give rise to moral issues. It is when the explicit content of the ought-judgment lodges a responsibility having a moral dimension that the judgment is a moral ought-judgment, not another kind. (Occasionally, of course, the recipient of such a communication resents more the fact that its originator is laying him under an *ought*—the implicit message—than he objects to the overt statement of the duty; he considers his challenger to be meddling. He may even agree on the content of the duty that has been identified for him.) In this new instance, the implicit content of the ought-judgment is as before, "I am telling you what your obligation is," and the explicit content is not placed in the aesthetic frame of the theater stage but has as its setting simply the social scene, in this case the reception where the lady is accosted. The statement will appear to her to involve her present conduct and to call for a change in it, and the change will be a change in her relationship to others, who are those before whom she might be said to "parade her good looks." When one person tells another how to act, under conditions where peer status rather than recognized authority of the one over the other is to be assumed, a moral relationship is involved, and if there is disagreement, the issue raised is a moral issue.

Let us summarize. A value-assertive proposition expressing only the *pure ought* will not *per se* contain an indication of who the performer might be who is assigned responsibility to see to it that the state of affairs or action expressed is realized. Next, it will be characteristic of a *moral* ought-judgment that an agent will be indicated, either explicitly or implicitly, but the assignment of agency in addition to expression of the pure *ought* does not suffice to constitute a judgment as moral, for an aesthetic ought-judgment, a prudential ought-judgment, and no doubt other kinds, may also have an agent indicated. What additionally is required is that the content of the proposition expressing the ought-judgment involve the moral dimension—the relationship of the performer of any mentioned act to others insofar as their well-being may be affected. Thus a judgment of obligation contains at least three components: an *ought*, an indication of a moral agent, and content that has the moral dimension.

Although for a judgment to be a *moral* judgment it is necessary that it contain something bearing upon the well-being of an affected human being,[1] it is with respect to the other moral issue raised by such a judgment that obligation (if any) arises. It is *I* who am told that I should not tell lies, when I hear the command "Do not tell lies." (The exception would be a command that is not a command *to* anyone—perhaps "Let freedom ring!"—but that sort of thing is rare.) If I hear this command from someone whom I regard as having adequate authority to impose ought-judgments upon me, then I am probably satisfied that I now know one of my obligations; but if I were told these words by, for example, a notorious liar, I might indeed resent his addressing me so, and might retort that he cannot make me—oblige me—to tell one kind of statement or another. That would be to address the other moral issue, the implicit one that inheres in a command, the issue whether the originator may bind the recipient. Although the explicit moral content of a moral proposition, rule, or command is what is heard, it is by an implicit allegation that the addressee or another moral agent, designated or implied, is laid under obligation; this being so, it is understandable that a hearer of a command or rule could readily believe that the obligatoriness simply lies somehow within that which he hears, the explicit moral teaching that is being expressed in words.

Now the problem is all the plainer. Is the ground of the moral ought-judgment simply the fact that some judge, in making a moral judgment, has identified an agent who is capable of executing the act or realizing the state of affairs mentioned? Does just any moral agent have the authority and the power to bind another in this way? Or does none of them possess such power and authority, so that I direct myself in my own actions *solely* upon my own authority? Are some moral agents but not others qualified to allocate responsibility? And if so, by what qualifications?

Paradoxically, my obligation arises out of my freedom. If I had no freedom, I would have no obligation, for I would automatically do everything I were compelled to do, and there would be nothing else that I would or could do. It is because I have freedom that there is room, so to speak, for obligation, i.e., for there to be any acts that are performed out of obligation as distinguished from compulsion. The acts that are performed out of compulsion raise no moral issue; those that are performed under conditions of freedom, including within them those that are moreover performed under obligation (or are omitted despite obligation), raise the moral issues. If I perform a blameworthy act, not being in any way obligated to perform it, I may be morally censured because of doing so. Further, if I am under obligation to perform an act that otherwise I am free to perform or not perform, and if being under obligation I nevertheless fail to perform it, perhaps performing some other act instead, I am also subject to moral censure. But the latter moral censure or its occasion may arise only under conditions of freedom; "'Ought' implies 'can.'"[2]

That being the situation with obligation, it now becomes evident that there is only one possible basis for my obligation. It cannot be something imposed upon me from without, for its first presupposition is my freedom, and it depends for its existence upon my freedom. The only way, then, for it to be brought into being, to be real, while at the same time for its presupposition to be satisfied, is for me in my freedom to make, myself, the move that lays that freedom aside. That move is to consent to obligation, to being bound to certain things and not others. The only basis under which I am laid under obligation is my consenting to the obligation, and the only way others may know whether I am obligated thus is by my behavior in words or deeds that communicate to them that I consent to and do consider myself obligated.[3]

The outward sign of my consent may of course have many forms. My signature on a contract is one of them, and law and the courts have formalized this one for what the common wisdom adjudges to be the common benefit. Socrates' continuing to live in Athens after reaching maturity was his communication to the city that he was obligated by its laws. The raising of a hand, a finger, a pencil, even an eyebrow, to an auctioneer signals voluntary obligation to pay a certain price. Continuing to seek out another's company, to act as a friend, places one under the obligation to perform the duties of friendship and is taken as a sign of voluntary obligation. Acceptance of benefits, however small, conferred by another, is a way I can acquire or acknowledge an obligation. To undertake a vocation or a way of life is to assume a large number of obligations. And for many of our obligations, the specific demands of the obligation may not all be known at the time of giving consent to it. How many of us who have been married for any significant number of years accurately envisioned, upon making our vows, the number and variety of acts that we were undertaking to perform?

Is any moral agent qualified to lay another under obligation without that other's consent? It appears that indeed there are cases in which this situation obtains, although it is not the general case. Predominantly it is true of the situation of the parent vis-à-vis the child. This is because, first of all, the parent was responsible for bringing the child, a new potential moral agent, into the community of moral agents. (It is not without reason that marriage in civilized societies is licensed.) The parent is obligated, by virtue of his continuation of residence in a community, to treat other members of the community as moral ends; hence, when he adds to its numbers he is obliged to assure that what he adds will be a moral end and agent, not a mere animal in the shape of a human. In order to do this, the parent must be in charge of the moral development of the child, and included within the lessons for it to learn are the knowledge of and attitudes supporting the institution of obligation. Obviously one of the ways to practice the child in the performance of obligations is to lay him under obligation. Hence the parent has the right to do so. Naturally, as the child develops into a fully responsible moral agent, the obligating by the parent will occur less and less, and the free undertaking of obligations by the child and youth will occur more and more. And just as the parent is in the relation, among others, to the child of having authority to oblige the child, any other situations in which one individual may lay a second under obligation are situations in which the first has charge of the moral development of the other. And each of them, like that of parent and child, will arise out of the moral relations internal to the society of moral agents within which they are present.

Our mention of parent and child gives us the occasion to notice the moral situation within a family. The family may of course be looked at in many ways, such as the physical, the economic, the psychological, and the sociological. Under the moral view of the family, at any given moment the situation is one of a network of obligations, of various strengths and durations, among all the various members, with diverse means by which they were entered into and by which they were communicated. At the foundation is the obligation of any member to any and all the others as members also of the human community; each must respect the humanity of every other, and is entitled to the respect of each other. Distinguishing the given family from other groupings is the marriage vow undertaken by the parents. Between these, some obligations are voiced, others spoken about obliquely, others set up solely by behavior and acknowledged solely by behavior, and still others probably never articulated either by word or behavior. Some are of utmost importance, while others are of so little weight that they may be abrogated by a mere mention. The importance of each differs with each marriage, and perhaps also from time to time within a marriage. The vow of sexual fidelity, for example, is for most marriages of utmost importance in the early years, for many into several decades, and for some until or even after the death of a partner. For other marriages the importance of fidelity diminishes relatively soon, and for still others it was secondary at the start. No doubt in some the vow itself was a mere meaningless ritual. When children arrive, they gradually learn to obligate themselves and to extract obligation from other members of the family just as the parents do, and their participation in obligation in either the role of originator or acceptor occurs more and more often as they become more morally mature. Meanwhile the parents are still responding to obligations toward *their* parents, some based on spoken understandings and others little mentioned or even—on account of *other* obligations—strictly *not* to be spoken of. And the children enter into obligations not only with their parents, but also with their grandparents, and with each other. All this is not to say that there are not other moral relationships within a family besides those that are obligatory; it is, rather, to emphasize that one aspect of the moral structure of the family is that of a network of ever-developing obligations, in a continuous process of being performed, discharged, and replaced by others.

Obligation as such, then, is not of itself an object of intuition to be found upon or within an act *qua* act. Rather, it is first a creation of rationality. We think ourselves in the condition of freedom. Reasoning concerning our acts, we conclude that it is the better situation for ourselves and for society that the institution of voluntary obligation exist than not. We recognize the benefits and compare them against the disadvantages, then opt for a society in which obligation arises through deliberate intent, and is maintained through observance of its requirements.

Thus we construct socially the concept of obligation. The mode of being that concepts participate in is not the same as the one that the deontologists impute to obligation. They would require concepts to be of lower rank, so to speak, than obligation; they would require the concept of obligation to be shaped and modified by the allegedly real external object, obligation, rather than having obligation itself shaped and modified by concepts, by thinking and reasoning. Once derived, of course, the concept of obligation and its relations may yield many intuitions, for concepts as well as other objects of attention possess qualities acceptable to intuition. The most evident proof that concepts and their relations may be objects of intuition is the functioning of the logical intuition, whose task is generally defined as the discernment of relations among ideas, that is, concepts. Evidence that this particular concept, *obligation,* may yield qualities is the different regard for it held by different individuals. Some find it to exhibit a character worthy of considerable respect; others find in it the occasion for loathing. The situation is much the same as that with many works of art! It is little surprising that there may be such a variety of responses toward obligation since it becomes known to us through our differing personal histories in myriad ways.

To describe obligation as a rational creation is not at all to deny that persons bow to it, employ it, and enjoy the benefits gathered from it, without having arrived at decisions about it rationally. Most of us have encountered obligation long before we were at an age to reason methodically or even consistently, much less to philosophize. Society has found supports to reinforce its institution of obligation, supports that are active far below the rational level. Things like that get worked out probably quite inarticulately, by the group's consciousness, long before some articulate person has put them into words. They are none the less forceful, and perhaps all the more so because of that.

Just as obligation has been employed in the role of justification by moralists and by moral agents, it has been cast also in the role of incentive, and particularly as compulsion. A person is told by another, "You must perform act *A*; it is your obligation to do so." Often, the hearer is persuaded (or coerced) to perform by this kind of statement, and frequently without considering whether he has consented, on either grounds of obligation or otherwise. The operative consideration may be the actual authority of the speaker (the policeman, the military superior) or his presumptive authority (he is a parent, or a clergyman, or a psychiatrist; even a few teachers once in a while are so regarded). Or it may be that further discussion, which is not necessarily rational deliberation, operates so as to induce the hearer to perform as the speaker has enjoined. This common situation shows us (each reader filling in instances from his own experience) that the concept of obligation, even or especially when not well understood, is invoked for persuasive purposes. The effect is to draw attention away from the true nature of obligation, which is necessarily a voluntary undertaking of responsibility, to give it the appearance of a compulsion—"You have to perform act *A*. It is your obligation; you have no choice."

Children learn of obligation early, through their experience with compulsion. They come to understand that some instructions are intended simply as suggestions or advice, whereas others are of the nature of orders, carrying the necessity to comply. "Do I *have* to?" is the question a child asks when given an instruction to do something he dislikes doing. This is his way of discovering which sort of instruction he has been issued, the compulsory or the noncompulsory. The ground of the compulsoriness in the earliest experience of the child is simply the physical force that the parent applies. He is, for example, put physically to bed in a barred crib, and is powerless to alter the fact. The toddler who is told to stay away from the fireplace but nevertheless strays toward it is simply picked up and physically removed. He can do no other than obey. At a later age, physical punishment may be the penalty for failure to obey an obligating instruction. Still later, direct physical punishment is replaced by psychologically efficacious punishment. And much later, the child realizes that in his home situation the force and punishment are no longer applied, but there are still some things he "has to" do while others remain recommended, or wished for, but noncompulsory. He has probably detached the ideas of force and punishment from the concept of the compulsory, which he originally constructed from them, and now he thinks of the compulsory as separate from these, but nevertheless in contrast with voluntary. Perhaps he reflects that if he fails to perform certain of the things that are in this sense compulsory, his parents will think less well of him, or that his parents will be looked down upon by other adults, or that some other undesired result, much less tangible and direct than physical or other explicit punishment, will ensue.

As the individual acquires contact and experience outside the family, the development of his understanding of obligation goes much further. He becomes able to see the advantages, to himself individually and to society at large, of maintaining it as an institution. Its advantages are obvious, and a whole list of them need not be put forward here. Essentially it is the institution of the contract, voluntarily entered into. In early childhood, the individual is placed in contractual relations—"If you'll go to bed without complaining, I'll read you a bedtime story," and the like. We see here and on all higher levels the replacement of physical compulsion by psychological compulsion, which is entered into voluntarily by the contracting party who is at a physical disadvantage. Thus the child learns to use his human power of free choice in accepting or rejecting an obligation. In his process of further development of the idea of obligation, he responds to many influences. Not only does the child react to the specific compliance of his obligated parent, when he has contracted for the bedtime story; he responds also to the pleasure the parent takes in the fact that the device has succeeded, to the evident affection of his parent in the situation, unimpeded by the necessity to resort to disciplinary devices, to the pleasure of hearing the story itself, to his own success at operating on a peer level—that of the free agent entering into a mutually beneficial contract—with the parent, and so on.

By the time the maturing individual has a wealth of social contacts, he has a pretty full conception of the social institution of obligation. He has intellectual comprehension of it, in the many forms in which he encounters it. He enters into contracts and covenants, fulfills them, and exacts fulfillment on the part of other contracting parties. But there are other ways in which he understands that he is bound by obligation. He knows, for example, that he is under obligation when dining at a restaurant and finding the service satisfactory, to leave a tip for the server. He knows that he is under obligation to appear when he has made an appointment, or else to notify the other party that he will break the appointment. If he fails to comply, the other party justly feels injured, and may exercise sanctions such as refusing to renew the appointment or embarrassing the defaulter by asking for an explanation. He considers himself under obligation to return some, not all, invitations, and it becomes a nice point of social understanding to know which ones. It is a favorable factor in one's reputation to have it said of him, "He lives up to his obligations," and for those who say it of him to intend that the unarticulated obligations as well as the explicitly verbal ones are included in the scope of what is said. In other words, it is simply a part of the pattern of behavior that the culture imposes upon the individual, in which he comes to share consciously and willingly, that there is a social institution that we may call "obligation," abstracted from a fabric of myriad specific obligations all related to one another by having as their point of focus the individual who bears them.

It is extremely important to notice in considering obligation that each of these separate, specific obligations has all of the many facets of any other incident of interpersonal contact. To the extent that the obligation is conscious, it will be apprehended intellectually and will be amenable to rational explanation ("I must play bridge today with Martha, not because I want to but because she helped me out by being a fourth when a member of my club suddenly took sick"). But there are also the many intuitive responses to the physical-object elements involved ("Is this car that I'm considering buying really large enough?"), and responses to the feeling-elements ("I really like the car, although I don't care much for the salesman. I'm not sure his service shop will really live up to what is said in the warranty"). These responses involve not only the elements acknowledged in the arrangement, but also the whole history of the individual's prior experience with such things. They affect the willingness to enter an obligation, the quality of the particular obligation, and the degree of strength one attaches to it. Here the experience of an actual obligation most nearly resembles, in its intuitional factors, the sort of experience that diverts the attention of the value intuitionist from the actual nature of obligation.

It must be admitted that various individuals have varying patterns of behavior relating to obligations, and varying conceptions of them. At one end of a scale is the individual who will honor a contract or other obligation even after the moment at which it has come to mean nothing to the other contracting party whether he does or not. At the other end is the individual who conceives of an obligation as a potential behavior pattern that is backed solely by social compulsion, so that if he attempts to default he will be detected and *made* to comply, whereas an arrangement that is not obligatory is one such that if he defaults and is detected, he will not be made to comply even though he is disapproved of by other members of society. This of course is hardly the understanding of obligation that deontological ethicists have adopted. Now we might ascribe this sort of conception of obligation to temperament, just as we ascribe certain repeated acts of lawbreaking to a psychopathic personality; but I do not believe that every defaulter is a psychopath. Rather, these are people who "know the difference between right and wrong," but have an attitude of performing in their own interest that which they can "get away with." Defaulters of this sort can be shamed, and can sincerely feel shame when their attitude is exposed and its deficiencies pointed out. Without attempting to explain how such people are molded, I should simply say that they do have a collection of beliefs that have arisen in their lives, taken as a whole, that have been fashioned out of the many incidents relating to others, each incident with its full complement of intuitions of external and internal objects of intuition, and that these beliefs include a substantial number of beliefs about obligation, although they are at odds, in some part, with the beliefs that give to the word its standard meaning in that society.

It cannot escape our attention that for each stage of the development of the individual's concept of obligation, there lurks in the background an "or else." If the willful schoolchild disobeys, punishment follows. If the adolescent disobeys, something he values is lost. This is to say what Kant expressed about all imperatives, save only one, that they are hypothetical imperatives—and Kant's critics have been long at challenging his claim of the one exception. Yet his example, that of the categorical imperative, can serve us[4] as clear evidence that man can indeed abstract from the specific situations in which he sees an undesired consequence to the concept of a perfectly abstract compulsoriness, independent of the thought of concrete consequences. An example of a hypothetical imperative that one might hear is, "If you wish to keep respect in the eyes of others, never tell lies." With the protasis removed, the imperative simply says, "Never tell lies." Kant urges that since this imperative is moral in nature, it is categorical. It is not, however, simple. It conveys an interpersonal context, in that when lies are told, they are told to other moral agents (or even to oneself as a moral agent); hence multiple human relations, those of agent and patient, are involved. Obligatoriness is still suggested in the imperative wording, strongly enough to encourage some modern ethical theorists to seek to found moral obligation upon the grammatical mode of command. By trimming away the protasis clause of a hypothetical compound proposition, Kant arrived at an ought-judgment without *that* kind of qualification; the categorical imperative in the Kantian ethic is the one command unqualified by any consequence or indeed by any limitation except that its employment is among beings who are rational. We can, then, arrive at a concept of independent obligatoriness through building up an abstract notion of penalty following failure to comply, then dropping that component to reach a final concept, that of *obligation without qualification*. It is this that many ethical theorists regard as the grounding of ethical propositions that they deem true, and whose explanation is the purpose of much of their inquiry.

The involvement of feeling-response with the internal and external objects of intuition in a situation involving obligation is surely strong, even—or perhaps especially—in the experience of the person whose temperament is the nearest to the favorable extreme in his behavior and concept connected with obligation. He will perform an acknowledged obligation seemingly for its own sake, or that is, without regard to those consequences that may be unfavorable to himself. But he has an inner experience in doing so that is far from the mere passing of a logical judgment ("I am under obligation to perform act *A*. Therefore I perform act *A*"). He notices the ill effects upon himself, such as the depletion of his finances or the risk of the disfavor of people around him, and he intuits the qualities of his anticipations of these. He summons to mind the reactions of the other party to his contract, and apprehends the qualities of these reactions. He intuits the qualities of the relation of the other party to himself, as at present and as it will change upon performance of his obligation. He conceives of or imagines the relations between that contracting party and others involved, such as members of his family, upon whom performance will impinge, possibly favorably, possibly unfavorably. He will consider the new nature of their relation to himself, and will gain intuitions of what that may be. He will be aware of the relation of the performance of this obligation to his performance of all the past obligations that he has discharged, of its effect of strengthening his habitual performance of obligations and of its reinforcement of the concept of obligation that he has constructed. He will be conscious of the effect of performance upon his reputation. He will feel pride in his possession of a reputation of being one who always performs his contracts, "no matter what" (whereas the individual at the opposite end of the scale will take pride that he got away without performing a contractual obligation). He will feel satisfaction in the relation that he apprehends between himself as a performer of all obligations and the other members of society, among whom the presence of performers such as himself is not only admirable but immensely advantageous. If the thought of defaulting upon his obligation should cross his mind, he intuits the shame that would fill his consciousness, and in fact his response might be so strong as to be felt as an actual shame—"Why, I was ashamed at the very *thought* of committing such an offense!" Just as pride in a reputation for fearlessness has sent many a hero to certain death, pride in one's reputation as honest, as a person of integrity, as a person of unflinching adherence to duty, will send some persons through the full performance of difficult obligations, no matter how disadvantageous to themselves.

Obligation clearly plays its part then in the making of moral ought-judgments, and reference to obligation has a proper and often sufficing role in the justification of many of them. However, it is no one ingredient on which the outcome totally depends, as bread depends upon flour; it is not a single element with which a judgment is made moral or without which it cannot be a moral judgment. Rather, in each mind there is a practically infinite complex of intuitions and rational cognitions resulting from experiences; these vary as the biographies of individuals vary; and the process of responding intuitively and rationally to the incidents of life are sufficient to explain the great variety of versions of it held by different individuals. The ought-judgments that call for change are founded on the judgments of moral agents, and are based on their estimates of the efficacy of potentially performable acts to bring about those envisioned states of affairs. When so understood, the deontologist's position collapses into that of the teleologist. We do not need to postulate obligation as a separate metaphysical real entity, in order to account for having the concept or performing in accordance with it. Rather, we see that society has gone from judgments in particular situations, "It is good that parties A and B undertake *this* obligation," to "It is good that the society itself (or its government) be party to obligations and fulfill them," to "It is good that society support, maintain, and enforce obligations contracted by itself and its members." It is an irony that society expresses such judgments, when it gets around to wording them, by calling an obligation an absolute necessity; it is precisely because there is nothing either metaphysically or practically necessary about it in the first place that makes it possible and attractive for persons to consent to be bound by obligation.

16

How We Test Moral Judgments:

II. Reason, Justification, and Universalization

The principle of universalization has become important to many rational moral systems as they have been developed. The importance of the rational step of universalizing ethical rules and judgments is recognized by such disparate ethical positions as that of the Christian ethic of the Golden Rule, that of Immanuel Kant, and that of utilitarianism. Kant considerably shored up the categorical imperative with it. Few later theorists have seriously questioned the universalizability doctrine unless they were (like the existentialists, for example) questioning all previous moral theory itself.

A first question arises when the notion of universalizing the application of a moral rule occurs to us. Why should we universalize its application? Leaving aside pragmatic aspects that may account for the actual origins of our thoughts of universalizing, we may give as the pattern of an answer the suggestion that we consider it proper to apply a rule uniformly to agents A, B, and C, because they are in some way themselves alike. They are similar in regard to the worth of their claims. If my moral universe consists of myself, A, B, and C, and I am applying the rule "Give to each an equal share of the available food," then I am treating them not necessarily as though they have equal appetites, but as though their claims upon the food are equally strong or well founded. It is in this way that "All men are created equal."

But now why are their claims equally well founded? Are we saying that I have an equal obligation to A, B, and C, and that each of them in turn has an equal obligation to the other three members of this community? There is no natural necessity for that, as we have seen in relating obligation to the freedom to undertake a covenant, for the stronger and more capacious member of the community could simply consent to be obligated to provide for the others only on the basis of a larger share for himself. Is there anything that the members of the moral community possess in common that renders them equal to each other with respect to the worth of their claims?

Immanuel Kant found the common characteristic in the worth and dignity of each rational being. This attribute grounds the categorical imperative. In my act, according to this rule, I am to treat each other rational being as an end in himself, not a means only. Thus the application of any other rule, such as that about sharing the community's food, treats them as having claims of equal worth. The imperative phrasing of Kant's rule may be reformulated into the descriptive phrasing embodying the pure rather than moral *ought*: "The world as it ought to be is one in which each rational being is treated as an end in himself, not as a means only." This formulation represents Kant's "kingdom of ends," the community of rational moral agents, which we cannot prove exists actually but which provides us with the ideal according to which we should *look at* the moral community. Since the original *is* an imperative, it asks persons to do something, and one of its chief merits is that what it asks of them is possible, even if difficult. According to it, although we cannot *know* that all other beings naturally possess claims of equal worth, we can *treat each one as* equal in this regard. Unswerving application of this rule by every rational being would bring it about that each rational being would have his claims honored equally with all the others, a result tantamount to his *being* equal to every other in the worth of his claims. It is possible only for rational beings to accomplish this, since their doing so hinges upon their free choice to do so (since the categorical imperative has nothing about it that is *naturally* compelling), and their freedom so to choose, as well as their ability to conceive of the persons as rational, is a corollary of their rationality.

The starting point for universalizing is self-knowledge. One begins to treat mankind morally by treating oneself morally, for each person directly knows his own purposes and rational means of achieving them; his own choosing activity; his espousal of consistency in a system of beliefs that is in turn a product of choice; his own freedom, without which in each person the whole arrangement of a moral community would be impossible and which is a necessary condition for bringing about morality. It is precisely in the freedom to choose, the dreadful freedom of the existentialists, that all men are alike; and it is upon their likeness by virtue of their humanity that they find in each other or project upon each other, that the morality of mankind is built.

G. C. Field, in criticizing Kant's doctrine of the end-in-itself, has succinctly summarized the relativity of the end. Field's statement, I think, encapsules our usual and widely held belief about the status of the ends of action:

> Being an end is not really a fact about the thing at all. My end in ordinary speech means my object or purpose, what I am aiming at or trying to get at or want or desire. It is made an end by being wanted, and if I cease to want it, it ceases to be my end. If no one wants it any longer, it ceases to be an end at all. That is, there is strictly no such thing as an end in itself unless we are going to attach an entirely new meaning to the word.[1]

So far as it goes, Field's description applies to whatever is an end in my own conception—an incentive to act, a value. I should point out an important distinction, however, that is crucial to make in the interpretation of end or value. That is the distinction between an understanding of the end in psychological terms and an understanding of it in rational terms. As described in the quotation from Field, the end can be understood wholly in terms of the biological and psychological factors in man's make-up, with no attention whatsoever to the moral and rational as such. This distinction is often missed, in a world where knowledge is frequently defined in operational and behavioristic terms; but it is what is crucial to understanding the moral and rational. Kant himself was well aware of it:

> The authors of this science [general practical philosophy] . . . do not distinguish the motives which are presented completely a priori by reason alone, and which are thus moral in the proper sense of the word, from the empirical motives which the understanding, by comparing experiences, elevates to universal concepts. Rather, they consider motives without regard to the difference in their source but only with reference to their greater or smaller number (as they are considered to be all of the same kind). . . .[2]

What I insist on is that there *is* such a distinction, that it lies at the root of all understanding of value as contrasted against merely organismic, biological, or psychological interpretation of the human being, and that in it we see the elevation of mankind above the animal level of existence. This of course is not to deny that we do intellectually reach a positive valuation upon things that our animal nature determines us to seek, but it means that we have a rational apprehension and appreciation of those things, and can extend it to other things not possible to apprehend and value without rationality. In the instance of ends as they enter into moral experience, the situation is that the rational is overlaid, as it were, upon the emotional and instinctive. Undoubtedly, in early human development family love and ethnocentric feeling were originally responsible for many patterns of "good" conduct unaided by reasoning, and were present in the primitive stages of human culture independently of the rational. However, man's strides toward rationality have enabled him to articulate and to rationalize (in the favorable sense, not the pejorative sense of psychological excuse making) the feelings that he has had. He has become able to form logical patterns and concepts from his feelings and feeling-dependent intuitions, then to manipulate them logically, finally in this fashion arriving at articulate propositions and principles that render his deliberations objective and relatively uncolored emotionally. Those deliberations that are unrelated immediately to biological goals, those of mathematics or natural science, for example, can be quite unbiased emotionally. This can be true similarly of deliberations upon interpersonal and moral subject matter also, though achieving objectivity here is much more difficult psychologically.

Kant in effect *did* attach an entirely new meaning to the word *end*. As he and later ethical theorists employ the word, there is an important shift in its meaning. This is not a fallacy, a hidden ambiguity. It is a deliberate extension of the meaning of the term, in the fashion of metaphoric extension. It will reward our effort to notice what the new sense is, while retaining our attention to the old one as well. The first sense is that just seen in the description by Field, an end-in-view, "what I am aiming at," a goal state of affairs. But when Kant uses the word *end* as in his famous phrase "kingdom of ends," he is using it in the extended sense, which becomes important for ethical theory. In this sense, a human being may be characterized as "an end in himself." The phrase has no meaning at all on the biological or anthropological level. Rather, the implication of goodness and value has been shifted from the product of action, the goal state of affairs, to the performer of the action, the moral agent. This is an important shift.

The shift that moved goodness from the goal state of affairs to the agent could have been made either by conceiving another agent as the one into whom the good was projected, or else, more easily for most, by conceiving oneself in that role. It is natural for an individual to take for granted his own purposiveness and its deservedness to be served, but also natural for him to have certain emotions toward others, such as love for members of his family and respect and affection for friends. The less intense the emotional tie, perhaps, the easier it is for him to be reflective about other persons seen impartially. Let us look at a situation of each sort to trace the development of the kingdom of ends, consisting of all rational beings, each as end-in-himself.

I see agent A carrying on rational activity so as to achieve an end, a goal state of affairs. I understand that he is acting for that purpose, for I myself perform the same acts and I know I do it in expectation of outcomes similar to the outcome A anticipates. A is a person whom I respect, and my thought of him is such as to approve of his action, possibly even to direct my own action toward assisting him, helping him achieve the goal state for which he is acting. In this fashion I can conceive that A is acting for such-and-such an end, and then that *I* am now acting for the purpose or end of A-achieving-such-and-such. Thus A becomes part of my own end, and shares value that the goal state has both for A and for myself. And if the other agent is one with whom I often interact, not a casual friend like A but my wife, B, or my son, C, then it can be a very important thing to me, eliciting much of my activity, that there can be in the world the state of affairs of B-achieving-her-ends or C-achieving his-ends. My conception of these loved persons becomes one entailing their achievement of their purposes, consequently their happiness. Thus I am conceiving B or C, the person at the center of the network of his or her ends, as that which is the real good in the envisioned state of affairs, that which is the locus of the worth in the collection of purposes and ends involved. I conceive of the person as an end in himself, not meaning that he as such is relative to nothing (an impossibility), but rather that he is a being who deserves to have his purposes served, and the reason he deserves it is that he is the worthy object of love. Finally, I universalize from "my" human beings, the objects of *my* love, to all human beings, who, treated thus as persons, are now regarded as equally worthy of love. Having first judged domestically, so to speak, that the objects of my love ought to have their purposes served, I now judge that humankind in general ought to have their purposes served, which is to say that they are the abiding-places of moral worth.

In a way similar to my generation of the concept of the worth of others, I can also trace the conceiving of moral agents in general as ends from my thought of myself as the first agent in whom worth is seen. In my natural role, I take my own being for granted—not only that I am, but what sort of being I am. I do not incline to question my own purposes as such, for the achievement of them comprises goods, that is, states of affairs that I, from my own standpoint, judge to be good. Thus, I conduct myself in the world in such a way as to realize these ends, to bring them about as realities. I take it for granted that I am worthy in myself to have these purposes served. The fact that the actions of others can favorably affect me is a strong force in bringing me to impute value to them, but insofar as I look on them as simply beings whose actions I desire to affect me favorably, in my own interests, I am not looking at them as persons worthy of being served, but rather as beings whose existence is good on *my* account. But natural conditions of life soon lead me to expand upon this conception of others in my world. Another wants me to serve him, just as I want him to serve me; therefore we enter an arrangement of mutual aid. This relationship may be the basis of community in the primitive family, tribe, village, or other grouping. Yet this still is not the essentially moral, for it is merely organismically self-interested. But when for some reason I am moved to reflect upon humankind in general, or perhaps only upon those humans who are members of my own community, I see them as *like* me in this; I project upon them my conception of what I take myself to be, namely, a being whose purposes deserve to be served. Thus, universalizing, either with others or with myself as the starting point, I come to regard my peers in my community as ends to be served. From this conception, we can define an "end" or "end-in-himself" as a being of worth such that his purposes deserve on his own account to be served, rather than by deriving his worth from something external to him. Such are the citizens of the kingdom of ends.

The shift made by extending the locus of value from the consequent state of affairs to the purposing agent is the more justified when we notice that ends in the sense of goals are precisely always relative, as Field shows, to a person who constitutes them to be ends. Hence the total state of affairs achieved by action is not simply the new situation, but *the new situation with the agent present* in relation with it. When I act, what I bring about is a total combination including some rearrangement of the world, but in the relation now existing I am a terminus of a relation whose other termini are elements of the state of affairs that my action, when completed, has brought about. Moreover, it frequently happens that these elements may eventually lapse, or lose interest for me, or change in some other way. When they do, I tend to continue to think in the fashion of regarding myself as continuing to be in-valuated, to bear value, just as I had clearly borne value as an element among others in the goal state that my former action had brought about. I can let the other termini of that relation go unmentioned, unnoticed, unremembered since they were ephemeral, but nevertheless it is easy for me to continue to constitute myself as an end, even if as one not entirely complete. But when the shift is made from the earlier meaning of *end* to its later sense, then I treat myself as an end in this new sense, a being whose purposes ought on their own account to be served, and not incomplete, not lacking in some factor of worth, but rather merely changing in respect to purposes held from time to time. The same is true also for those other members of my moral community.

The development of the concept of the kingdom of ends, of every person as equally the locus of moral worth with every other, on account of his rationality, was one form of Kant's universalizing moral principle or rule. Universalization is associated with the very foundation of morality, for it seems to subdue self-interested considerations to moral ones at a single stroke.[3] Moreover, universalization is possible only when the rational overlay is added to moral feeling and emotion, for these are virtually always associated with or addressed to particulars, not to generalities, much less to the generality of mankind. Here is the central reason that we may be sure morality is a relation existing between rational creatures, or better stated, between creatures insofar as—to the extent that—they are rational.

Universalization, whether undertaken in subscription to the doctrine of equality of deservingness or not, serves first as a test to use in selecting acts that impinge upon others. When we say that we will not take revenge on someone for an injury that he committed accidentally, we rule out the act on the basis that to do so would not treat him as a person, as a human being, an end in himself. On the other hand, to select acts of assistance toward him is to treat him as a person, as a being who deserves to have his purposes served. This is where Kant's ethical theory has been considered formalistic, i.e., the moral value of an action inheres entirely in the motive. However, the motive one has is a result of the decision one has made, the selection of an act; and the performance of the act is undertaken with the goal respecting agent A of bringing about the state of affairs of A-achieving-his-purposes. This analysis makes it about as correct a description to call such a doctrine teleological as formal, for the worth of the motive or of the act depends upon the goal state, A-achieving-his-purposes; that end is the justification of the act as the right act; and one may well say that it is done for the sake of the "end" when the "end" is an end-in-himself.

Thus universalization is not only a test of action but a justification to others for an act. In effect, the most often heard justifications of actions that are declared to be fair, and condemnations of actions declared to be unfair or unjust, rest upon universalization. They may start simply in reciprocity: "Don't do that to him, because you wouldn't want him to do that to you." With the involvement of more agents, this becomes pluralized, and in another step universalized: "Don't do that to anybody, because you wouldn't want anybody to do it to you." The doctrine is especially useful to those who object to an act before the act is committed, and is far more often used in this censor's role than in the positive role, in which it becomes "*Do* perform act *X*, because act *X* affects everyone (including yourself) favorably." The reason may be that questions of fact are difficult to establish when the factual assertion is about "everybody," the whole human species. We tend to doubt that there is any *one* good thing achievable by an act that everyone without exception would judge good, or even that impartial observers (who by the hypothesis would not exist) could judge good for every reason without exception.

There is, however, a further merit of universalization: Considering whether a principle or rule can apply universally, or whether an act could be consistent with the universal good, tends to guarantee that deliberation upon it goes to the fullest stage of completion. If we have not tested an anticipated act under the light of universalization, we must concede the possibility that an effect of the act which we have not considered will fail to treat some fellow rational being as an end. On the other hand, if we show that the principle, rule, or act can in the respectively appropriate way be universalized, then we surely must have deliberated long enough about its consequences, for there is nothing left to consider in this regard.

Seen logically, universalization carries out to completion the classification of humans as rational agents. The great psychological difficulty of it is reflected in the patterns of behavior of ethnic discrimination, persecution of minorities, nationalistic aggression, social snobbery, even simple egoism.[4] But the curbing of tendencies of these sorts is generally a victory for rationality, through the principle of universalization, which rests logically on the simple patterns of class membership and class inclusion. It occurs when moral agents become persuaded to acknowledge the inclusion not only of members of their own group but of *persons* of any identification whatever, within the kingdom of ends that they inhabit. Once they do that, they have removed the greatest obstacle toward acting to bring about the states of affairs indicated by the conclusions of moral arguments.

However, to have an enlightened view of the kingdom of ends, there are some qualifications. I must take into account the various desires of different persons. I come to learn that sometimes to treat the other as I want myself to be treated might *not* be how the other wants me to treat him. Rather, I must impute to him a worth that motivates me to regard him as having the right to enjoy this oddity. Further, it is not simply a case of assuming that everyone's purposes deserve to be served, *no matter what they are.* From this, moral chaos could result. Rather, it is a case of regarding the other individual as a moral agent who will himself engage in the imputation of moral worth to *his* others, including me, who will also regard my own and all other moral agents' purposes as worthy regardless of whether they are the same as or different from his. This teaches us to want, on our part, to fulfill only purposes that are compatible with the purposes of others and not destructive of them. Yet further, we are not bound to exhaust ourselves unto death in the attempt to fulfill others' purposes. Rather, it involves according to the other the willingness to "be reasonable about it," to adjust himself to the fact that not all of his individual purposes *can* be served, and to make decisions to select the ones that must await a later time, that must be abandoned because they are unfeasible (and also because they do not treat others morally), and that may justifiably be sought after. Finally, let us acknowledge that in the practical situation, universalization is never literally universal, because there can only be a proportion, never all, of mankind standing in effective moral relation with others. We deliberate therefore about effects of our judgments or actions "upon those (only) to whom it could make any difference." Thus, like teleological deliberation, universalization has cloture. To the extent that we find ourselves capable of moral thinking of this sort, capable of setting aside selfish purposes in favor of another, we impute the same moral capacities to others. They sense this attitude in us, and we in them, as they comport their outlook in the same way. When this happens, we can verify as actually present in them that worth which we project upon or impute to them, and they, in us. Mutually, we realize or actualize the kingdom of ends.

One consequence of the reasoning that is built upon the propositions that we assume in creating the moral order is that we come to see that there is nothing in itself unworthy about being self-interested, having interests of one's own. These after all are the direct outgrowth of our need to survive in the world in which we find ourselves. The purposes of others, which we serve, are more often than not their self-interests. However, we universalize here too; we see that our self-interests are on a par with theirs, and have the same proportion and place in the scheme of values that we and they may be assumed to share in common. The art of moral judgment and of attainment of wisdom consists in judging in favor of those outcomes in which the prudential interests both of individuals and the community coincide. So long as this occurs, community survival and the desired qualities of life for the individual will be preserved and promoted. It is when such judgments do not prevail that clashes destructive to society arise. The many factors that together comprise the qualities of life include those qualities intuited upon objects of attention and upon relationships among them, qualities that are in themselves pleasurable to entertain, as our pleasures in the arts attest. The moral way of judging, then, like that of judging works of art, is an instrument for each of us and for our society toward the end of ever-greater attunement to, and satisfaction in, life in the world.

I would not like to say, however, that the occurrence of something in our experience, which we take to be this satisfaction, is the test of the truth of the judgments that we arrive at in prosecuting our moral deliberations. The sound moral judgment in other words does not have the characteristic of truth in the pragmatist's conception, just as it does not in the conception of correspondence to an exterior reality. Rather, the attained satisfaction would be a probable sign, but not a conclusive sign, that our deliberations were as complete and our judgments as rightly reached as possible. It is always possible that there could be misinterpreted or wholly overlooked considerations whose discovery would set us back to work. And again, we tend from habit and association to think of our value-assertive propositions, even and perhaps especially those with moral content, as *true*; yet we must remember that we do not put facts from the world up against them to test their accuracy. Rather, what we "put up" to validate our moral judgments is not an external state of affairs, but respect and esteem in the eyes of ourselves and others. That is, we make value assertions on our own authority, and place our authority at risk. When we offer a fact-assertive statement and are found wrong, we lose esteem as an accurate observer and recorder of states of affairs; but when we offer a value-assertive statement and it is overthrown by a better-justified alternative, we lose esteem as a judge and critic. What is placed at risk is not our knowledge but our wisdom, a far more highly prized possession.

The price of this heightened satisfaction in life, our moral responsibility, is a corollary of the absence in nature itself, in the external (or "external") world, of value or values. We do not have the easy way out. We cannot justify our moral and other valuative judgments by taking the critic to the appropriate spot and saying, "There, look! There you see for yourself the determinant value necessitating that I should have judged as I did!" Rather, there are myriad items in that world upon which we can bestow the attribution of value, from within ourselves as it were, from our own thinking in terms of objects and properties that exist, of relationships among them, of probable future states of affairs into which they will enter, of all the qualities they give to our apprehension, and in fact of everything conceivable about them. The same item in the world is capable of being a reason for action *A* and a reason against action *A*, in the thinking of two different moral agents or in the thinking of the same moral agent at different times or under different conditions, and could be equally justifiable, and acceptably so, on each occasion. Thus, the absence of determinants in the world thrusts upon us, in our freedom, the burden of being determinants of actions, and therefore determinants of tomorrow's world, the world that our actions will make. This is what our responsibility consists in, and this is what actually occupies the place that we have yearned to give to a *value* that could be found—we wrongly hoped—within a reality existing apart from ourselves in the world.

17

How We Ought to Make Moral Judgments

It is the human condition that we must act in order to survive in our world, and that our acting affects others of our species who inhabit both of the worlds we posit, the moral kingdom of ends and the physical external world. Ethics is the branch of study that examines the relationships between these; thus, in a sense, ethics is the metaphysic of the relationship between self and world. Since we value at least some of the other rational inhabitants of our worlds, we want and need a principle, or perhaps a set of principles, for making our moral judgments and decisions upon action, and for resolving our moral perplexities "in good conscience." Our action shall go forward in some fashion, willy-nilly, so we want our ethics to supply a normative guide to shape our actions. And we know by now that we do not find such a principle in our environs, since the standards of what ought to be done or brought about are the results of our own judgments. We have warned ourselves against the naturalistic fallacy, which we would commit if we were to certify current practice simply because it is current; we have demanded of ourselves a more responsible role than that. Yet we can see that it would be equally egregious if we were to disregard the past practice of moral agents rather than to attempt to learn from it. We remind ourselves that it is possible to reach moral judgments, for they abound in our experience. But thus far, none of this produces the criterion called for by the question that has largely motivated our whole inquiry: *How ought we to make moral judgments?*

Evidently, then, the problem of validating moral judgments is not one of quantity, for there is no dearth of them, but rather of their quality—their rightness, their goodness, their fulfillment of appropriate standards. Do I dare to suppose that my own moral judgments are better than those of Jones or Smith? Better than those of persons from a religious background quite different from mine, or from a cultural tradition a world away? It has come to be regarded as quite bad science for an anthropologist, for example, to allow bias favoring his own culture to show through his professional descriptions. The attitude has become prevalent that since there are no objective yardsticks by which to measure, one must do the only fair thing and set all value judgments, including moral judgments, on the same level—to regard, or act as though one regards, all value judgments as equally good.

However, while this sort of fairness may suit one or another of the sciences, I submit that it is not necessary in the ongoing practice of life and it might be quite deleterious to human progress toward general happiness. Shall we preserve (say) cannibalism as a rite of passage, or sacrifice of the leader's first-born when battle looms, on the grounds that these are the right things to do (somewhere)? Rather, I believe that even while avoiding cultural or individual arrogance we can on occasion expect some moral judgments to be better than other ones. We must believe that this is possible if we are to get a normative moral theory, or even to make any sense while talking about one.

Moreover, I am convinced that it *is* possible to rate certain judgments above others as better arrived at or as sounder once delivered. While this flies in the face of the arbitrary neutralism of methods in the social sciences, it is as necessary a principle for value theory (and within it, moral theory) as its expurgation is to those sciences. And to establish the principle, I commend to attention a fact that lies in everyone's moral experience. Every adult has become aware that his own moral judgments have improved over a period of time. As we mature, we become able to make better moral judgments and to know the inferiority of the less-good ones of the past. All of us have at one time or another revised a past opinion about whether on a certain occasion we were sufficiently fair to another person, or whether a given act with a moral dimension was or was not good, or whether a moral plan under which we operated was the best possible. Even nations and whole societies have acknowledged that decisions made by their earlier members have been inferior to decisions made by those who came later. If we can do that to our own past moral judgments, then of course we can do it to our anticipated judgments and actions of the future, and to the judgments and acts of others; yet further, to the rules of action under which we subsume specific acts, and to the broad framing principles of our personal or public moral system itself. Thus, this common experience argues that we actually do make use of some criterion (or criteria) for assessing moral judgments, and that we may legitimately expect to locate and use such criteria as a basis for inferring how we should make our moral judgments.

This question, that feeling and reason together have led us to pose to ourselves, has a logic whose examination should help us toward what we seek. We have said that the meaning of *ought* arises out of comparison and contrast with the meaning of *is*. For anything that *is* (specific tense not considered), there is always an *ought*-question. It *is* thus-and-so; *ought* it to be that way? It *happens: ought* it to happen? Thus, we *do* justify our moral judgments in a certain way; *ought* we to justify them in that way? Semantically, our word *justify* in this last question conceals a regress, for "to justify" is "to tell why it ought." But in actuality this step cannot be repeated. There is no justifying of the justifying of justifying; we need not fear an infinite regress. For we have identified justification as a process of articulating the reasons for making the judgment that is being justified, and have affirmed that ideally the process of justifying the judgment is a perfect match, statement for statement, of the statements used for reaching that judgment. And there is, and can be, only one step from the inward, silent thinking that comprised the reaching of the judgment to the overt articulation of that reasoning. The making of the step itself may be justified: One asks, "Why ought I to justify my action to him?" and answers, "For his, or my own, satisfaction." But it is simply idle to go on justifying the justifying, that is, to make overt the reasoning for making overt the reasoning for the original judgment. The step of making the reasoning overt to another party or to oneself will either fulfill the need or it will not, and further justificatory statements for the *justification,* for trying to bring about the satisfaction, will not contribute to the satisfaction that is sought if the first justification, that of the judgment in question, has not done so. It has been useful to conceive of language, articulation, as an overlay upon the subarticulate thought that does the bulk of our intellectual work for us, but it is not useful, since our object of crucial interest is the making articulate of that thought, to suppose that the subarticulate is in turn an overlay upon a sub-subarticulate function, and so on in turn down to some micro-mind at the center of it all.

The involvement of our question with itself has another implication. The question is phrased as one that calls for an answer that is framed as an ought-judgment, not as a fact-assertive proposition. This may seem to be a begging of the question. In fact, however, the crucial step is not made in the asking of this particular reason but in generating, in the first place, the meaning of *ought* as against the meaning of *is,* which we have already traced in chapter four. The generation of this meaning is an expression of our fundamental recognition that to survive we must act, with its consequence, our attempt to know what act to perform. Although a critic might wish to satisfy himself that our question does not contain an illegitimate assumption of a belief about ought-judgments before the ought-judgments are justified, I should reply that this must be a confusion. For we are not investigating whether there *are* ought-judgments, a point not worth proving formally because it is evident in everyone's experience. But what is significant about the occurrence of the word *ought* in the question, calling for an ought-judgment in its answer, is that it calls for this part of value theory—namely, ethical theory—to yield normative statements rather than descriptions alone. Some of its practitioners say that for ethical theory to be useful it must be normative; it must not merely describe what happens but give positive guidance in coming to moral judgments, making moral decisions, solving moral perplexities. To say this is of course to make a value-assertion. But it would seem either cowardice or misconception to hang back at this point, on the principle that the ethical scholar must himself be value-neutral, whereas if we do press forward we may indeed do a service to those who want the aforesaid results. We may also find that there are further facts that enable us, without much deviation from wide moral and rational consensus, to suggest those results. Thus, the final fact about the logic of the question, "How ought we to make our moral judgments?" is that its answer is bound not only to be a value judgment but a moral judgment, for any answer to the question is going to affect persons through its consequences. This is as true of the claim that value-neutrality is a requirement for the ethical theorist as for any other response to the question. Even if his answer goes entirely unheeded by others, the normative-ethical theorist himself, assuming he is sincere in what he says, will be one moral agent who is guided by the content of the answer. Thus we cannot avoid making a moral judgment in the very decision whether to attempt or not to attempt to answer the question.

What we are striving to find, then, is a set of moral value judgments that will help us to make the best possible moral value judgments; and knowing that we cannot get them from outside ourselves, we recognize that they must issue from our own minds. To satisfy this requirement, all that remains possible for us to do is to produce for ourselves, in the content of our own consciousness, either from known practices or from imaginable or conceivable ones, all the procedures and principles that could be relevant, then to *judge them,* and thus erect the best structure of norms that we find it within our power to construct. While this may sound like sailing away in a hot-air balloon that is inflated only by the warm breath of our own exhalations, it can in fact be a much more successful venture. For since our judgments will be informed from that larger world in which we posit our place, through the intermediaries of its expression in linguistic, conceptual, and other symbolic ways that we have of uniting the features of the outer world together in a single construction that also includes all the moral agents who, with us, inhabit the kingdom of ends, we can believe that with these as our materials we may establish a solid and sturdy structure for both immediate use and later improvement.

To make a start, then, let us first look at the termini of the relation between self and world, and of the two, let us first consider the world. We inhabit a rather regular world. It matters little for our conclusions in this inquiry which of the following might be the case: (1) whether the regularity that our intuitions of our world disclose to us is the product of real regularity in a real external world, (2) whether there is a real external world but a haphazard one that we inaccurately intuit and interpret as though it possesses regularity, or (3) whether we wholly impose upon a real or merely postulated world a regularity that arises totally within ourselves. For if there is an environing world that only seems regular to man but is not *really* regular, there is nothing he can do about its real irregularity and any ensuing intractability of it, for on this hypothesis he cannot even know of it. On the other hand, if it is he who imposes order on an irregular universe that is real but is not ordered, then at least to impose a presumptive order has so far worked rather well for him, and has made possible a moral as well as a scientific or cognitive order within which he can effectively act. Thus, regardless of which metaphysical hypothesis actually obtains, the effects are the same, so far as man's actions are concerned, as though there really is an external world, that it really possesses regularity and order, and that man's cognitions of it correspond at least roughly and for practical purposes to what is really there.

Thus, man has in practice acquired a knowledge of much that is in his own world (which may or may not be the same as the external world), and is considerably aided in his accumulation of this knowledge by the regularity of pattern that he sees in the objects of his discovery. From what he knows of the features of the world in which he lives, he gains many concepts upon which to reflect, and therefore many propositions to regard as candidates for selection to be treated as reasons for preserving what he finds or for bringing about change. All of the existents and events encountered in his world and regarded as potential reasons for action are available material to be considered in constructing patterns for action, and in particular to be considered setting up moral rules and ethical principles.

At the other terminal of the relationship of man and world is man. Man is indeed free, but he need not see his freedom as irrational. He not only is able to exercise choice as his essential activity; he is able to choose according to criteria. Furthermore, he can exercise compound choices, as it were: He can choose his criteria, then choose other things according to his criteria. He himself is as much an existent thing as anything else, but he is more, for he is the most willful existent there is. He can alter things; he can make things. He can create universals, then structures of universals. If there were no rationality in the regularity found in nature, then man could and would create rationality of his own, and if in fact there is none, then he has actually done so. While some persons protest that there is not a rational order in nature, *the essentially human standpoint* is that of treating nature *as though* it has rational order. Adopting this standpoint has not only made nature greater than it is, but has also made man greater than he was to start with. Far from being absurd, all this is natural history, the natural history of mankind. I, for one, judge it to be not only factually the case, but—whichever way the facts fall—qualitatively good.

Man, moreover, can choose to treat this one undeniable existent— himself—as a reason. When one most fully loves a human being, either as one's fellowman or as the special object singled out among one's fellowmen for special love, one is treating that other person as end-in-itself, bearer of value, and reason enough for being served, maintained, and so far as possible, perpetuated. Man is able himself to constitute in the human being the value without qualification. Of course, he is also free to lay the same concept upon the pig, the hyena, the monkey, the sun, the world spirit, the Absolute. Somehow he knows that there are fitter objects for bestowal of it than the pig, the hyena, or the monkey. He has sometimes preferred to fasten it upon one of the other aforementioned beings rather than upon himself, recognizing the dangers of self-adoration; but in his present stage of development, his rationality can allow him with impunity to bestow value upon whatever rational beings there are, as Kant did, for example. And even within a framework that acknowledges a higher and more worthy being, he is still able to construe his own role as that of a citizen of a kingdom of ends, a being who among other like beings is deserving of having his purposes served.

In addition to seeing himself as an object of worth, man discerns innumerable beings, objects, states of affairs, and actions that he labels *good*. He finds among any of the ways of appearing in consciousness those items that he adjudges either to be as they ought to be or to be not as they ought to be. Of these he assembles structures that we call structures of values. The more complex his life, the more complex the structure of values he is likely to have. An individual's career is the history of his whole endeavor to establish as actual those things that he adjudges good, as they ought to be, and eliminate those that he adjudges bad, not as they ought to be. Moreover, an individual is never free of this interwoven net of goods, values, at whose center he is sited. His vocation is thus to act in such a fashion as to continue in action, realizing as many as possible of the goods, while alleviating as many as possible of the evils or negatively valued items, in his experience. Man necessarily acts in this fashion. He is born into a world, and if he is to survive in it, he simply must act. How is he to act? He is to act in a way that makes things be as he judges they ought to be—how else? Thus, man is free to act in freely chosen ways—but granting that he is to survive, he is not then free not to act at all.

To the extent that he is a physical being, man exhibits regularity and order just as the external physical world does. Man's biophysical behavior is in general highly predictable, even though he has much free choice within its limits. Routines of eating and sleeping and the like, even though interruptable and modifiable, are the basis of predictable behavior. But within the broad limitations of nature, man has wide choice as to the specific component actions of his behavior. Here his values, his envisioned realizable states of affairs, serve as the incentives to his specific actions and draw him on in action. Definitively, values are human incentives.

The regularity seen in the order of nature is highly influential in the ultimate shapes of moral systems and consequent ethical theories. Man, as an evolving creature in nature, is slowly but continually changing. We may, I think, legitimately regard him as presently in a transition from animality, a level in which he simply does what is determined by instinct or immediate feeling, related directly to bodily self-interest or family-unit or tribal survival, to the level of rationality, in which all outcomes are to be rationally warrantable outcomes, sometimes coinciding with the outcomes of instinct or bodily self-interest and other animal-level factors but implemented only when the criteria supplied by rationality are fulfilled. I concede that much that most people do in man's present stage is only partly rational or quasi-rational, if by *rational* we intend the sort of thing that is fully consistent with the criteria of logic and epistemology. With some of us, of course, emotion dominates reason, often to our own detriment; and with all of us emotions still play a great part in determining our beliefs, judgments, and actions. To the extent that they do so, man is still "reacting naturally," is living according to the regularities and forces of the natural world. But even in the reactions where emotion is most prominently manifested there is some shaping by reason, even if only by the agency of habit formed through the activity of rational factors in prior situations in which countervailing emotion was not strongly evoked.

Some of our experience and some of our interpretations of it seem to confirm that a special faculty or factor in the make-up of the human person does indeed lie at the base of the valuative judgments and is the determinant upon which the judgments are based. The formulation is suggested, "If persons *judge* alike, with respect to art or morals or any area of value judging, then inwardly they must *be* alike." One area of evidence seeming to support this formulation is that of the arts. It is seen that over a period of time the judgments on a certain body of works within a given art form settle down to something resembling uniformity. Few serious judges find much to impel them to claim, for example, that Shakespeare and Goethe were not great poets, or that Michelangelo and Leonardo da Vinci did paintings that were middling to poor. The art of our contemporaries may not receive wide immediate acceptance, but among those spectators who follow its development there usually is agreement upon who its best artists are. After a period of accustomization, acquaintance with the novel works becomes wider and consensus upon quality within its genre tends to grow more solid. Another area of evidence tending to support the suggested formulation is that of our dependence upon juries and panels in matters where evaluative judgments must be reached. We place our faith in the deliverance of twelve citizens chosen at random, to determine whether an action committed was a crime; we use panels of qualified persons to determine the best jar of pickles at the state fair, the best dog in the show, the best painting in the exhibition, the best film shown at Cannes. Finally, the most convincing body of evidence for the formula probably is simply the biophysical similarity of human beings, complex organisms that they are, which suggests a strong analogy; they are alike in so many obvious respects that it is well worth hypothesizing that they are also alike in whatever it is that yields their value judgments.

But these areas of experience do not strongly support the inference that in the judging faculty there is some one thing in all persons that determines the outcomes of specific judgments and that because of the likeness of this inner component among people we may count upon them to reach uniformity in moral and other value judgments. For although judgments in the arts do settle down in general, there is enough exception and variation from agreement that we do not deem the agreement or consensus to be a sufficient argument for an inner art-judging faculty or function that is alike in all of us. The matter of juries and panels is more an argument against rather than for an inner uniformity; often these panels are deliberately constructed to have an odd number of members, so that there can be no tie votes, a measure that hardly argues for uniformity of judgment among those judging. The conspicuous exception is the jury of twleve that sits in court; but here the number does not matter because law requires unanimity for a verdict to be reached. Finally, even though persons are biophysically much alike, the behavior that we see them carrying out is surely very diverse, weakening the analogy with respect to whatever it is about them that determines their behavior—and above the animal level, the determinant is value-judging. Consequently that argument by analogy loses credibility also.

The issue just discussed is substantially the one that was controverted in the eighteenth century when the "moral sense philosophers" were suggesting that an inner sense, present in all moral agents, was the touchstone by which the morally good and right was distinguished from the morally bad and evil. It is related to the notion of conscience, as an inner voice or other sort of determinant that compels or restrains this or that action. It would seem as though if the powerful philosophical minds of the eighteenth, nineteenth, and twentieth centuries were turned to the testing of this thesis, it should be rather better established by the present time than it was two hundred years ago—but this has not happened. A renewal of it was made, in the form of early twentieth-century moral intuitionism, which seems to have had its day and to have passed rather inconspicuously out of court.

Now we really have confessed ourselves to be in a dilemma. There are arguments for affirming uniformity of inner make-up, determining like outcomes of value judgings; and there are arguments for diverse make-up, based on actual diverse value-judgings. Neither is strong enough to carry the day. And whatever solution we find for the dilemma will not only have to be supported by good argument but will also have to accommodate the diversity, showing how this is possible when what we are striving to find is a correctness of method in moral value judgment; and that correctness, we insist, must surely be objective for every moral agent, no matter how diverse the moral agents are in inner make-up.

I have been insistent throughout the present inquiry that man is a free judge of values as well as being free in other ways. Now it is a disadvantage to him who asserts freedom that his thesis is formally unprovable, because a proof would be the establishment of a conclusion for reasons, and the reasons must function logically so as to determine the truth of the thesis. Further, the language in which the thesis is couched is descriptive, and in that respect is somehow thought to "match" or "copy" or "correspond" to reality. But if freedom is genuine, then it is something that is, by definition, *not* to be determined. Hence no reason can be found that will enforce the conclusion of freedom upon him who is opposed to this thesis. However, the latter party is in no better position, for he cannot exhibit arguments that will compel the believer in freedom to desist in his belief. It seems that either may choose not to accept the argument of the other. (And this last is one of the more convincing arguments *for freedom* of which I am aware.)

I have already allied freedom and reason as corollaries, opposite faces of the same coin, so to speak. But consistent with human freedom of reflection, moral judgment, and choice of action, it appears that the account for the relative uniformity, when it is present, of value judgments is indeed the similarity of the inner nature of persons, but in a qualified sense. The actual observational powers that man has are largely biophysical, at least at base (setting aside ways of performing interpretation), but the choosing is done either by virtue of the biophysical or of reasoning, or as a resultant of the two at work together. The standardization, so to speak, has its empirical side in the reception of sense data, and its rational side in the application of reasoning, whose logical objectivity is pretty demonstrable; but it has also its provision for variation in the freedom that reason itself presupposes. What actually obtains, then, we see, is that: (1) Insofar as their cognitions depend upon their sensory powers, there is relatively high uniformity among the findings of different persons, with some variation on account of different sensitivities. Where overt training in observation, such as that used to enhance the apprehension of X-ray photographs or of works of art, the deliverances of perceptual intuitions of various observers have an ever-diminishing margin of variation as training goes on and experience is accumulated. (2) Where cognitions and judgments make use of reasoning capacities, the objective rules of deductive and inductive logic apply. They can be learned by a moral agent from teachers and books, but also may be learned informally through use and reflection. (3) Where the acceptance of whole arguments (as contrasted with the conclusions of arguments from their evidence) is at issue, variance of outcome is normal and to be expected, because the human moral agent is essentially free to treat or not to treat this or that proffered belief or proposition as a reason; and he may reject that which his opponent in moral argument advances as a reason. While both concur in the validity or inductive soundness of the logical steps in one or another argument, they need not concur that the argument bears upon the outcome, for one party may decline to accept a premise (i.e., treat as a reason) a proposition upon which the other bases his conclusion.

Undoubtedly, human beings are physically much alike, although not entirely. Some are colorblind, while others are tone deaf or suffer from other sorts of insensitivities. Some are insensitive to the appeal of certain beauties that others respond to strongly and value highly. We may suppose that in a similar way some are insensitive to principles of right and wrong, or to relationships between conditions and prospective changes in those conditions, or other factors that could be associated with the psychopathic personality—

the "conscienceless" individual. However, on the whole, people's sensitivities are enough alike to be statistically significant. As to reasoning ability, of course some learn logic readily and others have great difficulty with it; but for workaday purposes, the inference that takes place "intuitively" and sub-articulately appears to suffice for nearly all of us. Not everyone can correctly analyze a long string of syllogisms, or even a single syllogism, but nearly everyone can inarticulately recognize the validity of a simple syllogism and employ its conclusion with confidence, quite correctly and objectively. Thus, reasoning—use of objective standards of inference—is an important way in which human beings are alike.

The account of the variety of moral judgments upon a single case is not, for the most part, then, to be explained in terms of the sensitivity or the reasoning processes underlying each, although some differences may, to be sure, come into the comparison from these areas. Rather, the greater portion of the variety is surely to be accounted for by the freedom that people enjoy, to regard or not to regard that X is good, and to regard or not to regard Y and Z as reasons, or premises, in the argument leading to the judgment that X is good. Now, when we are able to get deliberations on moral problems from a number of individuals, and providing that those delivering their own judgments are unaffected by the outcome (i.e., impartial), we do in fact find, rather encouragingly, that there is a fair amount of agreement. Most people will concur, for example, that on the whole no adult should casually leave a scene where a small child is in great danger. With respect to specific cases, there well may be disputes on what constitutes great danger, or what age is the age below which children are regarded as being not wholly competent to safeguard their own interests; but the general principle is surely recognized pretty much the world over.

The continuum from intuition, through perception, to reason is wholly engaged in our process of accumulating value-beliefs and arriving at moral judgments. An outline of this process in the case of a particular judgment would no doubt show that our information on "the facts of the matter"—the elements from self and world that will eventually be seen as being involved in the matter to be judged—are known to us first from direct intuition. We simply see (or hear, etc.) how things are. Fuller acquaintance with the situation shows us relationships, tendencies things have toward actions and reactions, and so forth. Sometimes quite immediately, we react with liking or disliking to what is immediately presented, and sometimes we make those responses as the situation becomes more complex for us, as we come to apprehend relationships, such as physical consequences of things and events with which we are acquainted, and we like or dislike the consequences. We become acquainted with impingements of these elements of the situation both upon ourselves and other persons. By the time we are doing this, we are no longer taking our read-off simply from the elements as they are first given; rather, we are construing or constructing them in certain ways. We are "thinking about them, thinking them over." Our intuitions are the more intellectual and rational the more we apprehend the situation in its gathering complexity. As it presents obstacles to us—things to take into account in selecting any actions we may undertake that will touch it—we pose the obstacles to ourselves in the form of statements of problems, or questions, and deliberately apply reasoning in order to assure ourselves of a rational outcome. We have, by this stage, collected many perceptual intuitions of the situation but also many rational, intellectual intuitions. We begin to subsume the situation or elements of it under moral principles or rules that we have found acceptable, as well as principles of cause and effect and other such things that may help us foresee outcomes. We will be invoking memory constantly, summoning up information as needed, very importantly including memories of the persons involved, and of the tendencies of the changing elements of the situation to affect persons. We will be taking intuitions from the remembered matter as well as the immediately sensed, and particularly we will be alerting ourselves to the impact upon other persons of any potential actions we can think of ourselves as taking.

Our results so far make it obvious that, in the popular sense of the word, it is good *judgment* that accounts for the correctness, the merit, the betterness, when we say that one of our value judgments was better than another. Rather than continue to search for an objective solution, valid the world over, to every valuational problem and especially every moral problem, let us put our results in the perspective of a wholly competent individual moral agent, whom we posit. We shall assume that he can be right about his appraisals of his own valuations, as to which are better, and which are worse. We shall ask what the factors are—when he is going through the process of arriving at a moral judgment and making a moral decision—that are likely to induce him to believe that its outcome is better than if those considerations were not considered. The list is long.

Factors that may operate at the very outset, as preliminaries before he has fully addressed himself to his particular problem, factors that tend to produce for our moral agent a favorable assessment of the quality of a given solution to his moral problem, may include that he has been through moral problems and perplexities before, and knows that he knows how to go about it. He knows that he has built a dependable habit of thoroughness in carrying on his deliberation, both the selecting of his moral judgments and choices of actions, and in their justification afterward to other moral agents who may have an interest in them. He knows that in this past experience he has disciplined and trained his emotions to develop those favoring rationality, and to enable himself to hold in abeyance those favoring irrationality. And he knows that at the moment of undertaking the new problem, he is capable of operating at his greatest level of ability compared to what he has attained in the past.

This agent knows that his sensitivity to relevant intuitions and his rational powers work closely together; they are actually indistinguishable from one another except by deliberate analysis of the process itself (such as may take place later, not during the actual process of solving the moral problem, at least not necessarily during it). He knows what it is to possess an openness of sensitivity, open to new intuitive information, even as he may be involved in reasoning or in verbalizing the other elements present to his consciousness. He knows that he keeps up his awareness to impressions of the ongoing process itself, so that there is nothing in his subarticulate thinking that, though clamoring for attention, fails to reach the level of the necessary verbal expression. He imaginatively projects himself far enough into the problem situation to give attention to every relevant element that may enter it. His self-discipline requires that he penetrate all possibilities both imaginatively and in deliberate conceptual projection, so that he intuits all the facets of each potential variable of the situation.

He is systematic in his making of projections, to assure that he leaves out no element that ought to be considered, with respect both to its present and its likely future state, under each possible choice of action. He includes in his projections both those things that will happen inevitably and those things that can be made to happen or not to happen by his own intervention, and he keeps well in mind the difference between the two. He estimates accurately the amount of control that he can have over the varying factors. He remains aware of which ongoing processes once begun are reversible or corrigible, and which are not. He considers not only all the physical consequences of actions but also the symbolic effects they may have—what they will mean, rightly or wrongly, to observers.

After imagining or conceiving of each possible action and projecting its likely consequences, this agent judges each sequence of act and consequence morally. On behalf of each individual who might be affected, he envisions how he himself would react if he were in the place of that individual, then estimates whether the individual would react the same or differently, and notes whether this brings to light any ground to adjust his view of the right thing to do. He asks whether, for each potential action, each affected person is being treated as a worthy moral end. He considers the effect not only on individuals but on the community collectively, as citizens of the realm of ends. He considers whether a prospective action will serve as a proper instructive example to persons observing it. He considers whether other persons, either those affected or those whom he respects as moral judges, would judge differently from his own prospective final judgment, and if so, why; he seeks to establish whether his own justifications would outweigh theirs, and why, or whether he should shift his position. Having done all these things, he knows that he has done as much as he can to apply the principle of the universalization of moral judgment and choice of action.

He is aware not only of the rational process of universalization but of other logical steps as well. He checks his reasoning to assure that it commits no missteps or logical fallacies. He reviews to see that every possible relevant thought from the subarticulate level has been articulated accurately, in exact wording. This is another measure by which he avoids deceiving himself and clears up any point on which he may previously have had a confused outlook. He checks his facts; he goes over his collection of factual data to assure that the reasons for believing each fact-assertive statement are adequate reasons. For instances where the factuality of the fact-assertive statements cannot actually be known, he assesses probabilities and reviews how the determination, one way or the other, would affect the choice before him, and he then selects needed fact-assertive beliefs according to the most complete practicable assessment of the probabilities.

He takes pertinent moral principles into account, the sort of second-level moral principle that is subordinate to those broadest principles, such as that of universalization. The sources of these are human experience in one form or another; he has gained them from his moral instruction in childhood and youth, and from his reading that has relevance to morals, as well as from his personal experience in the world together with his reflection upon it. These moral principles may be from one or another of the existing moral codes or systems or bodies of religious teachings, but those that he applies in making his own moral appraisals have themselves previously been submitted to his own process of criticism and justification. He retains his awareness that these are, as it were, competitive in the marketplace of ideas and actions, and that therefore his own selection of them is not unchallengeable, but rather that he must respect the collections assembled by others and accord to them the respect that is due to their own criticism and justification of their own bodies of moral principles. He is aware that for the competition among such codes and systems to serve the purposes of a kingdom of ends, the competition must have the form of rational reflection and deliberation of the part of all, and that the assumption by the partisan that his own position has final correctness, relegating that of another to second or lower position, is not morally justifiable because its outcome does not succeed in helping all moral agents to possess a body of the highest available moral criteria.

The moral agent functioning at what he knows to be his best level notices whether the outcome he decides to attempt to implement is the one that prudential judgment also would determine. He knows that at times the prudential judgment and the moral, other-oriented judgment may coincide, just as on many occasions they will not. He considers whether it has been self-interest rather than rational treatment of all factors, eminently including other persons and their interests, that has made him tend towards this judgment. If it appears that it may have been self-interested bias that inclined him, he reviews the entire case and attempts to put his own interest in its proportional importance and in its proper place with the other factors, not attaching undue importance to it because it happens to involve himself.

In making a final review before action, the effective moral agent confirms for himself that he has achieved his intentions about coming to his judgment. He has persisted at the information-gathering process so long as any new information germane to the result could be developed and so long as there is foreseeable prospect of any. He has used intellect to heighten sensitivity, and sensitivity to inform intellect. He has heeded his own and others' feelings, regarding their occurrence as fact to be considered, and their prospective occurrence as prospective fact to be considered, while not allowing the occurrence of an emotion itself and alone to determine his own belief. He has forecast possible outcomes of options as accurately as the available knowledge may permit. He has assured that the reasons for arriving at his judgment are articulated rather than subliminal, and are freely chosen.

The description thus far given has presupposed ample time for reflection, which unfortunately is not the common case. Our moral judgment and agent knows this, and knows by what time necessity will force action upon him. Consequently, he attacks the problem in a systematic time scheme, taking up the apparently most important points first, and less important ones later, in case the need for action cuts off deliberations before he has had the opportunity to apply all his competence to them. One result is that it appears to him that first he develops the main reasons for adopting a certain action, and next he develops supporting reasons that tend to confirm that that action is the one he should adopt. Only rarely should it occur, for an expert moral agent, that information developed late in the inquiry radically alters the trend of the whole prospective solution; however, this is far from impossible.

Thus we survey the method of arriving at the moral value judgment that the ideal, consummate moral agent would certify to us as his own best practice. It is the "correct" way, the way we ought to make value judgments, and its warrant to preference is that the moral agent himself judges it superior to less complete, less deliberate, less sensitive, less rational instances of his own experience. While we cannot expect more, what we have here is, I believe, something that most self-aware moral agents and judges would rate as very good.

Now that our statement of how moral ought-judgments should be made is before us, let us examine it critically. We will attempt to test how well it fulfills the requirements that we set out for it before it was introduced. To begin with, what is it, we may aptly ask, that is the distinctly moral factor about the deliberations that our excellent moral judge has recognized, in the solution of the problem that he faces? It is that the action to which the solution (whether carried out by himself or others, whether now or years later) will affect the well-being and the interests of others besides himself, others who are themselves moral agents, to whom he imputes worth as ends deserving in themselves. This is a logical, rational foundation, the visible face of which is the step we call universalization. Human feeling, particularly sympathy, may precede it as a guide to or determinant of the individual's conduct; but when clashes of emotion occur, such as when sympathies extend to two who are in conflict, sympathy is stultified and the only thing to which one can turn is reason, including its concomitant, universalization, the treating of all conceivable members of the class of moral agents as having the same defining property, that of moral worth constituting the citizen of the realm of ends. Our recommended method then is superior to the calls of emotion, and promises well to resolve moral questions with a proper balance of rationality as counterweight to distracting forces of emotion.

Does our prescription accommodate the apparent moral quality that seems to distinguish some episodes of our experience, to the point that we speak unhesitatingly of our having moral experience? Yes, and its structure, a pattern compounded of many elements, even suggests an account of that impression. We see from it that the moral quality of our moral experience, whose existence we do not question in our lives and whose occurrence motivates us to inquire into morals in the first place, is no one, simple property distributed over acts, or distributed over persons, or distributed over virtues. Rather, it is a complex of elements expressible in value-assertive propositions, the essential members of which have just been outlined. It is probably highly colored with the qualities of appropriate feelings, which we intuit as we feel these feelings in association with our concept of the moral worth of mankind; but moral quality itself does not consist in that sympathetic feeling alone, or even essentially. Rather, the construct that we devise, and which we project into situations in which there are persons (other human beings) whose interests our actions can affect and whom we value—it is this that imbues our experience with moral quality.

A critic may notice that the presentation of our method is in descriptive, even behavioral, language, scarcely marked by the common word-signals that identify value-assertions. Has the author, he may ask, lapsed into expression that is not true to his claims, or might even betray inconsistency in his thought? No, I deny those charges. Even though the idea of "ought" is contained not only in the title but in the very purpose of the chapter, I have been using descriptive language; I hope, however, that I have fooled no one in doing so. The chapter offers an incidental demonstration of one way we use language to express value judgments without confining ourselves to direct, literal ought-language, but I have substantial as well as stylistic reason for the device, which will become apparent shortly. To admit that the whole long list of judging competences constitutes valuative expression is for the author to confess that unlike the other chapters, chapter 17 is abundantly freighted with value judgments of his own. And from this, one consequence immediately follows: the author is hoist by his own petard, swept off the solid ground of provable assertions to the uncertain heights of individual venture, and depends for a safe return to earth upon the approving judgments of his peers, his readers. He can look nowhere else—not in the rocks and trees and creatures of nature, not in the tea leaves, not in the skies—for support. Like all value judges, he stands or falls on the apparent cogency of the array of ought-judgments that his descriptions of the ideal embody.

Let us therefore sample the list of steps or component processes of the method of moral judgment, to attempt to appraise its quality. Let us look at instances of the fifteen or twenty skills that our wholly competent value judge practices, and see what challenges of them would require. He has, we said, sensitivity to his emotions but discipline over them. What are the alternatives? Emotional insensitivity, or dominance by the emotions. Will a critic of this description prefer those to disciplined sensitivity? Again, we described the moral value judge as systematic in his projections of the effects of various available potential actions upon the states of affairs of the future. Would a challenger prefer that the value judge be haphazard rather than systematic, in these projections? Or that such projections not be made? We called for tolerance to the differing moral codes of those who might be involved in the outcome of his judgment. Should a rational person choose intolerance instead, or uncritical, partisan preference of one code over another? And so it goes, throughout the entire description of the ideal moral value judging process performed by the wholly competent moral agent. At worst, only one or two of its points would arouse a quibble from his critics. The merits attributed to him are as homely and as necessary as bathing. What is essential to it is not one or another crucial measure, but the combination of an adequate number of measures each of which is in itself commendable. Yet we suppose that few persons, on few occasions, ever fully achieve this ideal. Until we demand of ourselves that we do at least as well, until we invariably show our adeptness at practicing it, and until our self-criticism were to show us ways in which it were inadequate and could be further improved, we do better to attend to its application, rather than to seek some arcane formula or other external criterion for solving our moral problems.

A great merit of the list is that all its proposals, separately, are occasionally met in actual settings in the present. Thus, clearly not one of them is an impossibility. What is lacking is for the most part simply the awareness of them and of their fruitfulness when persistently put into practice. They do not require as a precondition the settling of one or all of the ongoing controversies in moral theory. They do not require any particular moral code as a grounding. Their practice can tolerate the adherence to any existing moral code as a starting place, and their statement is such that rational criticism will be applied to that code as to other factors entering a value decision; thus the code must fit within the total process, and cannot be elevated over it without destroying it. Unfortunately, there are moral agents to whom that requirement will be intolerable—but we may hope that the remainder of agents, while tolerating those, will excel them in justification of the choice of adhering to the ideal value-judging process rather than aborting it when a conflict with one's favorite predetermined code happens to arise.

The features of the ideal process do not require that the moral agent or moral critic accept as *true* a description of every other moral agent as a being totally worthy of having all of his purposes fulfilled, a consummation that it has now been shown can never be reached. Instead, it asks the agent to *treat* the other agent *as though* he were so worthy. *That* certainly *can* be done. It asks all moral agents so to treat all others—but not first to wait until everyone else has done the same. It asks him to consider worldly facts and moral ends as inclusively as possible; that, too, we all can do. It asks him to practice the openness of his sensitivities to all qualities, so as to fail in no way to have the materials at hand for his deliberations—again, not an unrealistic request, and one whose rewards have been pointed out. It asks him constantly to exercise at increasing his skills of deliberation and reasoning, which is readily possible, rewarding on its own, and hardly too much to demand. In a word, the necessary steps of consummate moral deliberation and decision are all within our reach here and now, and are reasonable to ask; they do not depend on our discovery of things we do not yet know. We have but to recognize the right relation of egoistic interest to the serving of the purposes of the members of the kingdom of ends—then to get busy at putting them into practice, as individuals, as groups, and as nations.

18

Retrospect, and a Bright Prospect

From all that has preceded us at this juncture, it is evident that value is neither a thing nor a property. In effect, value is not a predicate, just as existence is not a predicate. The unresolved and seemingly irresolvable controversy about value has surely come about because we have been attempting all these many centuries, in fact, millenia, to make *good* a something, a quality, a *what*ever. Our language has been considerably oriented to this assumption, yet far from totally. While there are many locutions and idioms that presuppose value to be this or that character or quality, there is also ample evidence in the contexts and discourses in which value-terms are embedded that the basic thing assumed about them is their instrumentality. This presupposes their relation to action, the movement toward a goal for which these locutions are instruments. And it is this movement toward a goal, a conceived state of affairs, that gives all the value terms their common meaning, and thus creates the value-aspect of things in the world.

This being so, the value-aspect is present wherever the being-aspect is present. Neither is really understandable without the other. I do not find it strange that those who apply a disciplined contemplation to pure being, rigorously excluding apparently extraneous considerations, can be constantly fascinated yet constantly unrewarded, constantly puzzled, by what Heidegger has called the most far reaching, deepest, and most fundamental question of all.[1] For if one contemplates pure being, without asking questions of the sort, "What is it good for? How might it be different? How ought we to change it? Into what ought we to attempt to convert it?" there is no frame of reference, no background, against which to orient it to something *else*. Thus, there is no understanding it, since it is by putting an X into relation with a *non-X* that (we say) we understand the X.

Rather, the field of "what ought to be" is metaphysically at least as broad as the field of "what is." Each of them is simply the universe treated in certain ways by humanity. The one is the universe treated as existential, and the other is the universe treated as criticized. The one is the universe treated as a mere given; the other is the universe treated as the arena of action. The universe as the arena of action is the general topic of value judgments; and since others as well as ourselves inhabit that universe, the entirety of it is the field of the objects of those value judgments that are moral value judgments. And since the very domain itself is defined under our awareness of our own potential to alter the existing, in the direction of something else, the field of ethics (which is what we call our attempts to explain this domain) must be viewed and described in such a way as to accord fundamental status to the valuative or critical principle, the concept of *what ought to be*, along with the existential principle, the concept of *what is*.

Life surely is characterized by the impulse to change. At its simplest, this is the impulse to ingest and digest, thus to continue life. Taking the definition of value as that which is conceived of as a state of affairs potentially to be reached, hence that which is an incentive to action, it is easy to see that the status quo itself, as merely the object of thought, is hardly an explanation of life. The living of the life is the continual changing undertaken by the living being, and beyond the perception of the status quo, this consists in the conception of other states as alternatives to it, the comparing of various alternative conceptions including that of the status quo, the selection of the conceived state that is preferred, and if that one is different from the extant one the undertaking of action to realize it. (And if it is the extant one, the taking of steps to preserve it.) Without this conceiving and comparing, the status quo would merely continue as the status quo and the living being to which it is present would simply remain inert until he was as lifeless as any other element in the status quo. *Thus, for existence to have a meaning, the value-aspect must be imputed to existent things along with their being.* This is true at a fundamental metaphysical level, just as it is also truistic in terms of workaday people who ask each other at cocktail parties or tête-a-têtes what is the meaning of life, and who invariably employ the value-aspect in offering an answer.

Through the ages, for reasons good or bad, we have constantly thrust aside various answers to the question of value. We have denied that value is pleasure, because we abhorred the idea that whatever is pleasing to the individual to do is what he ought to do—be a glutton, be promiscuous, treacherous, vicious, cruel, and the like. We have denied that value is salvation, because the concept has been made to depend on a constellation of propositions, all of which are systematized only by a process involving some myth making and no one of which is provably germane to the empirically or logically established or establishable elements of everyday states of affairs. We have denied that the life of reason is the good, for it would exclude too many of our fellow beings less privileged than ourselves. And the same is true for all the many suggestions as to what the good, or value, consists in. In all this, we have seemed to give ourselves an unanswerable question—"What is it that is the good? What is it that is value?" And so long as we have clung to these terms in which we have sought to conceive the answer, we have indeed posed to ourselves a question whose answer must be so inclusive of every suggestion and of every qualification of each suggestion, that it would surely be impracticable even if possible to give such an answer. But an answer is possible, in the quite different terms that I have suggested. According to this answer, that which unites all goods, all values, into *value* is no one quality discovered outside the person, but rather it is being the object of a certain treatment by persons themselves, simply in their own conception and action vis-á-vis the world. Thus value is imposed on the world, not found in it.

In the latter portion of this inquiry, emphasis upon moral theory has been heavy. Nevertheless, the topic of the inquiry is value, not morality per se. The culmination of value theory in a survey of the moral ought-judgment is appropriate, because the moral is the most complex as well as the most inevitable of ought-judgments. The title *Value, Language, and Life* puts life at the last in order to reflect this culmination, as well as to give life final emphasis.

The reader will have observed that a certain framework has functioned both as a device for exposition and as a pattern for inquiry. It is itself somewhat above the simple, being a compound, or better, a hybrid, of certain other familiar philosophic methods. Like most hybrids, it does not completely resemble either of its parents. The assumption of the basic framework of *consciousness* comprehending numerous ways of appearing, distinguishable from each other, is appropriated from the field of phenomenological inquiry. It is strongly influenced by the writings on the arts of the Polish philosopher Roman Ingarden,[2] but I have not made the attempt to reach the thorough and subtle level of description that Ingarden maintains. I have, however, exported my understanding and some of the vocabulary of Ingarden's descriptions of our cognitions of works of art to the life scene itself, for I find his descriptions both highly perceptive and highly accurate, and I assert from my own observation and reflection that we do in fact employ just such intuitions in our seeing of all the givens of life. In fact, the intuitions we have of our givens are intuitions of a whole tapestry-like fabric that we naturally observe in exceedingly various ways. These already have provided us with complex information for our inner, subarticulate thinking before we are at all well equipped with language for articulating them. This is why we eventually need training in the seeing of art, not the seeing of life. The kind of training that is touched upon in chapter twelve (pages 220-21) has the effect of separating out the more purely perceptual intuitions and relieving them of the interpretive overburden that from the standpoint of practical life we shall have already placed upon them. We have to learn to see with the "innocence of eye" of the painter, the draftsman, or the sculptor, because for purposes of art we normally see too much, rather than not enough. Indeed we normally see with those purposes which ultimately result in not only our aesthetic ought-judgments, but our moral ought-judgments and all the other, lesser sorts. It would be illegitimate to use art to illuminate life in such ways as to take the painter's color discrimination, the draftsman's coordination, the sculptor's weighting of masses, or other technical skills apt for one or another art, and then command that for moral success these must be applied in life. But rather, by using art as our test-tube sample we are able to observe in a purer form the gathering of our cognitions, unburdened by interpretations that we incline automatically to add to our perceptions as we live our practical lives in the moral sphere.

A question I have avoided, because I believe it is asked on a wrong basis and therefore leads to unwanted tangles and confusions, is the question, "Is value real?" The problem I believe is with the framework, not with value. To sidestep this question I have assumed consciousness, experience, as our framework rather than "reality" or existence. We long have regarded one obvious way of appearing, namely, that of the physical object, as the "real"; rather than make that assumption, I have regarded the physical or spatio-temporal mode of appearing merely as the paradigm of our concept of existence, and not as an absolute to which all other things are relative. I have worked as though it may safely be assumed that what this mode of existence has in common with all the other ways of appearing is that their objects appear, and that is all we need in the way of an assumption about existence in order to inquire into value and establish the nature of our concept of *value*. While for myself this procedure has succeeded, each reader can, and no doubt must, judge its success for himself. Among other ways, the device has been useful for providing an explanation of how linguistic or conceptual reference operates when the referent object is not present or is undetermined. It is my intention that the framework employed may be compatible with a variety of metaphysical doctrines, and need not presuppose only one. Of course, it is obvious that I have adopted a vaguely realist metaphysic, and have identified this assumption in appropriate places, but I have attempted to suggest also that the present doctrines regarding value are compatible with alternative metaphysical presuppositions.

Within the field of this phenomenologistic or at least quasi-phenomenologistic framework, I have planted some specimens of language analysis, in the manner of the largely British contribution to philosophy of linguistic analysis. However, there is one rather obvious difference from the practice of the analysts, namely, that I have given more attention to whole sentences and their meanings rather than to individual words and phrases. R. M. Hare, for instance, speaks of a class of "value-words," and acutely points out properties of and differences among these.[3] This method has the advantage of keeping other things the same: by exhibiting the difference the selection of first one word, then another, would make to a sentence, everything else in the sentence being held constant. However, I believe that the requirements of my inquiry have called for analysis and interpretation of whole sentences— as to specific word meanings and general purport and tone—including the broad and the subordinate framing concepts of the assertive sentences.

In working with fact-assertive and value-assertive propositions as such, in order to understand the difference between them, I found that I needed to know what was alike about them, and thus I was led to formulate the theory of the proposition that appears in the second chapter. It bases the proposition on those appearances in our consciousness that we know as sentences, whether written or spoken, and whether physically before us in one or the other concrete form or present only as remembered, or as imagined, conceived, or expected future material manifestations of the sentence. These are objectivities of our consciousness, available for our intuitive examination, while other conceptions of what a proposition is have often depended either upon an idealist-realism that is difficult to demonstrate, or upon simply the device of translating "proposition" into some other term whose explanation is recondite, such as "meaning."

There is much to say about *truth*, and I have said very little here. One thing I have done, however, is to treat truth as though it has little or nothing to do with existence per se, although both traditional and modern logic tend to tie truth to existence and make the one depend somehow upon the other. Rather, without attempting to attack the problem implicit in this, I have simply referred to our correctly attaching a *truth-sign* to a sentence or to a proposition. Whatever else may be true of truth, we do in fact do this, and the use of this fact has, I believe, been sufficient for my purposes.

From the description of the proposition, I was able in a fairly simple step to get to a description of the concept. An essential fact within that description is that we do not demand truth of concepts—that is, we permit ourselves to have accurate or inaccurate concepts, and do not demand that to say we are in possession of a concept is to say that everything we include within it is a true proposition. Now it may seem that if I have said that a proposition is *every* appearance of a certain sentence, when treated in a certain way,[4] I have made it something impossible for the mind to grasp. Then if to that I have added that a concept is a collection of related propositions, I have compounded impossibility into the preposterous. However, while the reality of the proposition *is* every one of its appearances to any consciousness (*as* a proposition, not merely as a sentence), the individual has no need of all that, much less any possibility of obtaining it. But he *can* recognize the new appearance of the proposition in a new sentence, say, one in a foreign language that he has learned or in a synonymous phrasing in his own language, and thus theoretically he could comprehend and use the proposition wherever and whenever he might find it. He does not have to know every single appearance of the proposition by firsthand acquaintance in order to use it fruitfully. The same, *mutatis mutandis*, may be said of the concept.

It is easily seen from the description of "value" that is based on the facts herein surveyed and on implications drawn from them that the word *true* cannot mean the same thing with respect to value-assertive statements that it means for analytic fact-assertive statements and for synthetic or empirical fact-assertive statements. We do not verify ("true-ify") value-assertive statements by holding them up to the same kinds of givens as those to which we take our analytic and synthetic statements. We cannot, for there is no such given. Two options are open to us, to put something in the place that verifying has for those sentences. Eventually, linguistic convention will probably come around to at least one of them, if not (perhaps unwisely) both. One is to redefine *true* so as somehow to keep it as the honorific title for the only assertions that we really want to have, but at the same time to be allocated according to some criterion entirely different from comparison with the concrete or abstract entity to which the proposition spuriously seems to refer. I do not hold out much hope for this approach, as I cannot see what criterion could be produced that would function practicably in this way. Majority opinion is what the makers of linguistic convention are likely to turn to, but majority opinion is at times a notorious deceiver. To use the concept of *truth* in any such diluted way, even for acknowledged matters of opinion, very likely would dangerously erode the usefulness of the concept when applied to the analytic and synthetic propositions to which it now, usefully, belongs. The second option open to us is to become sharply aware of the separate class of declarative statements, the value-assertive (popularly, "value judgments"), and form the habit of applying some other and more apt term to those that we find to be most worthy of acceptance, belief, and use. The term should have to connote "believable" and "justifiable" and "arrived at with maximum rationality." Suggestions like Dewey's "warranted" may be a start. Nowadays, one might even hope for the restoration of the little-used, indeed seldom thought-of word, "wise."

The nature of the value-assertive statements, we have seen, is such that there is no clear and direct test of them. Rather, their general warrant is the skill and wisdom of the value judge who originates them. For some fields of judgment, this may be a highly specialized expert, but for others, such as that of day-to-day dealings with our fellow man, it is simply ourselves as individuals, attempting perhaps to emulate the most experienced and wisest among us. The fact is, as shown in earlier chapters, that there *are* better and worse value judgments, wise and unwise ones; but the test of value-assertions and the judgments that they express is characteristically a highly complex test, involving the ascertainment first of many facts and, second, the judging upon each as to what actual or possible combinations of these should be made to be the case. In life situations, no single reason can be offered for the arrival at the value judgment; each value judgment is arrived at and justified by a whole set of reasons, one or more for each of its contributory parts, and these are constituted as reasons because people treat them as such, not because of any property of "reason-hood" inhering in them. But in the place of demonstrated rightness, such as may be the justification for the announcement of an empirical fact-assertion or a mathematical or logical fact-assertion, the assertor of a value-assertion places his own being and interests at stake. He lives at risk; he is held responsible both by nature and by society; he loses things that he desires to gain or to keep if he judges too unwisely. *Responsibility replaces truth as the credential of the value-assertion.* In this sense, the value theory presented here is a pragmatic theory, the ultimate test of a value judgment or a structure of value judgments being the success of the holder of it in achieving his purposes through it. But since he is rational, we do not decry this label as one that makes general value theory a license to be selfish. Rather, since the value judge is to some extent a rational agent, rationality, through its processes of treating ever-changing dynamic particulars as eternally unchanging, and of universalization from similar though non-identical particulars, induces the value judge to carry rational analysis to the point where the interests of the individual and of the species can without illusion be seen as the same.

In the progress of the inquiry, I have presented a broad definition of the term *intuition,* then I described it as a perceptual and cognitive process whereby we come to have knowledge through direct confrontation with that which we come to know. Thus I have tried to select one sort of intuition to describe and use, while rejecting others; I have selected one that I could to some extent explain, rather than one whose operation seemed obscure, mystical, or magical; it is one whose results can be replicated, intersubjectively verified, and corroborated by other, concomitant intuitions.

With this understanding of intuition, I have dealt with the naturalistic ethical doctrines, those views that make moral value somehow a given in the world. I have applied an empirical test, and found that the object sought is not found by the alleged means for finding it. I have put in the place of the naturalistic explanation of our acquisition of value structures the suggestion that they come from the opposite pole and move in the opposite direction, that is, they arise not in the world but in ourselves, and move not from outside to inside, but are first conceived in general meaning within ourselves, and then imposed upon or imputed to the givens of experience. This distinguishes the present theory from those heretofore called "naturalistic" by making it to some extent a "rationalistic," or I should prefer, "intellectualistic," theory. Yet man is a natural being, and in a legitimate sense of the adjective, we may say that it is natural for him to invent things to improve his lot. He has invented the concept of value and has invented, and goes on inventing, whole value structures. In that sense, the theory keeps man within nature, not outside of it; therefore in that sense and only in that sense, the present theory may come under an only slightly elastic blanket term of "naturalism."

The present work treats the theory of value as such, thereby touching upon metaphysics, epistemology, aesthetics, and ethics, but it is also a study of the language of value, and in that, it treats the philosophy of language. It explains why philosophers as early as Hume and Kant spoke of the difference between *is* and *ought,* and why the realization grew up that the former had to do with a world of fact, the latter with a world of value. I believe I have elicited the necessity of the relation between these two concepts, which materially speaking is in man's raw need for action in his given existential world, and logically is in the generation of a realm of *ought* by the imaginative and rational multiplication of possibilities from the particular givens of the realm that *is*.

I did not foresee when I first decided to write about value that I should become involved in a theory of the proposition and a theory of the concept. I do not believe that the theory of value given herein depends upon these two for its acceptability. However, these two linguistic theories do make me breathe easier when I am talking about value by finding the key to it in valuative propositions. If I had not come to a rather concrete notion of what a proposition is, I should have been uneasy about whether in fact I had achieved any explanation, or instead had just invoked a ghost of language in order to lay the ghost of value. Future research may reveal that there is indeed something more intangible about the proposition than I have portrayed; but whether or not there is more to it, there is at least as much to it as I have outlined, and that much is, I believe, enough upon which to rest concepts, among them container concepts, and among the container concepts the concept of *what ought to be*. I hope others may find sufficient stimulus in these theories to explore them further.

The ethical implications of this value theory may seem old-fashioned because rationalistic (although they are certainly not formalistic). I hope, though, that this conclusion will not be drawn, because I do not see that it follows, and because I see the implicit ethical theory, while rational, as firmly based upon human experience, its nature, and its contents. Yet it is clearly evident that the present one is not an empiricist ethical theory, for that would be a naturalistic ethic, already rejected. While the assumption is always in sight in the present work that the physical world is real, the withdrawal from it of privileged status as being thought to be the *only* reality and the placement of its phenomena on a level with all the appearances of other objects in all the other ways of appearing is a compensation, as it were, for any "loss of reality" that may be attributed to a non-naturalistic ethic. Morality was not waiting in the world for the advent of man. Rather, morality is something that man has built progressively, as *the* world became *his* world.

The view contained herein finds a place for the important aspects of value experience that we are certain it cannot do without. There *is* moral experience. Moral experience is not, however, a kind of experience that can be initiated and broken off. It does not start up, like an air conditioner on a thermostat, when we walk into a moral situation, and shut down again when deliberation has ceased and action has begun. Rather, the episodes that we label moral episodes, the situations that we label moral situations, and the problems that we label moral problems are those in which we are more intensely aware than usual of the qualities of intuitions that arise through the

presence of other rational beings. These qualities inhere in our sense perceptions of their physical appearance, but also in the qualities or character of
their actions and of our own actual or potential actions, of the conceptual
entities we discover among these, and of the perceptual and conceptual relations that we find them to exhibit to us. It is easy to take human sympathy—
for example, sympathy for a crying child—to be the felt moral quality itself.
Actually, the felt moral quality of a situation in which a child is crying is
much more complex and subtle than simply a feeling of sympathy. A large
component of it is probably the quality of the relation of the crying child to
the observing moral agent, who is aware that he is capable of doing something to relieve the child's distress. Moral quality itself, and especially that of
an episode in which one participates as contrasted to that of a scene one
momentarily witnesses, is a vast complex of individual elements, as a mosaic
is a complex of many individual tiles of stone, each one uniformly colored,
from which the mind makes pictures and derives feeling qualities. Successful
moral training enables the individual to receive these elements and their relations as they appear in his experience and become available to him for his
use in choosing new states of affairs for his world and its denizens.

When I affirm that value is not a predicate I do so in the sense that value
is not found in the world, is not given, but rather is a principle according to
which we classify the particulars of the given. And while value is not thus
found in the world, it would be utterly foolish to assert that value does not
exist—as foolish as to say that existence, not being a predicate, does not
exist. It is an easy parallel to see, when we notice statements like "Smallpox
exists now only in Ethiopia, but it ought not to exist even there." When over
a decade ago this sentence was true, it said nothing about the nonexistent;
rather, it made an affirmative assertion about a physical existent, and made a
negative assertion in the ought mode about the same class as that whose
instances then were existent in the physical mode.

The present value theory surely comes down on the side of teleological
rather than deontological ethics. While it extols the individual as the being of
ultimate moral worth, and calls upon all rational agents to treat him as such,
in order for this imperative to be meaningful there must be translation of it
into practical directives and there must be consideration of the results of
actions, both in the form of probability judgments about their potentially
realized effects and in the form of moral judgments on those effects as they
impinge upon the human beings affected. The analysis of the moral agent as
essentially a rational being, and the attribution of the process of universalization to the reasoning of the rational being as rational method, generates the
imputation of ultimate moral worth to the human individual (or other rational agent, if any). It is not because of what he *is* that he has ultimate moral
worth; rather, it is because of what he *does* and especially of what he *can* do,
that is, treat others, universally, in the same way that this imperative directs
us to treat him. In that actual or potential treatment of others, that under-

taking of actions for the sake of worthy ends, we see the real teleology of this view of moral value.

In the chapters on moral matters, I have surveyed how we actually do make and justify moral judgments. In this survey we by no means fall victim to the naturalistic fallacy, for what was surveyed was subjected to evaluative as well as logical criticism. And while the freedom to judge one way or another, being freedom, lends itself little to description (because description is predication), we can see from the survey that the general run of mankind has in effect been ahead of the moral theorists, in finding and using the ways of moral justification that eventually come to approbation in the present study. These are the ways that rationality itself seems to recommend, because rationality in fact depends upon them. They consist in the accumulation of a great number of inferences and of judgments, each preceded by an exhaustively thorough treatment of certain considerations as reasons for these numerous outcomes. It is patent that the theory acknowledges the pluralism of outcomes, a pluralism of potentially good and wise judgments, a result that to some will seem undesirable. However, the theory also recognizes what occurs far more often, a pluralism of outcomes of which only one is the best; and it accounts for how the best is selected and designated, when that happens, even though some agents involved are more narrow in their deliberations than others and consequently come to less fully justifiable judgments.

It appears to me that the present value theory can both accommodate and account for certain other doctrines that have been developed in the past. Its first purpose of course is to "tell what value is," or better said, to tell what we do when we use valuative expressions and state value judgments. It traces the idea of *value* explicitly to the idea of *ought*, a connection that has been assumed in some literature but not, so far as I am aware, both seen in its own proper nature and at the same time oriented to the larger whole of human experience. It sets forth the relationship of fact and value. It does not search for and find "the place for value in a world of fact," but takes the given world to be equally for man a world of fact and a world of value. Among the existents and events that partly compose the world of fact it gives an important place to emotions and feelings. These have much to do with valuative judgments but their occurrence does not in itself comprise valuative judgment or valuation. Rather, the occurrence of a feeling is a fact along with others, such as the height and weight and needs and aversions of him to whom the feeling occurs. The valuative judgment is, rather, a way for that individual to handle both the feeling and the need, to help him to decide what to do and then to do something about it.

In thus assigning a place for feelings among the givens, this value theory orients the naturalistic theories within a larger framework. It clarifies the naturalistic fallacy (as named by Moore and interpreted by later writers) by pointing out why or wherein there is an unbridgeable gap between *is* and

ought. It explains the error on which naturalistic ethics (affirming that goodness is itself in the world, awaiting to be apprehended by the human being) is
based, and supplies facts additional to those that are built into the scheme of
a naturalistic ethic so as to show how a more full and adequate value theory
incorporates these facts and others. The value theory replaces the "intuition"
of naturalistic intuitionisms with a more accurately described intuition, and
sets alongside it other processes also necessary to value judgment. Emotivist
value theory is accommodated and supplied with the missing element of
meaning that is present in the emotive statements that are actual assertions
rather than mere reactions, mere emotional outpourings. It shows the place
for those sympathetic feelings that we admire and have historically called the
moral feelings, on which various bodies of moral teaching have been based
and on which many ordinary individuals, innocent of study of morals or
ethics, operate from day to day.

One of the impulses to which many moral philosophers and aestheticians
have responded in essaying to produce value theories and moral theories is
the aversion to a mere relativism, a Protagorean "What the Thebans perceive
as right, *is* what is right in Thebes." Moralists throughout the ages have
believed that, for example, even if all Spartans regarded it right to expose
weak newborn infants to die, there is a principle higher than the law of that
state or of its neighbor that could show the moral error of the practice. The
term for the objectionable element in this sort of moral code is *relativism.*
What is objectionable about relativism includes lending itself readily to rationalizing or explaining away things that parties do or intend to do for
solely self-interested rather than morally justifiable reasons; its removal from
any adverse critic his basis for criticism; and its implicit denial that there is
such a thing as a moral consideration, a matter of a shared right-or-wrong of
mankind, above the self-interest of the individual or the state.

Indeed, the value theory and consequences for moral theory that emerge
from the present study are in some ways relativistic. One might readily
complain that it makes all value judging, including moral judging, relative to
the judge, and since it insists on the freedom of that judge it seems to provide
no criterion and no arbiter by which there can be a right and a wrong. This is
to a small extent true, although it is a great oversimplification. The element
of freedom is present for all valuations, and with that fact one might justly
maintain that the outcomes of moral and other value judgments are relative
to the judge. However, they are relative to some other things also, and while
those other things include no absolutes, they are largely objective and regular.
They include the facts of human life and survival, understood in terms not
only of the individual but of the society. And one of the constant factors is
that of responsibility of the moral agent, made evident to him through his
own rationality (although there is, to be sure, a small number of psychopaths
among us who cannot recognize this moral responsibility). We live at risk,

and the risks are much alike for each of us, and our responses are such that we tend to be much alike in the ways in which we meet them.

However, in this state of affairs—rather, at this stage of human development—I find more reason to be encouraged than to despair. I do not believe that exposure of the arbitrariness, in one sense, of man's moral rules and principles will lead to the breakdown of morality. Rather, I see in it the acknowledgment of the opportunity to make our present morality better than it is now ; to bring about its acceptability to society worldwide, not merely in this or that culture; to make it fully human rather than partial—in more than one sense of *partial*. This entails that there will be, despite varying heritages of different cultures, a practical uniformity, at least, in the major features of such a morality. Far from despairing that this will ever be achieved, I believe that we are constantly working our way toward it, often despite our conscious efforts to militarize, to nationalize, to "defend" ourselves by preemptive attacks and the like. Some deliberate international dealings tend to foster morality while others do not; but man's natural thrust, *the more he becomes rational*, is toward it, not away from it.

Our search has revealed to us no touchstone, but a situation and a broad response to it that is at once a criterion and a method for selecting our valuative beliefs and our actions. Granted, morality and other fields of value judging are susceptible to outcomes that are relative to each of us, rather than absolute for all of us. But that which stands by us and acts as our guide through this diverse, confusing, demanding life is that latest gift that binds us to one another—reason. I am content—in fact, comforted—knowing that this is the basis of value and morality.

The compensation to those who have wished for a touchstone by which to make their moral and other valuative judgments is rational justification. The justification for any moral choice is relative to the situation, of course, including the individuals who are in it. However, he who must make a judgment and initiate action has it within his power to perform his moral thinking well. He can deliberate thoroughly and skillfully to solve a given moral problem; he can discipline himself to do this work as well as his mind tells him it can be done, in the circumstances, instead of less well than that; and he can discipline himself to perform such thorough deliberation by habit for all situations, rather than only with an effort of resolve when an especially difficult situation appears. He knows that by these means he can improve the quality of his own fact gathering and judging, and that in all likelihood he shall have done so even for a new and perplexing situation. Finally, he knows that even though others may diverge from his judgment and may insist upon some absolute as the criterion that he ought to observe, they will recognize the quality of his deliberations and will respect his justification even if they do not accept or agree with it.

A great deal of the content of the study that is now drawing to completion has depended upon observation of life as lived, upon the intuitively grasped apprehensions of the given. It appears that these apprehensions are very much alike for most of us, and are even perceived or interpreted largely alike, although there are always differences, and differences apparently owing to different influences. Because of this nature of the empirical aspects of the study, it is to be expected that there will be some difference between the beliefs formed, as a result, by the author and by his reader. Very likely, however, the similarities will far outweigh the differences; we are usually much more aware of differences because they appear sharp against a background of similarities that goes pretty much unnoticed. However, to the extent that the theory of value given here depends upon empirical evidence and conclusions from experience, it is warranted only by the observation of those who receive it and by their extending of credence to him who transmits it. To the extent that it depends upon inference and reasoning, it is as good as the steps of inference and reasoning that develop its conclusions, and these may be tested objectively by anyone experienced in articulate logical discourse. If there are individuals whose intuitions simply are at variance, then I suppose the only appropriate thing for those who are at variance is simply to agree to disagree—to let intuitive matters rest on the intuitions of each. Not much more could be asked. However, all parties to disputes of that sort do well to keep their intuitive processes actively at work, rather than resting on accomplishments already attained, no matter how great.

Another source of disagreement might be the descriptive statements about linguistic usage and their interpretations (not to be confused with admitted conjectures). Each of us at any moment has a certain amount of knowledge and a certain degree of skill in observing, then using, his natural language. Here is another area where there is wide agreement but ample room for variation of interpretation of what happens. Once again, agreeing to disagree while investigations continue is probably the best way to reconcile conflicting interpretations.

With respect to the intuitionist schools, I believe that the value intuitionists are shown to occupy an untenable position. I welcome their efforts to persist, but I ask them to justify doing so by showing how that position, like this one, can be supported by replication and concomitant observation. If they were to succeed, which in my view none has done as yet, then we would have a semantic question to settle, about differentiating in our terminology between two sorts of intuition. But if they do not succeed, I hope they will fully explore the consequences of intuition as sketched herein, to see how such intuition is an adequate foundation for reasoned judgment.

I do not by any means believe that the great amount of good work in ethics and aesthetics that has already been done is to be disregarded. Most of the positions that are well known have deserved their renown by virtue of supplying at least partial explanations of human experience. The position of utilitarianism, for instance, has undergone many lashings from its critics and many ardent defenses by its supporters, and probably has actually been much used as a guiding principle for the actual making of moral decisions. It has been called the moral system of democratic government, in which each citizen has one vote to be cast in such a way as to tend to assure his happiness, and in that guise is tremendously influential in the world's democratic countries. Rather than attempt to drive it away, I prefer to affirm that it fits into the framework of the present value theory, while not telling the whole story of value and being based upon some misapprehensions of the criterion of value—in its particular case, "happiness." Its strong feature is that of universalization in the form of heed for "the greatest number" of persons. Those who apply it thoroughly will be getting pretty close to the same results as those who put into use and are guided according to the doctrine set forth in the present discussion. In a similar way, other moral doctrines of past history can find their place within the value framework outlined here, and to the extent that they do so, I regard them not as wrong or mistaken but as part of the whole truth.

Neither should it be thought that since a position reconciling the empiricist and the rationalist viewpoints, and yoking together the stout oxen of phenomenological and analytic methods is now available, nothing more need be added to value theory. Rather, without doubt a proper and fruitful criticism shall go forward indefinitely into the future. Because of the very open-ended character of this view, its lack of dependence upon any absolute, and its relativity to the minds of those who will not only be doing valuation but will be doing value theory, and because it may be criticized by its own principles, it will be found to be self-correcting. Room is left for wisdom. Not only that, wisdom is positively invited, by the rationality that is in each of us, to lead to ever-greater understanding of that which ought to be.

A self-correcting value theory will be a novelty under the sun. It asserts in an optimistic spirit that in moral belief and procedure, there is always room for improvement. Surely we should remember and apply this conjunction of principles as we look at life in the world around us, and see the irrational responses of many of our brothers and sisters, and indeed ourselves, to that life and its events. We see many of them making the weightiest decisions, of personal and public life alike, on bases that are nearly or wholly irrational. If *our* morality is to be self-correcting, we must universalize that principle and concede that *their* morality would be self-correcting also; if it appears to be highly irrational to us, we must grant to them that the possibility lies before them of improving their morality in the light of their rationality. We must recognize that *each individual, each nation, each society has a right to be irrational.* We must preserve their right to it, so far as doing so does not destroy our own right and ability to be as rational as we can. Irrationality precedes rationality. We must concede that free operation of the mind, rather than coercion, is what will bring about the replacement of irrationality by rationality, and the ever-improving quality of the other rational agents, individual and collective, in our world. We would ask it of

Notes

Chapter 1

[No notes for this chapter]

Chapter 2

1. The conceptual meaning has to do with what a user of a term thinks as he uses it, while the referential meaning of course is the object or objects denoted, physical or otherwise, to which the propositions comprising his conception apply. While there will not be a complete theory of meaning in this work, aspects of the nature of the concept will be examined in chapter 5, and aspects of reference will be looked into in chapter 6.

Chapter 3

1. J. Mark Baldwin writing on "Judgment" in his *Dictionary of Philosophy and Psychology* (new edition, 3 vols., [New York: Peter Smith, 1940]; orig. publ. 1901) makes the process-product ambiguity explicit: "Judgment. The mental function and act of assertion or predication; applied also to the resulting assertion or predication. . . . Logic . . . defined judgment in terms of verbal or some other sort of predication expressed in propositions." Gottlob Frege in several places, but most explicitly in "Compound Thoughts" (in P. T. Geach, ed., *Logical Investigations*, trans. P. T. Geach and R. H. Stoothoff, [New Haven: Yale University Press, 1977], p. 57 n), separates judgment as process from its product as well as from its object: "Logicians often seem to mean by 'judgment' what I call 'thought.' In my terminology, one judges by acknowledging a thought as true. This act of acknowledgment I call 'judgement.' Judgement is made manifest by a sentence uttered with assertive force. But one can grasp and express a thought without acknowledging it as true, i.e. without judging." The usage identifying judgment with assertion has persisted, however; R. M. Hare, for instance, could as easily be speaking about the sentence as about the judgment when he writes, "A judgement is descriptive if in it the predicate or predicates are descriptive terms and the mood is indicative" (Freedom and Reason [London: Oxford University Press, 1963], p. 10). The *product* of judging, one would suppose, may indeed have a

predicate and the features of grammar. The *act* of judgment or judging, rather, would have an agent and an object. Frege's breakdown is helpful in keeping the separateness of these things under our attention. Yet the important question concerning judgment as the acknowledgment or recognition that something is true remains before us: How is one to know whether a thought, when it is the object of judgment, is true?

2. Of course, in order to draw legitimate even if inexact conclusions from the frequency of occurrence of expressions in contexts of everyday language, we must set aside contexts which, like this one, are themselves discussions of these expressions.

3. Where convenient, I shall also use *fact-assertive sentence, fact-assertive statement, value-assertive sentence, value-assertive statement,* and the like derivatives, whose senses will be obvious.

4. Falsity does not define the lie, but rather, disbelief by the teller together with intent to deceive (see Sartre's short story, "The Wall").

5. This assertion is nothing new. Frankena not only finds it implicit in Plato but attributes recognition of it in the late nineteenth century to Alexius Meinong and Christian von Ehrenfels, the idea to be taken up in the early twentieth century by Max Scheler and Nicolai Hartmann, by British, and especially by American philosophers (William K. Frankena, "Value and Valuation," in *The Encyclopedia of Philosophy,* ed. Paul Edwards [New York: Macmillan, 1967].) Hare, without remarking its importance, assumes it in equating "This is a good strawberry" and "This strawberry is just as strawberries ought to be" (R. M. Hare, *The Language of Morals* [New York: Oxford University Press, 1964], first published 1952, p. 110). Here, what I hope will prove not only new but significant is my attempt to view the whole broad problem of the concept of value from this viewpoint and to work out the implications of this simple expression of the meaning of the value judgment.

6. Although it is unidiomatic to speak of an action as "existing," with the concept *what ought to be* we are not so much interested in proprieties of that sort as in the expression and communication of states of affairs and actions in terms of oughtness. While we usually say that objects or states of affairs *exist* and that events and actions *occur,* I do not discover that the difference of these usages makes any difference to our employment or our understanding of "what ought to be."

7. This is different from "One ought to have serenity," as those words normally would occur in context, for the language of this expression would often, perhaps usually, be both intended and interpreted as an imperative, not a declarative utterance.

8. See Karl Aschenbrenner's impressive survey of valuative characterizations in his work entitled *The Concepts of Value* (Dordrecht: D. Reidel, 1971). Moreover, very nearly any linguistic expression when occurring in certain linguistic and situational contexts and when intoned in certain ways can be made to express valuations rather than their more usual non-valuative messages.

Chapter 4

1. Some sentences of course can have a form of ambiguity such that they equivocally express either a factual assertion or a value judgment; for example, "The inn, old though it was, had a modern plumbing system." In such an instance, only the factual assertion, not the value-assertion, shall have been tested. That is, to the extent that *modern* is capable of meaning *good,* so much of what is said is valuative, and

that which is true of the valuative in general is true of it.

2. It is an unimportant point that an analytic value-assertion can be constructed, for example, "Sin is evil." When the subject and predicate terms are given the same meaning, then of course the sentence is tautologically true, but not very useful as a guide to let us know what to perform or avoid. Definitions of some value terms may more importantly exhibit this feature. This point was discussed in the text, p. 62.

3. "The notion of a naturalistic fallacy has been connected with the notion of a bifurcation between the 'ought' and the 'is,' between value and fact, between the normative and the descriptive. Thus Mr. D. C. Williams says that some moralists have thought it appropriate to chastise as the naturalistic fallacy the attempt to derive the Ought from the Is" (W. K. Frankena, "The Naturalistic Fallacy," *Mind* XLVIII [October, 1939]: p. 464-477). Frankena cites Williams ("Ethics as Pure Postulate," *Philosophical Review* XLII [July, 1933]: pp. 399-411).

4. This application in the field of aesthetics has been worked out more fully in my paper, "The Critical Fallacy," read to the California Division, American Society for Aesthetics, May 11, 1962.

5. It will be seen that the verb *ought* merits a qualification of the traditional definition of a verb, for ought expresses neither action, nor being, nor state of being. It is *sui generis*, although it functions grammatically in a way analogous to the verbs that do express these things.

Chapter 5

1. Anatol Pikas, in *Abstraction and Concept Formation* (Cambridge, Mass.: Harvard University Press, 1966), reviews the history of this problem.

2. The reason consistency must be that kind of an instrument is that *understanding* is ongoing through time, and must remain a single thing rather than changing and reversing itself. In this way the rational is temporal.

3. Or to ourselves at different times, as when we articulate our own thoughts to be remembered and entertained and perhaps put to work later. We should never overlook the vast importance of the self-communicative function of language.

4. *"That which all adequate conceptions of an object must have in common, is the concept of the object."* Susanne K. Langer, *Philosophy in a New Key* (New York: Penguin Books, 1948; first publ. Harvard University Press, Cambridge, Mass., 1942), p. 58. Emphasis is Mrs. Langer's.

5. Tarski, for example, in his famous essay "The Semantic Conception of Truth and the Foundations of Semantics" (*Philosophy and Phenomenological Research* [1944]; repr. in Herbert Feigl and Wilfrid Sellars, eds., *Readings in Philosophical Analysis* [New York: Appleton-Century-Crofts, 1949], pp. 52-84) attributes both extension and intension indifferently to the "term" *true*, the "word" *true*, and "the concept of truth" (p. 53 passim). Unless Tarski is being careless with language, evidently he accords the reference relation (in the form of possession by the concept of an extension) to concepts.

This relation probably deserves a term of its own rather than being included by metaphoric extension under a term *(refer, reference)* much more widely associated with, and perhaps by some users reserved for, the symbol-object relationship. A discussion below (pp. 112-13) of semantic couplings of symbol, concept, and referent object proceeds perhaps one step toward this goal.

6. One who says to another, "I agree with your letter" is instantaneously agreeing with the whole substance of the letter concerned, perhaps many propositions, and is *knowing* that substance, those propositions, while not being explicitly conscious of every one in all its precise statement. Again, a musician who can have Beethoven's Fifth Symphony as an object of thought can be said *to know* the whole symphony even though he thinks it only momentarily. Instances of this kind suggest that the mind holds its knowledge in an atemporal mode of existence rather than temporally, even though the knowledge may have been gained temporally and though (as in the case of a letter or a symphony) integral portions of the knowledge are organized temporally. Perhaps the things about mental operation that seem to us to be difficulties are made so by our acts of converting—or of supposing the conversion—of the atemporal to a temporal or discursive form. Thus, while as I say I cannot explain how memory can reproduce long passages of discourse, music, or imagery from "out of sight," noticing the power of the mind to operate with the atemporal seems to me to remove the difficulty in this respect which may seem to some to be implicit in the present theory of the concept.

7. See above, p. 100 and note 4.

8. In this illustration I am not shaving meanings so fine as to need strictly to maintain Moore's distinction between *good* and *the good* (G. E. Moore, *Principia Ethica* [Cambridge: Cambridge University Press, 1903], pp. 8-9).

Chapter 6

1. To the question, "Which nonexistent ampersand?" one might suggest the answer, "The one that eventually does get painted into the placard, once the ampersand is put in." But that of course resolves the indeterminacy by shifting from the identification of a nonexistent ampersand to the identification of an existing one, for once it is painted in, or even begins to be painted in, it is no longer physically nonexistent.

2. I owe the illustration to Roman Ingarden, *Untersuchungen zur Ontologie der Kunst* (Tübingen: Max Niemeyer, 1962), a translation of which, as *Investigations in the Ontology of Art*, by Raymond Meyer with my collaboration, is in press with Ohio University Press.

Chapter 7

1. This remark is not in conflict with that on page 46, about the greater number of appearances of identifications of value-assertions than of fact-assertions, because this remark is about the referents in the world, not about the instances of identification by explicit terms of the form of language by which we know them.

2. Above, in chapter 3, page 50.

3. See above, pp. 76-77.

4. Bertrand Russell, "The Elements of Ethics," in *Philosophical Essays* (New York: Simon and Schuster, 1967; copr. 1966 by George Allen & Unwin; first publ. 1910), p. 17. In a preface to the 1967 edition, Russell disclaims the position of this

essay.

5. With this point I am, I believe, at odds with the emotive-theory ethicists. So far as I can discern, C. L. Stevenson *(Ethics and Language* [New Haven: Yale University Press, 1944] *passim* but especially in chapter 4, "First Pattern of Analysis)", imputes current emotion or an existing attitude to the maker of the value-assertion, even though he attributes emotive meaning to value terms as a dispositional property.

6. H. A. Prichard, "Does Moral Philosophy Rest on a Mistake?" in Wilfrid Sellars and John Hospers, eds., *Readings in Ethical Theory* (New York: Appleton-Century-Crofts, 1957; orig. publ. in *Mind* 21 [1912]), p. 152.

Chapter 8

1. In connection with a proposition offered by a given authority, one may have grounds, perhaps quite good ones, for arriving at the separate value-assertive judgment, "I ought to believe the deliverance made by this authority." These grounds are, of course, also to be found among the items on the above list.

2. William James, "The Will to Believe," an Address to the Philosophical Clubs of Yale and Brown Universities. Published in the *New World*, June 1896; reproduced in Alburey Castell, ed., *Essays in Pragmatism* by William James (New York: Hafner, 1949), pp. 88-109, and in other collections of James's writings.

3. Gottlob Frege, "Über Sinn und Bedeutung," *Zeitschrift für Philosophie und philosophische Kritik*, 100, 1892; tr. as "On Sense and Nominatum," by Herbert Feigl in H. Feigl and Wilfrid Sellars, eds., *Readings in Philosophical Analysis* (New York: Appleton-Century-Crofts, 1949), pp. 85-102.

4. Alfred J. Ayer, *Language, Truth and Logic* (London: Victor Gollancz, 1950; first publ. 1936), p. 107.

5. Charles L. Stevenson, *Ethics and Language* (New Haven: Yale University Press, 1944). I discuss the first formulation only of Stevenson's interpretation of "This is good." His second pattern of analysis does not explicitly indicate the approval of the originator but expresses it obliquely by using the word *good*; it does however explicitly refer to the recipient's emotional approval:

"This is good" has the meaning of "This has qualities or relations X, Y, Z . . . . ," except that "good" has as well a laudatory emotive meaning which permits it to express the speaker's approval, and tends to evoke the approal of the hearer (p. 207).

Chapter 9

1. In *Webster's Third New International Dictionary of the English Language, Unabridged* (Chicago: William Benton, copr. G. & C. Merriam Co., 1971), see article "Color," associated color charts, and "Explanation of Color Charts and Descriptive Color Names."

2. Cf. Ewing, "An intuition must be regarded as a rational judgment, though not one based on argument, even if capable of confirmation by it, and not as a mere feeling." A. C. Ewing, *The Definition of Good* (London: Routledge and Kegan Paul;

New York: The Humanities Press, 1948; second impression New York: The Humanities Press, 1966), p. 22.

Chapter 10

1. The picture was originally drawn by the cartoonist W. E. Hill and published in *Puck* for November 6, 1915. It was copied from the halftone reproduction in *Puck* by Mrs. W. H. Hunt and published by Edwin G. Boring in *American Journal of Psychology* 42 (1930): p. 444, under "Apparatus Notes," where it was called "A New Ambiguous Figure." Hill had labeled it "My Wife and My Mother-in-Law."

2. I shall use the word *ideas* loosely to mean any sort of item in a way of appearing other than that of the way of appearing immediately of a physical object. It may be a memory or conception, etc., of a physical object, or a concept, an imagining, etc., of anything non-physical. Rather than its being a precise term, *ideas* is for me, here, merely a collective noun of considerable convenience.

Chapter 11

1. Gottlob Frege, *Logical Investigations*, ed. P. T. Geach, tr. P. T. Geach and R. H. Stoothoff, (New Haven: Yale University Press, 1977, orig. publ. in *Beiträge zur Philosophie des deutschen Idealismus*, 1918), p. 7. Also "On Sense and Nominatum," already cited.

2. Words like *prefer* and *approve* as used in everyday situations show no distinction whether the choice expressed is made mainly on emotive or rational grounds. *I like* chiefly expresses an affective response (though it may mask a reasoned conclusion, as when the sportscaster's "I like the Wolves" conveys "I predict that the Wolves will be the winners"). But *I judge* pretty uniformly expresses, and is used herein to express, a chiefly rational response in which the emotional factor present is reduced to negligible effect if it remains at all. Further, as with the other terms, *I judge* can be the prefix to either a fact-assertive expression, like "I judge that he is a little more than six feet tall," or a value-assertive expression, like "I judge his madonna to be a better painting than his crucifixion," or "I judge that I ought to buy a new car."

Chapter 12

1. *Feeling* and *emotion* in some usages are synonymous, and in other usages are distinct. Prescriptive authorities suggest that *emotion* is better applied to the more all-pervasive events, while *feeling* has a broader range of events of shorter duration and more immediate stimulus as its proper referents. I shall take feeling to refer to the latter—the simpler, more basic, and less extensive of the two.

2. The piece referred to is in the Staatliche Antikensammlungen, Munich.

3. However, after completion, some though not all artists can clearly verbalize at least some of their choices and their respective reasons. This is, however, a separate

activity from art-productive activity, and I should not judge an artist's performance in either one by the quality of his ability to perform in the other.

4. Here it is *not* my intention to speak of *value* in the way a painter would speak of it, having to do with the relative lightness or darkness of a brush stroke or other area of a painting—although that more or less accidental application of the word *value* is consistent with the usage I am employing, for lightness or darkness of an area do indeed act as incentives for further determinations by the painter.

5. Moore sets himself outside this tradition: " . . . when I call . . . propositions 'Intuitions,' I mean *merely* to assert that they are incapable of proof; I imply nothing whatever as to the manner or origin of our cognition of them. Still less do I imply (as most Intuitionists have done) that any proposition whatever is true, *because* we cognise it in a particular way or by the exercise of any particular faculty: I hold, on the contrary, that in every way in which it is possible to cognise a true proposition, it is also possible to cognise a false one" (George Edward Moore, *Principia Ethica* [Cambridge: Cambridge University Press, 1959; first publ. 1903], Preface, p. x). Ewing also gives up the self-certifying capability of intuitions: ". . . we must remember that ethical intuition, like our other capacities, is presumably a developing factor and therefore may be capable of error" (A. C. Ewing, *The Definition of Good* [London: Routledge & Kegan Paul; New York, Humanities Press, 1966; first publ. 1948], p. 22). These concessions tend to make the theory of value independent of that world which is the subject matter of our propositions, and move it toward the status of simply a system of propositional logic independent of other reality.

Chapter 13

1. Most often, the prudential *ought* is the first special type of *ought* overlaid upon the pure *ought* in our thinking. It may give way to the moral *ought;* or if compatible with the latter it may remain with the moral ought as an additional aspect of the ought-judgment ultimately adopted. All too often the prudential *ought* prevails over the moral *ought*, and the agent therefore performs an act that others disapprove morally, and that perhaps he will later acknowledge to have failed to meet moral standards.

2. The moral dimension includes the reflexive relation of the moral agent to himself; for example, he should not do to himself things that he ought not to do to other human beings. However, for simplicity of argument I use here the more minimal description of the moral dimension.

3. This point is argued above pp. 152-53, and below, p. 287.

4. It is reason, as Kant asserted, that accomplished the universalization of the moral imperative; for him this entailed that the moral dimension is partaken in only by rational beings. I shall explore this matter further in chapter 16.

5. I owe my awareness of the importance of this factor to William K. Frankena, who writes that "morally good or right action is one kind of excellent activity and hence is a prime candidate for election as part of any good life, especially since it is a kind of excellent activity of which all normal people are capable" *(Ethics*, 2d ed. [Englewood Cliffs, N.J.: Prentice-Hall, 1973], p. 115).

6. Recently Ann Landers in her syndicated advice column printed a letter from a woman who was greatly distressed to discover in the room of her twenty-two-year-old

son, who lived in the family home, photographs of himself and his girl friend nude and in pornographic poses; what, the mother was asking, should she do? But the columnist received a second letter from the woman before a reply to the first could be printed. Not waiting for the expected counsel, the woman had gone to the youth's room and torn up all the photographs. Now, she reported, she felt greatly relieved. Unfortunately for her self-content, one hopes, Landers's printed reply indicated to her that this solution was not morally right.

7. Adherents of the school of analytic philosophy enforce this problem for us; with relation to theory of value, see especially Everett W. Hall, *What Is Value?* (New York: Humanities Press, 1952).

Chapter 14

1. While we are taking clues from aesthetics, we must not overlook differences that obtain. A significant one has already been noted: A fundamental act of the artistic creation is bounding and framing the artwork so that its scope is established; but with moral conduct we can never fully and finally establish such a boundary. We must always remain open to the possibility that there are yet additional factors that we ought to consider, that our reasoning has not yet covered, affecting the moral outcome.

2. In the illustration, the justifier, Wilbur's mother, will be offering justification for a moral decision that issues in an avoidance rather than a positive action, but justifying this negative choice follows the same pattern as justifying a positive choice, such as "You ought to throw a coin to the beggar." It happens that our illustration entails the justifying of a negative choice because what it first showed us was an instance of the arrival at a *pure* ought-judgment, without a moral dimension so far as its maker was aware. In theory a pure ought-judgment can be justified, and justified in this typical pattern, but in practice it rarely undergoes actual justification, because no one's well-being is affected directly by the strand of the ought-judgment that is the pure "X ought to be." When an agent is specified a moral strand is added, and when a person is identified as being affected, then clearly the moral dimension participates in fixing the nature of the situation and its emergent judgment. Wilbur's mother is pointing out to him that he has not been free of this factor, but rather has overlooked it. The persons affected by breaking the garage window include those who may be endangered by broken glass, those who may be inconvenienced by the reduced efficacy of the garage, and those who must see to repairs. Moreover, Wilbur no doubt bestows personhood on his dog in respects such as this, an effect making for moral instruction that is intended by many parents who introduce pets into their families.

Chapter 15

1. If there are other moral agents in the universe, let "human beings" here include them. For example, the question of moral obligation toward animals may justify the inclusion of animals here. The point, however, is too special to be discussed in the present general treatment.

2. We make it compulsory by law—that is, "obligatory"—for the soldier to obey the lawful order of his senior officer. We do not charge the soldier with a crime, such as appropriating private food supplies in occupied territory, if he was clearly acting upon a lawful order. However, the instance of the *un*lawful order, for whose execution we do hold the soldier responsible and punishable, serves to show that the obligatoriness of the *lawful* order, on a par with it insofar as both are orders of the senior officer, is indeed a fragile thing. We expect the soldier to *dis*obey an unlawful order whose execution would perpetrate a crime. In effect, then, our arrangement is to remove from him the onus of misjudgment about what to do in the one case while requiring him to continue bearing it in the other—and also, to judge correctly as to which case is of which kind! Evidently no obligation or compulsoriness has inevitability about it. Rather, in the moral realm all obligation is relative to human judgment.

3. A friend in the business world, about to end a visit in order to fulfill his next obligation in his work, was asked by the eleven-year-old, "Do you *have* to?" He explained his affirmative answer by remarking, "If they tell you to, then you don't have to, but if you say you will, then you have to."

4. In a most unusual way, considered alongside the applications or uses made of it in most discussions of Kant. Kant's imperative is categorical only insofar as the commitment to rationality is made and adhered to. One *can* disobey it—one can be irrational. One's critic, condemning one's wrongful act, has his ground only in *his* commitment to be rational. This is, I believe, the central point of Kant's doctrine of the categorical imperative. It is an extremely strong point, for few of us renounce rationality.

Chapter 16

1. G. C. Field, *Moral Theory* (New York: E. P. Dutton, 1921), p. 49.
2. Immanuel Kant, *Foundations of the Metaphysics of Morals*, ed. and tr. Lewis White Beck (Indianapolis: Bobbs-Merrill, 1959), p. 7 [391].
3. Even when contemplating an action with a self-interested first motive, if one can apply the rule subsuming the act to all persons, one cannot then be accused of according special treatment to oneself, and performance of the act thus universalized becomes a reinforcement of the principle of universalization. Already with Kant the amenability of an act to be universalized was an adequate defensive justification for performing it.
4. In all but the last of these we see that universalization occurs *within* the membership of the group; the difficulty is in going *beyond its boundary* to include individuals who are obviously different, and systematically different, such as by color or by culturally or religiously founded behavior patterns Since the universalization only to the extent of the boundary of the group—"the people"—is unarticulated, and the differences being easily identified are generally articulated, the grounds of human worth become projected onto something other and lesser than humanity abiding in all humankind.

Chapter 17

[No notes for this chapter]

Chapter 18

1. Heidegger calls the question "Why are there essents [existents, "things that are"] rather than nothing?" the question that is first in rank because it is the most far reaching, the deepest, and the most fundamental of all questions. Martin Heidegger, *An Introduction to Metaphysics*, tr. Ralph Manheim (Garden City: New York, Doubleday, 1961), pp. 1-2.

2. Roman Ingarden, *The Literary Work of Art*, tr. George G. Grabowicz (Evanston, Illinois: Northwestern University Press, 1973); *The Cognition of the Literary Work of Art*, tr. Ruth Ann Crowley and Kenneth R. Olson (Evanston, Illinois: Northwestern University Press, 1973); and *Investigations in the Ontology of Art*, tr. Raymond Meyer with John T. Goldthwait (Athens, Ohio: Ohio University Press, forthcoming).

3. R. M. Hare, *The Language of Morals* (New York: Oxford University Press, 1964; first published 1952), throughout.

4. Rather, it is a *sentence* that is every appearance of a certain collection of linguistic symbols expressing a given sentential meaning. This, however, gives no one any trouble, for what is important to us is the meaning that we constitute upon encountering the appearances of this collection.

Index

VALUE
LANGUAGE
&
LIFE

Since his earliest days as a teacher, Professor John Goldthwait has regarded the problem of value as the most important philosophical issue of daily life. Now in *Value, Language, and Life*, he presents a fascinating new theory of value through which traditional attempts at definition are transcended in order to explore the human act of expressing value judgments. Pressing his inquiry where its emerging results require, Professor Goldthwait adapts a phenomenological method to examine presuppositions in metaphysics, theory of mind, epistemology, and theory of language—all of which bear upon cultural consciousness to influence the ways in which we speak of value.

Professor Goldthwait isolates and analyzes the differences between fact-assertive and value-assertive propositions, and in doing so produces a generic doctrine of value based on grounding all value claims on the central meaning of "ought." This common ground of value-assertive expressions unites ethics, aesthetics, and other value-laden disciplines on a single foundation that elicits a comprehensive